How to Do *Everything* with

Microsoft® Office PowerPoint® 2003

WITHDRAWN

Ellen Finkelstein

McGraw-Hill/Osborne

New York   Chicago   San Francisco
Lisbon   London   Madrid   Mexico City
Milan   New Delhi   San Juan
Seoul   Singapore   Sydney   Toronto

304032

APR 1 4 2005

The *McGraw·Hill* Companies

McGraw-Hill/Osborne
2100 Powell Street, 10th Floor
Emeryville, California 94608
U.S.A.

To arrange bulk purchase discounts for sales promotions, premiums, or fund-raisers, please contact **McGraw-Hill**/Osborne at the above address. For information on translations or book distributors outside the U.S.A., please see the International Contact Information page immediately following the index of this book.

How to Do Everything with Microsoft® Office PowerPoint® 2003

4567890 CUS CUS 01987654

ISBN 0-07-222972-1

Publisher	Brandon A. Nordin
Vice President &	
Associate Publisher	Scott Rogers
Acquisitions Editor	Margie McAneny
Project Editor	Carolyn Welch
Acquisitions Coordinator	Tana Allen
Technical Editor	Geetesh Bajaj
Copy Editor	Carolyn Welch
Proofreader	Claire Splan
Indexer	Claire Splan
Composition	George Toma Charbak, Tara A. Davis, Kelly Stanton-Scott
Illustrators	Kathleen Fay Edwards, Melinda Moore Lytle, Lyssa Wald
Series Design	Mickey Galicia
Cover Series Design	Dodie Shoemaker
Cover Illustration	Eliot Bergman

This book was composed with Corel VENTURA™ Publisher.

To MMY, who taught me how to dive deep within and find the foundation of happiness and success within me.

About the Author

Ellen Finkelstein has written several computer books on AutoCAD, PowerPoint, and Flash. Her previous book on PowerPoint was *How to Do Everything with PowerPoint 2002*. She writes numerous articles, especially on AutoCAD and PowerPoint, including a quarterly article, "Creative Techniques," in Presentations magazine. Ellen provides consulting on web site and presentation content. She maintains a web site of AutoCAD, PowerPoint, and Flash tips and techniques at http://www.ellenfinkelstein.com.

About the Technical Editor

Geetesh Bajaj, based in India, is a Microsoft PowerPoint MVP (Most Valuable Professional). He runs the Indezine.com and PowerPointed.com sites that contain extensive PowerPoint-related content including reviews, tutorials, and a bi-weekly PowerPoint Ezine. He's also a contributing editor for Presentations magazine.

Contents

Acknowledgments

The creation of any book is a group enterprise, and this book is no exception. You would not be reading it without the contributions of many people. Some of the important contributions, such as the design, layout, production, and printing of the book, were made by people whose names I don't know, but I thank them anyway.

First, I'd like to thank Margie McAneny, acquisitions editor, who offered me the opportunity to write this book. Margie was intimately involved with the book and answered my many questions patiently. Carolyn Welch, senior project editor, coordinated the editing and production of the book, including keeping track of zillions of figures and illustrations (and the difference between them), as well as editorial and production schedules. I don't know how you do it, but I'm glad you do. Geetesh Bajaj, a PowerPoint MVP (which means he knows a whole lot about PowerPoint), was my cheerful and competent technical editor. He came up with all sorts of good advice, which was incorporated into the book. Thanks, Geetesh!

Many people contributed presentations for this book. These presentations gave me real-world material to show you in the book's figures and illustrations, and I greatly appreciate them.

Last, but certainly not least, I must thank my family for supporting me while I wrote. My husband, Evan, shopped, did countless washes, and dragged me away from the computer when I needed a break. My kids, Yeshayah and Eliyah, managed to put up with my being endlessly in front of the computer.

I love you!

Introduction

Microsoft PowerPoint 2003 is a presentation program, which means that you create presentations that you develop and show on your computer. Presentations are like slide shows, but no physical slides are necessary. While almost all computer users are familiar with word processing programs and many know what a spreadsheet is all about, many computer users have never used a presentation program.

All that is changing. The use of presentation programs is increasing geometrically. While design professionals once created most presentations, presentation programs such as PowerPoint have now made it easy for anyone to create an attractive, effective presentation in a few minutes. There are enough special features—such as clip art, sound files, and animation effects—to help you create a professional-looking presentation if you want to invest a little more time.

PowerPoint is the most popular presentation program available. PowerPoint 2003, an integral part of the Microsoft Office XP suite, has been updated to provide greater ease of use and a number of new features. Here is a partial list:

- New design templates
- Normal view as the default interface layout
- Task panes to make commonly used commands more available
- Numerous improvements in graphic capabilities, such as more flexible transparency, image rotation, image compression, a new Clip Organizer, diagrams, and the ability to save anything on your slide as a separate image file
- More new animation types, including animation along a path and a timeline
- New slide transitions
- Multiple slide masters
- Print preview
- Document recovery and password protection
- Improved web and HTML features
- Smart tags to apply formatting and layout automatically (or let you reverse the feature)
- More collaboration features

Whether you're a new PowerPoint user or are trying to hone your existing skills, you'll find plenty about all of PowerPoint's features and how to use them to get professional results.

What's Special About This Book

How to Do Everything with Microsoft Office PowerPoint 2003 covers all the features you need to make using PowerPoint easy and productive, and then goes further to explain how to make your presentations truly professional. It includes tips, shortcuts, and notes to give you the extra edge you need to create presentations that communicate. Special How To and Did You Know boxes add information beyond the usual content of a book on PowerPoint.

I have designed this book to include not only the specific features of PowerPoint 2003, but also a great deal of information about designing and presenting slide shows that deliver the message effectively. You will see information on the use of color, laying out a slide, rehearsing, and many other related topics that directly affect the success of your presentation.

Who Needs This Book

I have designed this book for beginning and intermediate users who are familiar with Microsoft Windows. If you are just starting to use PowerPoint, *How to Do Everything with Microsoft Office PowerPoint 2003* explains the basics of presentation programs and brings you through the creation of your first complete presentation by Chapter 2. If you have already used PowerPoint but want to expand your skills, this book provides you with everything you need to know about PowerPoint and about creating presentations.

This book starts out with the basics and then presents the rest of PowerPoint's many features systematically and comprehensively. If you read it from cover to cover, it will bring you to an intermediate-to-advanced level of knowledge and skill.

How This Book Is Organized

The overall organization of *How to Do Everything with Microsoft Office PowerPoint 2003* is from simple to complex, from wholeness to specifics, and from start to finish.

Chapters 1 through 4 provide you with the basics you need to use PowerPoint. By Chapter 2, you know how to create a complete presentation using the AutoContent Wizard. Chapter 2 also demonstrates how to choose a background design and start a presentation from scratch. Chapters 3 and 4 explain how to edit a presentation as well as format bullets and paragraphs.

Chapters 5 through 10 describe how to add graphics, tables, and charts to a slide, including how to work with colors, borders, fills, and 3-D effects. I explain how to include repeating elements and how to make sure that all the slides in a presentation have a unified appearance. Finally, I discuss animation, slide transition effects, and multimedia—the use of sound and video.

Chapters 11 through 15 bring your presentation out of PowerPoint and into the rest of the world where it must inevitably go. I explain how to incorporate data from other applications, how to develop a presentation collaboratively, how to display a presentation on the Internet, and how to customize PowerPoint. I end the book with two chapters detailing the actual presentation process, including how to time and rehearse your presentation, use projection equipment, and actually deliver your slide show.

How to Use This Book

If you are a beginner, you should start from the beginning and read until you have enough information to create your presentation. Try out the features as you read. If you need to create a specific presentation, start creating it from the very first chapter. As you continue reading, you can improve and refine your presentation, using the chapters that cover the features you need.

If you have used PowerPoint before but want to improve your skills and increase your knowledge, scan the Note icons throughout the book because many of them highlight new features. You can then go directly to the chapters that contain the topics you need.

How to Contact the Author

Please contact me if you don't understand the material in the book or find any errors. You can contact me at ellenfinkl@bigfoot.com. However, note that I can't provide technical support for PowerPoint. Also, I welcome you to visit my web site at http://www.ellenfinkelstein.com.

Have Fun!

PowerPoint is great fun to use! However you use this book, enjoy the process and the satisfaction you will get from creating effective, professional presentations.

Part I

Create a Presentation

Chapter 1

Get Started with Presentations

How to...

- Get your message across
- Open a presentation
- View a presentation
- Get help when you need it
- Save a presentation

Microsoft PowerPoint is all about effective communication. PowerPoint gives you the tools you need to create a professional-quality presentation. No longer do you need to spend big bucks for a graphic artist or a slide bureau to create presentations for you. You can do it yourself. This book provides extensive coverage of PowerPoint features that will help you whether you are a beginner or an advanced user.

Get Your Message Across

Microsoft PowerPoint 2003 is a presentation program. A *presentation program* creates slide shows, which you can then show on a screen or monitor directly from your computer. A PowerPoint file is called a *presentation,* and the individual unit of a presentation is a *slide.* Each slide is equivalent to a page, as shown in the slide show pictured in Figure 1-1.

PowerPoint 2003 is light-years ahead of the traditional individual 35mm slides or overhead transparencies of yesteryear. For example, you can

- Add graphics, sound, music, animations, and short video clips to maximize your impact.
- Instantly make changes (as in any computer document).
- Animate text or other objects to emphasize your point.
- Create transition effects from one slide to another.
- Change the color scheme or background for an entire presentation or for a single slide.
- Add graphs (charts), tables, and diagrams to make your point visually and clearly.
- Create interactive and automatically looping slide shows—ideal when presenting at conventions and/or using a kiosk.
- Save your presentation in HTML format and publish it on the Internet or an intranet.
- Create an autorun CD of your presentation that can play on systems with no PowerPoint installed.

The purpose of a presentation is to communicate. Of course, you can also communicate with your word processing documents. Even your spreadsheets communicate something from their numbers. But in a presentation, the process of conveying the message is the point. You use

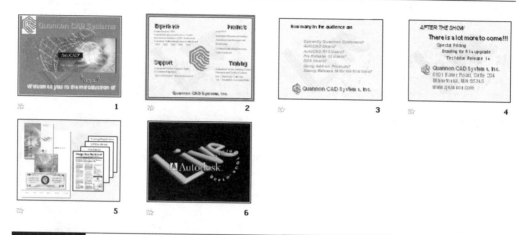

FIGURE 1-1   A presentation consists of a series of slides.

words, art, shapes, color, sound, and special effects to maximize the effectiveness of your message. It's called *multimedia,* and it's a hot, growing field. You may have never used multimedia tools before, but with PowerPoint, you easily get professional results. And with a little practice, you will soon be creating exciting, compelling presentations.

Because it is now so easy to create great presentations, the number of PowerPoint users has skyrocketed in the last decade. PowerPoint presentations are everywhere, but customers, managers, and peers expect an ever-higher level of professionalism in the quality of the presentations they see.

Open a Presentation

Opening a presentation, whether new or existing, is easy using the task pane that was introduced in PowerPoint 2002. The old method hasn't disappeared, though. The skills you learn in this

The Impact of Multimedia

Why use multimedia? A great deal of scientific research shows that visual aids and the use of color significantly increase the amount of material your audience understands and remembers. Moreover, presentations including visual aids and other multimedia effects have been shown to be more effective in convincing an audience to take the course of action suggested by the presenter. For full details, see Chapter 10: Use Multimedia.

section don't show up on your slides, but they do make your life a lot easier—and make creating your presentation a lot smoother.

Start PowerPoint

The first step is to open PowerPoint. An easy way to open PowerPoint is to double-click a desktop shortcut. If you don't already have a desktop shortcut for PowerPoint, here's how to create one:

1. Go to Start | (All) Programs | Microsoft Office and highlight Microsoft PowerPoint (without clicking it).

2. Right-click Microsoft PowerPoint, and choose Copy.

3. Right-click on the desktop and choose Paste.

4. Double-click the shortcut to open PowerPoint.

Of course, if you don't like shortcuts, you can open the PowerPoint icon by selecting Start | Programs | Microsoft Office | Microsoft PowerPoint.

Use the Getting Started Task Pane

Once you have opened PowerPoint, you see the Getting Started task pane shown in Figure 1-2, which segues you to the world of PowerPoint. The Getting Started task pane is one of several task panes that help you complete tasks more easily.

NOTE *The Getting Started task pane is new for PowerPoint 2003.*

The Getting Started task pane has the following features:

- To open an existing presentation that you have recently used, click its name beneath the Open list.

- To start a new presentation, click Create a New Presentation.

- To find templates on Microsoft's web site, click Templates on Microsoft.com.

Click More under the Open list to display the Open dialog box, discussed in the next section. You can use the top portion of the Getting Started task pane to search for information and news on Microsoft's web site.

When you click Create a New Presentation, the New Presentation task pane appears, shown in Figure 1-3. The New Presentation task pane has tools for creating a new presentation, as its name suggests.

The New Presentation pane lists five ways to start a new presentation:

- Choose Blank Presentation to start from scratch.

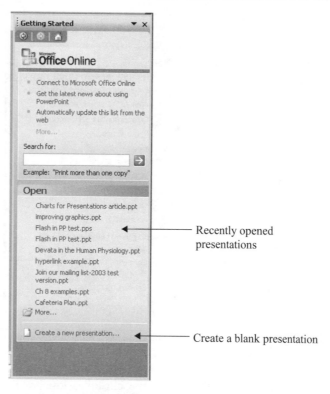

Recently opened presentations

Create a blank presentation

FIGURE 1-2   The Getting Started task pane offers a simple way to open a presentation.

- Choose From Design Template to select one of PowerPoint's many backgrounds (templates). You can then start creating your presentation.

- Choose From AutoContent Wizard to get assistance in organizing the content, that is, the text of your presentation.

- Choose From Existing Presentation section to choose an existing presentation and then use it to create a new presentation file. This method is similar to opening an existing presentation and choosing File | Save As.

- Choose Photo Album to create a presentation made up of photos or other graphics. (See Chapter 5 for details.)

These options are covered in detail in Chapter 2, where you learn how to create a new presentation.

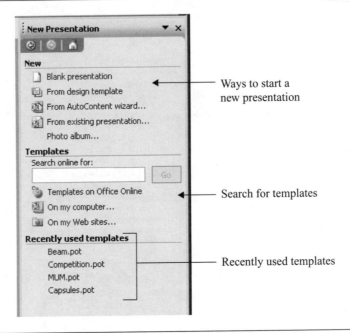

FIGURE 1-3   Use the New Presentation task pane when you want to create a new presentation.

When you're done with the task pane, click the Close box if you need the space to see your presentation. See "Use the Task Panes" later in this chapter for more information on task panes.

Use the Open Dialog Box

Another way to open an existing presentation is to click the Open button, shown here, to display the Open dialog box, shown in Figure 1-4 using the Preview view. Locate your presentation in the Look In drop-down list box, click the presentation, and click Open. Your presentation opens, displaying the last saved slide and view so you can pick up right where you left off.

Use the Places Bar for Document Management

Down the left side of the Open dialog box are five buttons that can help you find presentations and supporting files more quickly. Together, these buttons are called the *places bar*. The following list describes each button:

- **My Recent Documents** This button shows the most recently opened presentations. The History list is composed of shortcuts from the Recent subfolder, which is a subfolder in your Windows folder. If you keep presentations and supporting files all

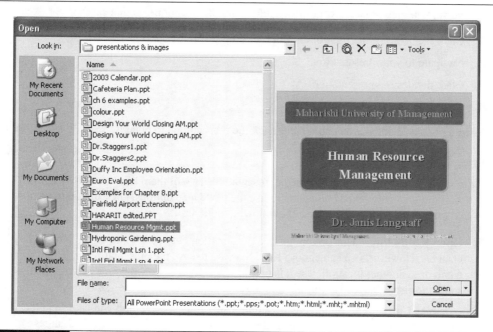

FIGURE 1-4   Use the Open dialog box to find existing presentations.

over your hard disk, the History button can be a savior when you're trying to find a file fast. Don't forget that the Home task pane also lists your most recently used presentations. It doesn't show as many, but if you can find a presentation there, you can skip the entire step of using the Open dialog box.

- **Desktop**   Click Desktop to display the shortcuts and files you have placed on your desktop. Some users keep shortcuts to their current projects on their desktop so they can open them immediately with a double-click.

- **My Documents**   This button shows you the contents of the My Documents folder. In this folder, you can collect the documents you are currently using for easy access. When you first open PowerPoint, My Documents is the default folder for opening and saving presentations. Unlike the Recent folder, you have to purposefully save and place files in My Documents.

- **My Computer**   The Open dialog box displays your drives so you can navigate to your presentation from any drive from there.

- **My Network Places**   This button shows you the contents of the network to which you are connected (if any). You can then open a presentation from the network.

Of course, you may organize your presentations in other locations. In that case:

1. Click the arrow to the right of the Look In drop-down list box.

2. Navigate to your presentation.

3. Click the desired presentation.

4. Choose Open.

Instead of steps 3 and 4, you can double-click the presentation to open it.

Use the Open Options

You have some hidden options for opening a presentation. Two of them are especially useful if you are working on a networked computer. To use the new Open options, click the drop-down arrow next to the Open button. You have the following options:

- **Open Read-Only**   This option opens a presentation but doesn't allow you to make any changes. However, you can choose File | Save As to save the presentation under another name or in another location. Use this option when you are working on a network and someone else is currently working on the same presentation.

- **Open As Copy**   This option creates a duplicate of the presentation you choose in the same folder as the original and opens the duplicate. You can then make any changes you need.

- **Open In Browser**   With this option, you can open a presentation saved in HTML format in your web browser.

Customize the Default File Location

If you often work from one folder, you may wish to make it the default folder for the Open and Save dialog boxes. No longer will you have to navigate to your presentations and other files on your hard disk or network. Whenever you want to open or save a presentation, your preferred folder will be active in the dialog box.

To set the default folder, choose Tools | Options, and click the Save tab, shown in Figure 1-5. In the Default File Location text box, type the path for the default folder you want. For example, type **c:\presentations**. Click OK.

Use a Presentation from the McGraw-Hill/Osborne Web Site

If you would like to practice the skills in this chapter but don't have a presentation to work with, you can download a sample presentation from the McGraw-Hill/Osborne web site. Agentha.ppt

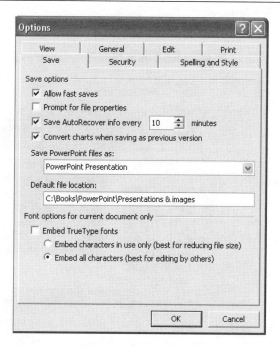

FIGURE 1-5   Customize the default location for saving and opening presentations.

is a simple presentation (about the advantages of investing in a fictional location) that you can easily work with. Go to http://www.osborne.com and click the Free Code link.

View a Presentation

Understanding PowerPoint's window and views helps you accomplish all your tasks more quickly. If you are familiar with PowerPoint 2002, you will feel comfortable immediately. If you have just upgraded from an earlier version, you will find some significant changes.

Look at the Screen

Figure 1-6 shows the PowerPoint screen and its elements. To understand the elements in this figure, refer to the bulleted list that follows the figure.

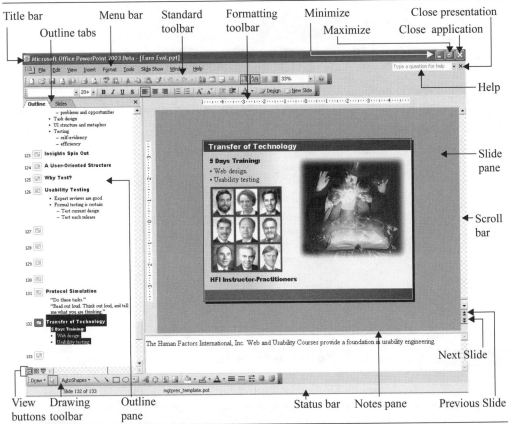

FIGURE 1-6   The PowerPoint screen. The Standard and Formatting toolbars have been placed on two separate rows so you can see them completely.

- The title bar tells you that you are in PowerPoint and displays the name of your presentation.

- The menu bar contains the commands you give PowerPoint.

- The Standard toolbar contains many of the most often used commands.

- The Formatting toolbar contains mostly common commands for formatting text.

- The application Minimize button allows you to reduce the application window to a button on the Windows taskbar.

- The application Maximize button allows you to make the application window smaller. Click it again to make the application window fill the entire screen.

- The application Close button allows you to close both the presentation and PowerPoint.

- The presentation Close button closes the presentation but not PowerPoint.
- The Type a Question For Help text box allows you to type a question to find help.
- The ruler helps you lay out your slide with precision and format text, especially bulleted text.
- The Slide pane shows the current slide.
- The scroll bars let you move backward and forward through your presentation.
- The Previous Slide button allows you to move to the previous slide.
- The Next Slide button allows you to move to the next slide.
- The Notes pane shows speaker notes that you have created.
- The status bar tells you which number slide is displayed, as well as the total number of slides, such as Slide 24 of 31. The status bar also displays the name of the *design template*, or background.
- The Drawing toolbar contains commands for creating and editing graphics.
- View buttons let you change views. Views are covered later in this chapter in the "Use the Appropriate View" section.
- The Outline pane shows your bulleted text or thumbnails of your slides.

The Outline pane has two tabs. The Outline tab displays the text on your slide and is a good way to organize the text content of your presentation. The Slides tab displays thumbnails of your slides so you can quickly find the slide you want.

Get the Most out of the Toolbars and Menus

You use the toolbars and menus to tell PowerPoint what you want to do with your presentation. When you first open PowerPoint, the Standard and Formatting toolbars are on the same row. Some of the buttons may not have room to be displayed. You can click the down arrow at the right of each toolbar to find them. A subtle *grab bar* at the left side of each toolbar enables you to drag the toolbar to a new location.

TIP *If you put the Formatting toolbar on its own row, beneath the Standard toolbar, you can see most, if not all, the buttons. You lose only a little real estate on your screen.*

You can customize the toolbars any way you like. For further options, see Chapter 14.

The buttons on the toolbars are discussed elsewhere in this book, in their appropriate chapters. For now, you just need to know these two simple features to make you a toolbar pro:

- Adding or removing toolbar buttons
- Displaying toolbars

Add or Remove Toolbar Buttons

Follow these steps to add or remove toolbar buttons. To add other buttons or create your own toolbars, see Chapter 14.

1. Click the down arrow at the right side of the toolbar. (The ToolTip says Toolbar Options.)

2. Move the mouse over the Add or Remove Buttons command, then over the name of the toolbar. A list of possible buttons drops down. Buttons currently displayed are checked. At the bottom of the list are other common buttons for that toolbar.

3. Click the button you want to add or remove.

4. Click anywhere off the toolbar to close the button list.

Display Toolbars

PowerPoint has additional toolbars that you can use. To display one or more of these toolbars, just right-click any visible toolbar to reveal a flyout menu with a list of toolbars.

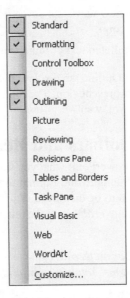

To display a toolbar, click any unchecked toolbar on the list. To hide a toolbar, click any checked toolbar. These toolbars are discussed throughout the book wherever they apply.

Use the Appropriate View

PowerPoint offers three ways to view a presentation. You choose a view based on what you are doing. Using the appropriate view provides the frictionless flow you need to get your work done.

Most commonly, you change views using the buttons at the bottom-left corner of your screen, just above the Drawing toolbar and the status bar. The view buttons are shown here:

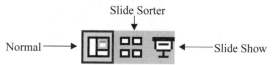

If you are upgrading from PowerPoint 2000 or earlier, you'll notice that Slide view and Outline view are gone. Normal view takes their place.

If you want, you can choose a view from the View menu.

Use Normal View

Normal view, shown in Figure 1-7, combines a large view of an individual slide, speaker notes beneath the slide, and your choice of an outline of the text of the presentation or thumbnail

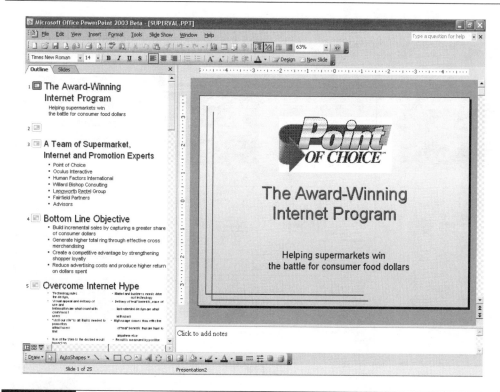

FIGURE 1-7   Normal view

images of the slides along the left side of the screen. Each section of the view is called a *pane*. Each pane has a scroll bar if it cannot display all the material so you can scroll to any part of the presentation.

NOTE   *Text created in a text box is not included in the text outline. It is treated as a graphic object. See Chapter 2 for details.*

Use Normal view when you are creating or editing a slide, organizing and writing text, or creating notes for the presenter to refer to when showing the presentation—which is most of the time!

TIP   *You can resize any of the panes in Normal view. Place the mouse over a pane border, then click and drag in either direction. For example, if you are working with the outline, make the Outline pane wider.*

Use Slide Sorter View

Slide Sorter view is quite different from Normal view. In Slide Sorter view, shown in Figure 1-8, you see a miniature view of all the slides at once.

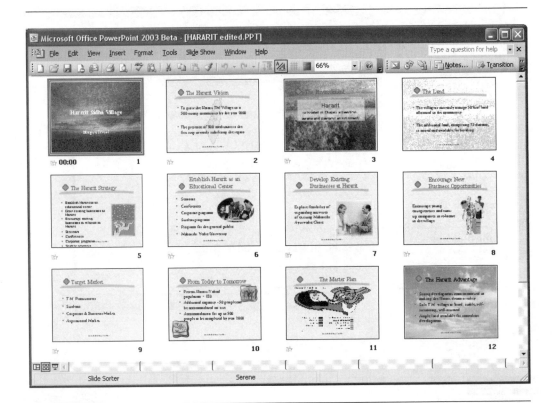

FIGURE 1-8   Slide Sorter view

Slide Sorter view is great when adding, deleting, and changing the order of your slides. You can also add timing and transition effects from one slide to the next. Therefore, when you switch to Slide Sorter view, PowerPoint displays a different Formatting toolbar, showing slide transitions, animation effects, etc.

TIP   *To quickly switch from Slider Sorter view to Normal view, double-click any slide.*

For details on adding, deleting, and moving slides, see Chapter 3. Transitions and animation are covered in Chapter 9, and timing is explained in Chapter 15.

Use Slide Show View

Slide Show view lets you look at your presentation like you would see it during an actual show. As you can see in Figure 1-9, the slide takes up the entire screen.

Here's where you get to see the results of all your labor! Use Slide Show view to evaluate the results of your work and rehearse what you are going to say. Of course, you also use Slide Show view when you actually deliver your presentation in front of an audience. Preparing for a presentation is the subject of Chapter 15, but here are the basic techniques for moving around in Slide Show view. It is important to know these techniques because there are no menus, toolbars, or other obvious navigation tools.

- ■ Press ESC to leave Slide Show view and return to your last view.

- ■ Click the mouse to move to the next slide (or the next animation effect). When you click the last slide, you see a black screen. Click again to automatically return to your last view.

FIGURE 1-9   Slide Show view

■ Click the icons at the lower-left corner or right-click to open the pop-up menu. These menus let you navigate to other slides, take notes or minutes, mark on the slide (temporarily) with an electronic pen as you present, change how the pointer looks and works, black out the slide, and end the show.

Use Notes Page View

To enter Notes Page view you need to use the menu; choose View | Notes Page. It's helpful to print out notes to use for reference while presenting. Chapter 16 gives details on printing notes and handouts. Each page contains one slide and the speaker's notes for that slide. Figure 1-10 shows a slide in Notes Page view.

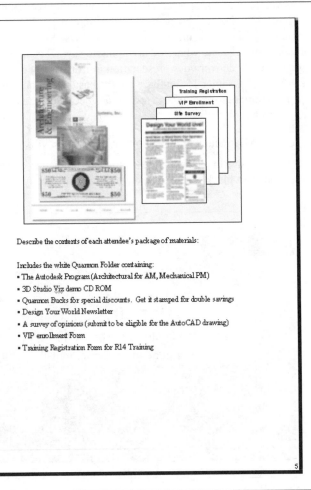

FIGURE 1-10   Notes Page view

1

Notes are designed to support you as you present. However, you can also use them to write notes to yourself as you create your presentation or to include comments on the presentation for your boss, colleagues, or clients. Use your imagination, and you'll find many uses for notes in your presentations.

Move Around a Presentation

Quick navigation through a presentation is always the hallmark of a pro. Here are some techniques:

- To move to a different slide, simply click the slide if it is visible, either in Slide Show view or on the thumbnail view of the Outline pane. You can also click the slide number in the Outline view of the Outline pane.

- Use the scroll bar in any pane. For example, to scroll through slides, use the Slide pane scroll bar. As you drag the scroll bar, a ToolTip tells you which slide you're up to. Stop when you reach the one you want.

- Use the Previous Slide and Next Slide buttons. (See Figure 1-6 earlier in this chapter.)

- Press CTRL-HOME to move to the beginning of the presentation and CTRL-END to move to the end of the presentation.

Use the Task Panes

Task panes, introduced in PowerPoint 2002, place a set of commands and options in one location to help you accomplish certain tasks more easily. PowerPoint 2003 has 16 task panes, several of them new for PowerPoint 2003. Although the pre-2002 dialog boxes and menu commands still exist, once you get used to the task panes, you'll usually find them more convenient.

Choose View | Task Pane to open a task pane. The task pane you last used appears. To change the task pane, use the down arrow at the upper-right corner and choose a task pane from the list. The individual task panes are discussed throughout this book as their tasks are covered.

 If your screen is big enough, you can drag the pane to the right of the PowerPoint window and keep it open all the time.

Get Help When You Need It

No matter how familiar you are with PowerPoint, you will use the Help feature at some time or other. You can access Help in three ways. This simplest way is to use the Help text box, shown here. Click the box, type a question or a few keywords, and press ENTER.

You can also use the Office Assistant, an animated image with a place to type in questions that is similar to the Help text box. To display the Office Assistant, choose Help | Show the Office Assistant.

TIP   *To customize how the assistant works, click it, and click Options. To turn off the assistant completely, clear Use the Office Assistant. Select the same box to turn the assistant back on.*

Finally, you can use the Help menu to get help. Choose Help | Microsoft PowerPoint Help, which is equivalent to pressing F1. The Microsoft PowerPoint Help task pane appears. Type a question in the Search text box and press ENTER or click the arrow button.

Whichever method you use, you get a list of related topics. Click the topic that seems most helpful, and the Help window opens.

At the bottom of the list of topics is a "Can't Find It?" heading, where you can find a link that offers search tips and another link that takes you to the Microsoft newsgroups where you can pose your question to other PowerPoint users. A second heading, "Other Places to Look," provides links that open the Clip Art and Research task panes and a link to Microsoft Office Support.

To close Help, click its Close button at the upper-right corner of the Help window.

Save a Presentation

You should save your presentation often as you work. As you have no doubt experienced, your computer system can crash or freeze—often destroying your most recent work. You should be especially careful to save before you print, switch to another application, or leave your computer to take a break.

NOTE   *PowerPoint 2003 (and all of Microsoft Office) contains a feature that helps save your work when your computer crashes. When you open PowerPoint again, the presentation is automatically displayed in a special Document Recovery task pane.*

The first time you save a new presentation, PowerPoint opens the Save As dialog box so you can name your presentation. Until then, your presentation is called Presentation1 (or a higher number if you have created more than one new presentation in a session). Figure 1-11 shows the Save As dialog box.

Remember, organizing your presentations and related files such as graphic files, sounds, and so on makes it a lot easier later when you need to find them. The following steps explain how to save a presentation for the first time using the Save As dialog box.

1. Use the places bar to save your presentation in one of the standard locations. If you don't use the places bar, click the Save In drop-down list to navigate to the desired folder.

2. Type the presentation's name in the File Name text box.

3. To save your presentation in another format, click the Save as Type drop-down box to choose the preferred type of document.

4. Click Save.

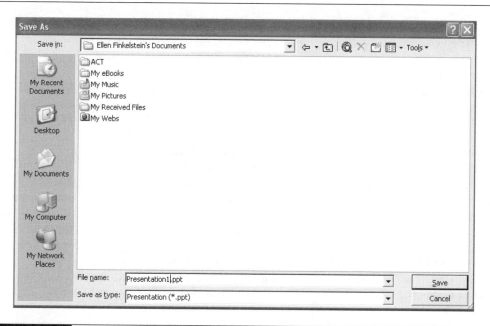

FIGURE 1-11   The Save As dialog box

For a discussion of the places bar, see "Use the Places bar for Document Management," earlier in this chapter.

PowerPoint 2003 (as well as all of Office) uses the same file format as PowerPoint 2002. As a result, you will find it easy to share presentations with colleagues who have not yet upgraded.

The Save as Type drop-down list offers a number of options for saving presentations, as explained in Table 1-1.

File Format Options	File Extension	Description
Presentation	.ppt	The default.
Single File Web Page	.mht or .mhtml	Saves an entire web site in one file.
Web page	.htm or .html	Lets you display your presentation on the Internet. HTML documents can be read by an Internet browser. Drawing objects are converted to GIF files.
PowerPoint 95	.ppt	Saves in PowerPoint 95 format; not able to be opened in later versions.
PowerPoint 97-2003 & 95 Presentation	.ppt	Saves in a format able to be opened in PowerPoint 95 and earlier versions by including both 95 and 97-2003 formats.

TABLE 1-1   File Format Options for Saving Presentations

File Format Options	File Extension	Description
Presentation for Review	.ppt	Saves the original presentation plus changes so you can incorporate changes made by others.
Design template	.pot	Saves the presentation as a template.
PowerPoint show	.pps	Opens, runs, and closes the show, and returns you to the desktop when a presentation is saved as a show and you open it from your desktop. If you open the file from within PowerPoint, it opens normally.
PowerPoint add-in	.ppa	Adds features to PowerPoint. (A third-party supplemental program.)
GIF (Graphics Interchange Format)	.gif	Saves the displayed slide as a GIF file—a common graphics format used on web pages. This format supports transparent backgrounds.
JPEG (Joint Photographic Experts Group)	.jpg	Saves the file as a JPEG file. JPEG (also called JPG) is a graphics format used on web pages. This format is best for photographs and detailed images.
PNG (Portable Network Graphics)	.png	Saves the displayed slide as a PNG file. PNG is a graphics format sometimes used on web pages. It compresses and downloads well.
TIFF (Tagged Image File Format)	.tif or .tiff	Turns the displayed slide into a bitmap graphic that you can import into other applications. Scanned images are typically in TIFF format.
Device Independent Bitmap	.bmp	Turns the displayed slide into a bitmap graphic that you can import into other applications.
WMF (Windows Metafile Format)	.wmf	Turns the displayed slide into a graphic that you can import into other applications. WMF is a vector format and resizes well.
Enhanced Windows Metafile	.emf	Turns the displayed slide into a graphic that you can import into other applications. EMF is an enhanced vector format that resizes well.
Outline/Rich Text Format	.rtf	Saves just the text of your presentation with most of its formatting so you can import it into a word processing (or other) application.

TABLE 1-1   File Format Options for Saving Presentations *(continued)*

You also use the Save As dialog box (File | Save As) any time you want to save a copy of a presentation under a new name or in a new location. If your presentation is a read-only file, meaning that you cannot make changes to it, you also use Save As to save the file under a new name.

After the first save, click Save on the Standard toolbar to save your presentation. PowerPoint saves only the changes you made since your last save. Saving only the changes takes less time, but the size of the file is larger.

Save So You Can Find It Fast Next Time

As you know by now, good file organization is definitely an advantage when you need to find your presentations, graphic files, text files, sounds, etc. The following tips provide efficient ways to find your presentations.

Add a Presentation to the My Documents Folder

As explained earlier in the "Use the Places Bar for Document Management" section of this chapter, you can use the My Documents folder to store files you use often. (For example, you might use your company's logo for every presentation you create.) The next time you want to open it, you can use the My Documents button on the places bar to find it quickly.

Customize Where and How a Presentation Is Saved

By default, when you first save a presentation, the Save As dialog box opens with the My Documents folder displayed in the Save In box. If you change the location, the presentation is, of course, saved in your chosen location each time you click the Save button. However, the next time you start a new presentation in the same session (without closing PowerPoint), the Save As dialog box displays the last location you chose.

If you want the Save As dialog box to open with another folder of your choice, you can change the default file location, as explained in the section "Customize the Default File Location," earlier in this chapter.

You can also specify a default file format for saving presentations. By default, PowerPoint saves your files as PowerPoint 2003 presentations. However, you can save your presentations in an earlier format. Choose Tools | Options, and click the Save tab. In the Save PowerPoint Files As drop-down list, choose the file format you want.

Back Up Your Presentations

No discussion of saving would be complete without explaining the importance of backing up, or *archiving,* your work. If you care about your work, back it up. While most computer users are accustomed to backing up files to floppy disks, many presentations are too large to fit on a disk, which holds a maximum of 1.44MB. There are many other options. Here are a few:

- Tape drives are fairly inexpensive and are large enough to back up an entire hard disk.
- Disk cartridges, such as those sold by Iomega (Zip disks) offer the convenience of a floppy disk but have more capacity.

- If you have a lot of presentations, a read/write CD-ROM drive lets you save your presentations to a CD-ROM.
- Optical drives have a long life and resist accidental erasure. Use them for long-term archiving, perhaps offsite.
- External portable hard drives ranging from 20 to 120 GB in storage allow quick and affordable backup.
- If you have broadband access, web storage can serve as a secondary backup.

The main point is not to walk away from your computer at the end of a day without backing up your day's work.

Summary

In this chapter, you learned the basics of PowerPoint: how to open a PowerPoint presentation, organize and find your presentations, view presentations most effectively, move around a presentation, get help, and save a presentation. In the next chapter, you get started with actually creating PowerPoint presentations.

Chapter 2

Create Your First Presentation

How to...

- Use the AutoContent Wizard
- Choose a background design
- Choose a slide layout
- Structure a presentation
- Write or import a text outline
- Use placeholders for text
- Place text in text boxes and AutoShapes
- Create fancy text effects with WordArt
- Eliminate spelling and style errors
- Create a summary slide
- Complete a presentation: tutorial

After learning the basics of PowerPoint in Chapter 1, you are now ready to create a great presentation. Creating a presentation involves a combination of preparing the text content and adding visual appeal. In this chapter, I explain how to structure the content of a presentation. You can also complete the quick tutorial to get a feel for the process of creating an entire presentation.

Create Your Presentation

You can create a presentation in PowerPoint using four methods. Your choice should depend on how independently you want to work:

- Use the AutoContent Wizard for professional help creating your text outline. This option provides the most support and structure. However, as you'll see, this method still requires a good deal of work on your part to customize the presentation to your needs.

- Choose a design template to create a background. PowerPoint's design templates include not only backgrounds, but also text styles and color schemes. For the content of the presentation, you're on your own.

- Start with a blank presentation when you want to work from scratch and create both the text and the background yourself.

- Use an existing presentation when you want to create a presentation that resembles an existing one.

The New Presentation task pane offers you these four options in the New section. Refer back to Figure 1-3 in Chapter 1 for an explanation of this task pane.

2

Use the AutoContent Wizard

The AutoContent Wizard cannot divine exactly what you need to say. Rather, it provides a general structure and suggested topics. Most professionals ignore it because, in most cases, a presentation needs to be designed individually, rather than from canned content. Rarely can the AutoContent presentations even come close to fulfilling your needs.

Then when should you use the AutoContent Wizard? The answer is when your needs loosely match one of the presentations and/or you need a presentation on very short notice. Or you may be the type of person who needs help organizing your ideas. Finally, you can use it as a learning tool, a training exercise to help you ask the right questions and clarify how to unfold a mature PowerPoint presentation. The complete presentations included with PowerPoint's AutoContent Wizard have been created by professionals to thoroughly cover a topic. You just need to replace the text with the specifics applicable to your situation. PowerPoint offers the following topics:

- **General**   Generic, Recommending a Strategy, Communicating Bad News, Training, Brainstorming Session, and Certificate
- **Corporate**   Business Plan, Financial Overview, Company Meeting, Employee Orientation, Group Home Page, and Company Handbook
- **Projects**   Project Overview, Reporting Progress or Status, and Project Post-Mortem
- **Sales/Marketing**   Selling a Product or Service, Marketing Plan, and Product/Services Overview

To start, click AutoContent Wizard in the New Presentation task pane to open the title screen of the wizard. Click Next. On the next screen of the wizard, choose a presentation type and a specific topic. Click Next. Here you see the topics available for the Corporate type of presentation.

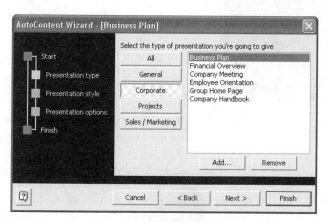

TIP   *Click Add to add an existing presentation to the list. You can use this feature to place in the AutoContent Wizard boilerplate presentations or presentation outlines that you use often. Click Remove to remove presentations that you know you will never use.*

The next screen asks you for the type of output, as you see here. Choose how you will display the presentation to your audience to get the right size and format. Then click Next.

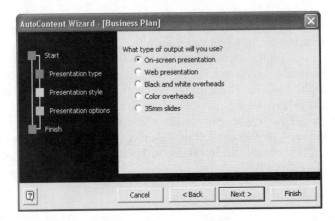

The next screen offers you some specific options for creating the presentation, as shown here. Enter a title for the entire presentation and any information that you want to appear on each slide. You can change any of these options later.

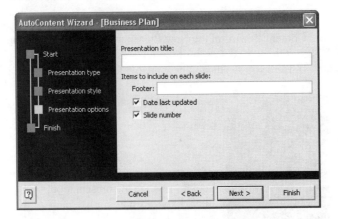

PowerPoint creates an entire presentation once you click Finish. In Figure 2-1, you see a complete presentation created with the AutoContent Wizard. The title slide has been customized to suit the company's needs.

Look at the outline in the Outline pane in Figure 2-1. It covers all the topics most companies need for an employee orientation but includes no specifics. Once you have created a presentation with the AutoContent Wizard, you need to edit the text for your specific situation and needs. (Chapter 3 covers editing text.) Nevertheless, it is a complete slide show with text and background, and may include other features such as footnotes, animation, etc. The slide show in Figure 2-1

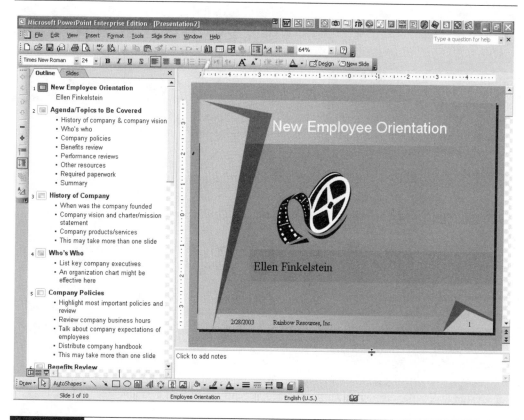

includes today's date and the slide number at the bottom of each slide. In addition, transitions and animation have been added to the slides. (Chapter 9 covers transitions and animation.) You can use the information in the rest of this book to finalize the presentation.

For creating a complete presentation quickly, there's nothing like the AutoContent Wizard. However, you will always need to customize your content.

Choose a Background Design

Let's say that you don't need any help with the text. You know exactly what you want to say and may already have prepared an outline. (Outlines are covered in the "Structure a Presentation from an Outline" section, later in this chapter.) In this case, choose a design template to create a new presentation.

To create a presentation from a design template, choose From Design Template in the New Presentation task pane and click OK. The task pane automatically switches to show you the

Did you know?

The Importance of Design Templates

Design templates are backgrounds for your slides. A *background* comprises both a colored background and design elements that appear on every slide. The template also includes other features such as a color scheme, bullet design, specific fonts, and font sizes. You can also add text animation to the template. Using a design template creates a unified look for your entire presentation.

> **NOTE** *Many new templates are available from the Templates Web site. To find them, scroll down to the bottom of the templates in the Slide Design–Design Templates task pane and click the Design Templates on Microsoft.com link.*

The truth is that if you hire outside professionals to make a slide show for you, they always create a background design from scratch. However, you can often find an appropriate design template that will give your presentation a professional look. Your choice of design template has a powerful effect on the impact of your presentation.Chapters 5, 6, and 7 are packed with helpful information and tips on graphic layout, color, and visual effects that can help you decide the best design template to use. Refer to Chapter 7 for details on creating your own design template.

Slide Design task pane, displaying currently used, recently used, and available design templates, as shown in Figure 2-2.

> **NOTE** *Since PowerPoint 2002, you can use as many design templates as you wish, by applying any design template to selected slides only. However, don't go overboard! Stick to one or two design templates.*

Use the scroll bar to view all the design templates until you find one you like. As you pass your mouse over a template preview, a down arrow appears. Click the arrow and choose one of the options:

- **Apply to Master** Appears as an option only if you have more than one design template in your presentation. Select a slide and choose this option to apply the design template to all the slides using the design template of the selected slide. See Chapter 7 for a full explanation of masters.

- **Apply to All Slides** Applies the design template to all existing slides in the presentation. If all your slides use one template, you can simply click the desired template to apply it to all the slides.

■ **Apply to Selected Slides**   Applies the design template to a selected slide or group of slides. You can select one or more slides in the Outline pane. If you are working in the Slide pane, the displayed slide is selected.

■ **Show Large Previews**   Increases the size of the thumbnail previews so you can see them better.

TIP *Use the Slides tab in the Outline pane to check the results when you are applying a design template to slides. You can quickly see which slides are affected by the change.*

FIGURE 2-2   Use the Slide Design task pane to choose a design template.

Start from Scratch

The third method of creating a new presentation is to start with a blank presentation. Choose Blank Presentation from the New section of the New Presentation task pane.

The main reason to start with a blank presentation is to create your own background design rather than use one of PowerPoint's design templates. Once you have created a design, creating a presentation from scratch is no different from using a design template. However, you can attach one of PowerPoint's design templates to your presentation at any time, using the Slide Design task pane as explained previously. Chapter 7 outlines the steps for creating your own design template.

The blank presentation comes with a number of default settings, such as the size of the title text, the type of bullets, and the color scheme. You can change these settings if you want to customize the blank presentation template for your own needs. You might also want to add actual content, such as your company's logo. These changes will affect all future presentations that you create using the Blank Presentation option. Here's how:

1. Create any presentation with the settings and/or content that you want.

2. Choose File | Save As.

3. In the Save as Type drop-down list, choose Design Template.

4. In the File Name box, type **Blank Presentation**.

5. Click Save.

6. Click Yes in the confirmation message box that PowerPoint displays.

Start a New Presentation from an Existing One

The fourth way to start a new presentation is to base it on an existing presentation. Follow these steps:

1. Click From Existing Presentation in the New Presentation task pane.

2. In the New from Existing Presentation dialog box, choose the presentation you want to use as the basis for your new presentation.

3. Click Create New.

You now have a new, unnamed presentation that is an exact duplicate of the original presentation. If you find yourself in slide master view, click Close on the Slide Master View toolbar. Save the presentation to name it.

Lay Out a Slide with AutoLayouts

Once you choose a design template or start a blank presentation, PowerPoint displays one slide on the screen, usually a title slide, containing space for you to enter the title of the presentation. You can start by designing this slide with its current layout or change the layout of the slide. Also, for each new slide you create, you need to choose a layout. A *layout*—or AutoLayout—specifies how the text, graphics, or other elements are laid out on the slide. PowerPoint comes with a large number of preset layouts that you can use. AutoLayouts are extremely helpful for creating slides. Picking the right one is essential for a legible slide that communicates instantly.

Whether you are changing the layout of an existing slide or creating a new slide, you specify the layout in the Slide Layout task pane, shown in Figure 2-3. This task pane automatically appears whenever you create a new slide. To create a new slide, click New Slide on the Formatting toolbar.

The Slide Layout task pane offers the following choices:

- **Title Slide**   Use this layout for the first slide of your presentation or for the first slide of each section. It includes a heading and a subheading.

- **Title Only**   As its name implies, there is only a heading. Title Only is best when you want to create your own layout. For example, this layout is great for a large photograph of your product.

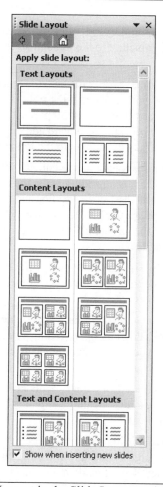

FIGURE 2-3   Choose an AutoLayout in the Slide Layout task pane.

■ **Title and Text**   This layout structures your text in a bulleted list. Use this layout when you have only a few items and the items need the full width of the slide. There is a heading at the top of the slide. A *bullet* is a small dot or other shape that appears before each item in a list. Look ahead to Figure 2-4, which shows this AutoLayout before any additions have been made.

■ **Title and 2-Column Text**   Use this layout when you have at least four items and each item is short. There is a heading at the top of the slide.

■ **Blank**   Use this layout if you like to work from scratch.

■ **Content**   This layout provides a set of clickable icons that you use to insert a table, a chart, clip art, a picture, a diagram or organizational chart, or a media clip—usually a movie/video file.

■ **Title and Content**   This layout is like the Content AutoLayout, but there is room for a title.

■ **Text and Content**   Several AutoLayouts offer various configurations of content icons. For example, you can insert a picture to the left and an organizational chart to the right of a slide.

■ **Title, Text, and Clip Art**   This layout puts bulleted text on the left and a place for clip art or any other graphic (that you provide) at the right. There is a heading at the top of the slide. Professionals suggest that at least 50 percent of your slides should include some kind of graphic. Chapter 5 explains how to add clip art and graphics to your slides. There is also a variation that puts the clip art at the left and the text at the right.

■ **Title, Text, and Chart**   Two layouts include bulleted text on the left and a chart (graph) on the right, or vice versa. There is a heading at the top of the slide. Use the layout with the text on the left when you will discuss the text first and then the chart, because it is natural for the audience to look from left to right. Use a chart when communicating trends or patterns in numerical data—such as annual sales over the last three years. Chapter 8 discusses adding charts to slides.

■ **Title, Text, and Media Clip**   Two AutoLayouts offer bulleted text on the left and a media clip placeholder on the right, or vice versa. A media clip includes various types of digital sound and movie files.

■ **Title and Table**   This layout lets you insert a table under a heading. Double-click the icon on the slide, and a dialog box opens letting you specify the number of columns and rows. Use a table when you need to communicate complex data and when a graph is not appropriate. Chapter 8 covers tables.

■ **Title and Diagram or Organization Chart**   This layout inserts a diagram or organization chart under a heading. Chapter 8 explains how to create diagrams and organization charts on slides.

■ **Title and Chart**   This layout is just a chart under a heading. Use this layout when you want the chart to be as large as possible and you don't need any supplemental text. If your chart is well designed, you often do not need any text beside it.

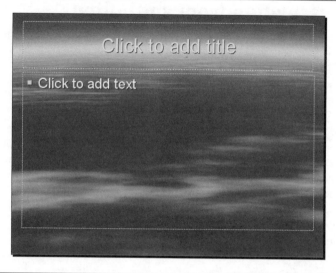

FIGURE 2-4   A new slide using the Title and Text AutoLayout

Figure 2-4 shows a slide after choosing the Title and Text AutoLayout. Notice the two dotted rectangles. These are called *placeholders,* and they hold the place for objects on your slide—in this case, text. Other placeholders are used for clip art, charts, and so on. Later in this chapter, in the "Add Text to a Presentation" section, I discuss how to use the placeholders to add text.

Complete the Presentation Structure

Once you have chosen a design template and an AutoLayout for your first slide, you can complete the structure of the entire presentation in one of two ways:

- Work in the Slide pane and enter text in the text placeholder(s), if any. Choose New Slide on the Formatting toolbar to add a new slide. As mentioned earlier, the Slide Layout task pane opens again to let you choose an AutoLayout. Then add text in the text placeholder(s) for the new slide. Continue in this way until you have completed your presentation. You can add graphics and animation as you work or complete the text first and go back to work on the artistic parts.

- Work in the Outline pane and create a text outline for the entire presentation. PowerPoint automatically creates new slides for you. Continue until you have completed your presentation. You can adjust the layout later. Of course, you will want to add graphics, animation, and so on.

The next few sections explain how to create outlines in the Outline pane as well as how to enter text in placeholders.

Structure a Presentation from an Outline

It would be nice to create a presentation without having to type text in the text placeholders on each individual slide. You can. In fact, the quickest way to create a complete presentation is to type an outline of your text on the Outline tab of the Outline pane. Working with the Outline pane is ideal for creating the text of your presentation because you can see most of the text at a glance. This strategy lets you view the flow of ideas from slide to slide. You can easily rearrange text later by moving it from one slide to another.

When you type your outline, PowerPoint automatically creates new slides for you as you work. You immediately see the results in the Slide pane at the right of your screen. When you have finished typing your outline, you have a complete presentation. All you need to do is refine it.

Bulleted text that you type in the Outline pane is placed in text placeholders. By default, PowerPoint uses the Bulleted List layout.

Figure 2-5 shows an outline in the Outline pane. Note that the Outline pane has been expanded by dragging to the right the divider between the Outline pane and the Slide pane. Work with the outline to help you to organize and structure your entire presentation.

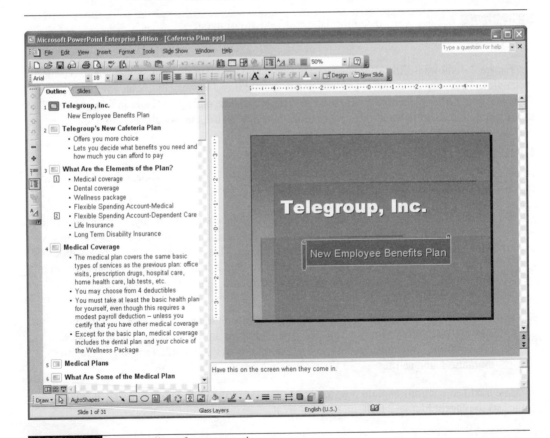

FIGURE 2-5 The outline of a presentation

Understand Outlines

An outline has *levels* of text, as shown in Figure 2-6. The level determines whether text becomes the title of a slide or a bulleted item (also called *body text,* because it makes up the body of the text on a slide). You can also create up to five levels of bulleted items. Each level of bulleted text is indented more than the previous one and generally uses a smaller type size.

Once you know the special terms that apply to the outlining function, you will feel right at home working with outlines. They are listed and explained here:

■ **Promote**   To make text one level higher. For example, second-level bulleted text becomes first-level bulleted text; first-level bulleted text becomes a slide title.

SHORTCUT   *Select bulleted text and press* SHIFT-TAB *to promote it.*

Slide number and icon   Slide title

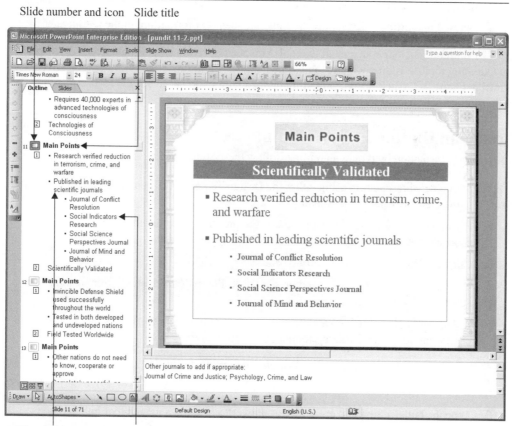

First-level bulleted text   Second-level bulleted text

FIGURE 2-6   An outline has levels of text

■ **Demote** To make text one level lower. For example, a slide title becomes first-level bulleted text, and first-level bulleted text becomes second-level bulleted text.

SHORTCUT *Select bulleted text and press* TAB *to demote it.*

■ **Move Up** To move selected text above the previous text.

■ **Move Down** To move selected text below the following text.

■ **Collapse** To hide all text lower than the slide title, for one slide only. Collapsing text lets you see more of your presentation so you can assess its overall structure. You can collapse text for one slide or for the entire presentation (Collapse All).

■ **Expand** To display all the levels of text, for one slide only. You can expand text for one slide or for the entire presentation (Expand All).

■ **Summary Slide** A slide containing the titles of your other slides. Use this slide for a table of contents, agenda, or ending (summary) slide.

■ **Show Formatting** To display the font and other text formatting in the Outline pane.

The Outlining toolbar contains all the tools you need to create an outline quickly. To display the Outlining toolbar, right-click any toolbar and choose Outlining. The Outlining toolbar is shown in Figure 2-7. Click Show Formatting on the Outline toolbar to see the text formatting in the Outline pane as you work.

Create an Outline in PowerPoint

To create a presentation by typing an outline, follow these steps:

1. Start a new presentation using either the Design Template or Blank Presentation option in the New Presentation task pane.

2. If you would like a slide layout for the entire presentation other than Bulleted Text, choose the AutoLayout you want in the Slide Layout task pane.

3. Click the Outline tab of the Outline pane.

4. Type the title of the first slide and press ENTER. PowerPoint creates a second slide automatically. See Figure 2-8a.

5. If you want bulleted text on a slide, press ENTER after typing the slide's title. Then click Demote on the Outlining toolbar. See Figure 2-8b.

NOTE *On a title slide only, if you click Demote, you create a subtitle.*

6. Type the bulleted text and press ENTER. PowerPoint starts a new line of bulleted text. See Figure 2-8c.

7. Continue to type bulleted text.

Promote
Demote
Move Up
Move Down
Collapse

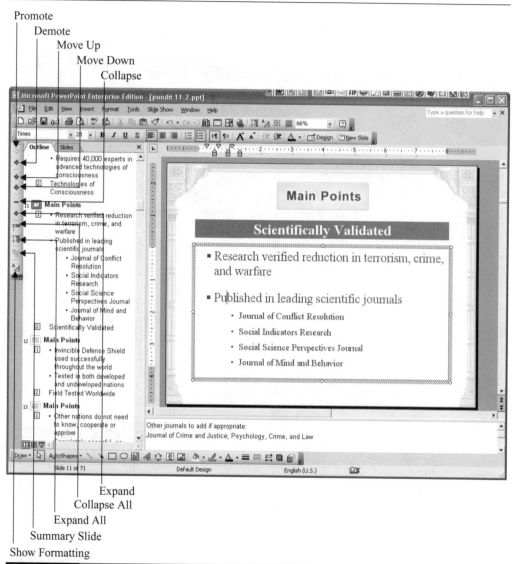

Expand
Collapse All
Expand All
Summary Slide
Show Formatting

FIGURE 2-7   The Outlining toolbar

8. To create second-level bulleted text, press Demote again. You can create up to five levels of bulleted text. See Figure 2-8d.

9. To return to a higher level of bulleted text (from second level to first level, for example), click Promote on the Outlining toolbar.

Type title of the first slide and press ENTER.

a

A second slide is created automatically.

On second slide, type slide's title and press ENTER.

b

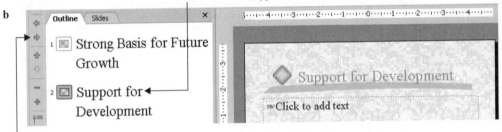

Then click Demote on Outlining toolbar.

Type bulleted text and press ENTER.

c

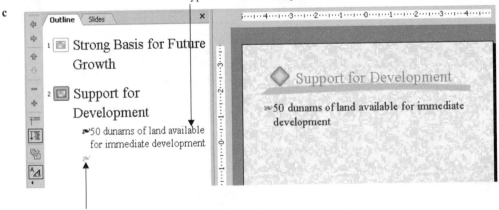

A new line of bulleted text starts automatically.

FIGURE 2-8 Typing an outline

2

d

To create second-level bulleted text, click Demote again.

When you have finished bulleted text for
a slide, press ENTER, and click Promote…

e

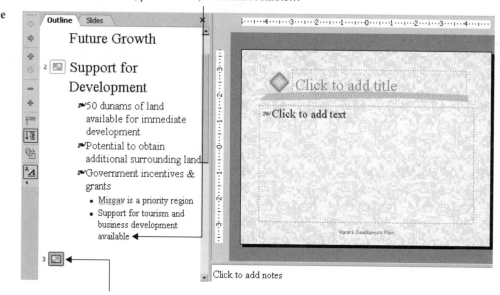

…until you see the New Slide icon.

FIGURE 2-8   Typing an outline *(continued)*

10. When you have finished typing the bulleted text for the slide, press ENTER and click
Promote until PowerPoint starts a new slide, as shown in Figure 2-8e.

11. If you want a different layout for the next slide, choose it from the Slide Layout task pane.

TIP

If you see that you will have too many bulleted items to fit on a slide, you may be able to fit them in two columns, as shown here. Open the Slide Layout task pane and choose Title and 2-Column Text. PowerPoint places a number 1 in a small box next to the text in the first column. Press CTRL-ENTER to move to the second column of text and continue typing. If you have already completed the text, select the text and drag it to the second column. Text in the second column is marked with a number 2 in a box, as shown here.

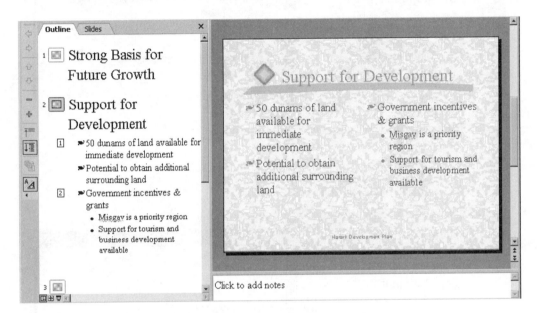

Chapter 3 covers techniques for editing existing outline text.

Import an Outline

You may prefer importing an outline created in a word processing program over creating the outline in PowerPoint. You may choose this option for several reasons:

- You can work faster in a word processing program.
- You need to collaborate with others who don't have or know PowerPoint in order to create the text for the presentation.
- You receive text for a presentation already created in a word processing program from a client, supervisor, or colleague.

Any time you have text already saved as a word processing document, import the text. There's no need to duplicate the effort of typing it.

Prepare the Outline

Before importing the text, you should review it so that you get the results you want. Most word processing programs have a feature called *styles,* which help you organize the formatting of your paragraphs. For example, in Microsoft Word, heading styles are used for headings. The Normal style is often used for the body of a paragraph. PowerPoint uses these styles, if they exist in your outline, to organize your text into a complete presentation. By creating the appropriate styles, you can determine exactly how your text will be organized on the slides of your presentation. Figure 2-9 shows an example. Here's how it works:

- Heading 1 style becomes the slide title.
- Heading 2 style becomes first-level bulleted text.
- Heading 3 style becomes second-level bulleted text and so on.

You can also organize your document by indenting the paragraphs. Paragraphs with no indentation become slide titles, and indented paragraphs become first-level bulleted text.

 Be sure that there are no blank lines in your outline because they are imported as blank slides.

If you need to import a plain text (ASCII) file, you can use tabs at the beginning of paragraphs to create your outline.

Chapter 3 explains how to insert all or part of an outline into an existing presentation.

Keeping our School Clean

Topics for Tonight's Discussion

The Problem

Existing Resources

Issues

Possible Solutions

The Problem

Graffiti on outside walls

Trash on grounds

Vandalism after hours, including broken fences

Landscaping

    Damage to bushes and trees

    Beautification

Existing Resources

Occasional volunteer projects

FIGURE 2-9   An outline in Microsoft Word prepared to create a presentation

 **Develop an Outline**

You should spend a lot of time and thought in creating your outline. It determines the content of your presentation—what you are going to say—and is the first and most important step in creating a presentation.

First decide the objective of your presentation, whether it's selling a product or service, explaining a program, or training employees. Then narrow your objective, such as training supervisors how to interview prospective employees.

Get as much information as possible about your audience. What do they already know? Why are they coming to the presentation? What do they want to gain? Then research your topic, always keeping in mind the objective of your presentation and the type of audience.

Next, decide on the structure of your presentation, the body of the presentation. Let's say you are recommending a strategy for reducing costs in the Human Resources Department. Your structure might be the following:

1. State the objective.
2. Explain the present situation.
3. List the possible strategies.
4. Analyze the advantages and disadvantages of each strategy.
5. Recommend one or more strategies.
6. Offer action steps for implementing the strategy or strategies.

Place your structure inside a broader framework:

- **Opening** Tell your audience the subject and, if appropriate, the objective of your talk.
- **Agenda** If appropriate, list the key areas you plan on covering.
- **Body** This is the main part of your presentation.
- **Examples and anecdotes** Give examples, tell anecdotes, and show pictures or video clips to add interest. These can be integrated into the body of the presentation.
- **Conclusion** Repeat the key areas you covered, including next steps to take.

Now write the outline, pouring the results of your research into the structure you want to use. When you are done, format the outline as explained in "Prepare the Outline." Use level 1 headings for main topics, the slides. Use level 2 headings for subtopics, the main bullets.

Edit and rewrite the outline until you are happy with it. You may want to run it by a colleague or your boss. Leave out anything that might not be clear or necessary. Of course, you can always change your text later.

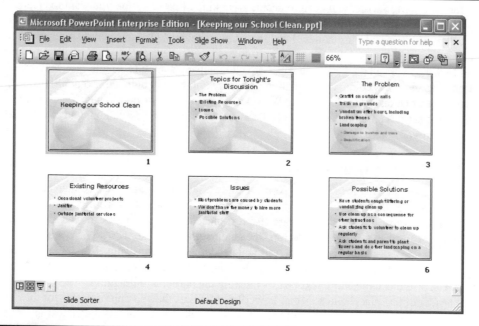

FIGURE 2-10   The outline after being imported into PowerPoint

Use the Outline

Once you have created and formatted your outline, you can create the presentation. Here are the steps:

1. From PowerPoint, choose File | Open.

2. In the Open dialog box, choose All Outlines from the Files of Type drop-down list.

3. Navigate to your outline and double-click the document that contains your outline.

PowerPoint creates the presentation. The next step usually is to assign a design template. Figure 2-10 shows the results. After that, you can add clip art, charts, and other design features.

Add Text to a Presentation

In the previous section, you learned how to add text to a presentation by creating an outline. However, you may want to add text directly on the slide or add additional text to an existing slide. For this reason, you need to understand all the ways to add text to a presentation. Text needs to be very clear—both visually and in content. In this section, you learn how to create professional-looking text.

Before you start to write, you need to decide what kind of presentation you want to create. Is your main goal to provide information, to tell a story? In that case, your text is very important, and you'll probably want to use bulleted text in text placeholders. Or suppose you really want to create an impression, a mood. Perhaps you want to excite sales reps about a new product feature but will follow up with all the details on paper or your company's intranet. In this case, text is less important than graphics, color, and animation. You may not use any bulleted text at all. Instead, you may use text boxes, AutoShapes, and WordArt. This book shows both types of presentations so you can see various possibilities. Once you know the goal of your presentation, you can choose the type of text you want.

Use Text Placeholders

The easiest way to add text is to click a text placeholder. Several AutoLayouts contain text placeholders. You can always recognize a text placeholder because it says, Click to Add Text. Placeholders for slide titles, which are also text placeholders, say, Click to Add Title. When you click inside a text placeholder, an I-beam cursor appears, showing where the text will appear, as you can see in Figure 2-11. All you need to do is start typing. The dotted border changes to a thick selection border and displays *handles,* which you can drag to resize the text box. You can also move the entire text box by clicking the border and dragging.

The beauty of text placeholders is that PowerPoint formats the text appropriately for the placeholder. For example, a title is usually centered and uses a larger font. Bulleted text is properly aligned to the right of the bullet and uses a smaller font. The design template controls

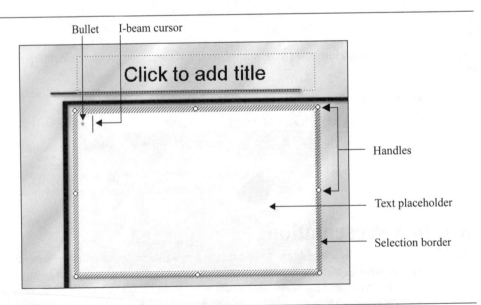

FIGURE 2-11   To add text to a slide, click a text placeholder and start typing.
Thanks to Digital Juice, //www.digitaljuice.com, for permission to use this design template.

this formatting, although you can change it. As a result, you get perfectly formatted text every time, for professional results.

To start a new paragraph in the bulleted text area, press ENTER. PowerPoint automatically creates a new bullet so you can continue typing.

NOTE
Only text that you type in a text placeholder is displayed on the Outline tab of the Outline pane. Other types of text, such as text in text boxes or WordArt, do not appear in the Outline pane.

The text in the text placeholder telling you to click to add text never appears on the slide during a presentation, even if you never add any text. The same is true of the dotted placeholder border. Therefore, if you insert a slide with a text placeholder and never place any text in it, at presentation you will have a blank slide that includes only the design template. Of course, if you don't need the text placeholder, you should probably delete it.

Figure 2-12 shows a slide with a title, bulleted text in a text placeholder, and some art. Using the text placeholder makes it very easy to create a slide like this.

Chapters 3 and 4 explain how to customize your text to look any way you want. Chapter 7 covers slide masters, the part of the design template that controls text formatting for the entire presentation.

Create Text Boxes

A common way to add text to a slide is to create a text box. Use a text box when you want to place text anywhere on the slide. For example, you can use a text box to create a caption for a graphic or to emphasize an important message. A text box is an *object,* which means that when

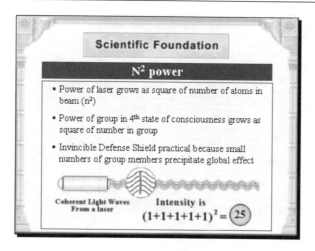

FIGURE 2-12   A slide with a title, bulleted text in a text placeholder, and some art

you click it, you can move and resize it. You can format the text in a text box in whatever way you wish, but this text does not appear in the Outline pane.

Figure 2-13 shows an example of text in a text box. This slide uses text boxes to create *callouts* (or labels) that point to the graphic at the center of the slide.

Like most objects in a PowerPoint presentation, a text box has its own properties, including a border, a background color or fill effect, and the text. The text boxes shown in Figure 2-13 do not have a visible border. A visible border is useful when you want to emphasize text; but on this slide, it would distract from the message. The fill has been eliminated so that the text looks like it has been written directly on the slide. Chapter 6 explains how to format borders and fills.

To create a text box, follow these steps:

1. Click the Text Box button on the Drawing toolbar. (You can also choose Insert | Text Box.)

2. Click and drag to create the text box. PowerPoint pays attention only to the width of the box you specify, not its length. Don't worry! The box now looks like a text placeholder.

3. Start typing to add the text. When you type enough text to get to the right side of the text box, PowerPoint automatically wraps the text to the next line. The box's length expands as you add text.

4. Click anywhere else on the slide to remove the selection border and handles.

To create the effect shown in Figure 2-13, create the text box using the steps just explained. To remove the border and fill, right-click the text box and choose Format Text Box from the shortcut menu. On the Colors and Lines tab, click the drop-down arrow in the Fill section and choose No Fill. Click the drop-down arrow in the Line section and choose No Line. The text box becomes completely invisible—all you see is the text.

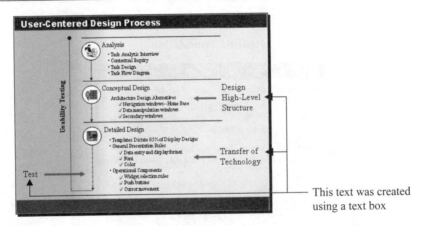

FIGURE 2-13   Use a text box when you want to place text anywhere on a slide.

Place Text in AutoShapes

PowerPoint includes a large number of shapes that you can add to a slide. These are called *AutoShapes.* You can use these shapes in many ways, but one way is to place and emphasize text. To insert an AutoShape, choose AutoShapes from the Drawing toolbar and use the menu that opens to choose an AutoShape. Then drag the shape onto a slide. To place text in an AutoShape, click the shape (if it isn't already selected) and start typing. Click outside the AutoShape to remove the selection border and handles. Figure 2-14 shows an example of text in an AutoShape. Here, Sony uses the text in AutoShapes for two purposes—to draw attention to a model number and to point to features of the remote commander. For more thorough information on AutoShapes, see Chapter 5.

Text that you type in an AutoShape is attached to that shape. You can move or rotate the AutoShape, and the text follows suit. Like text boxes, AutoShapes have a border and a fill color or effect. However, you rarely eliminate the border (unless you add a shadow or 3D effect) because the shape is then not apparent. As you can see on the slide, the distinctive shape and contrasting background color of the AutoShape help to make the text jump out from the rest of the slide.

To create the star-shaped AutoShape you see in Figure 2-14, choose AutoShapes | Stars And Banners on the Drawing toolbar and choose the top-left shape. On the slide, drag out the shape so that it is slightly wider than it is tall. To change the border, choose Line Color on the Drawing toolbar and then choose black. To change the fill, choose Fill Color, then More Fill Colors, and then whatever color you want. With the AutoShape still selected, type the text. The text will appear in the default font and size. Chapter 3 explains how to change the font and font size.

You can find the AutoShape callouts that point to the remote control in Figure 2-14 by choosing AutoShapes | Callouts on the Drawing toolbar. Choose the top-left shape, called Rectangular Callout, and drag it to the desired size on your slide. As described in the previous paragraph, change the fill color as desired and type the text. To pull out the pointer part, look for the yellow diamond. If you don't see it at first, click elsewhere on your slide, and then click the AutoShape again on its border. Drag the yellow diamond until the pointer points just where you want it. Voila!

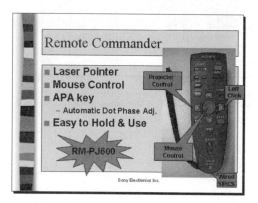

FIGURE 2-14   Text in AutoShapes stands out.

You can use AutoShapes instead of text placeholders. In the slide shown in Figure 2-15, all the text is in AutoShapes. The formatting of the AutoShapes you see here is repeated often throughout the presentation for a unified appearance. This slide is part of a distance education course on Human Resource Management.

Use WordArt

WordArt creates fancy text effects. It is ideal for text that you want to stand out. WordArt gives you much more control over the appearance of text than any other method of adding text to a slide. Figure 2-16 shows an example of WordArt text. Although WordArt is a powerful tool and adds a new dimension to your presentation, use it sparingly for maximum effect, and be careful that the words are still legible!

To create WordArt text, click Insert WordArt on the Drawing toolbar (or choose Insert | Picture | WordArt). WordArt opens its WordArt Gallery dialog box, shown in Figure 2-17. To choose a style, click one of the boxes and click OK. Notice that the right column contains all the vertical text styles.

WordArt now opens the Edit WordArt Text dialog box, as shown in Figure 2-18. Start typing to replace Your Text Here. Press ENTER whenever you want to start a new line. When you're done, click OK to close the dialog box.

Your WordArt now appears on your slide. You can move and resize the WordArt object as needed.

FIGURE 2-15   For a bolder appearance, you can use AutoShapes as a replacement for text placeholders.

FIGURE 2-16   The WordArt Gallery dialog box

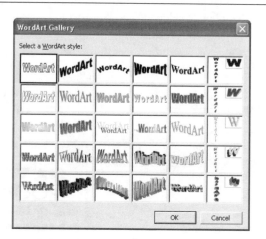

FIGURE 2-17   Use WordArt to create a powerful impression.

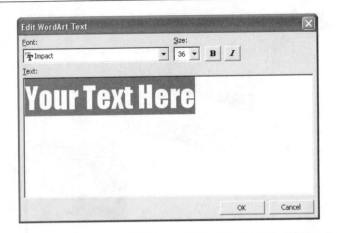

FIGURE 2-18   The Edit WordArt Text dialog box

Edit WordArt Text

When you place the WordArt object, the WordArt toolbar appears. The WordArt object remains selected so you can immediately use the buttons on this toolbar to modify the WordArt. The items on this toolbar and the available shapes are shown in Figure 2-19.

To edit any WordArt object, click to select it. The WordArt toolbar appears. (If it doesn't, right-click any toolbar and choose WordArt.)

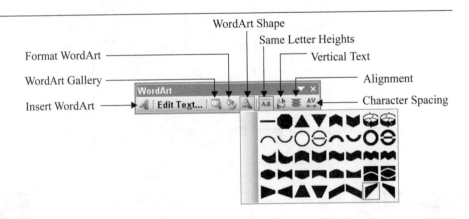

FIGURE 2-19   The WordArt toolbar and the available WordArt shapes

Many WordArt objects also display one or more yellow diamonds when selected. Point and drag on the diamond to change the special characteristics of the WordArt's shape. A boundary appears to help you see the changes as you drag, as shown here. Each diamond does something different, so you need to experiment.

Changes waviness of the letters

Shows effect of change as you drag

Changes how bottom curve matches top curve

The WordArt Gallery makes it easy to choose a predesigned text effect. However, you have total control of all these effects, using the WordArt toolbar. A WordArt effect is made up of these properties:

- **Text shape**   Choose WordArt Shape from the WordArt toolbar to change the shape.

- **Line color, type, and weight**   The line is actually the outline around the edges of the letters and the line type can be continuous, dashed, etc. Line weight means thickness. Choose Format WordArt and use the Colors And Lines tab to change the line's properties.

- **Fill color and fill effects**   Choose Format WordArt and use the Colors And Lines tab to change the fill. Refer to Chapter 6, which covers borders, colors, fills, and 3-D effects in detail. You can use all of the effects explained there for your WordArt objects.

- **Alignment**   Choose Alignment on the WordArt toolbar and choose one of the options. WordArt offers more alignment options than are available through PowerPoint's regular text formatting.

- **Character spacing**   Choose Character Spacing on the WordArt toolbar to specify the spacing between characters. Very tight sets the spacing at 80 percent, normal is 100 percent, and very loose is 150 percent. You can also type in a percentage in the Custom text box to set any character spacing you want.

TIP   *You can also edit WordArt using the Drawing toolbar, which is covered in Chapters 5 and 6. For example, you can add shadows and 3-D effects to your WordArt objects.*

Eliminate Spelling and Style Errors

Nothing screams "*unprofessional!*" more loudly than spelling errors in a presentation. PowerPoint not only lets you check your spelling, but also adds a *Style Checker* that checks for consistency and style.

Check Spelling

When you type a word that is not in PowerPoint's dictionary, you see a wavy line beneath it, appearing both in the outline and on the slide. To correct the word, right-click it to open the shortcut menu, as shown here.

Right-click any word with wavy red underlining.

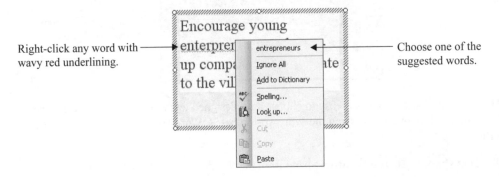

Choose one of the suggested words.

Words are often underlined inappropriately. For example, many names of people and companies are underlined because they are not in the dictionary, which can be most annoying. If you use these words frequently, you can add them to the dictionary, and they will never appear underlined again. If the words appear only in this presentation, click Ignore All, and they will no longer be underlined in the presentation.

The shortcut menu is enough for most needs, but if you want more detail, click Spelling on the shortcut menu to open the Spelling dialog box. Note that dialog box offers more options than the shortcut menu.

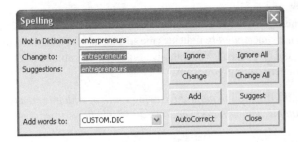

The Spelling dialog box lists the misspelled word and suggested alternatives. The Change To box displays the first alternative. You can choose any one of the suggested words or type another possibility in the Change To text box. The dialog box also contains the following options:

- **Ignore**   Ignores only the current instance of the word. This button changes and can appear as a Start or a Resume button, so you can start or resume a spell check.
- **Ignore All**   Ignores all instances of the word.
- **Change**   Choose a word from the Suggestions list and click Change to change the current word to the suggested word.
- **Change All**   Changes all instances of the current word to the suggested word.
- **Add**   Adds the word to the dictionary.
- **Suggest**   Suggests possible words. This is done automatically by default.
- **AutoCorrect**   Adds the incorrect and corrected words to the AutoCorrect list. Chapter 13 explains the AutoCorrect feature in detail.
- **Add Words To**   Specifies the dictionary to add words to.

CAUTION   *PowerPoint doesn't check the spelling of WordArt text or text in charts, documents, tables, and other elements that have been imported from other applications. You should therefore proofread this text carefully.*

If your misspelled word is actually a word, but not the one you want, the spell checker will not find it. Therefore, always proofread your presentation carefully and never depend on the spell checker to catch all your errors.

You can customize some options that specify how spell check works. For more information, see Chapter 14.

Use the Style Checker

One of the hallmarks of a professional presentation is consistency. The Style Checker ensures consistency of style throughout your presentation. It checks your presentation for consistency, style of sentence structure, and punctuation. To turn on style checking, choose Tools | Options and click the Check Style checkbox on the Spelling and Style tab. If you have the Office Assistant on, a lightbulb appears, reminding you of the style guidelines, as shown here. If the Office Assistant is not on, you cannot use style checking.

Click the light bulb to see information about the style guidelines, as shown here.

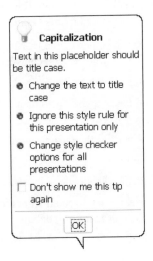

If you don't want the Office Assistant on while you work, turn it on (choose Help | Show the Office Assistant) when you have finished your presentation and want to review it for style. Scroll through the presentation, looking for lightbulbs.

The Style Checker checks for the following:

■ **Consistent capitalization**   Titles are checked for initial capitalization of each word and bulleted text is checked for capitalization of the first word.

■ **End punctuation**   Titles shouldn't have periods at the end, and bulleted text should be consistent—either always have periods or never have them.

■ **Maximum number of fonts**   By default, you should have no more than three font styles on a slide.

■ **Minimum font size**   By default, titles should be no smaller than 36 points and bulleted text no smaller than 20 points.

You can also check for the maximum number of bulleted items on a slide and the maximum numbers of lines in a title or per bullet. These settings are turned off by default, but you can turn them on. To customize all your Style Checker settings, choose Tools | Options and use the Spelling and Style tab. Click Style Options to specify the exact settings in the Style Options dialog box. For more information, see Chapter 14.

The style guidelines that appear when you click the lightbulb offer you several choices:

■ Change the text to adhere to the style rule. For example, the Style Checker can remove ending punctuation or change capitalization.

■ Ignore the rule only in the current situation.

- Change the rule for all presentations, which opens the Style Options dialog box.
- Turn off the rule, which you do by checking Don't Show Me This Tip Again.

When changing title text to conform to title *case, the Style Checker capitalizes the first letter of each word, which is not considered proper usage. In general, most people go by the following rule: in a title, articles (the, a), conjunctions (and, or), and short prepositions (with, from) are not capitalized. To follow this rule, always check titles that you have allowed the Style Checker to change and change the words that you don't want capitalized.*

Find Synonyms

If you're at a loss for words, you can find synonyms by using the thesaurus. This new feature provides you with a tool that Microsoft Word users have had for years.

The easiest way to find a synonym is right-click any word and choose Synonyms from the menu. Pass the cursor over the right arrow to display a list of synonyms, as shown in Figure 2-20. At the bottom of the synonym list, you can choose Thesaurus Dialog to display the Research task pane where you can find more options.

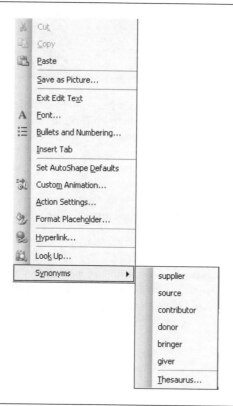

FIGURE 2-20   You can find synonyms by right-clicking any word or using the new Research task pane.

Create a Summary Slide

Audiences understand and remember a presentation better if they can grasp the wholeness of the message. For example, you may want to have an agenda slide near the beginning of your presentation so that your viewers know in advance all the topics that will be covered. A summary at the end of a presentation helps them to integrate all the material they have seen throughout. Both types of slides perform the same function—they summarize the topics covered in the presentation.

You can automatically create a summary slide in PowerPoint. A *summary slide* contains the titles of all the other slides, as shown here.

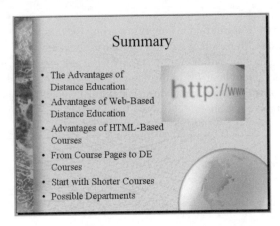

To create a summary slide, select all the slides you want to include in the summary slide. Then click Summary Slide on the Outlining toolbar. PowerPoint places the new slide in front of the selected slides. You can then move it wherever you want—for example, at the end of the presentation.

PowerPoint names the new slide Summary Slide. Don't forget to change this title to something more meaningful! Don't let the term *summary slide* fool you. You can use this feature however you wish. For example, you could change the title to Agenda, or Tonight's Topics, and use the slide at the beginning of the presentation—perhaps just after the title slide.

TIP
You can use the summary slide feature to create a list of slides at the end of the presentation and hyperlink each slide's title back to its slide. This strategy works well for a question-and-answer session. As someone asks a question about a slide, you can quickly go to that slide. Be sure to have hyperlinks on each slide back to the summary slide. For more information on creating hyperlinks, see Chapter 11.

Complete a Presentation: Tutorial

In this section, you create a short presentation to get an overview of the entire process. Throughout the tutorial, I refer you to the chapters that explain the feature in more detail. While the presentation is very simple, it contains many of the features you need to use when creating a presentation.

Develop the Framework

First you develop the framework for the presentation, including choosing a design template and adding a logo to the slide master.

1. Open PowerPoint. The Getting Started task pane appears at the right.

    NOTE *The Getting Started task pane does not appear if you have gone to Tools | Options, clicked the View tab, and unchecked Startup Task Pane. In this case, choose View | Task Pane to display the task pane.*

2. At the bottom of the Open section of the task pane, click Create a New Presentation to display the New Presentation task pane.

3. Choose From Design Template from the New section of the New Presentation task pane. The Slide Design task pane appears.

4. In the Slide Design task pane, choose any of the templates. The illustrations here show the Competition.pot template. The template appears on the first slide.

5. If you don't have a title slide on your screen, as shown here, click the down arrow at the top of the Slide Design task pane and choose Slide Layout. Choose the first AutoLayout, Title Slide.

6. To add a logo on all the slides, press SHIFT and click the Normal view button at the lower-left corner of the screen. The slide master view opens, as shown here. For more information, see Chapter 7.

7. From the Drawing toolbar, choose AutoShapes. (If you don't see the Drawing toolbar—usually at the bottom of your screen—right-click any toolbar and choose Drawing.) Then choose Basic Shapes and click the sun shape. Now click near the lower-right corner of the slide master to place the sun.

8. With the sun still selected, press SHIFT and drag any corner handle to enlarge the sun until it is about an inch in diameter. (The size will depend on your screen resolution but need not be exact for this tutorial.) If necessary, drag the sun so it is not too near the edge of the slide. Chapter 5 explains more about adding art and graphic objects.

9. With the sun still selected, click the arrow to the right of the Fill Color button on the Drawing toolbar. Choose one of the yellow colors that are part of the color scheme. The sun turns yellow. Chapter 6 explains how to work with color schemes and fills.

10. With the sun still selected, type **The Natural Gift**.

11. Select the text you just typed. Click Bold and Shadow on the Formatting toolbar. You read about formatting text in Chapter 3.

12. With the text still selected, click the Font Color button's down arrow (on the Drawing toolbar) and choose the darkest color in the color scheme colors. Click outside the text to see the results, shown in the next illustration.

13. Click the sun logo to select it and choose Edit | Copy to copy it to the clipboard.

14. In the Outline pane, you see two masters, one for the title slide and one for all other slides. Only the title slide master displays the logo. Click the other logo to display it in the slide pane. Choose Edit | Paste to paste the logo onto the master. It will now appear on all the slides in the presentation.

15. Click Close Master View on the Slide Master View toolbar to return to your first slide. You can see that your logo appears on the slide.

NOTE *To add a logo, you would most often insert an existing file by choosing Insert | Picture | From File.*

Add Slides

Once the framework is completed, you start to add slides to the presentation. You can either work on the slides in the slide pane or add text in the outline pane.

1. Click the text placeholder that says, "Click to add title." Type **Quarterly Sales Report**.

2. Click the text placeholder that says, "Click to add subtitle" and type **2nd Quarter, 2003.** Click outside the textbox to deselect the text and see how it looks.

3. Click Save on the Standard toolbar. Keep the suggested title of "Quarterly Sales Report." Navigate to the desired location and click Save.

4. Click New Slide on the Formatting toolbar. A new slide, using the Title and Text AutoLayout, appears.

5. Click the text placeholder that says, "Click to add title." Type **Overall Sales Up**.

6. Click the text placeholder that says, "Click to add text." Type **Total sales were up 6% from last quarter** and press ENTER. A new bullet appears.

7. Type **Gifts were up 15%** and press ENTER.

8. Type **Office supplies were down 14%**. Your slide should look like the slide shown here.

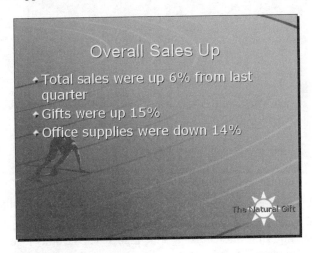

9. Click the Outline tab of the Outline pane. Place the cursor on the last line of the text and press ENTER.

10. Click Promote on the Outline toolbar to start a new slide. The new slide appears in the Slide pane.

11. Type **Our Competitors** and press ENTER. A new slide appears.

12. Click Demote on the Outline toolbar. The new slide disappears and the cursor is now beneath the previous slide's title.

13. Type **Our market share for gifts increased slightly** and press ENTER. A new bullet appears.

14. Type **Our market share for office supplies decreased slightly** but do not press ENTER.

Add a Chart

After creating some slides, you add a chart showing the details of the quarterly sales in graphic form. Charts and graphs are covered in Chapter 8.

1. Click New Slide on the Formatting toolbar. The new slide uses the Title and Text AutoLayout.

2. If necessary, display the Slide Layout task pane by clicking the down arrow of the task pane and choosing Slide Layout. (If no task pane is displayed, choose View | Task Pane.)

3. From the Content Layouts section of the task pane, click the Title and Content.

4. The middle of the slide displays six small icons. Click the top middle icon. (The tooltip says Insert Chart.)

2

5. You now see a chart (a graph) and a *datasheet,* a small spreadsheet where you enter your data for the chart, as shown here.

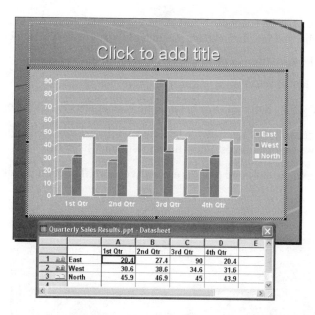

6. Complete the datasheet as shown here. To delete the "D" column, click the letter "D" (the column header) and press DEL. As you type, you see the chart develop on the slide.

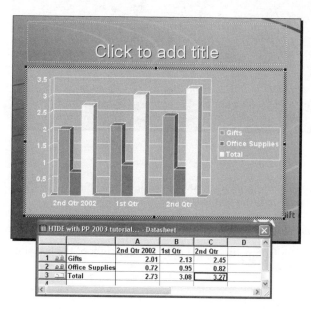

You can drag the bar between the column heads to resize the columns of the datasheet.

7. To change the chart type, choose Chart | Chart Type from the menu. In the Chart Type dialog box, choose Line, then choose the upper-left chart sub-type, Line. Click OK.

8. For each of the three lines in the chart, do the following:

   a. Click the line to select it.

   b. Choose Format | Selected Data Series. The Format Data Series dialog box opens.

   c. In the Line section of the Patterns tab, click Custom. From the Weight drop-down list, choose the bottommost line—the widest line. Click OK.

9. Click the title of the slide and type **Comparative Sales**. The chart is automatically deselected.

10. Click anywhere outside the slide to deselect any objects and see the result, shown here.

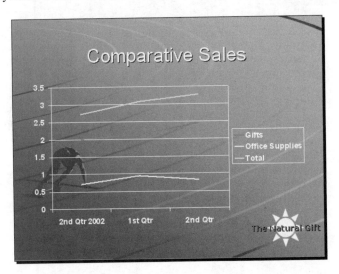

Move a Slide

Here you move a slide to a new position. You can add, delete, or move slides whenever necessary. Chapter 3 covers editing text and slides.

1. Click the Slide Sorter view button at the lower-left corner of your screen.

2. Click Slide 3 (Our Competitors) and drag it to the right of the last slide (slide 4).

2

Add Animation

Presenters often animate bulleted text so that they can control when each line appears. Here you add an animation scheme to the entire presentation. Animation is explained in Chapter 9.

1. With the presentation still in slide sorter view, click Slide Show | Animation Schemes. The Slide Design — Animation Schemes task pane appears.

2. From the list of Subtle animation schemes, choose Appear. At the bottom of the task pane, click Apply to All Slides.

View the Slide Show

Our simple presentation is complete and now is the time to view the results of your work. Chapter 15 covers techniques for delivering a presentation.

1. Click the first slide and click the Slide Show button at the lower-left corner of the screen. You see the first slide displayed fullscreen, as shown here. Only the first title appears.

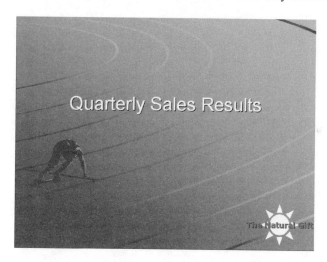

2. Click the mouse button. The sub-title appears in accordance with the Appear animation scheme you chose.

3. Click the mouse button again to see the next slide.

4. Continue to click the mouse button until you have seen the entire slide show. At the end is a black screen.

5. Click once more to leave slide show view and return to slide sorter view.

Congratulations! You have completed the entire presentation. This overview gives you a firm basis to go deeper into PowerPoint's features, which are covered throughout this book.

Summary

In this chapter, you learned how to create a presentation by using the AutoContent Wizard, by choosing a design template, by starting with a blank presentation, and using an existing presentation. You saw how to add text to a text placeholder, a text box, and an AutoShape. In addition, you learned how to create special text effects with WordArt. This chapter covered creating a text outline from within PowerPoint as well as importing an outline. Once you have created an initial draft of a presentation, you should check both the spelling and the style—this chapter explained how. You also learned how to create a summary slide. Finally, you created a complete presentation as an overview of the entire process that is developed throughout this book.

In the next chapter, you move on to the next step: editing a presentation.

Chapter 3

Edit Text

How to...

- ◼ Move and copy text
- ◼ Use the clipboard
- ◼ Expand one slide into two
- ◼ Edit placeholder text
- ◼ Edit text in AutoShapes and text boxes
- ◼ Edit WordArt text
- ◼ Add symbols to your text
- ◼ Use AutoCorrect to automate text changes
- ◼ Use the right font for the message
- ◼ Make the font bigger or smaller
- ◼ Work in Slider Sorter view
- ◼ Import slides from other presentations
- ◼ Keep a slide library

Once you have created your presentation, you will find that it needs to be edited, just like any other document. Editing a presentation is somewhat different than editing a word processing document, although there are many common elements as well. The differences occur because of the graphical nature of a slide. In this chapter, you learn about editing text as well as your presentation as a whole.

Edit for Clarity

Your main concern when editing text is clarity. Text on a slide is quite different from text in a word processing document. Bulleted text is often not in full sentences, yet it needs to be clear, nonetheless. Try reading the text on each slide aloud to see if it makes sense. When you deliver the presentation, you expand on the text and explain each item fully.

A second reason to edit text is aesthetic. If you created your presentation using an outline, you need to run through each slide to see how the text fits on the slide. Text may need to be cut. You may even want to add text for a balanced look.

The basic techniques for editing text are the same in all Windows programs:

- ◼ To add text, place the cursor where you want the new text to appear and start typing.
- ◼ To edit text, select the text you want to change and type the new text that you want.
- ◼ To delete text, select it and press DEL.

To change the case of text, select the text and choose Format | Change Case. You can change the case to uppercase, lowercase, sentence case, or title case.

SHORTCUT   *Select the text and press SHIFT-F3 to cycle through the case choices.*

I cover changing fonts in the "Choose Text with Style" section, later in this chapter. Formatting bullets and paragraphs is covered in Chapter 4. You can set text-editing options, such as whether text is automatically resized to fit in text placeholders, in the Options dialog box. See Chapter 14 for more details.

Move and Copy Text

Within a presentation, you can often move selected text by dragging it to the new location on the Outline tab of the Outline pane. Hold down CTRL to copy the text instead of moving it. However, if you can't see both the source and destination locations on the screen at one time, you should use the clipboard. Use the Cut, Copy, and Paste commands on the Edit menu or the buttons on the Standard toolbar.

SHORTCUT   *Use CTRL-X to move text and CTRL-C to copy text. Then place the cursor in the desired location, and use CTRL-V to paste the text.*

To copy text from another presentation or document, you can use the clipboard as well. Follow these steps:

1. Open the file that contains the source text.
2. Select the text.
3. Copy the text to the clipboard.
4. Move to the desired destination in the presentation, and place the cursor where you want the text to appear.
5. Paste the text from the clipboard.

You can also use drag-and-drop to move or copy text from one file to another. It's more fun but requires more dexterity than using the clipboard. Here's how:

1. Open both files. (It may help to close other, unnecessary files.)
2. Choose Window | Arrange All. You see both your presentation and the other document on your screen. Make sure you can see both the source and destination locations in each window.
3. Click in the source document, and select the text you want to move or copy.
4. To move the text, point to it, and drag it to the desired location in your presentation. To copy the text, hold down CTRL as you drag.

Later in this chapter, in "Import Slides from Other Presentations," I explain how to copy slides from other presentations.

Use the Clipboard Task Pane

Office now includes a Clipboard task pane that lets you place up to 24 items on the clipboard at once.

The Clipboard task pane automatically opens when you copy or cut items twice consecutively in PowerPoint. Otherwise, subsequent items are not automatically copied to the clipboard unless the Clipboard task pane is displayed. To manually display the Clipboard task pane, choose Edit | Office Clipboard.

You can collect multiple items when the Clipboard task pane is not displayed by opening the task pane manually, clicking Options, and choosing Collect Without Showing Office Clipboard. From then on, multiple items are invisibly collected on the clipboard, even when the task pane is not displayed.

Once the Clipboard task pane, shown here, is displayed, you simply copy a second item to the clipboard in the usual manner. You can then paste either item into your presentation. Each additional piece of data that you copy to the clipboard (up to 24 items) is added as a separate item. To paste an item from the Clipboard task pane, place your cursor wherever you want the item to appear and then click the item on the task pane.

You can use the Paste All button on the Clipboard task pane to collect text from several places and paste it all in a new location.

Edit Placeholder Text

Because placeholder text also appears in the outline, you can edit it either in the outline or directly on the slide. Editing placeholder text on the outline may be more familiar to you because it is quite similar to editing text in a word processor. If all you want to do is simple text editing, do it in the Outline pane.

However, you may want to edit text directly on the slide for several reasons:

■ The text is larger and therefore easier to see.

■ The slide may contain a graphic, and you may need to see how the text fits with the graphic. For example, you may want to edit your text because it covers the graphic.

■ You may be performing several editing functions at once, such as changing the placeholder's background color along with editing the text. Because you must change the placeholder's background color directly on the slide, it is easy to continue your work right on the slide.

■ You instantly and clearly see the results of your text attributes, such as color, shadow, font, and font style (such as bold or italic text).

When you edit placeholder text on the slide, two objects are involved—the placeholder and the text inside the placeholder. When you click any text in the placeholder, PowerPoint places the cursor where you clicked. The placeholder gets a selection border and handles to show you that it is selected. You can also drag to select the text you want to edit, which automatically selects the

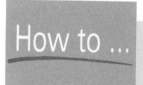

How to ...   Expand One Slide into Two

If you just can't make the text fit properly on a slide, try splitting the text onto two slides. If the text is in a text placeholder, you can accomplish this task easily on the Outline tab of the outline pane, as follows:

1. Position the insertion point at the end of the last bulleted item that you want to appear on the first slide.

2. Press ENTER.

3. On the Outline toolbar, click Promote until a New Slide icon appears.

4. Type a title for the new slide. You may have to adjust the bulleted text to get it to the proper level.

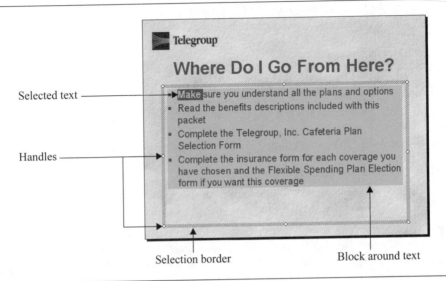

Selected text ————

Handles ————

Selection border

Block around text

FIGURE 3-1   Editing text in a placeholder

placeholder as well. You also see a block in a different color than the background that shows the overall boundaries of the text. You are now in Edit Text mode, shown in Figure 3-1. Although the placeholder is selected, your changes affect only the text within it.

To delete an entire bulleted item, place the cursor over the bullet. The cursor changes to a cross with arrows, as shown here. This technique works only when the placeholder is already selected. Click to select the entire bulleted item, and then press DEL.

- Make sure you understand all the plans and options
- Read the benefits descriptions included with this packet
- Complete the Telegroup, Inc. Cafeteria Plan Selection Form
- Complete the insurance form for each coverage you have chosen and the Flexible Spending Plan Election form if you want this coverage

If you backspace to delete the text in a bulleted item, or select only the words in an item, you may be left with just the bullet. With the cursor next to the bullet, press BACKSPACE twice to delete the bullet and the empty line. To add a bulleted item, place the cursor after the previous item, and press ENTER. You can then type the text.

To move a bulleted item above or below another item, follow these steps:

1. Place the cursor over the bullet.

2. Click and drag to the desired location. A long cursor line appears, showing you where your bulleted text will appear, as shown here.

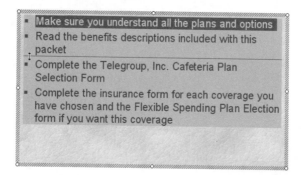

3. When the cursor line is where you want it, release the mouse button to move the text.

In this illustration, the first bulleted item will be moved below the second item. These techniques work on the Outline tab of the Outline pane as well.

In Chapter 2, I explained how to import an outline. You can also insert an outline into an existing presentation as part of the editing process. Follow these steps:

1. On the Outline tab of the Outline pane, click the slide you want the new text to appear after.

2. Choose Insert | Slides from Outline.

3. In the Insert Outline dialog box, shown in Figure 3-2, locate your outline and select it. Notice that the Files of Type drop-down list is already set to All Outlines.

4. Click Insert.

Work with Placeholders

Once you click a placeholder, you enter Edit Text mode. Any time you press DEL, text is deleted. In this case, how do you delete the placeholder itself? The answer is not very obvious. Here are the steps:

1. Click the border of the placeholder to exit Edit Text mode.

2. Press DEL again to delete the placeholder.

TIP   *Another way to exit Edit Text mode is to press* ESC.

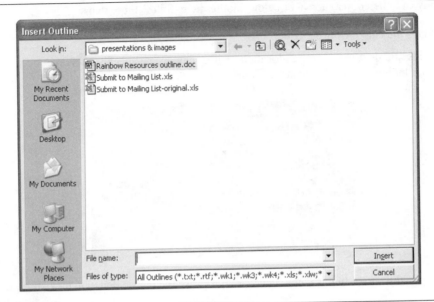

FIGURE 3-2 Use the Insert Outline dialog box to insert an outline into an existing presentation.

Here are some other things you can do with placeholders:

■ Once you have exited Edit Text mode, you can duplicate the placeholder. From the menu, choose Edit | Duplicate. You now have twin placeholders. Move the new placeholder so it doesn't overlap the first one.

 *Press* CTRL-D *to duplicate a placeholder.*

■ You can cut (or copy) and paste a placeholder to a new slide. Again, you need to exit Edit Text mode. Then press CTRL-X to cut or CTRL-C to copy. Move to the new slide and press CTRL-V to paste the placeholder.

■ To move a placeholder, select it and place the cursor anywhere over the selection border until you see the crossed arrows cursor. Then click and drag the placeholder to its new position.

■ To resize a placeholder, drag one of its handles. The placeholder grows or shrinks in the direction you drag.

In Chapter 5, I explain how to position and resize any object on a slide more precisely. See the section "Lay Out Your Slides with Precision."

Find and Replace Text

You can search for text throughout the entire presentation. You can also specify replacement text. You are probably already familiar with the Find and Replace feature of your word processor. To find text, choose Edit | Find (or press CTRL-F). The Find dialog box shown here is displayed.

3

Select Match Case to find *Governor* but not *governor,* for example. Select Find Whole Words Only to find *and* but not *sand.* PowerPoint highlights the text it finds in text placeholders only in the Outline pane but displays the equivalent slide so that you can work on either the outline or the slide. However, PowerPoint highlights text in text boxes and AutoShapes on the slide, because it doesn't appear in the outline. Click Find Next to continue to search for other instances of the word.

 The Find and Replace commands cannot find WordArt text. Be sure to check WordArt text carefully.

You can go directly to the Replace dialog box, shown here, by clicking Replace in the Find dialog box. Otherwise, choose Edit | Replace or press CTRL-H.

Type text you want to find ——

Type replacement text

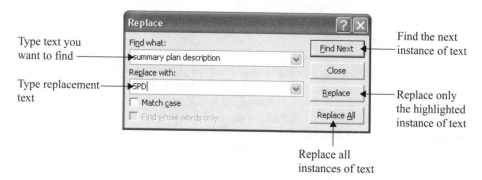

Find the next instance of text

Replace only the highlighted instance of text

Replace all instances of text

Change Text Case

For a professional look, pay attention to proper use and consistency of *case,* that is, capitalization. PowerPoint's Style Checker (covered in Chapter 2) looks for case. For example, the slide title usually uses title case and bulleted text uses sentence case. When you want to make changes, the

Change Case command can help you quickly change the case of text. Just select the text, and choose Format | Change Case. Here are your options:

- **Sentence case** Starts with an uppercase letter. All the rest of the letters are lowercase, and the sentence ends with a period.

CAUTION *When changing text to sentence case, PowerPoint also changes proper nouns to lowercase. For example, "We Go To School On Monday" becomes "We go to school on monday." You need to manually correct any such mistakes.*

- **lowercase** Contains all lowercase letters.
- **UPPERCASE** Contains all uppercase letters.
- **Title Case** Capitalizes the first letter of each word. But you'll still need to review the results—if you don't want short words such as *with, and,* and *a* capitalized. See the discussion of the Style Checker in Chapter 2 for more information.
- **tOGGLE cASE** Reverses the case of each letter.

When you have made your choice of case, click OK to close the dialog box.

Edit Text in AutoShapes and Text Boxes

Editing text in AutoShapes and text boxes is very similar to editing placeholder text. When you select the text, you are also selecting the object that contains the text, and a selection border and handles appear around the object.

TIP *If any word is underlined, right-click it to get the Spelling shortcut menu, where you can quickly correct the spelling.*

When you place text in a text box, the text box expands as you type. The text box similarly adjusts when you edit text. If you delete enough text, the text box will shrink accordingly.

If you add text to an AutoShape, it will overflow the boundaries of the shape. Right-click the shape and choose Format AutoShape from the shortcut menu. When the Format AutoShape dialog box opens, click the Text Box tab, as shown in Figure 3-3.

The Text Box tab of the Format AutoShape dialog box lets you format all the qualities of the AutoShape that pertain to text, as shown in Figure 3-3. You can format text in a text box in exactly the same way—the only difference is that the dialog box is called Format Text Box. These dialog boxes are the key to good-looking text in AutoShapes and text boxes.

TIP *To fit more text on an AutoShape or in a text box, reduce all four margins on the Text Box tab to zero. Here you see "before and after" examples of text in an AutoShape formatted using some of the settings of the Text Box tab in the Format AutoShape dialog box. As you can see, these settings are very important for obtaining professional results. For example, text that overflows the boundary of an AutoShape looks sloppy, but you can easily fix it by checking "Word Wrap Text in AutoShape" on the Text Box tab.*

3

Before adjusting settings

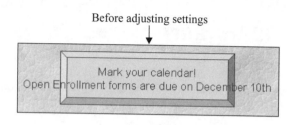

After adjusting settings

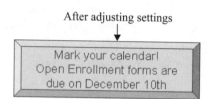

Wraps text to a new line to fit in the AutoShape

Specifies how text is centered in AutoShape

Resizes
AutoShape
based on size
of text

Sets margins
between text
and edge of
AutoShape

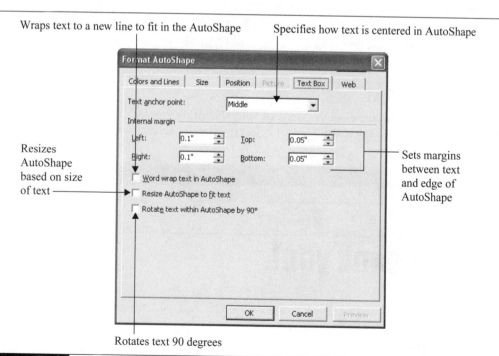

Rotates text 90 degrees

FIGURE 3-3 Use the Text Box tab of the Format AutoShape dialog box to specify how text fits in an AutoShape.

Did you know?

Uses for AutoShapes, Text Boxes, and WordArt

Text used in conjunction with meaningful AutoShapes or WordArt can help make your point—if you don't get carried away. For example, to show that sales went up 15 percent, put the text **15%** on an AutoShape of an arrow pointing diagonally upward about 15 degrees. Here are some guidelines:

- Use AutoShapes to organize your text for the audience. For example, if you set up two columns and three rows of text, in which direction are readers supposed to look first— down the first column or across the first row? You can place AutoShapes behind groups of text that you want readers to consider all at once.

- When you place text in AutoShapes and text boxes, make sure these objects are aligned with each other to avoid a chaotic effect. Chapter 5 explains how to perfectly align objects.

- Don't put too many AutoShapes with text on a slide. Sometimes simple bulleted text is easier to follow.

- WordArt is great fun, but use it sparingly. Use WordArt for short phrases that are separate from the rest of the text, such as "See you there!" or "Don't forget!"

Remember, too many effects make your text less readable, so use common sense.

Edit WordArt Text

To edit WordArt text, double-click the WordArt object. The Edit WordArt Text dialog box opens, shown here. You can also select the WordArt object (by clicking it once) and click Edit WordArt on the WordArt toolbar.

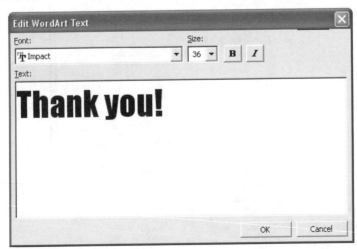

You can replace the entire text by typing new text. Otherwise, click to place the cursor or select part of the text to edit. When you have finished editing the text, click OK.

You can use the WordArt toolbar to edit any feature of the WordArt object in the same way you created it. (See Chapter 2 for a discussion of how to create WordArt.)

Add Symbols

To insert a symbol into new or existing text, choose Insert | Symbol. PowerPoint opens the Symbol dialog box, shown here:

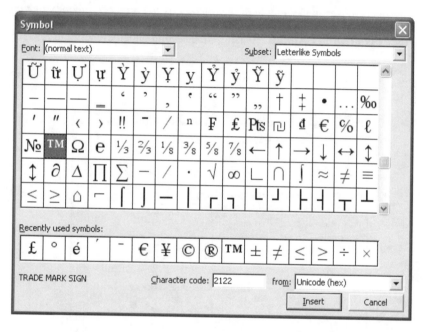

First, choose a font from the Font drop-down list. The default is Normal Text. Choose the symbol you want and then click Insert to insert the symbol. The dialog box stays open so you can insert other symbols. Click Close to close the dialog box.

Besides choosing technical symbols such as the degree symbol (°), the diameter symbol (ø), and the plus-minus symbol (±), you can find arrows, check marks, stars, and other more whimsical symbols. You may especially want to check the Wingdings and Monotype Sorts fonts.

| NOTE | *For complex equations, use the Microsoft Equation Editor. Choose Insert | Object and choose Microsoft Equation 3.0. (If the Equation Editor is not there, you need to install it.) Create the equation. (The Equation Editor has its own Help file.) Then choose File | Exit and Return to Presentation. The equation is always black text, so if you have a dark background, place a light-colored rectangle behind it.* |

Use AutoCorrect

AutoCorrect is a feature that automatically corrects misspelled words. You can also use AutoCorrect as a shortcut for typing long, difficult words or phrases. To set up AutoCorrect, choose Tools | AutoCorrect Options to open the AutoCorrect dialog box, shown in Figure 3-4. Settings you make in the AutoCorrect dialog box also apply to Microsoft Word and Excel.

NOTE   *AutoCorrect does not apply to WordArt, so be sure to check WordArt text carefully.*

Use the five check boxes in the middle of the dialog box to correct common typing errors:

- **Correct TWo INitial CApitals**   Changes the second uppercase letter to lowercase.

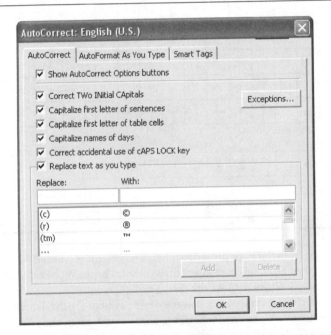

FIGURE 3-4   The AutoCorrect dialog box settings determine how PowerPoint corrects text as you type.

- **Capitalize First Letter of Sentences**   Changes a lowercase letter to uppercase when PowerPoint thinks you have started a new sentence, usually after a period. See the following discussion regarding exceptions for this setting.

- **Capitalize First Letter of Table Cells**   Changes a lowercase letter to uppercase when it is the first letter in a table cell. See the following discussion regarding exceptions for this setting.

- **Capitalize Names of Days**   Automatically capitalizes the first letter of the days.

- **Correct Accidental Use of cAPS LOCK Key**   Reverses the case of letters when PowerPoint notices one lowercase letter followed by several uppercase letters.

The last check box, "Replace Text as You Type," lets you add your own AutoCorrections. Type the incorrect spelling in the Replace box, type the correct spelling in the With box, and click Add. To delete an item, choose it and click Delete.

TIP   *Use AutoCorrect to help you type long or difficult phrases. For example, type **hrd** in the Replace box and **Human Resources Department** in the With box. Then, every time you type "hrd," PowerPoint replaces it with the full version. Be sure to use a shortcut that you won't type in any other situation.*

Click Exceptions to open the AutoCorrect Exceptions dialog box, shown in Figure 3-5. The First Letter tab specifies exceptions to the Capitalize First Letter of Sentences setting. Because PowerPoint bases its concept of a sentence on anything after a period, you may find that it incorrectly capitalizes words after an abbreviation that you follow with a period. By adding abbreviations that you commonly use, you can avoid this problem.

The INitial CAps tab fine-tunes the Correct TWo INitial CApitals setting. If you type words where the first two letters should be capitalized, add them to this list.

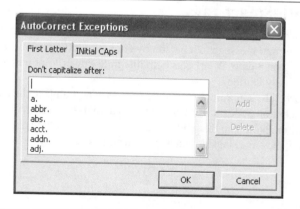

FIGURE 3-5   Use the AutoCorrect Exceptions dialog box to fine-tune the AutoCorrect feature.

Whenever the AutoCorrect feature changes text, the AutoCorrect Options button appears as a small rectangle near that text when you point to it, as shown here.

We look forward

Point to the rectangle and it changes to display a drop-down arrow. Click the arrow and it opens a menu, as shown here.

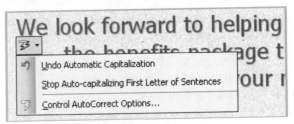

The AutoCorrect Options menu offers the following choices:

- **Change Back To**   Choosing this option allows you to undo the change.
- **Stop Automatically Correcting**   Choosing this option changes the setting in the AutoCorrect dialog box.
- **Control AutoCorrect Options**   Choosing this option displays the AutoCorrect dialog box so you can change the settings.

Normally, the AutoCorrect Options button is available whenever you pass the cursor over any text that has been corrected using the AutoCorrect feature. You can disable the button by unchecking the Show AutoCorrect Options Buttons check box in the AutoCorrect dialog box.

Act on Data with Smart Tags

Smart tags help you take actions on certain types of data and labels. For example, you can use this feature to send an e-mail message to a person by clicking on the person's name or set up an appointment by clicking on a date. Smart tags help integrate PowerPoint with other Microsoft Office programs, especially Outlook.

Smart tags are marked by a purple dotted underline. When you place the cursor over the text, the Smart Tag Actions button appears. Here you see a date marked as a smart tag, along with its Smart Tag Actions button. Note that this underline is not always easily visible against a dark background. Of course, the smart tags do not appear in slide show view.

Setting Smart Tag Options

You may have to activate smart tags to use them, if they are not active already. To activate smart tags, choose Tools | AutoCorrect Options and click the Smart Tags tab, shown in Figure 3-6.

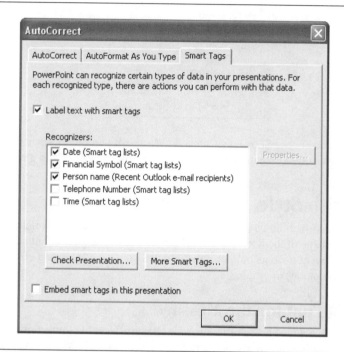

FIGURE 3-6   Use the Smart Tags tab of the AutoCorrect dialog box to specify smart tag settings.

To activate smart tags, check the Label Text with Smart Tags checkbox in the AutoCorrect dialog box. You can also specify which types of data PowerPoint recognizes. From the list, check the smart tag types you want PowerPoint to use.

To check the presentation for smart tags, click Check Presentation. This procedure sometimes reveals smart tags that were not marked.

NOTE   *Click More Smart Tags to go to Microsoft's web site. Click Find other great Smart Tags on the web page to go to a list of companies that provide a variety of solutions using Smart Tags at http://www.officesmarttags.com/.*

Check Embed Smart Tags in this Presentation if you may need to move the presentation or give it to someone else. Embedding smart tags increases the size of the presentation file. Click OK to close the AutoCorrect dialog box.

Using Smart Tags

To use a smart tag, place the mouse cursor over a smart tag until the Smart Tag Actions button appears. Click the button to display the action list and choose one of the actions. In the following illustration you see the list for a date.

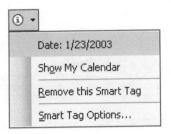

For example, if you choose Show My Calendar, Microsoft Outlook opens with the calendar on the date in the smart tag. You can then see if your schedule is clear or add a reminder.

Choose Text with Style

Part of editing text is formatting it. Fonts are an important feature of text formatting. The font type determines the shape of the letters in a font. You can also change the font size of any font. You can apply a font *style*, such as bold or italic. Finally, you can add certain effects to your text—underlining, a shadow, or embossing.

Use the Right Font for the Message

PowerPoint offers you a wide choice of fonts. Your choice affects the impact of your message on the audience. For guidelines on choosing the right font, see "How To Make Text Count" later in this chapter.

Sans serif fonts have no extraneous lines and are good for titles and text that you want to stand out. The most common sans serif font in Windows is Arial, which comes in several variants. Some examples of sans serif fonts are shown here.

Sans-Serif Fonts
• Arial
• **Arial Black**
• Century Gothic
• Comic Sans MS
• **Impact**
• Lucida Sans
• Tahoma
• Verdana

Serif fonts have small extra lines at the ends of letters. They are considered most readable for paragraph text. Times New Roman is the most common serif font in Windows. Some examples of serif fonts are shown in the next illustration.

3

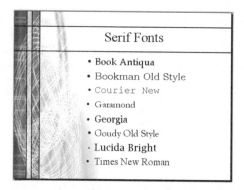

When you select text, its font appears in the Font drop-down list on the Formatting toolbar. To change a text's font, select the text and choose a new font from the drop-down list. A very helpful feature of this drop-down list is that fonts are displayed as they will appear, as shown here.

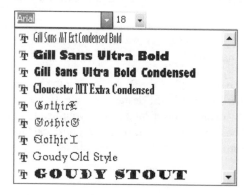

To replace a font throughout an entire presentation, choose Format | Replace Fonts. Type the current font and the new font you want to use, and then click Replace. Even new slides use the new fonts you have chosen. The slide master (see Chapter 7) fonts also change.

TIP   *To change the default font and size for new text boxes that you create, deselect everything (click outside the slide), then choose a font and font size. The next time you create a new text box, it uses the font and font size you selected.*

To change the font for WordArt text, double-click the text and choose a new font from the Font drop-down list in the Edit WordArt dialog box.

Make a Font Bigger or Smaller

Changing the font size is as easy as changing the font—select the text and choose a new size from the Font Size drop-down list on the Formatting toolbar. (The Edit WordArt dialog box has its own Font Size drop-down list.)

TIP *If you don't care exactly which size you choose but just want to make your text a little bigger or smaller, use the Increase Font Size and Decrease Font Size buttons on the Formatting toolbar, shown here. Your text quickly goes to the next setting on the Font Size drop-down list, either smaller or larger, according to which button you click.*

SHORTCUT *To increase font size, press* CTRL-SHIFT->. *To decrease font size, press* CTRL-SHIFT-<.

As you have no doubt discovered, typical font sizes are much larger on slides than in word processing documents. Fonts are usually measured in points. A *point* is 1/72 of an inch.

While 12-point text is typical in a word processing document, it is much too small for a slide. In general, you should never use text that is less than 18 points—and then only in a pinch. You will find that 24-point text is appropriate for most bulleted text, and your slide title should be larger than that.

NOTE *A presentation meant for the Web can use smaller text than a presentation shown on a screen in front of an audience.*

As mentioned earlier, in the section "Use the Right Font for the Message," the default font size is stored in the slide master that comes with the design template. However, if you type more text than can fit in a placeholder, by default, PowerPoint resizes your text to fit into the placeholder. You can turn this feature off by choosing Tools | AutoCorrect Options, and then click the AutoFormat As You Type tab. Uncheck AutoFit Title Text to Text Placeholder and AutoFit Body Text to Text Placeholder.

Add Font Effects

Add a font style to your text to emphasize it. To format text with a font style, select it and choose Bold or Italic from the Formatting toolbar. You can also add underlining or a shadow effect from the Formatting toolbar. Here you see some text using font styles and effects. To create an embossed effect, which looks like raised text with no color, choose Format | Font and choose Emboss in the Font dialog box.

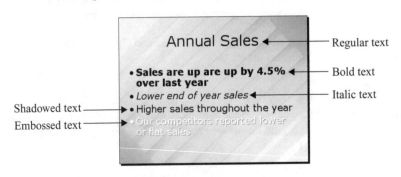

Note that you can also create shadows for objects. In general, you should use the Text Shadow button, shown here, on the Formatting toolbar for text and the Shadow button on the Drawing toolbar for objects. For example, if you change the shadow settings from the Drawing toolbar while placeholder text is selected, PowerPoint applies the settings to all the text in the placeholder because the placeholder is one object.

TIP *By default, the shadow for text is gray, so it does not show up well on a gray background. Shadows for objects are covered in Chapter 6.*

3

Use the Font Dialog Box

Until now, I have described the easiest and most common ways of formatting text. However, there is another way—the Font dialog box. The Font dialog box puts most of the settings for formatting text in one place, and is shown in Figure 3-7.

To change existing text, select it and choose Format | Font to open the Font dialog box. Choose a font, font style, and font size from the drop-down lists. From the Effects section, you can choose Underline, Shadow, Emboss, Superscript, or Subscript.

To change the text's color, click the Color drop-down list and choose a color. To choose from a full range of colors, choose More Colors from the drop-down list.

You can also change the default settings for new text. Follow these steps:

1. Format some text the way you want it.

2. Select the text.

3. Choose Format | Font to open the Font dialog box.

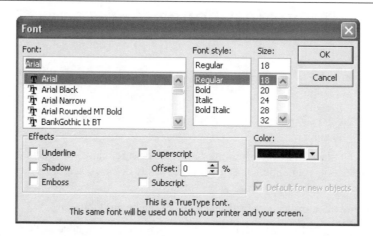

FIGURE 3-7   The Font dialog box contains in one place most of the settings for text formatting.

4. Choose Default for New Objects.

5. Click OK.

For any setting in the Font dialog box, you can click Preview to see the results before you click OK. However, because you are frequently working on selected text, which is highlighted, it is often hard to see the results precisely until you click OK and deselect the text.

Copy the Look with Format Painter

Sometimes you see text formatting that you like and you want to format other text in the same way. Figuring out the exact formatting and changing the text can be time-consuming. Format Painter was designed for just this situation. To format text with the Format Painter, follow these steps:

1. Select the text with the formatting you want.

2. Click Format Painter.

3. Select the text you want to format.

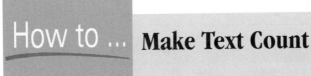

To format several selections of text with the same formatting, double-click Format Painter. You can then select text as many times as you want. Click Format Painter at the end (or press ESC) to stop formatting.

How to ... Make Text Count

The first rule for making text count is readability. Here are some pointers that will help you ensure your text is legible:

■ Shadowed text can make text stand out, but make sure it looks good on your background color.

■ When you place text over a full-color graphic, be sure that the text is readable everywhere on your slide. If the graphic has many colors, some of its areas may blend in too well with your text.

■ Be careful about rotated and vertical text—it can be hard to read.

■ To get text to stand out, concentrate on the right font, the right size, the right color, and a contrasting background instead of using all capital letters or a very fancy text effect. One of the text styles (bold, italics) or effects (shadow, embossed) can also work wonders.

3

- Don't use more than three fonts on a slide. The effect is chaotic and therefore distracting. A better choice is to limit yourself to one or two fonts.
- Associate a font with a type of element. For example, make all your slide titles the same font.
- Keep the font type fairly simple for legibility.
- Have someone else read your presentation, on paper or on-screen, to make sure the flow of ideas is clear. For example, if you set up two columns and three rows of text, in which direction are readers supposed to look first—down the first column or across the first row?

In Chapter 9, I explain how to animate text—another good way to emphasize it. You can make text appear when you want it to, as well as have lines you've already presented dim or disappear.

Add, Delete, and Rearrange Slides

Another aspect of editing a presentation involves adding, deleting, and rearranging slides. You do this editing in Slide Sorter view, where you can see most or all of your slides at once. To enter Slide Sorter view, click the small Slide Sorter View button at the bottom-left corner of your screen or choose View | Slide Sorter. In Slide Sorter view, you look at the wholeness and flow of your presentation, rather than the details on each slide. (Figure 1-7 in the first chapter shows Slide Sorter view.)

Work in Slide Sorter View

In Slide Sorter view, you select a slide by clicking it. The selected slide has a black border. You can drag that slide to any new location. To copy the slide, press CTRL as you drag. You can also move a slide by cutting and pasting. Follow these steps.

1. Select the slide.
2. Press CTRL-X to cut the slide and place it on the clipboard.
3. Click where you want the slide to go, between two other slides. PowerPoint uses a long vertical line to indicate the cursor between the slides.
4. Press CTRL-V to paste the slide.

To duplicate a slide, select the slide and press CTRL-D. The new slide appears after the original slide.

You can delete a selected slide by pressing DEL. When you move or delete a slide, PowerPoint automatically renumbers all the slides.

To add a new slide, click between two slides. Choose New Slide from the Common Tasks button on the Formatting toolbar. You can then choose a slide layout. The new slide automatically takes on the design template of the rest of the presentation.

Import Slides from Other Presentations

You may want to use a slide (or slides) from another presentation. You may even be able to build most of your presentation from slides in other presentations. Because the design template is attached to the presentation, not the slide, when you import a slide, it takes on the current template and fits seamlessly into your presentation.

Use the Clipboard to Import Slides

The most common technique for importing a slide is to use the clipboard. Here's how it works:

1. Open the presentation containing the slide or slides you want to use.
2. If you want only one slide, click its icon in the Outline pane. If you want a series of slides, click the first slide's icon, hold down SHIFT, and then click the last slide's icon.
3. Press CTRL-C or click Copy on the Standard toolbar to copy the slides to the clipboard.
4. Open your current presentation. If it is already open, click its button on the Windows taskbar to display it. In the Outline pane, click the icon of the slide you want the other slides to follow.
5. Press CTRL-V or click Paste on the Standard toolbar. PowerPoint places the new slide (or slides) after the selected slide.

This method of copying slides from one presentation to another is the easiest if you are copying a consecutive group of slides, but what if you want to copy several slides that are not together? You can do this easily in Slide Sorter view:

1. Click the first slide.
2. Press and hold CTRL as you select the rest of the slides you want to copy.
3. Click Copy on the Standard toolbar.
4. Put the cursor where you want to place the slides.
5. Click Paste on the Standard toolbar.

You may also find it easier to paste slides in Slide Sorter view because the long vertical cursor between the slides makes it clear where your slides will appear. Click between two slides and paste. You can also click before the first slide or after the last one.

Use Drag-and-Drop to Import Slides

You can also use drag-and-drop to copy slides. Drag-and-drop works best when you are copying a small group of slides; otherwise, it is hard to see all the slides without scrolling. Make sure you have only the two presentations open, and follow these steps:

1. Choose Window | Arrange All. You now see both presentations on the screen.
2. Click one presentation and change to Slide Sorter view.
3. Click the other presentation and change to Slide Sorter view.
4. Click the presentation whose slides you want and select them.
5. Press CTRL and click any of the selected slides.
6. Drag the slides to the desired destination in the other presentation. Use the vertical cursor as a guide.

Use the Slide Finder

PowerPoint offers yet another way to import slides—the Slide Finder. Use the Slide Finder when you're not sure which presentation contains the slides you want to import. First, select the slide that you want to insert the other slide(s) after. Then open the Slide Finder dialog box, shown in Figure 3-8, by choosing Insert | Slide from Files.

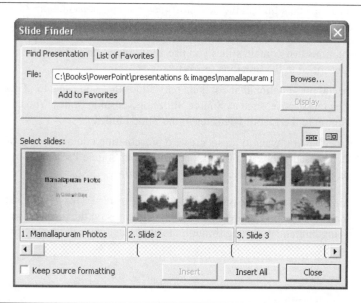

FIGURE 3-8   The Slide Finder lets you preview slides from other presentations so you can decide which ones you want to import.

If you don't find the slide you want, choose another presentation. The Slide Finder makes it easy to browse presentations on your hard disk or network.

TIP   *When you find a presentation containing slides that you might use again, select it and click Add to Favorites. To retrieve any of the slides, open the Slide Finder again and click the List of Favorites tab.*

Make Adjustments to Imported Slides

By default, new slides take on the design template of the current presentation. To keep the template and formatting of the source presentation, choose Keep Source Formatting in the Slide Finder dialog box. Even if you want your new slides to take on the design template of the current presentation, you may have to make other adjustments. Templates come with a color scheme that includes colors for the slide background, the text, bullets, and fill colors. If you have changed the color of any item in the source slide, such as the text color, the result in the destination slide may not be what you want. You might even find that the text disappears because it is the same color as the background! You can solve this problem by clicking a few times where you expect the text to be until you see handles and a selection border. Whew! You can now select the text and use the Font dialog box (choose Format | Font) to change its color.

To import individual slides, select them and click Insert. Click Insert All to insert all the slides. When you are done, click Close to return to your presentation.

Keep a Slide Library

Ever wonder how professionals find all the neat stuff they put into presentations? One secret is organization. If you reuse slides a lot, you can create a slide library. Here are a few techniques:

- Add presentations that contain slides you use a lot to the List of Favorites in the Slide Finder, as described in the previous section.

- Create a special presentation that contains only slides that you use a lot. Give it a name that identifies its purpose, such as Source Slides or Reusable Slides. You can then add that presentation to the List of Favorites in the Slide Finder.

- For each slide that you want to reuse, create a presentation containing that slide alone. Place all such presentations in a folder, perhaps called Source Presentations. Name each presentation in a way that describes the slide it contains.

If you wish, print handouts of these presentations (see Chapter 16 for details), and keep them in a book. Mark the name of the presentations and their locations on the printouts and keep them in a folder or three-ring binder. By leafing through the handouts, you can quickly find the slides you need.

Summary

This chapter showed you how to edit text in a presentation, including moving, copying, changing, and deleting text. It discussed techniques for editing placeholder text, text in AutoShapes and text boxes, and WordArt text. Some special techniques included finding and replacing text, changing text case, and adding symbols.

You learned how to set PowerPoint's editing options to meet your needs and to use AutoCorrect to correct errors as you type, including certain spelling errors. You saw how to use smart tags to quickly act on certain types of data, such as names and dates.

This chapter covered all the ways to work with fonts, including changing the font type, size, and style. The Font dialog box gives you more control over formatting. You saw how to use Format Painter to copy text formatting.

The second part of the chapter discussed how to add, delete, and rearrange slides, usually in Slide Sorter view. You can also import slides from other presentations, using the clipboard, drag-and-drop, or the Slide Finder. This chapter ended with some techniques for creating a slide library of slides that you use regularly.

In the next chapter, I explain how to format paragraphs and bullets.

3

Chapter 4

Format Bullets and Paragraphs

How to…

- Choose and change the bullet type
- Format a bullet's size and color
- Use a picture as a bullet
- Create numbered lists
- Understand paragraph formatting
- Use the ruler to align and indent text
- Work with tabs
- Align paragraph text
- Adjust line spacing

In many presentations, the majority of text is placeholder text. By default, this text comes with bullets. The purpose of bullets is to create a list of items. Each item is a paragraph of text. You can change the formatting of bulleted text to make it more readable or emphasize certain items. You can create bullets from pictures if you want to get really flashy. On the other hand, sometimes you might want to eliminate the bullets and work with regular paragraphs. Knowing how to format bullets and paragraphs is essential to creating a professionally designed presentation.

Create a Bulleted List

When you stand up in front of an audience, you talk to the audience. Why do you need text on a slide? The purpose of bulleted text is to create a visual confirmation of your message. Bulleted text should be short and to the point. The more quickly the audience grasps the text, the sooner the audience will turn its attention to you and what you are saying.

If your text is not bulleted, you can add bullets by selecting the text and choosing Format | Bullets and Numbering.

 *Click Bullets on the Formatting toolbar to add bullets. Click Bullets again to remove the bullets.*

Choose a Bullet Type

Each design template comes with a default style of bullets for each level of heading (except for heading 1 text, which creates the title of the slide). Here you see a sample of five levels of bulleted text.

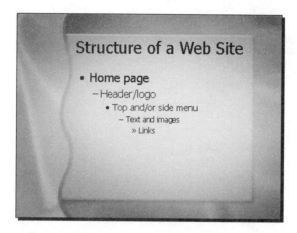

Thanks to Digital Juice at www.digitaljuice.com *for permission to use this background.*

In this illustration, the template uses three different styles of bullets and varies their sizes as well. Another template might use varying colors to distinguish between the heading levels. You can change every feature about any bullet to suit your taste and needs.

Of course, you don't want your bullets to distract from your text. Use those flashy bullets only when they have a meaningful purpose. For example, if you are selling floral ribbon to florists, you might want to use a picture of a rose as a bullet. In that case, use the rose bullets throughout the presentation. They make the point that you know the floral business, but they don't distract because they're on every slide and your audience soon knows to ignore them and pay attention to the text. Another good use of an unusual bullet is for occasional use—to draw attention to only one or two items.

To choose a bullet type for an item of text, select the text and choose Format | Bullets and Numbering to open the Bullets and Numbering dialog box, shown in Figure 4-1. The Bulleted tab should be active. Any change you make applies to all of the selected text.

In Figure 4-2, you see a slide at the end of a presentation for a graduate class in artificial intelligence. This slide is the bibliography, and the student used file folders as bullets to indicate that each reference is a container of information.

To create a similar effect, select the text and choose Format | Bullets and Numbering. Then click Customize and choose a "dingbat" type of font such as Wingdings from the Font drop-down list. Find the dingbat element you prefer (the presenter in the example shown in Figure 4-2 used the open folder), select it, and click OK. Dingbat fonts offer a wide range of small images and symbols.

Set Bullet Size and Color

You change a bullet's size as a percentage of text size. When you change a bullet's size, let consistency be your guide. Generally, a higher-level item, such as a level 2 heading, should not have a smaller bullet than a less important item, such as a level 3 heading. Also, items of the

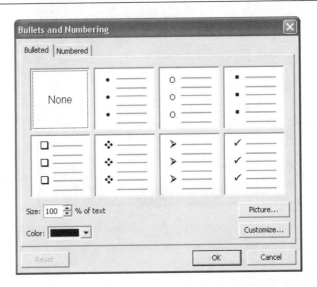

FIGURE 4-1 Use the Bulleted tab of the Bullets and Numbering dialog box to choose a bullet for your text.

same level should usually have the same size bullet, unless you are making an exception for emphasis. To change a bullet's size, click the bullet and choose Format | Bullets and Numbering. In the dialog box, change the number in the Size % of Text box, shown in Figure 4-1.

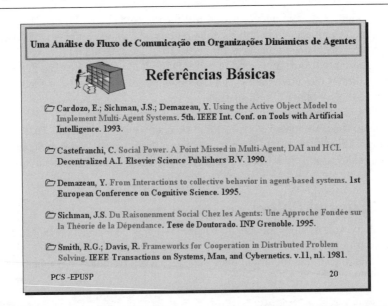

FIGURE 4-2 This slide is a bibliography of a graduate presentation on artificial intelligence.

 *Right-click the bullet and choose Bullets and Numbering from the shortcut menu.*

When you click the Color drop-down list box in the Bullets and Numbering dialog box (see Figure 4-1), you see the choices shown here.

Default color ——

Colors in the color scheme ——

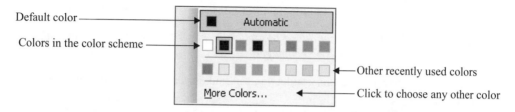

————— Other recently used colors

————— Click to choose any other color

4

Choose the color you want, and click OK to close the Bullets and Numbering dialog box. Like a bullet's size, a bullet's color should generally be consistent within a heading level unless you are using color for special emphasis. Color schemes are covered in Chapter 6.

Use an Image as a Bullet

For more variety, you can use an image as a bullet. Follow these steps:

1. Select the text that you want to have the new bullets.

2. Click Picture in the Bullets and Numbering dialog box. PowerPoint opens the Picture Bullet dialog box, shown in Figure 4-3.

3. To use one of the bullets displayed, choose it and click OK.

Your new bullet is now in place.

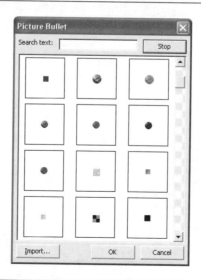

FIGURE 4-3   PowerPoint offers a large selection of images that you can use as bullets.

Did you find PowerPoint's choice of picture bullets boring? What if you want a bullet that is more exciting, one that specifically relates to the topic of the text that follows it? Are you selling computers? Why not use computers for bullets? You can create your own bullets from any bitmap file. Examples of bitmap file types are .bmp, .tif, .gif, and .jpg files. Windows metafiles (.wmf) work as well.

To use your own bitmap as a bullet, click Import in the Picture Bullet dialog box. The Add Clips to Organizer dialog box opens, shown in Figure 4-4. Choose the image you want and click Add.

TIP *In the Add Clips to Organizer dialog box, click the Views button on the toolbar and choose Preview so you can see the images.*

Don't have a field day and use every bullet you can find. Instead, choose one appropriate bullet and use it consistently.

To create bullets from your own images, you usually have to jump through a few hoops. Many images are not suitable for bullets when you first find them. Often, you need to manipulate the graphic file. You may be able to do so right in PowerPoint. Refer to Chapter 5 for more information on working with graphic files.

First import the image into PowerPoint, by choosing Insert | Picture | From File. Select the image and click Insert. For example, you may want to do the following:

- **Rotate the image** With the image selected, hover the mouse over the green dot until you see the rotate cursor, shown here, then click and drag in the desired direction.

- **Make the background transparent** Choose Set Transparent Color from the Picture toolbar and click the background.

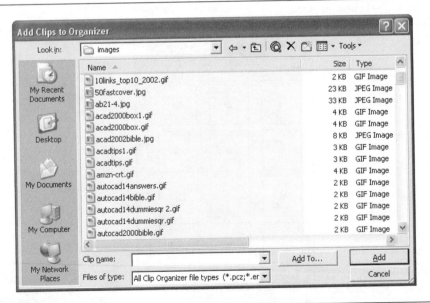

FIGURE 4-4   Use the Add Clips to Organizer dialog box to find image files to use as bullets.

> **TIP** *If the Picture toolbar doesn't appear when you select the image, right-click any toolbar and click Picture. For more information about the Picture toolbar, see Chapter 5.*

- ■ **Adjust the brightness or contrast**   Use the Brightness and Contrast buttons on the Picture toolbar.
- ■ **Crop the image**   Use the Crop button on the Picture toolbar and drag in from any of the four sides.

When you are done, you need to save the image as a file:

1. Right-click the image and choose Save as Picture.
2. In the Save as Picture dialog box, type a name for the image and choose a location.
3. Click Save.

To use the image as a bullet, select the desired text and choose Format | Bullets and Numbering. Click Picture. In the Picture Bullet dialog box, choose Import. Find the image file, choose it, and click Import.

Click the picture and click OK. PowerPoint creates the bullets.

> **TIP** *You often need to adjust picture bullets. With the text still selected, choose Format | Bullets and Numbering and change the size. Click OK. To change the bullets for an entire presentation, you have to change the slide master. Slide masters are covered in Chapter 7.*

Create Numbered Lists

Use a numbered list when your items have a logical sequence. To create a numbered list, select the bulleted items you want to number and click Numbering on the Formatting toolbar. PowerPoint knows to restart numbering for subheadings, as shown here. You can change the numbering back to bullets by clicking Bullets on the Formatting toolbar.

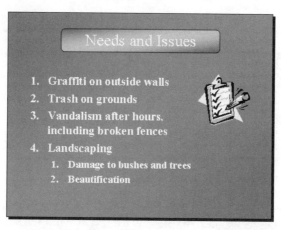

To format the numbering, select the text and choose Format | Bullets and Numbering. Then click the Numbered tab, shown in Figure 4-5.

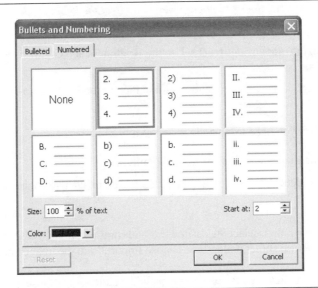

FIGURE 4-5 Use the Numbered tab in the Bullets and Numbering dialog box to format numbered text.

The AutoFormat as You Type feature starts a numbered list when you type the number **1**, a period, a space, and some text. Instead of the number 1, you can type **A**, **a**, **I**, or **i**. You can also use a closing parenthesis in place of the period. If you don't want automatic numbering, choose Tools | AutoCorrect Options and click the AutoFormat as You Type tab. Uncheck Automatic Bulleted and Numbered lists, and click OK.

 **Use Bullets and Numbering in AutoShapes and Text Boxes**

You can create bulleted text in AutoShapes and text boxes. For best results, the text should be left-aligned. To left-align selected text, click Align Left on the Formatting toolbar.

To add bullets to selected text, click Bullets on the Formatting toolbar. To add numbering, click Numbering on the Formatting toolbar. To create bullets or numbering as you type, click Bullets or Numbering first and then start typing. Click Bullets or Numbering again when you want to return to regular text. You can use all the features of the Bullets and Numbering dialog box as described earlier, including custom bullets. Select the text and choose Format | Bullets and Numbering.

There is no automatic way to create bullets in WordArt text. You can, however, insert a bullet symbol and use this technique to create bulleted text in WordArt. See Chapter 3 for instructions on inserting symbols into WordArt.

Work with Paragraphs

In Chapter 3, I explained how to format the characters in your text—by choosing the fonts, font size, and so on. A different aspect of formatting text involves formatting it as paragraphs. Paragraph formatting includes indentation, tabs, alignment, and line spacing. To lay out text on your slide in a pleasing, legible manner, you need to know about paragraph formatting.

A *paragraph* is any single line of text or multiple lines of text followed by a return. A *return character*, which moves text to the next line, is created when you press ENTER on your keyboard.

4

> **TIP** *Occasionally, you may want text to be treated as one paragraph but look like two paragraphs. You can start a new line without using a return by pressing SHIFT-ENTER (instead of just ENTER) at the end of a line. PowerPoint interprets both lines as one paragraph. For example, to create a separate, unbulleted line within bulleted text, as shown in Figure 4-6, you press SHIFT-ENTER.*

Understand Paragraph Formatting

Before leaping in, you may want to understand some terms that are commonly used for paragraph formatting:

- **Margin**   The space between the edge of your working area and your text. In a text placeholder, the margin is the space between the edge of the placeholder and your text. The left margin of a paragraph is the left edge of the text.

- **Indent**   The amount that text is moved to the right of the left margin.

- **First line indent**   An indent for the first line of a paragraph. Subsequent lines are not indented.

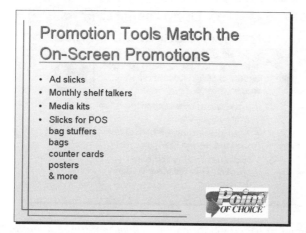

FIGURE 4-6   You can create an unnumbered line within bulleted text by pressing
            SHIFT-ENTER at the end of the line.

- **Hanging indent** A first line that is indented less than the subsequent lines of a paragraph. The first line "hangs out" from the rest of the paragraph. Bulleted text is formatted as a hanging indent. The bullet is at the left margin and hangs out from the rest of the paragraph, which is indented, as shown in Figure 4-7.

- **Tab** A place where the cursor stops when you press the TAB key. Tabs are used to align text.

- **Left-aligned** A paragraph in which the left side of every line is lined up.

- **Centered** A paragraph in which the center point of every line is lined up.

- **Right-aligned** A paragraph in which the right side of every line is lined up.

- **Justified** A paragraph in which both the left and right sides of every line are lined up.

- **Line spacing** The spacing between the lines in a paragraph. You can also separately control the spacing before and after paragraphs.

Figure 4-7 shows some examples of paragraph formatting.

Use the Ruler

PowerPoint comes with a top ruler and a side ruler that can help you format paragraph text. To view the rulers, choose View | Ruler. Choose View | Ruler again to hide the rulers—this menu item toggles the ruler on and off. You cannot format paragraphs unless the rulers are displayed.

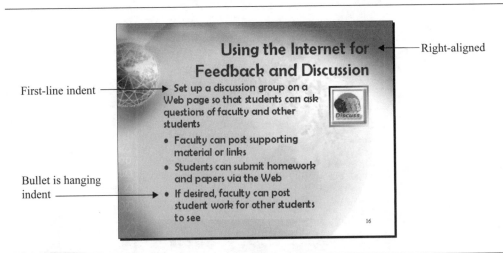

FIGURE 4-7   Examples of paragraph formatting. *Thanks to PresentationPro* (http://www .presentationpro.com) *for permission to use this template.*

The display of the rulers depends on which object you select. If you select any object other than a text placeholder, the rulers look like this.

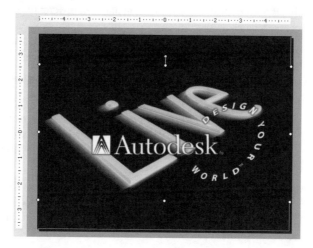

This kind of ruler is called a *slide ruler*. It has a zero point at its middle and measures the entire slide. You can use this kind of ruler for judging layout and distances for objects. In Chapter 5, I explain how to lay out and align objects on a slide.

If you select a text placeholder, the rulers look like those shown in Figure 4-8.

First Line
Indent marker

Hanging Indent marker

Left Indent marker

Sets type
of tab

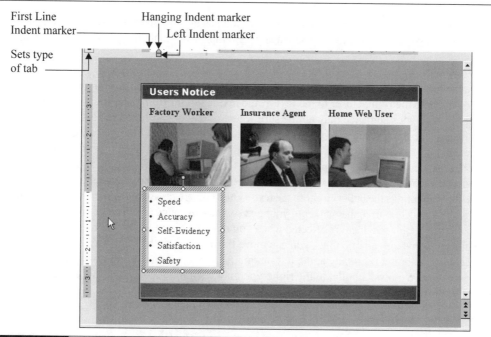

FIGURE 4-8   Use the top ruler to format indentation and set tabs.

These rulers look like the rulers you see in your word processor. The zero measurement starts from the left or the top and continues from there. The white portion measures only the area of the text. The ruler's length adjusts automatically if you click on another, differently sized placeholder.

Unlike most word processors, such as Word, PowerPoint has no dialog box that you can use to format paragraphs. You must format paragraph text using the top ruler. The side ruler is used mostly to judge size and distance and contains no controls. The top ruler has the following indent controls:

- **First Line Indent marker**   Drag to the left or right to control the indentation of the first line. This marker moves independently of the other two markers.

- **Left Indent marker**   Drag to the left or right to set the left margin of the entire paragraph, except for the first line. This marker is always with the Hanging Indent marker. When you drag it, the Hanging Indent marker comes along with it, so that the relationship between the two is always the same.

- **Hanging Indent marker**   Drag to the left or right to set the indentation for subsequent lines of a paragraph. This marker is always with the Left Indent marker. However, when you drag the Hanging Indent marker, the First Line Indent marker does not move, letting you change the relationship between the two.

There's something of an art to dragging the markers because they are so small. It's easy to grab the Left Indent marker (the rectangle) instead of the Hanging Indent marker (the lower triangle). After a little practice, you'll get better at it. Until then, remember the Undo button on the Standard toolbar!

Indent Text

The most common use for the ruler is to move bullets and to change the spacing between a bullet and its text. However, you can use the ruler to indent any paragraph text—in to the right or out to the left.

Move Bullets

While the default distance between the bullets and text is usually acceptable, you may want to move the bullets to the right, closer to the text. If the text is too far from the bullets, it seems disassociated, and your audience may not be sure where one item ends and the next begins.

In bulleted text, the first line of a paragraph is the line with its bullet. To move a bullet, first select the text placeholder containing the bullet. Then drag the First Line Indent marker to the right. The First Line Indent marker (the upper indent marker) moves independently of the other markers, so the indentation of the rest of the paragraph is unaffected. Therefore, moving the First Line Indent marker to the right brings the bullet closer to the text. While you are dragging the marker, PowerPoint places a dashed guideline from the marker to your text so you can gauge the effect of your dragging. All the bullets in the placeholder are affected when you drag the First Line Indent marker. If you have numbered items instead of bullets, you can move the numbers in the same way.

By default, the bullet is already at the left margin, so you can move it only to the right. Of course, once you've moved a bullet to the right, you may want to move it back to the left again. In that case, drag the First Line Indent marker to the left.

Indent Paragraph Text

Instead of moving the bullets, you may want to move the text. The Hanging Indent marker controls the alignment of the text, which controls the indentation of lines in a paragraph after the first line.

However, because the text of the first line (after the bullet) also aligns with the subsequent lines, you actually affect the entire paragraph.

To move the text, drag the Hanging Indent marker to the left or the right. Be careful not to drag the rectangular Left Indent marker.

The Left Indent marker (the rectangle) maintains the relationship between the first line and the subsequent lines of a paragraph. Therefore, the indentation of the entire paragraph changes as you drag the rectangular marker. As you drag, both the First Line Indent and Hanging Indent markers come along for the ride.

When your slide has more than one level of bulleted text, PowerPoint shows upper and lower indent markers for all the levels, as shown here. You can therefore adjust the indentation of any level of bulleted text you wish.

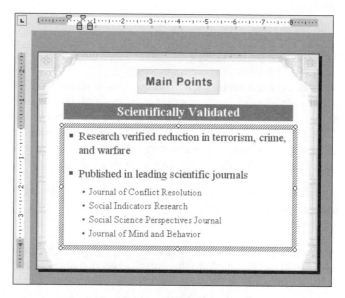

Create Paragraphs with No Hanging Indent

Sometimes you may want plain block text instead of bulleted text. For example, you might have only one statement to make on a slide, as shown here.

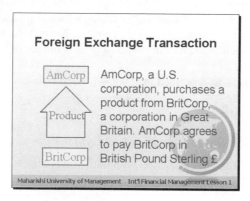

While it's easy to remove bullets if you don't want them, you'll still have a hanging indent unless you change the paragraph formatting. You usually don't want a hanging indent without bullets, but getting rid of the hanging indent can be frustrating. Here are the steps to change bulleted text to block paragraphs:

1. Select the text placeholder for which you want to create block paragraphs.

2. Click Bullets on the Formatting toolbar to remove the bullets.

3. Drag the First Line Indent marker to the right until it is aligned with the Hanging Indent marker. Now the hanging indent is gone, but the paragraphs are indented.

4. Drag the Left Indent marker (the bottom rectangle) to the left until the paragraphs are at the left margin again.

Change the Margins in a Text Placeholder

In Chapter 3, I briefly mentioned how to change the margins for both text placeholders and objects that contain text. Here I explain the concept more fully.

The *margin* is the space between the text and the edge of the placeholder. If you want to center the text better in the placeholder, you can increase the margins. By default, the margins are .1 inch on the left and right and .05 inches on the top and bottom. These settings might sound like small margins, but because the borders of the placeholder are usually invisible on your slide, it doesn't make any difference. However, if you choose to place a visible border around your text, you may wish to increase the margins. (Chapter 6 covers creating borders.)

 The text margins are used when text is wrapped to the next line. You can often fit more on a line by reducing the text margins. The empty space between the text and the placeholder's border is generally useless, especially when the border is invisible.

To change the margin between the text and its placeholder, right-click the placeholder and choose Format Placeholder. In the Format AutoShape dialog box that opens, click the Text Box tab, shown in Figure 4-9. Change any of the numbers in the Internal Margin section and click OK. This technique works for all types of AutoShapes, not just text placeholders.

Set Tabs

You probably don't use the TAB key on your keyboard to align text anymore. That was its original purpose, but now that word processors offer tables, which align text more easily, TAB is used mostly to move the cursor from cell to cell in a table. Nevertheless, you may sometimes wish to use a tab to align a small amount of text when a table is not needed. (Tables are covered in Chapter 8.)

There are four types of tabs, as described in Table 4-1. Each type has its own marker at the left of the ruler.

To set a tab, follow these steps:

1. Select a text placeholder. Tab markers are not displayed unless a text placeholder is selected.

2. Click the tab button at the left of the top ruler until you see the type of tab you want.

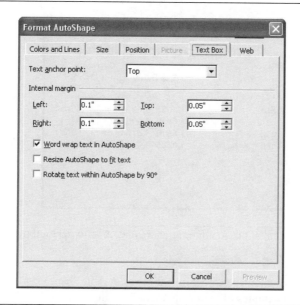

FIGURE 4-9   Use the Text Box tab of the Format AutoShape dialog box to change the margins between the placeholder and the text.

3. Click the ruler where you want to place the tab.

4. Press TAB before the text that you want to align at the tab.

To remove a tab, select a placeholder and drag the tab marker off the ruler.

Align Text

Aligning text refers to how the text is lined up in reference to the margins. Bulleted text is left-aligned by default. However, you may sometimes want to use another alignment. For

Tab Position	Icon	Description
Left	**L**	Aligns the left edge of text with the tab.
Center	**⊥**	Centers the text at the tab.
Right	**⌐**	Aligns the right edge of text with the tab.
Decimal	**⊥.**	Aligns decimal points with the tab. Figure 4-10 shows an example of text aligned with a decimal tab.

TABLE 4-1   The Four Types of Tabs

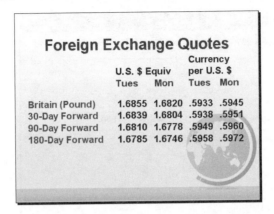

Use a decimal tab to align numbers that contain decimal points.

example, it is common to center titles. Text in text boxes or AutoShapes is also often centered. Figure 4-11 shows some examples of various paragraph alignments.

The procedure for aligning text is the same for placeholder text, text in text boxes, and text in AutoShapes.

Left-Align

To *left-align* text, select the text and click Align Left on the Formatting toolbar (or press CTRL-L).

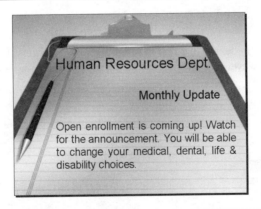

You can center, right-align, and justify paragraphs.

Center

To *center* text, select the text and click Center on the Formatting toolbar
(or press CTRL-E).

Right-Align

To *right-align* text, select the text and click Align Right on the Formatting toolbar
(or press CTRL-R).

4

Justify

To *justify* text, select the text and choose Format | Alignment | Justify. (There is no
toolbar button for justifying text.)

   Refer to Chapter 2 for instructions on aligning WordArt text, which has additional
alignment options not available for any other text.

Use Anchors

In Chapter 3, I explained how to change the text anchor point of text in text boxes and
AutoShapes. You use the Text Box tab of the Format Text Box or Format AutoShapes
dialog box. The anchor point is also a form of text alignment. You can choose from the
following anchors:

- Top
- Middle
- Bottom
- Top Centered
- Middle Centered
- Bottom Centered

When working with text in text boxes or AutoShapes, you may want to consider both types
of alignment to get the exact result you need.

Set Line Spacing

The final aspect of paragraph formatting involves setting how much space you want between
lines within a paragraph and between paragraphs.

Set the Spacing Within a Paragraph

Do you need to fit more text into a placeholder, text box, or AutoShape, without decreasing the font size? The solution may be to squeeze the lines of text together, as shown here in the right column of text.

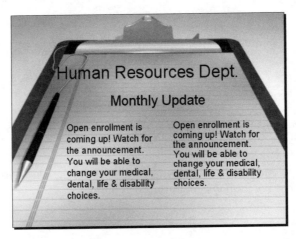

Of course, you don't want to put the lines too close together or your audience will have trouble reading the text.

To set line spacing within a paragraph, select the text and choose Format | Line Spacing. The Line Spacing dialog box opens, shown in Figure 4-12. Type a number in the text box. You can choose to measure line spacing by lines or points in the drop-down list. Click Preview to see the results. Click OK if you like what you see.

Set the Spacing Between Paragraphs

You can also specify how much space PowerPoint places before and after paragraphs. You may want to increase the spacing between paragraphs to separate them in your audience's awareness or simply to spread them out pleasingly on the slide.

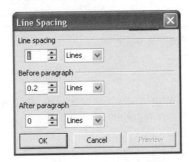

FIGURE 4-12   Use the Line Spacing dialog box to set the spacing between lines within a paragraph as well as the spacing between paragraphs.

To set the spacing between paragraphs, you use the Line Spacing dialog box, shown in Figure 4-12. The controls are the same ones you use to set line spacing within a paragraph. You can measure by lines or points. You can separately control the spacing before and after a paragraph. You probably don't want to add extra spacing both before and after a paragraph, because the two measurements are added together. Add spacing before *or* after your paragraphs, but not both.

Here you see an example of the effect of increasing the space following a paragraph. Compare the left and right columns.

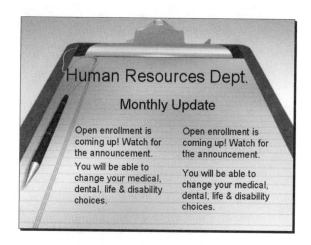

By adding one line space after the first paragraph, the second paragraph stands out more. You could obtain the same effect by adding one line space before the second paragraph.

Summary

In this chapter, you learned all about bullets and paragraph text. PowerPoint gives you a great deal of control over bullets. You can choose from various types of bullets, change their size and color, or use no bullets. You can choose a picture to use as a bullet or create your own bitmap files and make bullets from them. You can also create bulleted text in text boxes and AutoShapes. You can create numbered lists, too.

To format paragraph text, you use the top ruler. When a text placeholder is selected, the ruler shows indent markers and tabs. You drag the indent markers to align the text, move the bullets, or move the text relative to the bullets. You can remove the hanging indent automatically created for bulleted text and create blocked text.

Tabs are used to align text. PowerPoint lets you choose from four types of tabs: left, right, centered, and decimal. To add a tab, choose the type of tab you want on the tab button to the left of the ruler and click anywhere on the ruler.

PowerPoint offers four types of paragraph alignment. You can left- or right-align text, center it, or justify it.

You can squeeze lines in a paragraph together to fit more on a slide or spread them out to make them more readable, using the Line Spacing dialog box. You can also add space before or after a paragraph using the same dialog box.

This chapter ends Part I. Part II explains how to work with art, objects, color, 3-D effects, and slide masters—all the finishing touches you need to make your presentation truly professional.

Part II

Add Multimedia Elements to Your Presentation

Chapter 5

Add Art and Graphic Objects

How to…

- Find clip art
- Create a clip art collection
- Insert picture files
- Create a photo album
- Use PowerPoint's basic editing tools
- Use the Picture toolbar
- Edit graphic files
- Use the Drawing toolbar
- Insert AutoShapes
- Format and edit drawing objects
- Lay out slides with precision

Until now, you have mostly worked with text, but a presentation is much more than words. Without adding appropriate art and graphic objects to your slides, you cannot create the impact needed for an effective presentation. The visual effect of art helps your audience remember and understand your message more quickly and easily. In fact, one of the main differences between amateur and professional presentations is the quantity and quality of the graphics. This chapter is all about graphics, including clip art, photos, and shapes.

Create an Impact with Graphics

When your viewers first see a slide, they scan it quickly before focusing on specific elements. The mind first focuses on large, simple shapes. Shapes can include the AutoShapes that come with PowerPoint but can also include lines, rows of bullets, and borders. Then viewers move to shapes and patterns that are more complex, and finally they focus on the text. You can use this tendency to increase your audience's understanding of your material. If you ignore this pattern, your audience is likely to be confused or slow to comprehend your point.

In addition, graphic elements wake up your audience by grabbing their attention. Perhaps from our continual immersion in television and movies, we're used to constantly changing input. A presentation consisting of only text soon becomes boring, and viewers tune out. Offering a changing menu of shapes and pictures keeps your audience engaged. A good guide is that at least half of your slides should include graphics. Note that graphics that are displayed on each slide, such as a company logo, don't count here. The audience learns to ignore repeating graphics—they soon become as boring as the text. You need to create a balance. On one hand, contrast and newness can work wonders. On the other hand, overloading a presentation with graphics or extremely varying styles soon negates the alertness effect. Vary your presentation so that there is some alternation between quiet and active slides while maintaining some continuity of style—and your audience will take note. Here you see a slide on the topic of web page design that uses a strong graphic of an eye, a brain, and a hand.

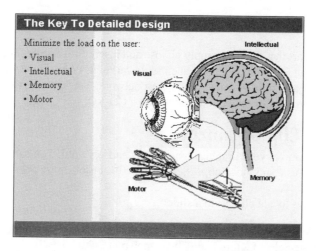

Art has a more subtle effect than simple graphic shapes. The right art can evoke a mood that supports your message. Think of how your audience might react to the following:

- A flag
- A dollar sign
- A happy family
- A pastoral farm scene
- Traders on the floor of the New York Stock Exchange

Each picture has a different effect. Even the manner in which the art is rendered has an effect—a photo makes a different impression than a rough sketch. An example of a photo used to explain an employee benefit feature covering medical costs is shown here.

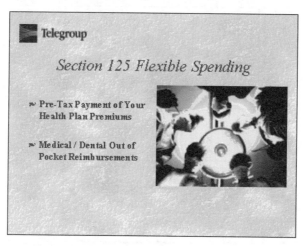

The colors you use are important too. Chapter 6 is all about using colors and other effects.

Use Clip Art

Clip art is ready-made art that you can simply choose and insert onto a slide. The Clip Organizer is shared by all Microsoft Office applications, such as PowerPoint, Word, Excel, and Publisher. You probably have other art available on your computer or network. You can also find clip art on the Internet or buy your own clip art collection, usually on a CD-ROM.

Find Art in the Clip Organizer

The Clip Organizer organizes your graphics by category and keyword. You can also use the Clip Organizer for sounds/music and video clips. See Chapter 10 for lots more about sound, music, and video.

There are three ways to add clip art to a slide:

■ Choose a slide layout that includes a clip art placeholder. Then click the Insert Clip Art icon to open the Select Picture dialog box, shown in Figure 5-1.

■ Open the Insert Clip Art task pane and choose any clip art, as explained next.

■ Click Insert Clip Art on the Drawing toolbar (or choose Insert | Picture | Clip Art) to open the Insert Clip Art task pane, shown in Figure 5-2.

The Select Picture dialog box has fewer options than the Insert Clip Art task pane. In the Select Picture dialog box, you can enter a keyword to search for clip art and import files into the Clip Organizer. To insert clip art, type the word that best describes the art you want, such as *flower*, and press ENTER or click Search. The results of the search are then displayed in the window.

FIGURE 5-1   Use the Select Picture dialog box to insert clip art onto a slide.

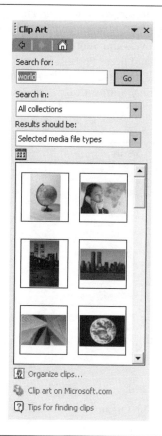

FIGURE 5-2   You can use the Insert Clip Art task pane to find and insert clip art.

In the Insert Clip Art task pane, you can not only search for clip art by keyword, but you can also specify where to look. In the Search In drop-down list, you have three choices:

- **My Collections**   Clip art collections that you have created. Creating collections is covered later in this chapter, in the "Create Your Own Clip Art Collection" section.
- **Office Collections**   Clip art collections that come with Microsoft Office.
- **Web Collections**   Clip art collections on an intranet or the Internet.

To save time searching for clip art, you can uncheck any option that doesn't interest you.

CAUTION   *By default, both the Select Picture dialog box and the Insert Clip Art task pane look on the Internet for clip art. Some users have had difficulty with this feature when they are behind a firewall or even without one. If you have problems with this feature, you may need to disconnect from the Internet when using the Select Picture dialog box. In the Insert Clip Art task pane, you can use the Search In drop-down box to uncheck Web Collections.*

You can also restrict which type of clip art you want to find in the Results Should Be drop-down list. You can choose Clip Art, Photographs, Movies, and Sounds. If you are interested in only Clip art and Photographs, uncheck Movies and Sounds.

Once you type in your keyword and press ENTER, PowerPoint displays the related clip art in the task pane. Click a piece of art to insert it or drag it onto your slide. For more options, pass your cursor over an item to display a drop-down arrow. Click the arrow to open this shortcut menu.

You can use this menu to do the following:

- Insert the clip art.
- Copy the clip art to the clipboard.
- Delete the clip art from the Clip Organizer.
- Open the clip in another program. The Open With dialog box opens, and you can choose a program. Use this when you want to edit the clip art in an image-editing program.
- Use Microsoft's tools on the Web. Go to Microsoft's web site, where you can find updates, articles, tips, a template gallery, and more.
- Copy the clip art to a collection. Collections are discussed in the next section.
- Move the clip art to a collection of clip art, without leaving a copy in its original location.
- Edit the keywords for the clip art. Clip art is organized by keywords so that you can search for them by typing a keyword.
- Find similar-style clip art.
- Preview the clip art and view its properties. Choosing this option opens the Preview/Properties dialog box, shown next. Properties include file name, file type, resolution, size, location, date created, orientation (portrait or landscape), and keywords, as well as others.

NOTE *Unfortunately, you cannot edit keywords for Office collections, only those for your own collections.*

Create Your Own Clip Art Collection

The Clip Organizer is a convenient place to store clip art that you use regularly—a company logo or a purchased clip art collection are good candidates. You can add this clip art to the Clip Organizer, place it in a category, and give it searchable keywords. You can then use this clip art in any of the Microsoft applications that share the Clip Organizer. Clip Art is organized into *collections*, and collections that you create are called *My Collections*, as opposed to Office Collections and Web Collections.

To add your own clip art to your collection and organize it, open the Clip Organizer by clicking Organize Clips in the Insert Clip Art task pane. The Clip Organizer is shown in Figure 5-3.

You can click any item of clip art to display the drop-down arrow, which opens the same menu available from the Insert Clip Art task pane shown in Figure 5-2.

To add graphic files to a collection, choose File | Add Clips to Organizer. You can then choose one of three options:

- **Automatically**   Searches your hard disk or folders that you specify and creates collections
- **On My Own**   Lets you specify individual files
- **From Scanner or Camera**   Activates your scanner or digital camera and inserts the resulting file into the Clip Organizer

You can add your own pictures to the Clip Organizer in the following formats:

- Windows Metafile Format (.wmf), a vector format that looks good even when scaled
- Enhanced Metafile Format (.emf), a vector format

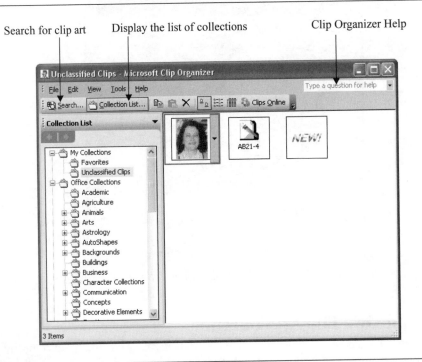

Search for clip art   Display the list of collections   Clip Organizer Help

FIGURE 5-3   The Clip Organizer lets you organize clip art into a collection.

- Bitmap (.bmp)
- Graphics Interchange Format (.gif), the most common graphics format on the Web
- Joint Photographic Experts Group (.jpg)
- Portable Network Graphics (.png)
- Macintosh PICT (.pct)
- Tagged Image File Format (.tif)
- Vector Markup Language (.vml)

In addition, special filters let you import several other file types.

NOTE   *To install filters, close all open programs, choose Start | Settings | Control Panel, and double-click Add/Remove Programs. Choose Microsoft Office (or Microsoft PowerPoint, if you installed PowerPoint as an individual program), and click Change or Add/Remove (depending on your Windows version). Follow the instructions on the screen.*

If you have an Internet connection, click Clips On Office Online at the bottom of the Insert Clip Art task pane. If you usually connect by dialing from a modem, you are prompted to make the connection, or you can connect in advance. PowerPoint seamlessly transports you to the new Clip Art and Media Home Web site, a Microsoft web site where you can find and download picture, music, sound, video, or animation clips. The site includes thousands of high-quality images in various styles and covering various topics, including seasonal graphics. Click the Templates link and do a search on the word "PowerPoint" to find PowerPoint design templates.

NOTE *You need to accept the license agreement before you can access the graphics.*

You can search the web site by keyword or choose a category. The web site then displays the applicable clips. Choose the ones you want and follow the instructions to download the clips. PowerPoint automatically places them in the Clip Organizer under Downloaded Clips.

5

Did you know?

Finding Additional Clip Art

It's easy to find clip art for your presentations. Some is free, and some you have to pay for. You can find individual pieces of clip art or entire collections containing thousands of files. Here are a few sources I've collected for clip art:

- **Freeze.com**   This site offers about 5,000 free images for private use. Go to the clip art section and find some clip art by topic. For $23.99 annually, you can access 15,000 images for commercial use. http://www.freeze.com

- **ClipArt.com**   Over 2.5 million clip art images are collected at ClipArt.com, including photos and lots of fonts. You pay from $2.88 to $7.95 per week depending on the length of your subscription. The collection is continually being updated so that you can always find something new. http://www.clipart.com

- **DigitalJuice**   You can purchase a huge selection of PowerPoint backgrounds, photos, and animations. I've used a number of their backgrounds for figures in this book. http://www.digitaljuice.com

- **ExpressIt**   This site has free clip art as well as a collection of a million images for $19.99 per year. http://expressit.broderbund.com

- **Barry's Clip Art Server**   Barry's offers a good selection of free clip art collections on certain topics. You can drag clip art directly onto your slide. http://www.barrysclipart.com/clipart

To save images from a web site, right-click the image and choose Save Picture As (Internet Explorer) or Save Image As (Netscape Navigator). Otherwise, follow the instructions on the web for downloading the images.

To drag clip art onto a slide, you can use one of two methods:

- Adjust the size of your browser window so you can see the slide at the same time and drag.
- Drag the clip art down to the Windows taskbar onto your presentation's button, wait until the presentation appears, and drag directly onto the slide.

Insert Picture Files

You don't need to use the Clip Organizer to insert a picture. You may never want to use a particular graphic again, so there's no point adding it to the Clip Organizer. To insert a picture:

1. Choose Insert | Picture | From File to open the Insert Picture dialog box. You can also click Insert Picture on the Picture or the Drawing toolbar.

2. Navigate to the file you want to insert.

3. Double-click the file.

In most cases, PowerPoint automatically places the image in a location on the slide that corresponds to one of the AutoLayouts. You see the AutoCorrect symbol (which I explained in Chapter 3 in relation to text). Click the symbol's arrow to choose to undo the automatic layout of the picture or turn off the feature for all images. You may want to resize or move both the image and any existing text placeholder.

> **TIP** *You can insert multiple images at once. To insert multiple images, open the Insert Picture dialog box as just described and select all the images you want to insert. Then click Insert. To select a group of files that are together, press SHIFT and click the first file in the group, then press SHIFT and click the last file in the group. To select files that are not together in a group, press CTRL and click the additional files you want to add. They all appear stacked on the same slide, and you can then move them to the desired location.*

Create a Photo Album

You can create a presentation that contains a series of photos with captions, called a photo album. The Photo Album feature (introduced for PowerPoint 2002) automates inserting photos from files, a scanner, or a digital camera into a specially formatted PowerPoint presentation. You can show your friends your summer vacation pictures or publish your album on the Web.

To create a photo album, choose Insert | Picture | New Photo Album or choose Photo Album from the New task pane. The Photo Album dialog box appears, as shown in Figure 5-4.

To create a photo album, follow these steps:

1. Click either File/Disk or Scanner/Camera to choose the source of your images.

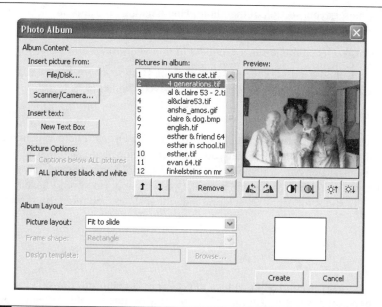

FIGURE 5-4   The Photo Album dialog box contains the settings for creating a photo album—a presentation containing a set of images.

2. If you choose File/Disk, a dialog box opens where you can choose the images you want to add. You can choose one or select a group. Click Insert.

TIP *To select a group of files, press* SHIFT *and click the first file in the group, then press* SHIFT *and click the last file in the group. To select files that are not together in a group, press* CTRL *and click for each additional file you want to add. You can press* CTRL *and click a selected item to unselect it.*

3. If you choose Scanner/Camera, a dialog box opens in which you can choose the device (scanner or camera) and the quality (web or print). Click Insert if you are inserting from a scanner. Click Custom Insert if you are inserting from a digital camera.

4. Continue to add images following the previous steps. As you add images, they appear in the Pictures in Album list. You can select any image, rotate it, and adjust its brightness and contrast using the buttons. These buttons are similar to those on the Picture toolbar and are covered later in this chapter in the "Use the Picture Toolbar" section. You can also remove an image and change the order of the images.

5. To add a text box, click New Text Box to add a text slide. When you return to your photo album, you'll see a text box with the words Text Box. Click the words and type a caption or description of a picture. This text box is on its own slide.

6. In the Picture Options section, you can check the checkboxes to add captions below all the pictures or to make all the pictures black and white.

7. In the Album Layout section of the Photo Album dialog box, choose a layout. The layout specifies how many images fit on a page.

8. You can also select a frame shape from the Frame Shape drop-down list.

9. If you wish, choose a design template by clicking Browse, choosing one of PowerPoint's templates (or a template you have created and saved), and click Select.

10. Click Create.

To edit a photo album, choose Format | Photo Album. The Format Photo Album dialog box is just like the Photo Album dialog box that you use to create the photo album. You should make any adjustments in this dialog box. A photo album contains special formatting and may not function properly if you try to edit it like you would a regular presentation. However, I have had success adding text boxes to slides for captions, deleting individual slides, and reordering them in the usual way.

Edit Pictures

The truth is that you may need to edit graphics to get the look you want. PowerPoint offers more options than ever before for editing your images. You may be able to get the results you want right in PowerPoint. In the next few sections, I explain how to edit images.

Use PowerPoint's Basic Tools

You may be able to edit the graphic from within PowerPoint. Sometimes the type of editing available depends on the type of graphic—bitmap or vector. I cover the options in this section.

Resize and Duplicate Graphics

When a graphic—clip art or other graphic file—appears on your slide, it may be much too big or small. You can quickly resize it using the handles. To maintain the proportion of the picture, click it to select it and drag one of the corner handles in the desired direction.

 Although PowerPoint 2003 does a reasonably good job of keeping images clear, remember that resizing always affects the resolution of bitmap graphics.

You can duplicate any selected graphic by choosing Edit | Duplicate or pressing CTRL-D. PowerPoint creates a copy of the graphic slightly overlapping the original. Drag it to a new position. You can also copy it to the clipboard and paste it—either on the same slide or another one.

Group and Ungroup Graphics

Some vector-based art can be ungrouped into individual drawing objects. (Drawing objects are discussed fully later in this chapter in the "Create Drawing Objects" section.) Right-click the graphic, and choose Grouping | Ungroup. (Or choose Draw | Ungroup on the Drawing toolbar.) Sometimes you can even ungroup the art twice: once into a few larger objects and again into many smaller ones. When you choose Ungroup for an imported picture, you see the message shown here. Click Yes to convert it to a Microsoft Office drawing.

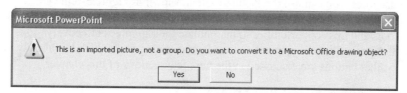

You can manipulate the art in unusual ways using this technique. For example, in Figure 5-5, you see an image of two leaves on the left. This picture had to be ungrouped twice before all the elements were separated. Then the elements in each leaf were selected together and grouped. On the right, the leaves have been resized, duplicated, and moved—something that you can do only by ungrouping the picture.

CAUTION   *If you ungroup a picture into individual components, you often have hundreds of tiny pieces that can easily be deleted or moved inadvertently. Don't forget to regroup the picture for easier handling. In Figure 5-5, each leaf was grouped to create two objects.*

Occasionally, you may also lose the colors when you ungroup pictures. While you may be able to recolor the object from scratch, that process can be difficult and not entirely satisfactory, so be cautious.

TIP   *Always save your presentation before you start making major changes to a graphic, and then you can have a little fun. If you don't like the results, you can undo all your changes or close the presentation without saving it.*

FIGURE 5-5   You can manipulate vector art by ungrouping it and converting it to drawing objects. *Thanks to Digital Juice for permission to use this background.* www.digitaljuice.com.

Use the Picture Toolbar

For more precise tools, you can use the Picture toolbar, shown in Figure 5-6 in vertical position. The Picture toolbar is your key to editing graphics. Many users are not aware of the depth of these editing tools and miss opportunities to manipulate their graphics effectively.

The first tool, Insert Picture, opens the Insert Picture dialog box, which has already been discussed. The other buttons are discussed in the next few sections of this chapter.

Adjust Color, Contrast, and Brightness

You can convert images to grayscale, black and white, or a washout. A washout is often called a *watermark*—a light-toned graphic—and is used as a background behind text. When you select a picture and click Color on the Picture toolbar, PowerPoint opens a short menu with these options:

- **Automatic**   Uses the image type that came with the graphic. The default.

- **Grayscale**   Changes the graphic to shades of gray. Colors are assigned a shade of gray in relation to their intensity.

- **Black & White**   Converts your graphic to black and white, with no shading.

- **Washout**   Creates a light-toned graphic. An example is shown in Figure 5-7. A washout is not transparent, and you may need to move it behind text, as explained later in this chapter in the "Reorder Objects" section.

You may want to fine-tune the brightness and contrast slightly as well. If you want the image to appear as a background on every slide, save it as a file (right-click and choose Save as Picture) and place it on the slide master, as explained in Chapter 7.

The next two buttons on the Picture toolbar, More Contrast and Less Contrast, increase and decrease contrast. Increasing contrast makes dark colors darker and light colors lighter. Increase

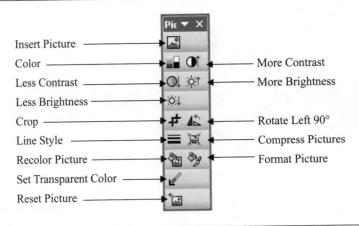

FIGURE 5-6   Use the Picture toolbar to edit your images in PowerPoint.

Original   Washout

FIGURE 5-7 You can change a graphic to a washout, also called a watermark. *(Courtesy of U.S. Fish and Wildlife Service Photo by Craig Blacklock)*

contrast when a graphic is not clear enough. Decreasing contrast makes dark colors lighter and light colors darker. If you continue to decrease a graphic's contrast, you end up with all grays. Decrease contrast when you want a softer effect.

Figure 5-8 shows a graphic before and after adjusting contrast. The contrast was originally very high but the presenter reduced the contrast to get a softer look and clearer details. Note that

High-contrast   Lower contrast

FIGURE 5-8 You can get a softer, more detailed look by lessening contrast.

this graphic was created using an image-editing program—as a result, there are other special effects that cannot be created in PowerPoint.

The fourth and fifth buttons, More Brightness and Less Brightness, increase and decrease brightness. Increasing brightness lightens all the colors in the graphic. You can increase brightness to correct a dark graphic. Decreasing brightness darkens all the colors. You may find that a graphic looks good on paper, but your screen is too bright when you shine it on a wall screen with an LCD projector—in that case, decrease its brightness.

Crop a Graphic

You often want to use only a portion of a graphic to emphasize the main focus. For example, you may want only the flower without its surroundings. Another good use for the crop tool is to get rid of an unwanted black border. Choose Crop on the Picture toolbar. The cursor changes to look like the Crop button. The cursor may change again to a T shape as you pass it over the picture's border. Move the cursor to one of the handles on the graphic and drag inward. Release the mouse button when you have cropped enough. The Crop button stays depressed so you can crop from more than one side. When you are done, click Crop again to stop cropping. Figure 5-9 shows an example of a graphic before and after cropping.

Rotate

You can use the Rotate Left button on the Picture toolbar to rotate any image 90 degrees to the left. Continue to click the Rotate Left button to rotate the image to any increment of 90 degrees.

For the ultimate in flexibility, use the green Free Rotate dot at the top of any selected image, as shown next. Place the cursor over the dot and it changes to the free rotate shape. Click and drag to rotate the image to any angle you want. See the section, "Lay Out Your

FIGURE 5-9 If you need only part of a graphic, you can crop it.

Slides with Precision" later in this chapter for another way to rotate images or AutoShapes precisely.

Change Line Style

You can place a border around a graphic. PowerPoint calls this border a *line,* and you can choose the color, weight (thickness), and type of the line. In practice, most graphics do not use a border because it looks formal and artificial. On the other hand, a border can set off text and give it a neat, tailored look, as shown in this text box.

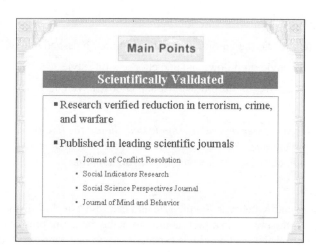

To place a border around an image, right-click it and choose Format Picture. The Format Picture dialog box appears, as shown in Figure 5-10, with the Colors and Lines tab on top. In the Line section, click the Color drop-down list. Choose a color and click OK. To remove a border, select No Line.

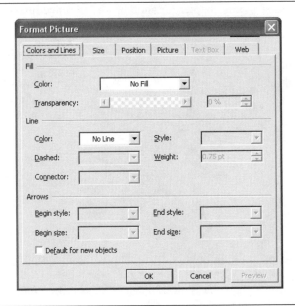

FIGURE 5-10   The Format Picture dialog box lets you format many properties of a picture.

Besides choosing the color, you can choose from these options:

- **Dashed**   Click the Dashed drop-down list and choose a dashed line type.
- **Style**   Click the Style drop-down list and choose a line style.
- **Weight**   Click the Weight drop-down list and choose a weight. Line weight means line thickness.

 *To quickly place a border around a graphic and choose the line style, click Line Style on the Drawing toolbar. Choose a line style from the list. To quickly place a border and choose the color, click Line Color on the Drawing toolbar.*

Compress Images

Large images in a presentation increase the file size and can result in slow display during a slide show. You can compress the images in a presentation to make the entire presentation smaller, so that it loads more quickly. This functionality is especially important for presentations that you place on the Internet.

TIP *The ideal situation is to create the images using a low resolution. Additional adjustments always affect quality. For onscreen presentations, 72 dots per inch (dpi) is usually fine. (PowerPoint compresses such images to 96 dpi.) Printed presentations require a much higher resolution, generally 300 dpi.*

To compress an image, select it and click Compress Pictures on the Picture toolbar. The C2ompress Pictures dialog box opens, as shown here.

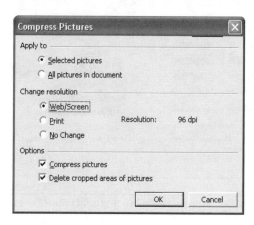

You can choose to compress only selected images or all the images in a presentation. Choose whether you want to compress for onscreen or print use. You can also choose to delete cropped areas of pictures. PowerPoint remembers the full image so you can restore it if you decide you don't like the cropping effect. Deleting the cropped area results in a smaller presentation, although it probably won't make a huge difference unless you have cropped a lot of images. When you click OK, you see a message warning you that compression can reduce the quality of your images. Click Apply to compress them.

 If you don't know the origin of your images, it's not a good idea to compress all of them at once. You may lose details that you need.

Recolor Pictures

 What if you find a graphic that is perfect in its subject but the wrong color? The colors of a graphic should blend nicely with the colors of the rest of the slide. (For more about color, see Chapter 6.) PowerPoint can change the colors of a vector graphic, color by color, giving you incredible control. Recoloring pictures can be indispensable when you have a picture that does not look good against the presentation background or if you need a series of color-coordinated images. To change the colors in your picture, click Recolor Picture on the Picture toolbar. PowerPoint opens the Recolor Picture dialog box, shown in Figure 5-11.

NOTE *You cannot recolor bitmaps in PowerPoint. You need to use a separate image-editing program, as discussed later in this chapter in the section "Edit Graphic Files." If you try to recolor a bitmap, PowerPoint displays a message telling you to use an image-editing program.*

PowerPoint defines a picture as having lines, fills, and backgrounds. Lines create edges—when you draw a picture with a pencil you are creating lines, even if they are curves. Fills and

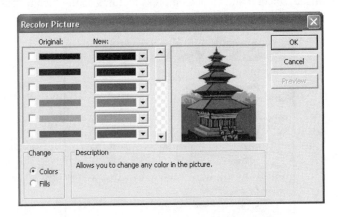

FIGURE 5-11 Use the Recolor Picture dialog box for total control over colors in your graphics.

backgrounds fill in enclosed spaces created by lines. The Recolor Picture dialog box lets you work with all these colors (choose Colors in the Change section) or only fills and backgrounds (choose Fills). The purpose of working only with fill colors is so that you can exclude lines of the same color. For example, if your picture has black lines and black fill—a common situation—by choosing the Fills option, you can change the black fill to another color, yet leave the black lines alone. (For more on colors, borders, and fills, see Chapter 6.)

To recolor a picture, follow these steps:

1. Select a vector image. The most common format is Windows Metafile Format (.wmf).

2. Click Recolor Picture on the Picture toolbar.

3. Choose Colors to change all colors in the picture, including lines, fills, and backgrounds, or choose Fills to change all colors except line colors.

4. Click an original color here to change it.

5. Click an arrow in the New column, and choose a new color.

6. Continue to change the colors as desired. If necessary, scroll down to see all the colors.

7. Click OK when you are done.

Format Pictures

 For general graphic editing, click Format Picture on the Picture toolbar to open the Format Picture dialog box, as shown in Figure 5-10.

 *You can also right-click any picture, and choose Format Picture on the shortcut menu. The Picture tab is displayed initially.*

Use the Colors and Lines tab to format fill color. In this instance, *fill color* refers to the background of the image. Generally, you can add a fill color only for vector graphics. When you click the Color drop-down box, you see the menu shown here. (Fill effects are covered in Chapter 6.)

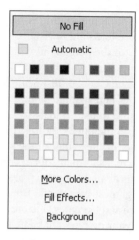

From this drop-down menu, you can change the fill in the following ways:

- **Eliminate fill**   Choose No Fill.
- **Fill with default fill color**   Choose Automatic.
- **Fill with a color in the color scheme**   Choose one of the colors in the row below Automatic.
- **Fill with a recently used color**   Choose one of the colors below the color scheme row.
- **Fill with any other color**   Choose More Colors to open the Colors dialog box.
- **Fill with a gradient, texture, pattern, or picture**   Choose Fill Effects to open the Fill Effects dialog box.
- **Fill with the same color as the slide background**   Choose Background.

Often, adding a fill makes a graphic look awkward and stilted, as shown here (left). Without the fill (right), the graphic seems to be an integral part of the slide.

The Size tab of the Format Picture dialog box is shown in Figure 5-12. Use this tab to precisely specify the size and scale of your picture.

You can type a height and width in inches to get precisely the measurement you need, or rotate the picture by choosing an exact rotation. Rotation is calculated clockwise, so that as you increase the rotation number, your picture turns clockwise.

In the Scale section, choose a scale for the height and width. Check Lock Aspect Ratio to keep the height and width in proportion. Check Relative to Original Picture Size to calculate the scale based on the original picture size. Choose Best Scale for Slide Show to set the screen resolution you will use for the slide show, and size the picture appropriately for that resolution. Click the Reset button to return the picture to its original size.

The Position tab lets you precisely set the position of the picture vertically and horizontally. You can measure from the top-left corner or the center of the slide.

The Picture tab lets you use precise measurements for cropping. You can also choose the image type here, duplicating the controls available on the Color button of the Picture toolbar. Finally, you can control contrast and brightness by percent. Buttons for recoloring and compressing the image bring you to the Recolor Picture and Compress Picture dialog boxes discussed previously.

When you have completed editing your picture, click OK to return to your slide.

NOTE *You cannot crop, group, or change the fill, border, shadow, or transparency of an animated GIF image with the Picture toolbar in PowerPoint. Use an animated GIF-editing program, and then insert the file on the slide again.*

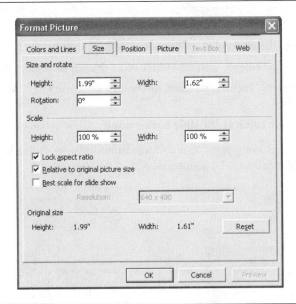

FIGURE 5-12   The Size tab lets you set the size and scale of your picture.

Set Transparent Color

You can create a transparent area on some types of images. The most common image type that supports transparency is the GIF format. To create a transparent area, choose Set Transparent Color on the Picture toolbar, and then click on the color in the picture that you want to be transparent.

Reset Picture

When you make changes to a picture, PowerPoint remembers all the original settings. Click Reset Picture on the Picture toolbar to return the picture to its original state.

Edit Graphic Files

Unfortunately, you may not be able to get the results you want within PowerPoint. When you want a more sophisticated way to edit graphic files, you need to find a graphic-editing program that can do the job and can save the results in a file format that PowerPoint can accept. Fortunately, there are many such programs. Most professionally created presentations include images that have been edited using separate software. The premier example of this type of software is Adobe Photoshop (http://www.adobe.com/products/photoshop/main.html), a high-end graphic file-editing program that can create just about any effect you want for a bitmap graphic.

If you don't have Photoshop, other less expensive, simpler alternatives are available that allow you to do almost everything you want, such as the following:

- ◼ **Adobe Photoshop Elements**   As the name says, contains elements of Photoshop (http://www.adobe.com/products/photoshopel/main.html)
- ◼ **Ulead PhotoImpact**   Image-editing from Ulead (http://www.ulead.com/pi/runme.htm)
- ◼ **Microsoft PictureIt!**   Image-editing from Microsoft (http://pictureitproducts.msn.com/default.asp)
- ◼ **Jasc Paint Shop Pro**   Image-editing from Jasc (http://www.jasc.com/products/psp)
- ◼ **CorelDRAW and Corel PHOTO-PAINT**   Drawing and editing programs from Corel (http://www.corel.com)

Use Photo Editor

If you have Microsoft Office, you already have a program you can use to edit graphics—Microsoft Photo Editor. (If you don't have it installed, use Office Setup to install it.) Despite its name, Photo Editor can edit any bitmap image. It contains a number of tools that are not found in PowerPoint for manipulating bitmap images. Photo Editor specializes in the types of effects often used on photographs, but you cannot change colors or modify individual pixels in the image. Start Photo Editor by choosing Start | Programs | Microsoft Photo Editor. You can then open any bitmap image, edit it, and save it. Return to PowerPoint, and choose Insert | Picture | From File to open the graphic.

5

TIP *From within PowerPoint, you can choose Insert | Object (on the expanded menu), and choose Microsoft Photo Editor Photo. Once in Photo Editor, open the graphic, and edit it. Then choose File | Exit and Return To at the bottom of the menu (your presentation name will be inserted on the menu) to return to PowerPoint.*

The following bullet points provide a brief overview of the features of this application. For more information, consult Photo Editor's help system.

- To change image type, choose File | Save As. In the Save as Type drop-down list, you can choose a new file type. For example, you can change a .tga image to a .gif image in this way.

- To convert an image's color type (true color, 256 color, grayscale, or monochrome), choose File | Properties, and choose from the Type drop-down list. Click OK.

- Use the Image menu to crop, resize, rotate, transpose, invert, or mirror an image.

- You can create transparent areas in an image, using the Set Transparent Color tool on the toolbar. (You can also do this in PowerPoint.) If you don't want the background of your graphic to show up on your slide, make the background transparent.

- Choose Image | Balance to adjust brightness, contrast, and gamma. While you can adjust brightness and contrast in PowerPoint, *gamma,* which controls contrast in dark areas, is a Photo Editor feature that gives you increased control over your images.

- To cut out an internal area of your picture, use the Select tool to select a rectangular area anywhere within your picture. Then choose Edit | Cut.

The most exciting features of Photo Editor are its way-cool artistic and special effects, which you find on the Effects menu. The first set of commands—the *artistic* effects—are Sharpen, Soften, Negative, Despeckle, Posterize, and Edge. The second set are the *special* effects—Chalk and Charcoal, Emboss, Graphic Pen, Notepaper, Watercolor, Stained Glass, Stamp (like an ink stamp), and Texturizer. The best way to get familiar with these effects is to take a couple of pictures, and try them all! You can get some very artsy results. Here you see an original photo and a version that has been embossed in Photo Editor to give a three-dimensional effect.

Work with Color in Microsoft Paint

One more tool for editing bitmaps is Microsoft Paint, which is included with Windows. Paint is a simple program, but it is especially useful for coloring in black-and-white clip art. As long as an area is enclosed, Paint can fill it with color. You can also easily touch up a drawing by adding your own freely drawn lines. To open Paint, choose Start | (All) Programs | Accessories | Paint.

TIP *When you are trying to fill an image with color, Paint works best with BMP files. To use a GIF or JPEG file, open it in Photo Editor, choose File | Save As, and save it in .bmp format. You can then open it in Paint.*

To fill in an area with color, choose a color from the Color palette at the bottom of the screen. Click to choose a foreground color and right-click to choose a background color. Then choose the Fill with Color tool. Then click in any enclosed area of the picture to fill with the foreground color and right-click to fill with the background color. To enclose an area, choose a color, and use the Line tool.

TIP *To add a custom color, choose Options | Edit Colors, and click Define Custom Colors in the dialog box.*

Here you see a drawing in its original black-and-white form and after being colored using Paint.

To create the graphic, fill in each area in Paint, using the procedure previously explained. Save the graphic, and import it into PowerPoint. Then use the Set Transparent Color tool on the Picture toolbar, and point to the white background. (Many graphics come in with a white background.) Finally, resize, crop, and place the graphic as desired.

TIP *Not all formats support transparency. If necessary, bring the image into Photo Editor and save it as a GIF file, a format that supports transparency.*

Vector files can usually be edited with success within PowerPoint, but drawing programs such as CorelDRAW, Adobe Illustrator and Macromedia Freehand can edit vector files as well and may have better tools.

Create Drawing Objects

Microsoft Office has its own drawing tools that you can use to create graphics on your own. While you won't be able to create sophisticated drawings or artwork, you can create some useful shapes to add focus and impact to your slides. In addition, you can manipulate these shapes to create some great effects, such as shadows and 3-D.

Use the Draw Toolbar

The Drawing toolbar, shown in Figure 5-13, is your gateway to creating drawing objects. By default, it is at the bottom of the screen. In this chapter, I explain most of the tools on the Drawing toolbar. Note that a few of the features of the Drawing toolbar relating to text—text boxes, WordArt, and font color—were discussed in Chapters 2 and 3. The tools relating to colors, borders, fills, and 3-D effects are covered in Chapter 6.

The next section covers inserting AutoShapes from the Draw menu. The following section tells you how to draw your own shapes using the tools on the Draw menu. The section "Edit Drawing Objects" covers the Draw menu tools that deal with manipulating existing drawing objects.

Insert AutoShapes

You use the Drawing toolbar to insert AutoShapes, which are shapes that you can easily resize and color. AutoShapes are surprisingly flexible, and there are loads of them. Here you see a slide that makes creative use of AutoShapes: one is a curved arrow that is repeated and rotated to create a

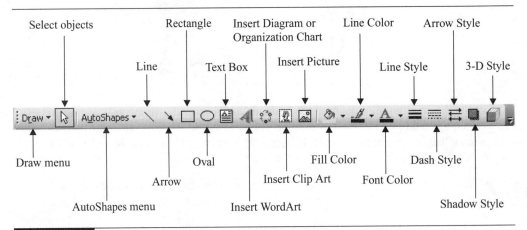

FIGURE 5-13   The Drawing toolbar

circular shape, and the other is a series of squares that have been combined to create a step shape with the number 2 inside, indicating the second slide.

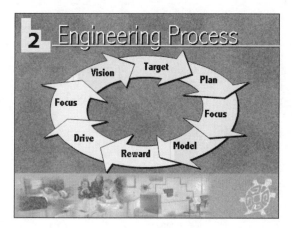

Thanks to Jennifer Rotondo (jennifer@creativemindsinc.com) for this slide.

To create this circle, follow these steps:

1. Insert the curved arrow AutoShape, as explained in the next section, "Draw Lines, Arrows, and Curves."

2. Reshape it (as explained later in this chapter in the section "Insert Basic Shapes, Block Arrows, and Stars and Banners"); then resize and place it as desired.

3. Choose Edit | Duplicate to create a second arrow, and rotate it.

4. Choose Draw | Order | Send Backward to move the second arrow behind the first, and move it so it appears to come out of the first arrow.

5. Select both arrows, and choose Draw | Group to group the two arrows.

6. Duplicate them, and repeat the process of sending it backward, rotating it, and moving it.

7. Continue until you are finished.

8. Ungroup (Draw | Ungroup) all the arrows.

9. The last arrow needs to be retouched so that its point appears to be above the end of the first arrow. To block out the end of the first arrow, insert a diamond-shaped AutoShape with no line that is the same color as the arrows. Resize, rotate, and place it so it covers the end of the first arrow.

10. Use the Line tool to draw over the arrow point of the last arrow so it appears to be on top. You can barely see where this was done to the point of the arrow labeled *Vision* in the previous illustration.

5

11. Finally, fill the arrows with a slight gradient to represent the process being described.

12. Add the text last.

If you group the entire circle, you can then resize and move it easily on the slide. Select all the objects and choose Group on the Draw menu of the Drawing toolbar.

The step shape at the top of the slide is simply six squares, with no line. Place each shape so they touch and look like one shape.

Click AutoShapes on the Drawing toolbar to open the AutoShapes menu, shown here.

Each item opens to a submenu with thumbnail pictures of the AutoShapes. (The Action buttons on the AutoShapes menu are covered in Chapter 11.)

Choose More AutoShapes to display more shapes, including a number of office objects.

Draw Lines, Arrows, and Curves

Use lines and curves to create your own shapes or touch up existing ones. On the Drawing toolbar, choose AutoShapes | Lines to find the lines and curves. Each tool works slightly differently— sometimes leading to a frustrating experience. Here are precise instructions to make it easy.

■ To draw a single line, choose the Line tool, move the cursor to your slide, then click and drag. The end point of the line is where you release the mouse button.

■ To draw an arrow, choose one of the arrow tools. Click and drag to create the arrow. The endpoint of the arrow is where you release the mouse button.

■ To draw a curved shape, choose the Curve tool. You can create a multicurved shape. First click at the desired start point. Then move the cursor to either the desired endpoint or to where you want to create a curve that changes the direction of the line, and click. You can continue to click at curve points. Double-click to end the curve. Here you see a curve with two vertices. To create this curve, click at the start point, move the cursor to a bend point, and click again. Click again at the second bend point and double-click at the end. The arrow was added separately.

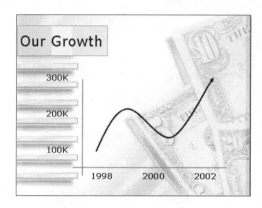

Thanks to Digital Juice at http://www.digitaljuice.com *for this background.*

■ A *freeform shape* is a multisegmented shape that can contain both curves and lines. Choose the Freeform tool. Then click at the desired start point. To create a line segment, move the mouse to the desired endpoint, and click. You can continue drawing line segments in this way. To draw freeform shapes, which are usually curved, drag the mouse. The shape follows the cursor, as if you're drawing with a pencil. To end the freeform object, double-click.

■ A scribble follows the cursor as you drag with the mouse. Choose the Scribble tool. Click at the desired start point, and drag, drawing as you go. Just release the mouse button to end the scribble.

To close a shape, click near its start point. PowerPoint automatically connects the endpoint to the start point.

The Line tool is also directly on the Drawing toolbar. There is one special advantage to using this tool. To draw several individual lines, double-click the Line tool on the Drawing toolbar. It stays depressed, and you can draw any number of lines, without reclicking the Line button. Click the Line button again to stop drawing lines. The same applies to the Arrow tool on the toolbar.

Create Flowcharts and Process Diagrams

The AutoShapes menu lets you insert a variety of flowchart shapes and connectors. *Connectors* are used in flowcharts and process diagrams to connect shapes. Figure 5-14 shows a simple flowchart.

NOTE   *You can create a variety of pre-set diagrams, in addition to organizational charts. These are explained in Chapter 8.*

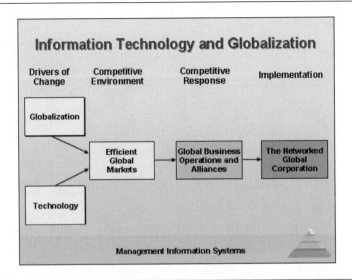

FIGURE 5-14 A flowchart diagram. *Thanks to Maharishi University of Management,* http://www.mum.edu, *for this slide.*

To insert a flowchart shape, choose AutoShapes | Flowchart, and choose a shape. Then click and drag on the slide to obtain the desired size.

TIP *You can also insert an AutoShape by choosing it from the menu and then simply clicking on the slide. PowerPoint inserts the shape using a predefined size.*

Once you have your shapes in place, you can use the connectors to show how the shapes relate to each other. Choose one of the connectors by selecting AutoShapes | Connectors.

When you place the cursor near one of the flowchart shapes, PowerPoint displays tiny blue boxes at appropriate points on the shape. Click, and the connector snaps exactly to one of the boxes. Now drag to the second shape, and the blue boxes appear on that shape. Click to snap the end of the connector to one of the boxes.

You can easily edit flowcharts and process diagrams because connectors know what they are connected to and try to remain stuck to their shapes. If you move one of the flowchart shapes, the connector readjusts its length and direction accordingly.

Insert Basic Shapes, Block Arrows, and Stars and Banners

PowerPoint has a generous selection of shapes that you can insert onto your slides. From the Drawing toolbar, choose either AutoShapes | Basic Shapes, AutoShapes | Block Arrows, or AutoShapes | Stars and Banners to see the menus shown next.

As you can see, the choice ranges from utilitarian to whimsical. To insert one of the shapes, choose it. Then click and drag on the slide until the shape is the size you need. To insert a shape with its default size, simply click the slide without dragging.

 *To draw a circle or oval, use the Oval tool on the Drawing toolbar. To draw a circle, either press* SHIFT *as you drag, or click the slide without dragging. Likewise, to draw a square or rectangle, use the Rectangle tool. To draw a square, press* SHIFT *or click without dragging. Double-click either tool to draw several shapes at once.*

Some of the shapes display a small yellow diamond when selected. Dragging this marvelous diamond gives you extra control, enabling you to create an infinite variety of shapes. Initially, the effect of dragging the diamond in a specific direction may not be obvious, so experiment! Figure 5-15 shows some examples of these variations on a theme.

Insert Callouts

A *callout* is a combination of a text box and a line, which points to an object. Here you see an example.

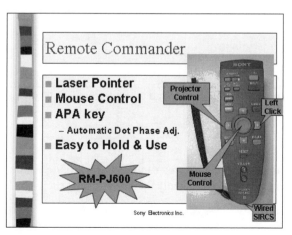

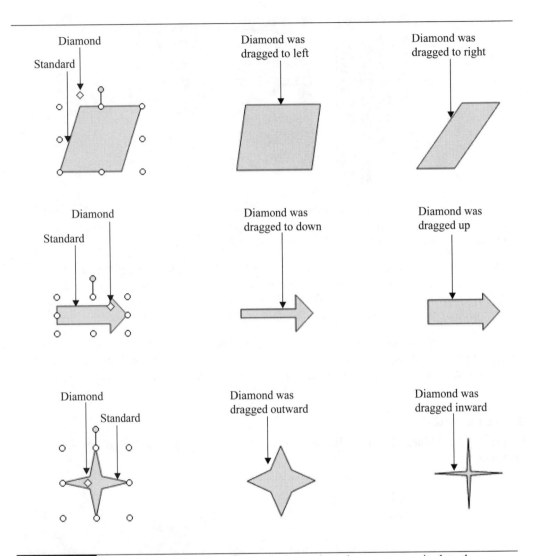

FIGURE 5-15   If a shape has a yellow diamond when selected, you can manipulate the shape's features.

The callout choices are shown next. As you can see, there is quite a variety. The callouts with a dotted box do not display a box—you see only the line and the text.

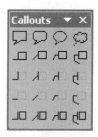

You probably won't know the right size for the callout until you have typed its text. Therefore, the easiest way to insert a callout is to follow these steps:

1. Choose the callout you want.

2. Click on your slide. PowerPoint inserts the callout using its default size and configuration.

3. Type the text for the callout.

4. Drag on the handles to adjust the size of the callout to fit the text.

5. Move the callout to its desired location.

6. Drag the diamond(s) until the line points to the appropriate spot.

Format Drawing Objects

Once you have inserted an AutoShape, you usually want to format it in some way. You can change the size and shape of arrows, change the line style, or create a dashed line directly from the Drawing toolbar. You can also use the Format AutoShape dialog box to specify the properties of your AutoShape. In Chapter 6, I cover formatting AutoShapes and drawing objects with color, fills, shadows, and 3-D effects.

Format Arrows

To change an arrow type, select the arrow, and choose Arrow Style on the Drawing toolbar. Choose one of the options. If you don't find the arrow you want, or if you want more control over arrow size and shape, choose More Arrows at the bottom of the menu to open the Format AutoShape dialog box shown in Figure 5-16.

Once you've selected an arrow, this dialog box opens with the current parameters showing in the Arrows section. Because an arrow is a combination of a line and an arrowhead, the settings in the Line section of the dialog box affect the arrow as well. The Line section controls the part of the arrow that applies to all lines:

■ Choose a color from the Color drop-down list.

■ From the Dashed drop-down list, you can choose from a variety of dashed and dotted lines.

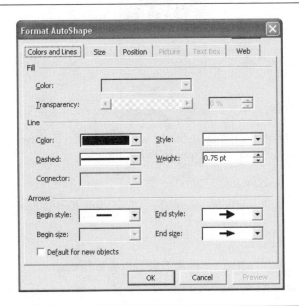

Use the Colors and Lines tab of the Format AutoShape dialog box to control arrows.

■ The Style drop-down list lets you choose from various line widths (weights) as well as a few double and triple lines.

■ The Weight drop-down list also controls line weight (width), but you can specify an exact width in points.

NOTE *Increasing the line weight affects both the arrow and the line.*

Use the Arrows section to control the part of the arrow that is specific to arrows:

■ Use the Begin Style drop-down box to create an arrow with an arrowhead at its beginning.

■ If the arrow has an arrowhead at its beginning, use the Begin Size drop-down list to choose the type and size of the arrow.

■ Use the End Style drop-down list to choose the type of arrow at the end. The choices are the same for both the beginning and the end of the arrow.

■ Use the End Size drop-down list to choose a size for the arrowhead at the end of the arrow.

TIP *If you wish, you can create your own arrowhead using the triangular basic AutoShape and a solid fill.*

Format Lines

You format lines in the same way that you format arrows. Choose Line Style on the Drawing toolbar to choose from various line weights and a few double and triple lines. Choose More Lines to open the same dialog box shown in Figure 5-16.

Choose Dash Style on the Drawing toolbar to choose from various dashed and dotted lines.

Lay Out Your Slides with Precision

The Format AutoShape dialog box, shown earlier in Figure 5-16 with the Colors and Lines tab on top, also gives you precise control over the size and position of an AutoShape.

Use the Size tab, shown in Figure 5-17, to specify the height and width of an AutoShape in inches. You can also rotate an AutoShape in a positive or a negative direction, with a precision of 1-degree increments. Use the Scale section to scale an AutoShape—you can separately control the scale of the height and the width.

The Position tab lets you position the AutoShape on your slide in inches, measuring from either the top-left corner or the center. Use the rulers to judge the setting you need.

TIP   *You can position by millimeters by typing **mm** after a measurement and by points by typing **pt**.*

If the AutoShape contains text, you can use the Text Box tab to control settings that affect the text, as explained in Chapter 3.

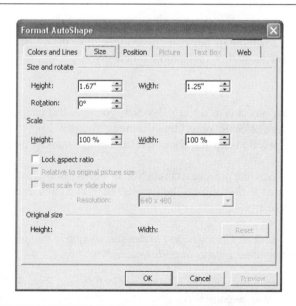

FIGURE 5-17   The Size tab of the Format AutoShape dialog box

Add Drawing Objects to the Clip Organizer

When you create drawing objects using the tools on the Drawing toolbar, you can add them to the Clip Organizer. If you spent quite a bit of time creating them and might use them again, by all means, place them in the Clip Organizer. Here's how:

1. First create the drawing object or objects.

2. Select the objects.

3. Press CTRL-C, or click Copy on the Standard toolbar.

4. Click Insert Clip Art on the Drawing toolbar. PowerPoint opens the Insert Clip Art task pane.

5. Click Organize Clips.

6. Choose a category.

7. Press CTRL-V. You may have to scroll down to see the new item.

> **TIP** *Don't forget to add keywords to help you find the drawing object again. Pass the cursor over the object's thumbnail, click the down arrow, and choose Edit Keywords.*

You can also save drawing objects as a separate graphic file. Select them, right-click, and choose Save as Picture. Once you have saved it, you can choose Insert | Picture | From File to insert the picture onto a slide.

Edit Drawing Objects

You will, of course, have to make changes to your drawing objects, sooner or later. No project ever seems to be completed without its fair share of changes. Take the time to learn these techniques well, and your work will go much more efficiently.

Select Objects

The first step in editing any object is to select it. By now, you have had enough experience with PowerPoint to know that you select an object by clicking it. You may have to click an AutoShape on its border to select it. A selected drawing object has handles that you can use to resize or reshape the object.

You can choose more than one object at a time. You can then reformat all the objects with one command. First, choose the first object. Then, press SHIFT, and click a second object. Keep on going as long as you like.

> **TIP** *Press SHIFT, and click a selected object to deselect an object that you selected in error, without deselecting other objects already selected.*

Another way to choose multiple objects is to use a selection box. First click at one corner of the rectangular area you want to enclose. Be careful not to click an object—click only empty space on the slide. Then drag to the opposite corner of the rectangle. PowerPoint displays a dashed rectangle as you drag. Release the mouse button when the rectangle encloses all the objects you want to select. In this situation, too, you can press SHIFT, and click any of the selected objects to deselect them. This is a great technique when you want to select all the objects in an area except one or two.

To select all the objects on a slide, press CTRL-A or choose Edit | Select All.

Objects are often layered on top of each other. You may find it difficult to select the object you want if it is behind another object. If the slide does not have too many objects, you may find it easier to cycle through all the objects until the object you want is selected. To accomplish this task, first select any object. Then press TAB repeatedly until the object you want is selected.

Group and Ungroup Objects

5

If you want to work with certain objects together more than once, you should group them. Grouped objects act like single objects. Common uses for grouping are text in a text box placed in a flowchart, WordArt text in an AutoShape, or a caption for a graphic image. In these instances, you want a set of objects to remain together. Grouping is especially important when moving objects.

To group a set of objects, select them all. On the Drawing toolbar, choose Draw | Group. All the handles displayed by the individual objects are replaced by one set of handles for the whole group.

You can always ungroup a group. Select the group, and choose Draw | Ungroup on the Drawing toolbar. Some objects have been grouped twice and you may need to ungroup them twice to get to the individual components.

For maximum flexibility, you can also select one object in a group without ungrouping. First select the group, and then click the object you want to select. You see a special set of handles, as shown in Figure 5-18. You can then modify the individual object in the group.

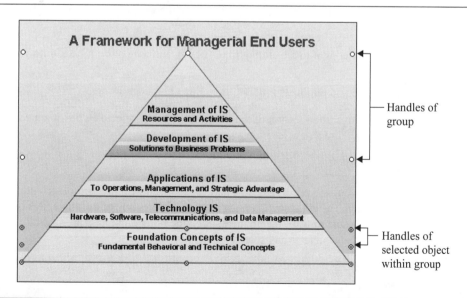

A special set of handles indicates a selected object that is part of a selected group.

Reorder Objects

As mentioned earlier, it is common to have objects that cover one another. You often place objects on a slide in a certain order, only to find that the wrong object is on top. Reordering objects lets you determine which object appears on top. To reorder an object, select it, and choose Draw | Order from the Drawing toolbar. Choose one of these options on the submenu:

- Bring to Front brings the selected object to the front of any other objects it overlaps.
- Send to Back sends the selected object behind any other objects it overlaps.
- Bring Forward brings the selected object one layer toward the front.
- Send Backward sends the selected object one layer toward the back.

In Figure 5-19, you see a slide containing several layers of pictures. On the right side of the first slide, the pictures are obviously in the wrong order.

Move Objects

You have already moved many objects in PowerPoint. Generally, you select the object, move the cursor over the object until you get the cross hairs, and then drag the object. You can precisely position an object using the Position tab of the Format AutoShape dialog box. (Right-click any object, and choose Format AutoShape.) In the section "Lay Out Your Slides with Precision," later in this chapter, I explain other techniques for positioning objects precisely.

Duplicate Objects

When you want two objects to be the same size and shape, you should draw the first object and then duplicate it, rather than try to draw it exactly the same the second time. There are two ways to duplicate objects:

- Select the object, copy it to the clipboard (CTRL-C), and then paste it back onto your slide (CTRL-V).
- Select the object, and duplicate it (CTRL-D or Edit | Duplicate).

You have no control over the location of the duplicate, but it is selected when it appears so you can immediately drag it to a new location.

Delete Objects

To delete an object, select it, and press DEL. In Chapter 3, I discussed how text placeholders are in Edit Text mode when you select them. Pressing DEL just deletes one of the characters of the text. Callouts follow the same rule. To delete them, click the border and then press DEL.

Pressing BACKSPACE also deletes any selected object or objects.

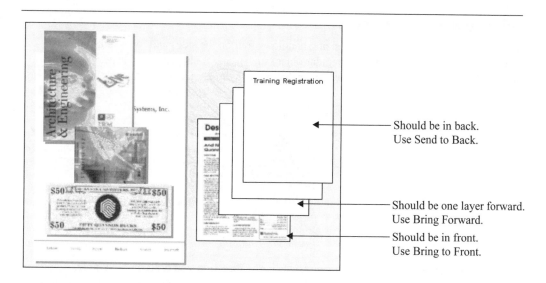

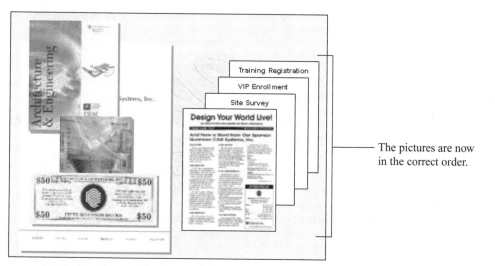

FIGURE 5-19   By reordering the objects on this slide, you can ensure that important information is not obscured. *Thanks to Quannon CAD Systems at* http://www.quannon.com.

When you press CTRL-X (or choose Edit | Cut), the selected object is deleted and moved to the clipboard. You can then paste it on another slide or even in another application.

Resize and Scale Objects

When you select an object, it has eight sizing handles—four on the sides and four on the corners—creating a selection rectangle. For an irregular object such as a star-shaped AutoShape, the handles are placed on an imaginary rectangular border that bounds the object, as shown here.

When you drag on a handle, the shape resizes in the direction you drag. For example, if you drag outward on either the left or right handles, the shape becomes wider. The side of the object *opposite* the handle you drag remains fixed. The center and all other sides of the object are moved.

You can also resize an object so that the center remains fixed. To do so, press CTRL while dragging a handle.

You may want to scale an object. When you scale an object, you have the option to maintain the shape without any vertical or horizontal distortion. PowerPoint calls this *resizing proportionally* because the vertical and horizontal remain proportional to each other.

■ To resize proportionally from a corner, drag the opposite corner handle.

■ To resize proportionally from the center, press CTRL and drag any corner handle.

As explained earlier in the "Lay Out Your Slides with Precision" section, you have exact control over the size of the object by using the Size tab of the Format AutoShape dialog box. You can also scale the object by percentage on the Size tab.

Lines, arrows, and connectors have only two handles when selected. When you drag one handle, the other end remains fixed. You can change the endpoint's position freely, so that both the length and angle of the line are changed.

You can resize a line from its center by pressing CTRL as you drag. When you press SHIFT and drag, the line's angle is held constant, and you can change only the line's length.

Rotate and Flip Objects

There are several ways to rotate an object. To rotate by dragging, select the object's green rotation handle, and drag in the desired direction. Release the mouse button when you like what you see.

For quick rotation by 90 degrees, choose Draw | Rotate or Flip from the Drawing toolbar, and choose Rotate Left or Rotate Right. For precise rotation, return to the now familiar Format AutoShape dialog box, and click the Size tab. Here you can set the rotation to any degree, as mentioned earlier in this chapter.

To mirror an object (called *flipping*), select the object, and choose Draw | Rotate or Flip from the Drawing toolbar. Then choose Flip Horizontal to mirror around a vertical line, or Flip Vertical to mirror around a horizontal line. You can create a mirror image of vector-based clip art by converting it to a PowerPoint object. Select the clip art, and then choose Draw | Ungroup on the Drawing toolbar. Immediately select Draw | Group, and flip the object.

 *To create a symmetrical shape by mirroring an object, copy the object and paste it. Choose Draw | Rotate or Flip. Move the copy next to the original. You can then group the two objects, and create a perfectly symmetrical shape.*

Here you see two examples of images created by copying and flipping.

Edit Points

Curve, freeform, and scribble objects are created with vertices that are located where you clicked as you created the object. You can edit these vertices to reshape these objects. Select the object, and then choose Draw | Edit Points on the Drawing toolbar (or right-click and choose Edit Points). PowerPoint now displays all the vertices, as shown here. You can drag any vertex in any direction. This method is great for making minor corrections in these objects, as you can see on the right of the example here.

Edit Connectors

Connectors have several unique properties that make them different from lines. First, there are three types of connectors—straight, elbow (angled), and curved. You can change any connector's type by right-clicking it and choosing a different type of connector from the shortcut menu.

To disconnect one end of a connector from its object, drag the handle at that end. You can then drag the handle to another object. To move the entire connector, drag its middle, and both ends become "undone."

PowerPoint can automatically reroute connectors so they travel the shortest distance. Right-click a connector, and choose Reroute Connectors from the shortcut menu. This command is also available on the Draw menu on the Drawing toolbar.

Change One AutoShape to Another

Would you like to switch AutoShapes? Maybe you think another shape would look more attractive or fit around the text better. It's easy:

1. Select the AutoShape you want to change.

2. Choose Draw | Change AutoShape on the Drawing toolbar.

3. Choose a type of AutoShape, and choose the shape you want.

Lay Out Your Slides with Precision

For you control freaks who like to lay out a slide precisely, a number of tools are designed especially for you. I have already discussed some of the techniques, such as using the Format AutoShapes dialog box to exactly position an AutoShape on a slide. Here are a few more pointers.

Use the Rulers

The rulers are very helpful when laying out a slide. As you move the cursor, the top and side rulers each show their position with a line. By observing the lines as you point to an object, you can know its position. You can use this information to position other objects.

The rulers as they apply to text are covered in Chapter 4.

To show the rulers, choose View | Ruler on the expanded menu.

Use Guides

The guides are one of the best tools for placing objects. Guides are fine horizontal and vertical lines that cross the entire slide. To view the guides, follow these steps:

1. Choose View | Grid and Guides. (You can also find the same menu item on the Draw menu of the Drawing toolbar.) The Grid and Guides dialog box opens, shown in Figure 5-20.

2. Check the Display Drawing Guides on the Screen check box.

3. Click OK.

The default guides appear through the zero mark of each ruler. If you added or moved guides, you see the last guide setup you created.

You can use the guides to measure distances. To do so, drag a guide. The measurement from the guide's start point appears. To properly use guides, you often need more than one in each

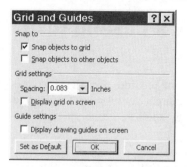

FIGURE 5-20 The Grid and Guides dialog box

direction. To add a guide, press CTRL, and drag any guide. PowerPoint creates a new guide. Use the measurement to place the new guide precisely, as shown here.

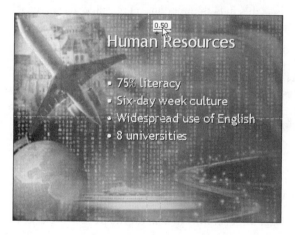

Thanks to Geetesh Bajaj for this presentation. www.indezine.com.

One reason that guides are so useful is that objects snap to them as you move them. To try this, place a guide, and drag any object near the guide. You will see that the object's edge snaps to the guide.

To delete a guide that you have added, drag it to its corresponding ruler. Drag horizontal guides to the top ruler, and vertical guides to the side ruler.

> TIP
> *Many slides use an asymmetric layout, and the center of the slide is not obvious. Use guides often to make sure that objects are properly centered.*

Snap to the Grid and to Objects

PowerPoint slides have a grid that you can use to control the placement of objects. By default, the grid is invisible, but you can display it and control its spacing.

 **Create a Custom Grid**

If the standard grid that PowerPoint provides doesn't suit your needs, you can create your own, with varied spacing and a margin, for instance. One way to create a grid is to draw it on the slide master using the Drawing toolbar:

1. First create your guides.

2. Then draw a line along the first guide. (Grids are traditionally light blue.) By default, the line snaps to the guide.

3. Choose CTRL-D to duplicate the line and drag it to the second guide.

4. Now continue to duplicate the last line you've created, and PowerPoint gets the message, placing them automatically on your guides.

5. When you've done this in both directions on the slide master, use the Rectangle tool to create a margin all around the slide.

6. Select all the lines and the rectangle, and group them.

Return to your presentation, and you will see the grid on all your slides.
You can create a template containing only a slide master with this grid and use it for all your presentations. Or once you've created this grid, you can copy it from one presentation to another. When you have finished the presentation, go to the slide master, and delete the grid.

By default, whenever you draw, resize, or move an object, it *snaps* to this grid. As a result, objects tend to line up easily, without much fuss.

TIP *Sometimes you want total control. To temporarily disable the grid snapping, press* ALT *as you drag or draw an object.*

You can also snap one object to another. To set this up, choose Draw | Grid and Guides to open the Grid and Guides dialog box, shown in Figure 5-20. Check the Snap Objects to Other Objects check box. When Snap to Shape is on, shapes that you draw or drag automatically snap to nearby shapes.

Use the Grid Settings section of the dialog box to set the grid spacing and display the grid. If you like to work this way all the time, click the Set as Default button to keep your settings for other presentations. Click OK when you're done.

Constrain Shape and Direction

As mentioned in the "Resize and Scale Objects" section earlier in this chapter, you can constrain lines to be horizontal or vertical by pressing SHIFT as you draw. You can also press SHIFT to create a circle using the Oval tool and a square using the Rectangle tool. Refer back to that section for an explanation of how to resize objects proportionally to prevent horizontal and/or vertical distortion.

To constrain the movement of objects to the horizontal or vertical, press SHIFT as you drag the object.

Nudge Objects

Do you find it difficult to move objects a very short distance with the mouse? You're not alone. PowerPoint lets you *nudge* objects, which means to move them a short distance. To nudge an object, select it, and choose Draw | Nudge on the Drawing toolbar. Then choose Up, Down, Left, or Right from the submenu. PowerPoint moves the object one grid unit in the direction you chose.

For quicker access, you can also use the arrow keys on the keyboard to nudge objects.

TIP *If you want super control, press CTRL as you use the appropriate arrow key. PowerPoint moves your object in increments of .02 inches. Remember that you can also press ALT while dragging to disable the grid completely.*

Align and Distribute Objects

PowerPoint enables you to automatically align objects and distribute them evenly across an area or the entire slide.

To align two or more objects, first decide how you want to align them. If the objects are lined up approximately vertically, you can line them up along their left sides, right sides, or through their center. If the objects are lined up approximately horizontally, you can line them up along their top sides, bottom sides, or through their middle.

To align objects, first select two or more objects. Then choose Draw | Align or Distribute. Choose one of the options on the submenu.

Here you see objects that need vertical aligning. Notice the position of the "Product" arrow in relation to the rectangles above and below it. On the right you see the result of using the Align Center option.

Another slick trick is to distribute three or more objects equidistant from each other, either horizontally or vertically. This saves you lots of calculations and is often a must for a neat-looking slide. To distribute objects, first choose three or more objects. Then choose Draw | Align or Distribute on the Drawing toolbar. From the submenu, choose either Distribute Horizontally or Distribute Vertically. Here the objects on the left have been redistributed on the right to have an equal amount of space between them.

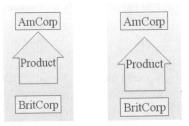

To arrange objects equal distances from each in relation to the entire slide, first click Relative to Slide on the expanded submenu of the Align or Distribute menu. Then start again—choose Draw | Align or Distribute | Distribute Horizontally or Distribute Vertically.

Tips on Design and Layout

Graphic designers use many principles that help to create a slide that looks balanced, easy-to-understand, and professional. The following sections discuss several of these principles.

Make Text Simple and Consistent

Pay a great deal of attention to consistency and legibility of text. As much as possible, stick to the same type family throughout the presentation. For example, you might consider using Arial, Arial Bold, Arial Black, and Arial Narrow. Don't use more than three fonts. Include font styles in your counting, because Times Roman regular and Times Roman italic appear as different fonts to your audience. Even different font sizes can sometimes give the impression of a different font. Use common sense, and keep it simple.

Consider the old belt and suspenders principle: you don't want to wear both to hold up your trousers—it's either one or the other. You don't need to use large type *and* make it bold. The point comes across clearer if you choose one or the other and give your presentation a more homogeneous look.

The line length of your text should never be more than 45 to 55 characters, including spaces. More than that is difficult for audiences to read. In most cases, the type will be large enough so that this is not a problem. The general principle is to use shorter lines rather than longer lines of text.

When mixing two different fonts, consider the *x-height* of the font: the height of the lowercase *x* as well as of many lowercase letters, such as *a*, *c*, and *e*. Two fonts may be the same point size but have different x-heights. For example, Garamond has a much smaller x-height than Arial. As a result, the entire font looks smaller and is harder to read. To compensate, you could increase the font size of the Garamond text. Here you see an example of both fonts side by side for comparison.

Follow a Simple Plan

Organize the elements of your slide in advance. Decide which elements are most important and which least important, and design them accordingly. Numbering and footnotes should be least important. If your headings are 44 points and bold and body copy is 28 points, create footnotes that are 18 points. Don't forget to stand back, and take a look at your slides. If some minor element jumps out at you, adjust it as necessary—remove the bold, make it smaller, or change the color.

Create a visual theme. A visual theme allows the graphic representation to express the content. For example, if you're giving a lecture on herb gardening, you might want to use natural-looking colors that emphasize the illustrations and photographs, leaf borders, leaf bullets, or pictures of finished recipes that express the theme visually.

If your slides are busy, with lots of text and graphics, make the background simple. The more contrast you create between your text and your background, the easier your slides are to read. If you use a 3-D or shadow effect, use it as emphasis. It's the belt and suspenders principle again—don't overdo special effects, or they lose their impact. The same principle works for highly saturated colors—use them in small areas for emphasis.

Consider Color and Rhythm

Audiences naturally read from left to right and from top to bottom. Audiences also notice dark or bright areas before light ones. So place and emphasize items with those two principles in mind. If you have a dark background, lighter areas stand out more because of the brightness and contrast.

Use cooler, muted colors for backgrounds, light or dark. Brighter warmer colors are "sweet,"—they're hard to look at for a long time. Light text on a dark background looks a little larger than vice versa. But don't be afraid to use lighter backgrounds with dark text—they create a softer look that is appropriate for many messages.

Think about the rhythm of the entire presentation. Like a piece of music, your presentation should have a regular beat without getting boring. For example, your slides could go like this: text, text, image, text. You can also create a rhythm such as large image, text, text, smaller images, text, text. To give the eye a rest and keep your audience attentive, you need to create variety.

Finally, do a usability test. You can even learn from a six-year-old's comments on your work. Then do the same with your colleagues at work. These people can point out issues that you missed, such as "This slide is about gardening. Why are the slides red?" Or "This part is too small for me to read." You'll get a lot of useful feedback and bring in an important element of objectivity. Don't be shy—people love to tell you what they think!

Thanks to graphic designer Stuart Friedman for these tips. He can be reached at graphics@iowatelecom.net.

Summary

In this chapter, you learned all about graphics. The first part of the chapter covered how to insert clip art on your slides. I discussed using the Clip Organizer, finding clip art, inserting graphic files, and editing pictures. You can edit many pictures using the Picture toolbar. Other tools often available are Microsoft Photo Editor and Paint.

The second part of the chapter covered AutoShapes, including inserting, formatting, and editing them. I also described the functions of the Drawing toolbar in detail. Finally, I reviewed some special techniques for laying out a slide with precision.

The next chapter is all about colors, borders, fills, and 3-D effects.

Chapter 6

Work with Colors, Borders, Fills, and 3-D Effects

How to…

■ Choose a color scheme

■ Customize a color scheme

■ Create gradient, texture, and pattern backgrounds

■ Create a picture background

■ Change fill color

■ Format fills

■ Create shadows

■ Use the shadow settings

■ Create 3-D shapes

■ Control 3-D settings

Color is an essential element of a presentation. Different colors send different messages to your audience. By using colors in borders, fills, backgrounds, and the slides as a whole, you can transform a ho-hum presentation into a forceful one. Add fills, shadows, and 3-D effects to realize the full power of your message.

Work with Color Schemes

Every design template includes a default *color scheme*: a set of eight colors that are automatically applied to the following features:

■ Background

■ Text and lines

■ Shadows

■ Title text

■ Fills

■ Accent

■ Accent and hyperlink. The color is applied to hyperlinked text, not to objects.

■ Accent and followed hyperlink. The color is applied when a hyperlink is clicked to show that the hyperlink has been followed. (Hyperlinks are covered in Chapter 11.)

In addition, design templates include a set of alternate color schemes that you can choose. The purpose of a color scheme is to ensure that your presentation has a coordinated look—not only should all titles look the same, but the colors should work well with each other.

You don't have to do anything to work with the default color scheme for your design template. PowerPoint automatically assigns the appropriate colors to the elements in your presentation based on the color scheme.

Choose a Color Scheme

You can imagine that you would not want to use the same color scheme for selling vacation packages to Hawaii as for selling long-term care insurance. Even the same presentation might use different color schemes for different situations. For example, if a presentation to employees on their employee benefits program is good news, you might use brighter colors compared to the softer colors you would use if the new program represented a cutback.

To choose a different color scheme, choose Format | Slide Design. The Slide Design task pane opens. Click Color Schemes to open the Color Scheme task pane shown in Figure 6-1. Note that some templates offer more color scheme options than others.

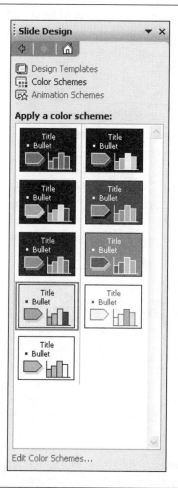

FIGURE 6-1   Choose Color Schemes on the Slide Design task pane to choose a color scheme for your presentation.

6

To see the colors in the color scheme more clearly, click the down arrow on any color scheme and choose Show Large Previews.

As you look at the color schemes, you'll see that the colors in each scheme are related. One scheme might feature blues, greens, and grays—soft colors—while another uses warmer greens, oranges, and browns. One color scheme is usually in shades of gray. Each color scheme is designed to create an overall impression that applies to your entire presentation.

To choose a color scheme, click any scheme to apply it to all the slides in your presentation. To apply the scheme to selected slides, follow these steps:

1. Select the slides that you want to have the new color scheme.

2. Hover the mouse over the color scheme you want to use. A drop-down arrow appears.

3. Click the drop-down arrow and choose Apply to Selected Slides from the menu, as shown here.

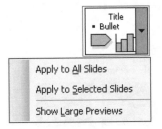

Be consistent with color schemes in your presentation. If you want to use more than one color scheme, do so only in a limited way. For example, if you have four parts to your presentation and each presentation has a slide to introduce the new part, use a different color scheme only for these part slides and perhaps your overall title slide. The other slides should then all use the basic color scheme.

Factoring in Lighting and Mood

Conventional wisdom is to use a dark background for presentations shown on a screen and a light background for overheads and printed handouts. The full truth is more complex. In a dark room, dark backgrounds with light text show up well, but in a light room, a dark background appears faded and the light text does not show up as well. Instead, use dark text against a light background.

The purpose of the presentation is another consideration. Yellow or white text against a dark background can appear harsh. When you want a softer impression or perhaps to convey bad news, use a lighter background. A light to medium green or blue with dark text often works well. However, be sure that the text contrasts sufficiently with the background for good legibility.

Create Your Own Color Scheme

You may think that the color schemes are pretty ugly or they simply may not suit your sense of style and design. Luckily, you have the flexibility to create any color scheme you can think up. To create a custom color scheme, click Edit Color Schemes at the bottom of the Slide Design task pane. The Edit Color Scheme dialog box opens, shown in Figure 6-2.

The Edit Color Scheme dialog box shows the eight colors of the color scheme you selected. To change a color, choose the color you want to change and click Change Color to open the dialog box shown in Figure 6-3.

Each of the dialog boxes for changing colors in a color scheme has both Standard and Custom tabs. To choose a color on the Standard tab, choose a hexagon from the Color palette and click OK to return to the Edit Color Scheme dialog box. You can make changes to other items of the color scheme or click Apply to return to your presentation.

You may not find the color you want on the Standard tab. Many companies have exact specifications for company colors. When it comes to color, the Custom tab, shown in Figure 6-4, is where the fun is.

The simplest way to create a color is to click a color in the main panel. The narrow bar at the right changes the *luminosity*—the brightness. You can also use one of the more formal systems for determining color: RGB or HSL.

- Use the red-green-blue (RGB) system to define a color by the amount of each primary light color. You can type in a number for each color or use the arrows to change the color by small increments. The numbers must be from 1 to 255; when all three colors are 255, you get white.

- Use the hue-saturation-luminosity (HSL) system to define a color by hue (the color), saturation (the intensity of the color), and luminosity (the brightness of the color). In the HSL system, you also set all three values at 255 to get white.

Click OK to return to the Edit Color Scheme dialog box.

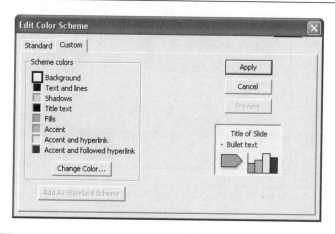

FIGURE 6-2   Use the Edit Color Scheme dialog box to create your own color scheme.

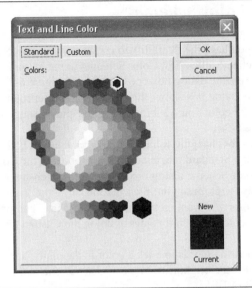

FIGURE 6-3   Use the Standard tab to choose a color from the color palette.

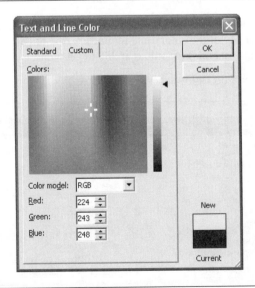

FIGURE 6-4   The Custom tab lets you specify any color.

NOTE

The RGB and HSL systems are used by PowerPoint (and all Microsoft Office applications) whenever you need to choose a color. For example, if you click the Fill Color arrow on the Drawing toolbar and then choose More Colors, you get the same dialog box.

Did you know?

The Effect of Color

Never sacrifice legibility merely for the sake of a pleasing color combination. Very light backgrounds can cause an uncomfortable glare. Similarly, avoid using strong primary colors, such as yellow or red, as backgrounds.

Due to the way our eyes work, and because color-perception deficiencies are common, avoid the following color combinations: red/green, brown/green, blue/black, and blue/purple.

Handle red with care. It can elicit such emotions as desire, passion, and competitiveness. However, it also carries negative connotations, such as financial loss. Red works best as an occasional accent color to make an item stand out.

Don't forget basic black. Often overlooked, black is a color with useful connotations; it suggests finality and simplicity.

Green is another background color with positive associations. Researchers believe that it stimulates interaction, which makes greens and teals good colors for trainers, educators, and those whose presentations are intended to generate discussion.

Blue is commonly associated with a calming and conservative effect. However, due to blue's popularity for business presentations, some business audiences now equate blue backgrounds with staleness and unoriginal thinking. When corporations specify blue backgrounds, professional presentation designers typically try to infuse them with some originality. Purple can imply immaturity and unimportance, while brown connotes uneasiness and passivity.

While background colors help set the emotional tone for your presentation, the colors you use for text, tables, charts, and other graphic elements have a bearing on how well the audience understands and remembers your message. Research has shown that the effective use of selective contrast, known as the *von Restorff effect* (or *isolation effect*), makes audiences remember the outstanding item—and even your entire message—better. An example of this technique is to make certain text larger or brighter than most text or to put it in an AutoShape.

Most experts agree that your color scheme should include one or two bright colors for emphasis—but to preserve the power of these colors, use them with restraint.

Change Backgrounds

Each slide has a background. The background is the bottom-most layer and is not an object that you can manipulate. You can never place anything behind the background, and it always covers the entire slide. A background can be a solid color, or you can use one of the fill effects discussed in the next four sections. Backgrounds certainly don't have to be dull! Here you see some examples.

 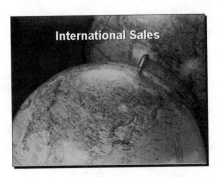

You can change the background color in the Color Scheme dialog box, but you have many more options if you choose Format | Background (or right-click the background of any slide and choose Background) to open the Background dialog box shown in Figure 6-5.

You see the color scheme so that you can see if your new background will match and contrast appropriately with the other elements on your slide. You can also click Preview, but if the current slide does not contain all the elements, you could miss a potential problem.

Click Apply to change only the selected slide or slides. Click Apply to All to change all the slides.

The background is one aspect of the slide master, which controls the look of all the slides in your presentation. Masters can include graphics and text. The Background dialog box lets you suppress the master's graphics and text—select the Omit Background Graphics from Master check box at the bottom of the dialog box. (Slide masters are covered in Chapter 7.)

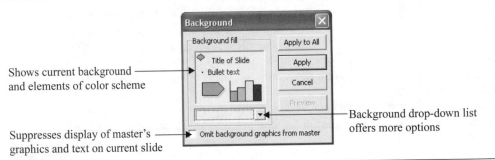

FIGURE 6-5 The Background dialog box offers many ways to create a background for the slides in your presentation.

When you click the down arrow beside the drop-down list in the Background dialog box, you see the menu shown here.

This small menu hides a world of opportunities! To choose a color not available on this menu, click More Colors to open the Colors dialog box, where the tabs look like the ones you saw in Figures 6-3 and 6-4. To create a more elaborate background, choose Fill Effects to open the Fill Effects dialog box, shown with the Gradient tab on top in Figure 6-6.

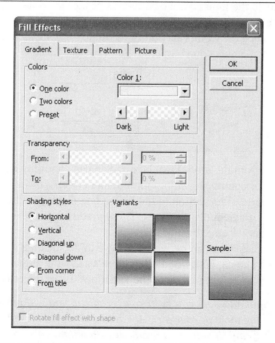

FIGURE 6-6   The Fill Effects dialog box lets you create backgrounds with gradients, textures, patterns, and pictures.

Create Gradient Backgrounds

In a *gradient,* the colors vary across the slide. In a one-color gradient, the intensity of the color varies. In a two-color gradient, the background changes from one color to the second. Choose Preset in the Fill Effects dialog box to give yourself the choice of a number of preset gradients, with names like Early Sunset, Nightfall, and Desert.

The one- and two-color gradients also offer a number of shading styles that determine the direction of the shading. Each shading style then has two to four variants. For example, in Figure 6-6, you see a one-color gradient using the horizontal shading style. The four possible variants are the following:

- The base color on top
- The base color on the bottom
- The base color on the top and the bottom with the lighter or darker variation in the middle
- The base color in the middle with the lighter or darker variation on the top and the bottom

Once you choose a type of gradient, new opportunities appear in the Colors section of the dialog box. If you choose One Color, the Colors section appears as shown in Figure 6-6.

Click the Color 1 down arrow to choose from color scheme colors, recently used colors, or any color in the Colors dialog box. Then choose how the gradient varies the base color by using the Dark/Light slider bar. If you slide the box all the way toward dark, the base color grades to black. If you slide the box to the light end, the base color grades to white. A setting in the middle eliminates the gradient because the color grades with itself.

If you choose Two Colors, the Colors section of the dialog box looks like this.

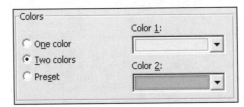

Choose the two colors from the drop-down boxes. You can choose two similar colors to create a subtle impression or contrasting colors for a bolder effect.

If you choose Preset, the Colors section of the dialog box displays a drop-down box letting you choose from any of 24 gradient backgrounds. These gradients range from soft to exciting. Some of the preset gradients are quite beautiful.

Whichever type of gradient you choose, you still have to decide on a shading style and one of the variants. With so much choice, it's a good thing there's a sample at the bottom-right corner of the dialog box. Feel free to try out several of the variations to see the effect they produce.

CAUTION   *If you combine light and dark colors in your gradient, you will probably have trouble with the contrast for some of your text. Always be aware of the color of your text when choosing a background. If you use a gradient with a light color at the top and a dark color at the bottom, you can counteract the legibility problem by making your titles dark (black or navy blue) and your main text light (white or yellow).*

After you choose a gradient, click OK. Then click Apply or Apply All in the Fill Effects dialog box.

Create Texture Backgrounds

Texture backgrounds look as if you have placed your slide on a physical object with a texture, such as wood, marble, or water droplets. Textures are pictures, and you can find your own, if you like. To use a texture background, click the Texture tab of the Fill Effects dialog box, shown in Figure 6-7. Choose one of the textures and click OK. Textures generally provide an understated, dignified impression.

To create your own texture from an image file, click Other Texture to open the Select Texture dialog box. Select any image file and click Insert.

Not all graphic files work as textures. If you try a large file, PowerPoint displays a message that the file is too large to use as a texture. I've tried .bmp, .jpg, and .gif files with success. Although a background may show as only a strip in the Sample box of the dialog box, PowerPoint tiles it to create a background covering the entire slide. Because of this tiling effect, the best graphics for textures are simple and repetitive, like the samples provided with PowerPoint. If you use a photograph of a flower, the background displays several copies of the flower, depending on the size of the image.

6

TIP   *To use an image of a distinct object as a background, insert it as a picture, not as a texture. See the section later in this chapter, "Create Picture Backgrounds."*

After you choose a texture, click OK. Then choose Apply or Apply All in the Fill Effects dialog box.

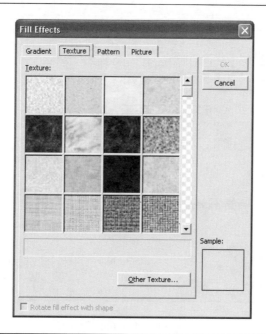

FIGURE 6-7   Use the Texture tab of the Fill Effects dialog box to create a textured background for your slides.

You can find more than 800 free seamless textures at http://www.indezine.com/back/.

Create Pattern Backgrounds

Pattern backgrounds are created from repeating patterns of lines or dots on a background. You choose from the patterns shown in Figure 6-8. You can choose the background and foreground colors. The foreground color generally creates the lines or dots, although some of the patterns are in reverse—see the second column of patterns in Figure 6-8.

Using contrasting foreground and background colors gives you a different effect than using similar colors. Be careful to check that your text is fully legible on a patterned background. The finer patterns work better than the more obvious patterns.

After you choose a pattern, click OK. Then click Apply or Apply All in the Fill Effects dialog box.

Create Picture Backgrounds

The last tab of the Fill Effects dialog box, shown in Figure 6-9, lets you use a picture as a background. Clicking Select Picture opens the Select Picture dialog box, where you navigate to the picture you want and click Insert. Your picture then appears on the Picture tab. Click OK, and then click Apply or Apply All in the Fill Effects dialog box.

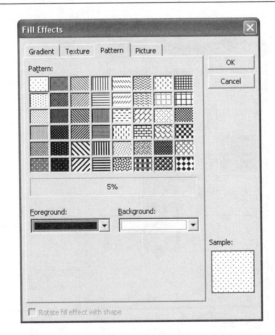

FIGURE 6-8   Choose a patterned background from the Pattern tab.

FIGURE 6-9   Use the Picture tab of the Fill Effects dialog box to choose any graphic file as a background.

Like with any background, you need to make sure that your text is legible. In Chapter 5, I discussed ways to turn a picture into a watermark, which reduces the contrast in the picture. See Chapter 5 for more ways to manipulate pictures in PowerPoint and other image-editing software.

PowerPoint automatically stretches your picture to cover the entire slide, so you don't need to worry about its size.

NOTE *You may want to keep the picture from being distorted when it fits on the slide. On the Picture tab of the Fill Effects dialog box, check Lock Picture Aspect Ratio. If this doesn't give you the result you want, you may be able to crop the picture to the proper shape.*

Experiment to get the effect you want. Have fun! A picture can create a sophisticated effect on a slide, so it's worth the effort. Figure 6-10 shows an example of a scenic picture used as a background.

FIGURE 6-10   Here a beautiful photo is used for the background. To increase text legibility, a semi-transparent AutoShape was placed behind the text.

 **Remove a Picture Background**

The Picture tab of the Fill Effects dialog box offers no obvious way to remove a picture background. You can substitute one picture for another by choosing a new picture, but how do you remove a picture altogether? The secret is to restore the automatic default background. Here are the steps:

1. Choose Format | Background. If you were looking at the Picture Background tab of the Fill Effects dialog box, click Cancel to return to the Background dialog box.

2. Click the drop-down list and choose Automatic on the top row.

3. Click Apply to remove the picture from one slide, or click Apply to All to remove the picture from all slides.

You now see the background defined by the slide master. Chapter 7 explains all about slide masters.

Format Lines and Borders

Every color scheme includes a color for text and lines. To consistently change the color of text, change the color in the color scheme as explained in the "Create Your Own Color Scheme" section earlier in this chapter. You can also change the text color for various levels of placeholder text on the slide master, explained in Chapter 7.

 You can also change the color of individual items of text. You can change the text color in the Font dialog box by selecting the text and choosing Format | Font. A simpler way is to use the Font Color button on the Drawing toolbar. Click the button to change the text to the most recently chosen color, or the down arrow to choose any color you want.

The *Lines* item in a color scheme includes the edging around an AutoShape and the border around a text box, text placeholder, or picture. The line color also applies to lines that you draw using the tools on the Drawing toolbar. You can change the line color or choose not to use a line at all.

The easiest way to format a line or a border is right-click the object and choose Format AutoShape (or Format Text Box or Format Picture, depending on the type of object). PowerPoint opens the appropriate dialog box. In Figure 6-11, you see the Format AutoShape dialog box with the Colors and Lines tab on top.

Most of the features of this dialog box related to formatting lines are covered in the section "Format Arrows," in Chapter 5. Following are a few additional suggestions from the point of view of color.

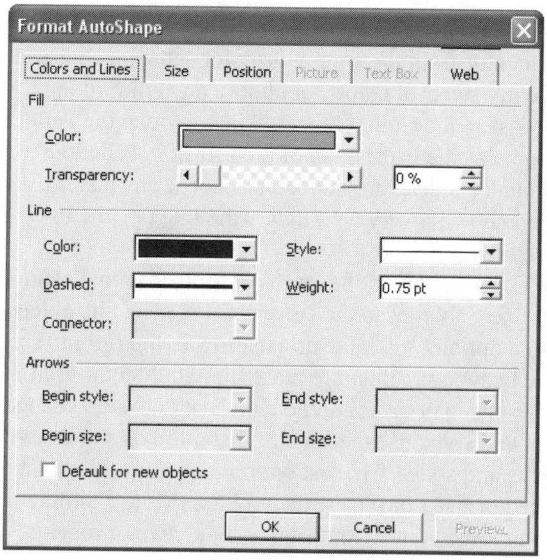

6

FIGURE 6-11   Use the Line section of the Format AutoShape dialog box to format the color and style of the edging around the AutoShape; the same section formats the border around text boxes and pictures.

When you click the Color drop-down box, you see the now-familiar choices shown here. The top choice is No Line, which is often the right choice. You rarely want a border around a picture unless, for example, you want to create a picture-frame effect. Text placeholders usually don't have borders, but text boxes can go either way: use a border when you want the text to stand out from the rest of the slide's text. Omitting the line in an AutoShape creates a subtle effect; on the other hand, a line can make the AutoShape more powerful.

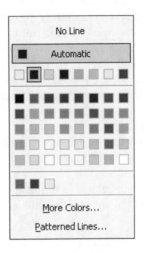

As previously explained in the "Work with Color Schemes" and "Change Backgrounds" sections, you can choose a color from the automatic color scheme, choose another color in the color scheme, choose recently selected colors, or choose any color in the Colors dialog box.

Patterned Lines is the last of the Color choices. Click to open the Patterned Lines dialog box, which looks exactly the same as the Pattern tab of the Fill Effects dialog box, shown earlier in Figure 6-8. Choose foreground and background colors, choose any pattern, and click OK. However, note that line patterns don't show up very well unless the line is quite thick. Use the Weight drop-down box to create a thick line.

You can use the Line Color button on the Drawing toolbar to make quick, simple changes to line color. To change any line or border to the current color, select its object and click the main part of the button. For more options, click the down arrow at the right to see options for more colors. The options on the Drawing toolbar are more limited than those in the Format AutoShape dialog box; you can choose any color or a patterned line, but you can't change line weight or style.

To change line weight and style, use the Line Style button on the Drawing toolbar. Choose from the list of line weights and styles. The last option includes a More Lines item that brings you to—guess what?—the Format AutoShape dialog box. (Moral: Simple line changes are easier to make from the Drawing toolbar, but if you want to make two or more adjustments with full control, open the Format AutoShape dialog box.) Figure 6-12 shows some AutoShapes using various line options.

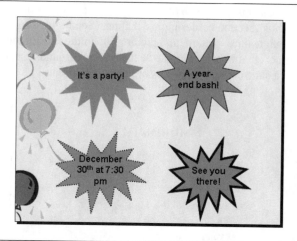

FIGURE 6-12   Each of the AutoShapes uses a different line format.

Work with Fills

A *fill* fills an enclosed space, such as the inside of an AutoShape or a text box. Every color scheme includes a fill color, but you can change any fill. You can also use the same fill effects for object fills as you can for backgrounds—gradients, textures, patterns, and pictures.

Change Fill Color

To change the fill color quickly, use the Fill Color button on the Drawing toolbar. Beneath the image of the paint can is a line filled with the current fill color. To change any fill to the current color, select the object and click the button. For more options, click the down arrow at the right to see the options shown here.

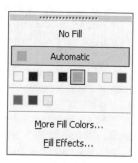

By now, you are familiar with these choices. You can select No Fill or Automatic, select from the set of color scheme colors or recently used colors, or choose More Fill Colors to open the Colors dialog box. Choose Fill Effects to open the Fill Effects dialog box, which I introduced in the "Change Backgrounds" section earlier in this chapter. (See Figure 6-6.)

You can create gradient, texture, pattern, and picture fills in the Fill Effects dialog box. In other words, the same effects that I covered in the "Change Backgrounds" section are available for any fill. Here you see a slide containing two examples of fill effects.

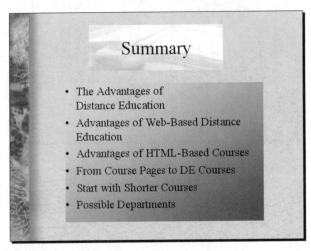

This slide uses a one-color gradient, with the Diagonal Up shading style and the top-right variant as well as a picture fill.

Format Fills in the Dialog Box

Two additional options are available only by using a dialog box. For the greatest control, right-click any object and choose Format AutoShape (or Format Text Box, etc.). You've already seen the Format AutoShape dialog box in Figure 6-11. When you click the Color drop-down box in the Fill section, the color choices are similar to those available on the Drawing toolbar. However, one new choice, Background, is now available. Choose Background to set the fill to the same color (or effect) as the slide background. Be careful, though. If your object has no line, it promptly disappears because you can't distinguish it from the background! If you don't like the result, click Undo on the Standard toolbar.

A special feature for solid and gradient fills applies only for AutoShapes and other objects, not for backgrounds. They can be transparent, with a range from 0 percent to 100 percent. In the Fill section of the Color and Lines tab of the Format AutoShape dialog box (refer back to Figure 6-11), drag the Transparency slider bar or type a percentage. Use transparency if you want objects behind the selected object to show through. Your slide background will show through as well. Look back to Figure 6-10 to see a slide that uses a 40 percent transparent text box over a picture background. The fill makes the text more readable but still lets the beautiful picture background show through.

It's always a good idea to use the Preview button before clicking OK, although you can undo any change you make. If you don't like the result, you can try something else. Move the dialog box to see the slide, if necessary.

Create 3-D Effects

PowerPoint can create 3-D graphics for you on the fly. A simple type of 3-D is shadows, which give the impression that the AutoShape or other object is raised off the slide's surface. True 3-D effects are more complex and actually draw a third dimension. Both shadows and 3-D effects come with loads of options and settings and can quickly improve the quality of your presentation's graphics.

Create Shadows

Shadows create a subtle, yet effective 3-D impression. You may have noticed that PowerPoint displays slides on your screen with a slight shadow. Here you see a slide with several graphics. The ones on the left use shadows and look much more three-dimensional than the newsletters on the right.

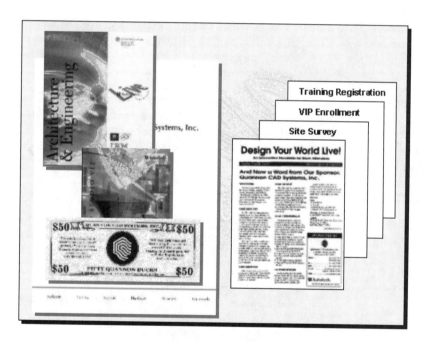

The graphics here were created by scanning the actual documents, inserting them as pictures, and then adding shadow effects, as discussed next.

To create a shadow, select any object (except text), and use the Shadow button on the Drawing toolbar. (To shadow text, use the Text Shadow button on the Formatting toolbar.) PowerPoint displays the choices shown in the following illustration. Choose No Shadow to eliminate a shadow you have created previously. Otherwise, choose any of the options. Notice that the options come in groups, which are generally based on four different lighting angles—top left, top right, bottom left, and bottom right. Even within these angles, there are variants. Generally, you will need to try a few shadows out before you find what you like.

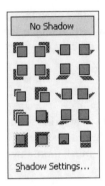

NOTE   *If you want to add a shadow to more than one object on a slide, you should generally add the same type of shadow to all, so that it looks like the light is coming from the same angle for all the objects. When you create 3-D effects, they should mimic the real world to some extent; otherwise, the effect will be confusing to your audience.*

Some colors and shapes show up a shadow better than others. A shadow that looks great on an orange, rectangular AutoShape may be scarcely noticeable on a green, star-shaped AutoShape. Semitransparent fills let the shadow show through, which can be confusing.

The color of the shadow is important. Often the shadow's color is too similar to either the object's fill or the slide background. Every color scheme has a shadow color, but you can change the color.

Use the Shadow Settings

If a shadow doesn't turn out to your satisfaction, you still have a lot more options. On the menu that pops up when you click Shadows on the Drawing toolbar, choose Shadow Settings to display the Shadow Settings toolbar shown in Figure 6-13.

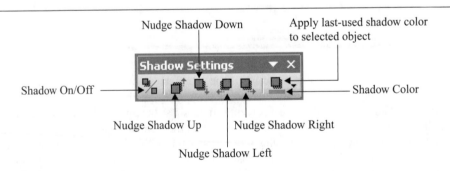

FIGURE 6-13   Use the Shadow Settings toolbar to fine-tune your shadows.

Nudging a shadow makes it bigger or smaller. If the shadow appears to the right of the object, nudging its shadow to the right makes the shadow bigger. Nudge the same shadow to the left to make it smaller.

When you click the down arrow to the right of the Shadow Color button, you see the typical color selections shown here. Usually shadows are gray and darker than the object, as you have probably noticed in real life. However, other colors can create a fun effect. Remember that to be noticed, the shadow needs to contrast with both the object's fill color and the slide's background. On the other hand, you don't want the shadow effect to distract your audience from the shape. Remember that the main purpose of a shadow is to make the shape itself appear to stand out from the surface of the slide.

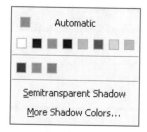

Choose More Shadow Colors to open the Colors dialog box. Nothing is new here except that for the first time, you might notice quite a nice selection of grays at the bottom of the dialog box. (Figure 6-3, earlier in this chapter, shows the Text and Line Color dialog box, which looks the same.) These grays are great for shadows. You may want to choose a lighter gray for a dark background or a darker gray for a light background. Figure 6-14 shows four of the available shadow effects.

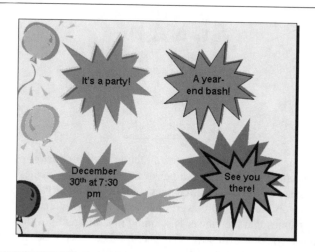

FIGURE 6-14   You can create both subtle and dramatic shadow effects.

Create 3-D Shapes

You can take a further step and create realistic 3-D shapes. A 3-D shape displays sides and shading like a real three-dimensional object. Here you see a slide with a 3-D AutoShape.

This is the final slide of the presentation and invites the audience to "test drive" the new software that the company is selling. This 3-D AutoShape was easily created by inserting a rectangle, choosing a solid fill color and no line, and then adding a 3-D effect, as discussed in this section.

You always start with a 2-D shape. (You can also use an imported vector graphic that you have ungrouped. See "Group and Ungroup Graphics" in Chapter 5.) Select a shape and choose the 3-D button on the Drawing toolbar. PowerPoint displays the pop-up menu shown here.

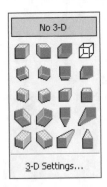

The 3-D options come in groups based on the direction of the *extrusion*—the side of the object that appears pushed out into the third dimension. The extrusion creates the depth of the object. The choices have rather unhelpful names such as 3-D Style 1, 3-D Style 2, and so on. Choose one of the options and let PowerPoint create the 3-D effect for your object.

Each 3-D option assumes that the viewer is standing in a different position vis-à-vis the object. As with shadows, you don't want to use different 3-D effects on several objects on a slide—it could give your audience vertigo! You can create classy effects using 3-D, but use it with constraint.

Choose No 3-D to remove the 3-D effect on the selected object or objects. The top-right effect, 3-D Style 4, creates a wire-frame effect as if the shape is made of wire and has no solidity. You will probably try out a few effects before settling on one you like.

Control 3-D Settings

To have more control over a 3-D effect, choose 3-D Settings to display the 3-D Settings toolbar shown in Figure 6-15. You'll find quite a bit to sink your teeth into on this little toolbar, but the settings are actually fairly simple. After all, PowerPoint is not like a professional rendering program where you can specify the lighting location of dozens of lights by x, y, z coordinates accurate to six decimal places. So here goes!

Tilt a 3-D Object

The four tilt buttons on the 3-D settings toolbar change the rotation of the object. Imagine holding a cube in your hand and tilting the side facing you up, down, left, or right—now you have the idea. The only thing that changes about the object is its position relative to your eyes. Try selecting an object and clicking these buttons, and their functions will soon be clear. Here you see the original 3-D star created using 3-D Style 1 and the result of tilting down, to the left, and to the right.

The effect of tilting depends on the original 3-D style you chose. For some styles, a certain tilt looks good; for others, it doesn't.

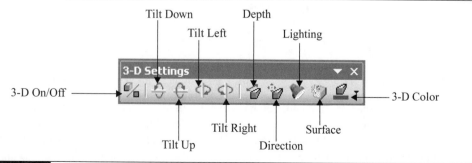

FIGURE 6-15   The 3-D Settings toolbar lets you control every parameter of the 3-D effect.

Change a 3-D Object's Depth

When you click Depth on the 3-D Settings toolbar, you see the options shown here. When you change an object's depth, you are actually changing its characteristics. The tilt stays the same, but the depth of the object that extrudes into the third dimension becomes greater or smaller. You specify the depth in points—remember that 72 points equals one inch. You can type any point value you want in the Custom box. Again, try out a few settings, and see what you like. Once you find what you want, you can use the same setting for other objects. Here you see some examples using different depth settings.

Change the Direction

When you click the Direction button on the 3-D Settings toolbar, the options shown here pop up. The effect of these options is to change the viewer's position relative to the object. It's like holding a cube steady and moving your head in one of eight directions. That might be hard to do in real life, but in PowerPoint, it's as easy as clicking one of the options.

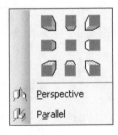

NOTE *As with other 3-D effects, you should use the same direction for all the objects on a slide. If you represent a source of light on a slide, all shadows should recede away from the light.*

At the bottom of the pop-up menu, you have two different view choices—Perspective or Parallel. In a perspective view, parallel lines—in this case, the lines that create the depth of the object—converge as they go off into the distance. The typical example is railroad tracks appearing to touch in the distance. In a parallel view, parallel lines always remain parallel.

Try out both types of views—you'll be surprised at the difference. Here you see two AutoShapes—the one on the left uses a parallel view, while the shape on the right uses a perspective view. In most cases, the parallel view appears more "normal" to us.

Set the Lighting Direction and Brightness

When you choose Lighting on the 3-D Settings toolbar, PowerPoint opens the pop-up menu shown here. At the center is a cube that represents your 3-D object. The current lighting is depressed, and the cube shows the result. Without clicking, move your mouse cursor from light to light and watch the difference on the cube. Click when you like what you see. At the bottom, you have three brightness options: Bright, Normal, and Dim.

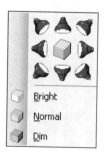

If you include shadows on the same slide with a 3-D object, you might want to coordinate the two. If the light on your 3-D object is coming from the right, sides facing left will be darker. Shadows will be thrown to the left as well.

Choose a Surface Type

The Surface button offers these four options: Wire Frame, Matte, Plastic, and Metal. A wire frame has no solidity—it looks like you fashioned the shape out of wire, as you can see here.

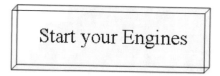

Start your Engines

A matte surface, the default, is bright but has no reflection. A plastic surface shows a slight reflection along one edge. The metal surface is the darkest, for some reason.

6

Set the 3-D Color

You can change the color of the extrusion portion of the 3-D object, the part that shows the object's depth. The 3-D Color tool works the same as other color tools you have worked with in this chapter. Click the tool to apply the most recently chosen color or click the down arrow for a greater choice of colors.

The 3-D color does not affect the color of the front face of the object, which is controlled by the fill color. However, the wire frame display shows only the wire frame without any fill—there is no color.

> **TIP**   *Regardless of the 3-D effect, you can fill the front face of the object with any of the PowerPoint fill options mentioned in the section "Change Backgrounds" earlier in this chapter.*

Summary

This chapter started off by exploring color schemes and how you can use them to create a uniform look in your presentation. Then I explained how to create any background you want—from plain colors to gradients to textures, from patterns to pictures.

I discussed formatting lines and borders for AutoShapes, text boxes, and pictures. Then I covered how to work with fills. You can create a fill of any color and use the same fill effects that are available for backgrounds.

The simplest 3-D effects are shadows, which give the impression that an object is raised off the surface of the slide and therefore casts a shadow. The chapter ended with a complete discussion of 3-D objects, including the various 3-D styles and all the settings on the 3-D Settings toolbar.

The next chapter explains how to coordinate elements throughout an entire presentation with slide masters.

Chapter 7

Coordinate Presentations with Slide Masters

How to...

- ■ Understand and manage slide masters
- ■ Control a presentation's look
- ■ Understand the title master
- ■ Format title slides
- ■ Understand the handout master
- ■ Format the handout master
- ■ Understand the notes master
- ■ Format the notes master
- ■ Set page size
- ■ Create your own design template
- ■ Add a custom design template to the AutoContent Wizard

The past few chapters have focused a lot on creating a presentation, but PowerPoint has a secret hidden beneath the text and objects you add to each slide. A slide master is a layer that's underneath all the slides in your presentation. In this chapter, you learn how to use masters to coordinate and polish the look of an entire presentation.

Understand the Slide Master

A slide is made up of three major layers: the background, the slide master, and objects. The background was discussed in Chapter 6; it is a rectangle at the bottom-most layer of each slide. Objects are the top layer; you can easily move, resize, or format them. Objects include AutoShapes, text boxes, graphics, and WordArt. The object layer is the default mode of functioning in PowerPoint. When you work on your slide, you most often work on this object layer.

The slide master is between the background and the objects. You need to go into a special Slide Master view to access the master.

The slide master includes any text or graphics that you want to appear on every slide. You use slide masters to create uniform features throughout a presentation. For example, you may want a company's logo on each slide. Although the logo is an object, because you insert it on the slide master, it appears on each slide and you cannot select or manipulate it in any way except from Slide Master view.

In addition, the slide master acts like a template to control most text properties, such as font, font size, color, bullet style, and shadowing effects. These properties are attached to the text placeholders, which are also on the slide master. However, you can move, resize, and delete the text placeholders as if they were objects on your slide. Of course, because text is on the object layer, you can change these properties directly on each slide. However, to make global changes to the entire presentation, you need to use the slide master.

The settings on the slide master are saved with each design template. You can make changes to a slide master and save the resulting presentation as a design template. Then, each time you start a new presentation based on that template, your text is formatted the way you want. Any other changes you made to the slide master, such as inserting a logo, slide numbers, or your name, also appear in the new presentation. PowerPoint templates are saved as .pot files. In the section "Create Your Own Design Templates" at the end of this chapter, I explain how to use the master to create your own design template.

You don't need to use the slide master to create a presentation. Often, the design template is all you need. You can also make changes to the color scheme and background and quickly apply them to the entire presentation, as explained in Chapter 6. Because you need to know all about slide formatting to work with slide masters, I waited to explain them until I explained all the essential PowerPoint features.

However, when you decide to use the slide master, you should use it early in the creation process. Set up the global features you want first and make as few exceptions to individual slides as possible. This procedure saves you from making changes to many individual slides. It also ensures a uniform look for the entire presentation.

> **NOTE**   *Since PowerPoint 2002, you can create as many slide masters as you want. Of course, if you use a different master for each slide, the effect is the same as having no slide master. The best policy is to stick to one or two masters.*

Enter Slide Master View

To enter Slide Master view, press SHIFT and click the Normal View button, which appears with other view buttons at the bottom-left corner of your screen. You can also choose View | Master | Slide Master. PowerPoint opens the Slide Master view, shown in Figure 7-1. You can control formatting for your entire presentation from this view.

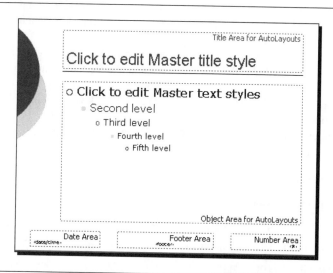

FIGURE 7-1   The Slide Master view controls repeating elements and placeholder text formatting for the entire presentation.

When you enter Slide Master view, the Slide Master View toolbar appears, as shown here. This toolbar is helpful for working with slide masters.

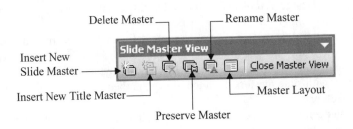

Manage Slide Masters

In PowerPoint 2003, you can have more than one master. When you enter Slide Master view, the New Slide button on the Formatting toolbar changes to become the New Slide Master button, as shown here.

You can also choose Insert | New Slide Master or choose Insert New Slide Master from the Slide Master View toolbar.

To delete a master, select the master in the Outline pane and click Delete Master on the Slide Master View toolbar.

Normally, a master is deleted when all slides using the master are deleted or when you choose a new design template and apply it to all the slides in the presentation. You can prevent a master from being deleted automatically by preserving it. Select the master you want to preserve in the Outline pane and click Preserve Master on the Slide Master View toolbar.

You can rename the master, which is the same as renaming the design template. You see the change immediately on the status bar. Click Rename Master and type a new name in the Rename Master dialog box. Click Rename.

If you delete components of the master, such as a text placeholder, you can reinsert them. Click Master Layout on the Slide Master View toolbar and choose the component you want to reinsert.

To exit Slide Master view, click the Normal View icon or click Close Master View on the Slide Master View toolbar.

Adding a design template automatically adds a slide master to your presentation. You can control how a design template is added to your presentation:

1. Go to Slide Master view.

2. Choose Design on the Formatting toolbar.

3. Choose one of the templates from the Slide Design task pane.

4. From the drop-down list that appears, choose one of the three options:

   ■ **Replace All Designs** Applies the design template to all slides in your presentation. The slide master for the new design template replaces the previous slide master.

- **Replace Selected Designs**   Applies the design template to selected slides in your presentation. The slide master for the new design template is added to the previous one. (This option appears if you already have more than one master. First select one or more of the masters in the outline pane.)
- **Add Design**   Adds a new slide master for the design template without applying it to any slides.

If you have more than one slide master and wish to make changes that apply to every slide, you need to separately change each slide master. For example, if both slide masters use black text and you want all the text to be navy blue, you need to change the text color in both slide masters.

Change the Background and Color Scheme

Although the background can be considered its own layer, you can format it from the slide master to affect the entire presentation. The relationships between the background, the color scheme, the design template, and the slide master can be confusing at first, but make a lot of sense once you understand the concept.

The design template contains the settings for the master, including the background and the color scheme. When you assign a design template, PowerPoint always remembers that template and displays the design template name on the status bar. PowerPoint continues to remember the design template even if you end up changing everything about it—the background, the text properties, and so on. However, as explained earlier, you can rename the design template—the slide master—if you wish. The design template can be applied to any presentation, but the master applies only to the presentation containing it.

If you change the background from the Master Slide view (by choosing Format | Background), your changes affect every slide, even if you click Apply, not Apply to All. Your presentation may no longer look anything like the original design template, but that's OK. If you change the background from Normal view, the background affects only the active slide, unless you choose Apply to All.

However, the color scheme controls the master, not vice versa. If you change the color scheme for text, background, and titles from any slide, for example, and click Apply to All, the entire presentation is affected. If you view the slide master, you will see that it has been changed to reflect your changes. If you try it the other way around—view the master and change the background, title color, and bulleted text color   the changes affect all your slides but the color scheme does not change. If you have a presentation whose slides don't reflect the color scheme, remember—someone could have made changes to either the master or to individual slides that overrode the color scheme.

Format Headings and Bulleted Text

At the top of the master, in the area labeled "Title Area for AutoLayouts," you format slide titles. The text, "Click to Edit Master Title Style," not only gives you an instruction, but also shows you the current text properties. Text color, font, size, alignment, and case (capitalization) are some of the properties you can change. You make the changes as you would on the object level. The techniques for editing text properties were discussed in Chapter 3. The only difference is that any change you make affects every slide in the presentation.

7

In the middle of the master is an area called "Object Area for AutoLayouts." Here, you find the formatting for five levels of bulleted text. You can format the text and the bullets, as well as the paragraph alignment and indentation. See Chapter 4 for information on formatting bullets and paragraphs. If you like fancy bullets and want to use them throughout your presentation, here's the place to create them.

Add Placeholders

You may have wondered why there is no way to add a text placeholder. Suppose you delete one from the slide master. How do you get it back? Earlier in the "Manage Slide Masters" section, I explained how to perform this task using the Slide Master View toolbar. You can also choose Format | Master Layout to open the Master Layout dialog box shown here.

NOTE *You can use the Master Layout dialog box only when you have deleted a placeholder and are in the slide master.*

Only the placeholders that you have deleted are available. Check any placeholders that you want to reinstate, and click OK.

Add Repeating Objects and Animation

You can add any other objects to the slide. A company logo is probably the most common example, as shown in Figure 7-2. To create this effect, open the slide master and choose Insert | Picture | From File. Locate and choose the graphic file and click Insert. Then move and resize the graphic as necessary.

Remember that you can't see the actual text on each slide on the slide master. Because the logo will appear on every slide, be careful to place the object where it won't interfere with your text. Remember to double-check this placement after you have completed the presentation. The easiest way to check is to go to Slide Sorter view, where you can get a bird's eye view of the entire presentation. If the object collides with text on one or more slides, return to the master and move it to a better location.

TIP *Insert the logo on the slide with the most text. If it fits, press CTRL-X to cut it to the clipboard, open the slide master, and press CTRL-V to paste it onto the master in the same location.*

Because objects that you insert on the slide master are not on the object layer, you cannot select them unless you are in Slide Master view. If you are unable to select an object, try going

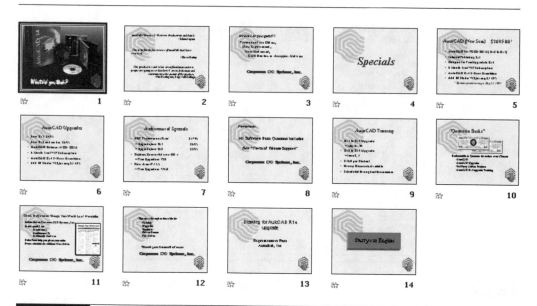

FIGURE 7-2   Any object that you add to the slide master appears on every slide.

to Slide Master view. The Office Assistant may advise you of this if you try to click a slide master object from one of the other views.

You can also add animation on the slide master. This animation appears on all slides. For example, if you animate the text of the master, all text in the presentation uses the same animation. You can also add a slide transition to the master. For more information on animation, see Chapter 9.

Add a Footer

The slide master comes with placeholders for the date, a text footer, and the slide number. Many users add the date for documentation purposes. A text footer can specify your name or department without being obtrusive. Slide numbers are especially helpful if you might need to go back and forth in your presentation while you present. Slide numbers are also invaluable in the creation process, while you are still deciding on the order of your slides. You can change the location and formatting of these footers directly on the slide master.

Add Footers to the Entire Presentation

To add or change the footer, display the slide master and choose View | Header and Footer. PowerPoint opens the Header and Footer dialog box shown in Figure 7-3 with the Slide tab on top.

To use the Header and Footer dialog box, follow these guidelines:

■   Check the Date and Time check box if you want to place the date and time on each slide.

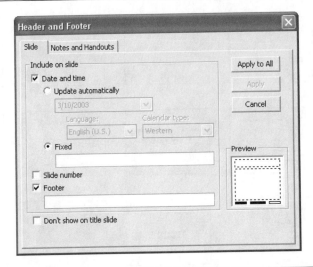

FIGURE 7-3   The Header and Footer dialog box lets you add the date, slide number, and a text footer to all your slides.

- Choose the type of date and time. The Update Automatically drop-down list displays the current date and time. Click the drop-down list to choose the format. You can choose a format that includes the time. If you select Fixed, it always displays the date that you enter.
- Check Slide Number to add a slide number to each slide.
- Check Footer to include a text footer and type the text in the box.
- Check "Don't Show on Title Slide" to omit footers on any slide using the Title Slide AutoLayout.

Click Apply to All when you are finished making all the settings you want.

TIP   *There are no separate headers, but you can move the footer placeholders to the top of the slide master and turn them into headers.*

Add the Date or Slide Number to One Slide

To add the date or slide number on only one slide, follow a different procedure. (Of course, you don't want to add the date or slide number to a slide if you've done so on the slide master, because you'll end up with the date or slide number twice on a slide.)

1. Click Text Box on the Drawing toolbar.
2. Drag across to create a text box.
3. To insert a slide number, choose Insert | Slide Number. PowerPoint inserts the slide number in the text box.

4. To insert the date, choose Insert | Date and Time to open the Date and Time dialog box shown here.

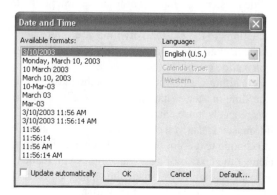

5. Choose the format you want. Check Update Automatically to always show today's date.
6. Click OK when you're done.

TIP   *If you run a presentation through several revisions and collaborate with others to create the final version, place the date and time on the first slide, leaving the Update Automatically check box blank. Include instructions to each reviewer to enter the current date and time just before they pass on the presentation. In this way, everyone instantly knows when the presentation was last saved, without having to look at the file information in Windows Explorer—many people do not display these details in Explorer. Don't forget to delete the text box when the presentation is finalized.*

Change the Starting Slide Number

Occasionally, you may want your slide numbers to start with a number other than one. Perhaps your presentation is the second half of a larger presentation. To change the starting slide number, choose File | Page Setup to display the Page Setup dialog box shown in Figure 7-4.

Under Number Slides From, type a new starting number or use the arrows to change the starting number. Click OK.

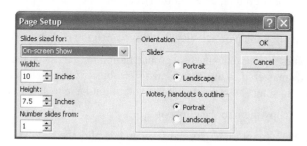

FIGURE 7-4   Use the Page Setup dialog box to change the starting slide number, as well as slide size and orientation.

Make Exceptions

You aren't locked into the slide master. You may want to make exceptions to the formatting you have created in the slide master. In fact, most of the formatting already covered in this book has had the effect of making exceptions to the master. Any time you reformat bulleted text on a slide, change font color, or change the background for a slide, you are creating an exception to the master.

Any change you make on a slide overrides the master. Even if you change the master, your changes remain. That's because although the slide master is the master of the presentation, you, the user, are the master of the slide master. What you say goes. Therefore, if you make changes to a slide, PowerPoint always respects those changes.

The advantage of the slide master is that you can make changes that affect the entire presentation. It is certainly much easier to change text color once than to change it individually on each slide. Moreover, if you need to change the text color again, as long as you made the change on the master, you need change only the master. If you made the change on each slide, guess what? Now you have to go back to each slide and change it individually.

Hide the Background Graphic on a Slide

Suppose you want to create a slide without any background graphics. You might want to do this for a great image that will look best taking up the entire slide. Just follow these steps:

1. Display the slide.
2. Choose Format | Background.
3. Check Omit Background Graphics from Master in the Background dialog box.
4. Click Apply so that the background graphics are omitted only from the active slide.

This technique deletes all the background graphics from the slide, including the graphics that make up the design template and any graphics you may have added to the master. This all-or-nothing approach may not work in your situation. Let's say you want to see the design template's graphics but not a graphic you added, such as your company's logo. (Perhaps it doesn't fit on one slide.) Here's how to accomplish the task:

1. Display the slide you want to work on.
2. Choose Format | Background, check Omit Background Graphics from Master, and then click Apply.
3. Press SHIFT and click the Normal View button to open the slide master.
4. Select the graphics that make up the background design for the design template. Remember that on the slide master, they are objects just like objects you create on a slide. Press SHIFT and click to select additional objects. You might have to select several objects.
5. Press CTRL-C to copy them to the clipboard.
6. Click Normal View to return to Normal view and display the slide you were working on.
7. Press CTRL-V to paste the graphics onto the slide. You now have your background graphics but not any additional objects you added to the master, in this case, your company's logo.

Understand the Title Master

The title master is just like the slide master, but it applies only to slides that you created using the Title Slide AutoLayout. Just like the title page of a book often has a different format from the rest of the book, title slides often use different formatting from the rest of your presentation. Most presentations have only one title slide at the beginning, but you can have as many as you want. Section titles and ending slides often use the Title Slide AutoLayout. Changes made on the title master affect only title slides.

The title master is connected to its slide master. If you are using more than one slide master, you see the slide-title master pairs connected by a line in the Outline pane when you are in Slide or Title Master view, as shown here.

7

Enter Title Master View

To enter Title Master view, you can press SHIFT and click the Normal View button just like you do to enter Slide Master view. You may need to scroll up or down to find the title master, especially if you are using more than one master. You can also choose View | Master | Slide Master.

If you open a blank presentation, there is no title master. To create one, press SHIFT and click the Slide View icon to enter the slide master. Then choose Insert | New Title Master.

SHORTCUT   *Choose Insert New Title Master on the Slide Master View toolbar.*

If you have more than one slide master, you should attach to one of the existing slide masters a new title master that you create. Enter Slide Master view and select the slide master you want to use from the Outline pane. Then click Insert New Title Master on the Slide Master View toolbar.

FIGURE 7-5   Use the title master to format slides using the Title Slide AutoLayout.

Figure 7-5 shows a title master. As you can see, it looks much like a slide master, except that there is no placeholder for bulleted text. Instead, the title is centered vertically on the title master, and there is a subtitle. This formatting reflects the typical structure of title slides.

To exit Title Master view, click the Normal View icon or click Close Master View on the Slide Master View toolbar.

Format Title Slides

You format title slide masters in the same way you format slide masters. However, bear in mind that the slide master controls the title master to some extent. For example, if you change the color of the title text on the slide master, you will find that the title text will also change on the title master. The opposite does not hold true—changes to the title master have no effect on the slide master.

While this concept can be confusing, the general rule is to change the slide master first. Then make changes to the title master. If you make changes to the title master first, you may find them overridden by changes you subsequently make to the slide master.

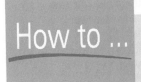 **Control a Presentation's Look**

The slide master is the framework of your entire presentation. It is a powerful tool for coordinating all the elements of a presentation when you use it fully.

PowerPoint has two main masters that control the look of the presentation: the slide master and the title master. The title master defines the elements only for slides that use the

Title Slide AutoLayout—usually used to open the presentation or perhaps at the start of a section. The slide master defines every other type of layout. On these masters, you define the format for the entire presentation, so that when you change something on the master, it affects the whole presentation. Working with the slide master lets you do less and accomplish more. On the master, you should do the following:

- **Format the background**   Insert your background here. The background automatically shows on every slide. An added bonus is that inserting the background once helps keeps the file size small. (See Chapter 6 for more information.)

- **Specify the color scheme**   Format your slide color scheme on the master. Here, in one location, you decide all the colors of the presentation. Define the colors of the text, shadows, fills for charts, and even hyperlink colors. (See Chapter 6 for more information.)

- **Select fonts and bullets**   Apply your fonts to the slide masters. These will automatically take effect for any slide in the presentation. You should also select which bullets you want in the body text. (See Chapters 3 and 4.)

- **Add animation**   Use the slide master to specify consistent animation for the entire presentation, including slide animation and slide transitions. (Animation is covered in Chapter 9.)

- **Add logos or slide elements**   Anything you need on every slide should be placed on the master. A company logo, slide numbers, copyrights, and so on—all of these should be placed once on the master, so they will be displayed on every slide. (See Chapter 5 for information on adding graphics.)

Slide masters are powerful tools. They increase your efficiency and improve the quality of a presentation. Incorporate into the masters all consistent components for your presentation.

Understand the Handout Master

You can create printed handouts of your presentation to give to your audience to take home or to show your boss during the approval process. Handouts show your slides in groupings of two to nine per page. Handouts are covered in Chapter 16. However, because we are on the topic of masters, you may want to know about the handout master.

The handout master controls the formatting of handouts. You can add art, text, the date, and page numbers to your handout master, and they will display on the handouts, in addition to your slides, which are automatically included. Settings on the handout master have no effect on your slide master or slides.

Enter Handout Master View

To enter Handout Master view, press SHIFT and click the Slide Sorter View icon at the bottom left of your screen. You can also choose View | Master | Handout Master. Figure 7-6 shows a typical handout master, formatted to print six slides per page. By default, the handout master contains a header area for text, a date area, a page number area, and a footer area for text.

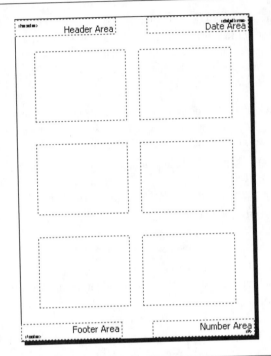

FIGURE 7-6   The handout master controls the formatting of printed handouts.

Format the Handout Master

When you open the handout master, PowerPoint automatically displays the Handout Master toolbar shown here. The toolbar lets you easily change the number of slides that the handouts include on a page. The three-per-page choice prints lines to the right of each slide so the reader can jot down notes. You can also print the outline. Click the format you want, and the handout master will change automatically.

You don't have to limit yourself to the standard format. You can add graphics, text boxes—anything that you can add to a slide. For example, you can create captions for each slide or callouts pointing out features of a slide. You can add your phone number or e-mail address—the possibilities are limitless.

To add a header, footer, the date, or page numbers, choose View | Header and Footer while in Handout Master view. PowerPoint opens the Header and Footer dialog box, with the Notes and

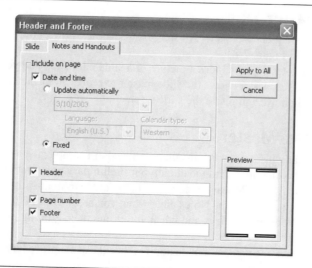

FIGURE 7-7 Use the Notes and Handouts tab on the Header and Footer dialog box to create headers and footers for your handouts.

Handouts tab on top, as shown in Figure 7-7. This tab is almost the same as the Slide tab. The only differences are the following:

- You can specify both a header and a footer.
- You must choose Apply to All. You cannot separately format the various pages of the handouts.

Refer back to Figure 7-3, in the section "Add Footers to the Entire Presentation," for more information on using this dialog box. When you have finished formatting your handouts, return to any view by clicking its icon.

Understand the Notes Master

As explained in Chapter 1, you can create notes to accompany your presentation. Traditionally, notes are used by the speaker during the actual presentation. For example, notes are a good place to put your jokes so that you won't forget the punch lines. Printed notes contain one slide per page and a large area for text—your notes. However, you can use notes for other purposes, such as to write down ideas for the presentation as you are creating it, or to create and print comments for your supervisor who is reviewing the presentation.

You create the notes by typing in the Notes pane. Chapter 16 contains more information about creating and using notes.

The notes master formats these notes. Notes are generally text, and PowerPoint provides an outline format that is similar to the slide master.

Enter Notes Master View

To enter Notes Master view, choose View | Master | Notes Master. PowerPoint opens the Notes Master view, as shown in Figure 7-8.

Because the actual notes page includes a picture of a slide on the top and your notes at the bottom, the top of the notes master shows the slide master to represent the actual slides that will be printed. You can only move and resize the slide master.

Format the Notes Master

Although notes are usually just text, you can add graphics. For example, if you are preparing a presentation for a client, you might send the client your preliminary presentation for review in the form of notes pages. You might want to add your company logo in the notes area. Graphics, headers, and footers don't appear in the Notes pane when you are in Normal view. You see them on the notes master, in Notes Pages view, and when you print notes. Printing notes is covered in Chapter 16.

To add a header, footer, the date, or a page number, use the same procedure explained previously for the handout master.

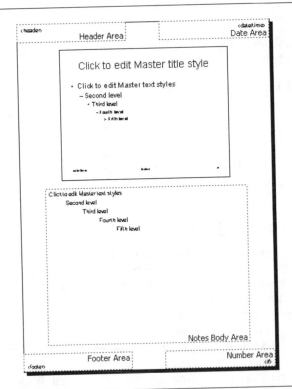

FIGURE 7-8   Notes Master view lets you format the look of your notes when printed.

Set Page Size

Another way of formatting an entire presentation is to set the page size. Choose File | Page Setup to display the Page Setup dialog box shown earlier in Figure 7-4. By default, PowerPoint sizes your slides for an onscreen slide show. Slides are 10 inches wide by 7.5 inches high. When you click the Slides Sized For drop-down arrow, you see the choices shown here. Once you choose the type of presentation, you can customize the size using the Width and Height text boxes.

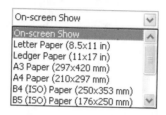

 If you want to change the default slide size and orientation, do so before you start working on your presentation; otherwise, text and graphics may not fit on each slide as you expect and may be distorted as well.

7

On the right side of the dialog box, you can set the orientation of the slides separately from the notes, handouts, and outline. By default, slides are in landscape orientation (the width is longer than the height), and everything else is in portrait orientation.

Create Your Own Design Templates

Now that you understand masters, you have the tools to create your own design templates from scratch.

Most design templates are simply a slide master, including a background. The background can include graphics that make up a design like the ones in PowerPoint's design templates. If you create your own slide master, you can save it as a design template. You can then use that template for other presentations. You can include fonts, bullets, a color scheme, and other formatting in your template. You can even include text and shapes—in other words, you can develop some actual content for your template that you may want to reuse in the future.

Creating your own design template is really a must if you create a lot of presentations and want the highest-quality results. Having your own template means that everything is already set to your specifications and you can start to work right away. Here are the steps you need to take:

1. Open a blank presentation. From within PowerPoint, choose New on the Standard toolbar.

2. Open the slide master.

3. Choose Format | Slide Design. In the Slide Design task pane, choose Color Schemes. Choose the color scheme closest to the one you want. Then click Edit Color Schemes at the bottom of the Slide Design task pane and change the colors as you wish. Click Apply. You immediately see the changes on the master. (See Chapter 6 for details.)

4. If you want to add a fill effect to the background, choose Format | Background. In the Background dialog box, click the down arrow and choose Fill Effects. Create the effects you want. Click OK and then Apply. (See Chapter 6 for more information.)

5. Now add any graphics that you want to appear on every slide. These can be a creative design, a company logo, or both. Format the graphics with color, fill effects, shadows, and/or 3-D effects. (Chapter 5 explains more.)

6. Change the font if you like. Choose Format | Replace Fonts to globally change the font.

7. Change the font color and size if you want.

8. Format the bullets and the indents.

9. Resize and format the text placeholders.

10. If you want footers, choose View | Headers and Footers and choose the options you want. You can also delete any of the footers from the master.

11. To create a title master, choose Insert New Title Master from the Slide Master View toolbar.

12. Use the same procedures described in the previous steps to format the title master.

13. Choose File | Save As. In the Save as Type drop-down list, choose Design Template (*.pot). In the Save In box at the top of the dialog box, navigate to the desired folder. By default, design templates are in C:\Program Files\Microsoft Office\Templates\ Presentation Designs.

14. Type a name for the template in the File Name text box and click Save.

> **SHORTCUT** *You can also open an existing presentation that has many of the features you want and modify it.*

If you wish, you can add content to your template. A template with suggested text is called a *content template.*

To use your template, start a new presentation. On the Formatting toolbar, choose Design. If the design templates don't appear, click Design Templates in the Slide Design task pane. Choose your template.

> **TIP** *It's sometimes hard to find a template by scrolling through so many thumbnails. Instead, click Browse and navigate to the template by name. Choose it and click Apply.*

Figure 7-9 shows some examples of slides created using custom-made design templates and their slide masters.

If you want the extra professional touch that a graphic artist can provide, you can find a professional who specializes in creating PowerPoint presentations. You can also purchase design templates. Here are four useful sources:

- PresentationPro: http://www.presentationpro.com
- Digital Juice: http://www.digitaljuice.com
- CrystalGraphics: http://www.crystalgraphics.com
- Powerpointed: http://www.powerpointed.com

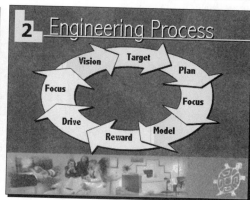

| FIGURE 7-9 | You can modify one of PowerPoint's design templates or create your own. Here you see two examples of a slide master and one of its slides. |

Add Your Template to the AutoContent Wizard

You can add a template of your own to the AutoContent Wizard. Here's how:

1. Display the New Presentation task pane.
2. Click From AutoContent Wizard.
3. Click Next.

4. Choose a category except for All. (The All category automatically contains all the templates in the other categories.

5. Click Add.

6. In the Select Presentation Template dialog box, choose your template and click OK.

7. Click Cancel if you don't want to continue with the AutoContent Wizard at the present time. The next time you will be able to choose your template from the AutoContent Wizard. Or choose the new template and click Next to start a new presentation using the template.

Summary

In this chapter, you put together all the knowledge you have learned about creating presentations and put it to use to create masters. Masters control the overall look of a presentation.

The slide master controls all slides except for those using the Title AutoLayout. In the slide master, you can change the background, format titles and bulleted text, insert objects and graphics that will appear on every slide, and add footers.

The title master is like the slide master, but it only controls slides using the Title Slide AutoLayout. This chapter also explained how to use handout masters to format handouts and notes masters to format notes.

The Page Setup dialog box lets you format the size and orientation of your slides.

Once you can create masters, you have the tools you need to create your own design templates. The chapter ended with a description of how to create design and content templates.

In the next chapter, you learn how to incorporate graphs, tables, and organization charts into your presentations.

Chapter 8

Incorporate Graphs, Tables, and Organization Charts

How to…

- ■ Create a graph from within PowerPoint
- ■ Import data from a spreadsheet
- ■ Choose the right chart type
- ■ Format a chart
- ■ Add a table to a slide
- ■ Import a Word table
- ■ Create diagrams
- ■ Add an organization chart to a slide

Effective presentations sometimes require more than pictures, and PowerPoint lets you add graphs, tables, and organization charts to your slides. In this chapter, you learn how to present complex data as simply and clearly as possible.

Present Data Simply

The more complex the data you need to present, the more you should plan ways to present that data so that your audience can comprehend it at a glance. While long tables of data are OK for printed reports, they are not effective on slides. A slide is not big enough, and the audience doesn't have enough time to read through lots of numbers. You may need to present less data, but you may also be able to find a way to format the data more simply. For example, the table shown next doesn't make the trends immediately obvious.

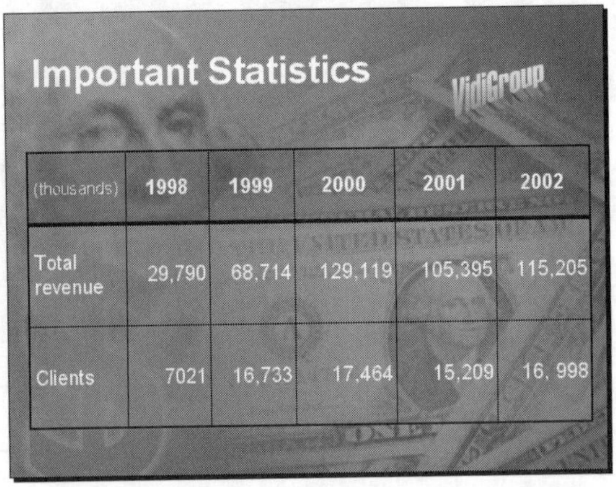

Important Statistics — VidiGroup

(thousands)	1998	1999	2000	2001	2002
Total revenue	29,790	68,714	129,119	105,395	115,205
Clients	7021	16,733	17,464	15,209	16, 998

Thanks to Digital Juice for permission to use this background. www.digitaljuice.com

If your point is the growth of the company, you could split the data onto two slides and use the following two charts instead.

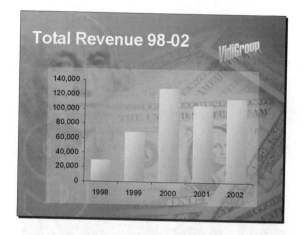

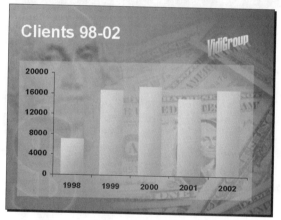

8

Your audience doesn't see the exact numbers, but the overall message is much clearer. The audience can immediately see the trend.

Add Graphs to a Slide

A graph visually portrays a series of numbers. Graphs are usually more effective than tables when the figures show a trend. Your audience can see the direction of the trend at a glance rather than have to figure out the trend by analyzing the numbers in a table. The most direct way to add a graph to a slide is to use a graph placeholder and PowerPoint's own graph module. Later in this chapter, in the "Insert a Chart from Microsoft Excel" section, I explain how to import a graph from a spreadsheet application such as Microsoft Excel.

To create a graph using a graph placeholder, create a new slide with one of the Content Layouts. The content icons on these layouts let you choose from a variety of content types, including charts. PowerPoint uses the term *chart,* which is another word for graph. (I use the terms interchangeably throughout this chapter.) PowerPoint displays the new slide, shown in Figure 8-1. The instruction is clear—click to add a chart.

Insert Chart icon

FIGURE 8-1   Any of the Content Layouts lets you add a chart (graph) by clicking the Insert Chart icon.

Another way to insert a chart is to click Insert Chart on the Standard toolbar. To create a custom AutoLayout, use one of the existing AutoLayouts, and click Insert Chart on the Standard toolbar. You usually have to resize existing objects and the chart so they fit together on the slide.

Once you have the proper layout, you can create a chart. Although the order of the steps you use to create a chart is flexible, in general, you should proceed as follows:

1. Resize the chart placeholder to the desired size on your slide. Resizing a placeholder after you have created the graph often does not provide satisfactory results.

2. Enter the data you want to use.

3. Choose a chart type to create the chart.

4. Format the graph.

Enter Data on the Datasheet

Once you have sized the placeholder appropriately, it's time to enter your data. When you click the chart placeholder, your screen looks like Figure 8-2. (The placement of the datasheet might be different.) Where did those numbers come from? The datasheet opens with dummy data already filled in.

The *datasheet* is a place to insert your data and looks like a worksheet in any spreadsheet application. This data is the basis for your chart. Columns are labeled A, B, C, and so on, and rows are numbered 1, 2, 3, and so on. A *cell* is one of the rectangles that contains data and is called by its column and row, so that the active cell in Figure 8-2—the one with the black border—is A1. Unlike most spreadsheets, however, PowerPoint's datasheet has an unlabeled first column and top row that you use for labeling the columns and rows.

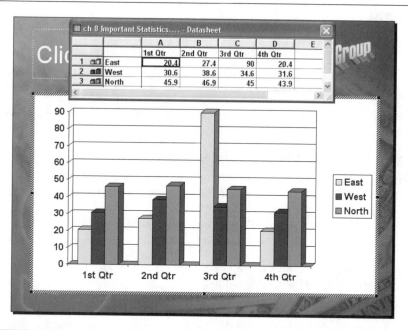

FIGURE 8-2   When you click a chart icon, PowerPoint opens a dummy chart and datasheet.

To enter your own data, you can delete all the dummy data first, by clicking in the top-left corner cell and pressing DEL. Alternately, you can simply go from cell to cell and replace the data. Move from left to right across a row by pressing TAB, or click the cursor in any cell to type there. If you need to enlarge the datasheet to see more of your data, place the cursor over an edge or corner and drag outward. You can also drag column dividers to change column widths. As you type, PowerPoint modifies the graph so that you instantly see the results of your data. However, the graph usually needs to be formatted for legibility and style.

In most cases, the column headings of the datasheet relate to time (such as 1st Qtr and 2nd Qtr) and become the x axis, which is usually the *category axis*. The row headings contain the types of data for each time period and become the y axis, which is usually the *data axis*. When you start formatting the chart, you will find it helpful to keep these terms in mind.

While you are working in a datasheet, you might notice that PowerPoint's toolbars have changed and two new menu items, Data and Chart, have been added. The new menu and toolbar items are especially for working with graphs. These items are covered throughout the rest of the section on graphs.

Import Data

Of course, if you already have the data in a spreadsheet application, such as Microsoft Excel, you don't need to retype it. You can choose from two ways to import existing spreadsheet data:

- Import the spreadsheet data into the PowerPoint datasheet and continue to work in PowerPoint.
- Insert a spreadsheet as an object and modify it using the original spreadsheet's menus and toolbars.

Import Spreadsheet Data into the Datasheet

When you import data into the datasheet, PowerPoint places the data right into the datasheet. Once you've imported the data, PowerPoint automatically creates a chart that you can format directly in PowerPoint.

You can import data from Microsoft Excel, Lotus 1-2-3 (with a wk* filename extension), and several types of text data files. Here's how to import your data:

1. In PowerPoint, double-click the chart to open it. If the datasheet is not visible, click View Datasheet on the Formatting toolbar.

2. Choose Edit | Import File.

3. In the Import File dialog box, check the file format in the Files of Type drop-down list and, if necessary, change it. Navigate to the file you want to import and double-click it.

   - If you selected a Microsoft Excel workbook created with version 5.0 or later, the Import Data Options dialog box appears, as shown in Figure 8-3. Choose which sheet you want to import and how much of it (a range or the whole sheet). Check the Overwrite Existing Cells check box to replace the current data if desired, and click OK.

   - If you select a text file format, such as CSV, TXT, and PRN, follow the instructions of the Text Import Wizard.

Insert a Spreadsheet as an Object

When you insert, or *embed,* a spreadsheet as an object, you edit the object by double-clicking it. The menus and toolbars change to those of the original spreadsheet application, which you use to make changes. Here's how to embed a spreadsheet:

1. Display the slide where you want the spreadsheet.

2. Choose Insert | Object.

3. To create a new chart, click Create New, and then choose your spreadsheet from the list. For example, choose Microsoft Excel Chart if you have Excel. To insert a chart you've already created, click Create from File, and then click Browse. Locate and double-click the file. (If you created a new Excel chart, you see dummy data and a chart, similar to the datasheet.)

FIGURE 8-3   Use the Import Data Options dialog box to specify exactly which data you want to import and how.

You can now use your spreadsheet's tools to edit the data and the corresponding chart. When you're done, click anywhere outside the chart to close it.

Choose the Right Chart Type

While you have the datasheet open, the entire graph object is open and available for formatting. One of the first tasks is to choose the chart type. By default, PowerPoint creates the column chart you saw in Figure 8-2. However, not every chart type is suitable for the type of data you have, and you have a wide array of options.

The key to choosing a chart type is to understand your data and the strengths and weaknesses of each chart type. The ideal chart type for your presentation is the one that presents the data most clearly. In the next few sections, I give you the information you need to understand each chart type.

To change the chart type, right-click inside the graph's border. Choose Chart Type from the shortcut menu. You can also choose Chart | Chart Type to open the dialog box shown in Figure 8-4. If your graph is not currently open, you must double-click it to open it before you can access the Chart Type menu item.

You can't always use any chart type you want. Some types of graphs are suitable for data with several rows; others shouldn't have more than one row. Several are used only for scientific data. If you aren't sure which kind of chart to use, try several to see which one seems to make the point most clearly.

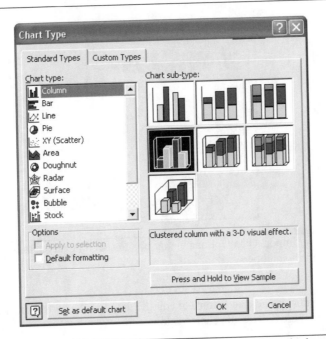

FIGURE 8-4   The Chart Type dialog box is the place to choose from the long list of chart types and subtypes.

Column

Column charts are among the most common. You often see them showing financial data over time, where quarters or years are the column categories in the datasheet. On the graph, these time categories are shown across the bottom (on the X axis) and the data for each time category is along the left side (on the Y axis). If you are showing data for more than one item (such as several products or locations), you will see as many vertical bars as you have items. Figure 8-5 shows an example of a datasheet and its corresponding column chart showing income for both sales and service over four years.

If you want to show the relationship of your data to totals, try one of the stacked column charts. And if you have more than one series and want to show relationships across both categories and series, try the last 3-D Column subtype.

Bar

Bar graphs also compare data across categories, but the categories are shown along the left (Y) axis and the data is shown along the bottom (X) axis, as shown next with the Stacked Bar subtype. This graph used the same datasheet as the column graph.

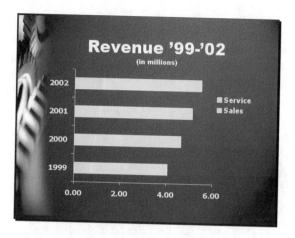

Column and bar graphs are visually impressive and easy to understand. You can use fill effects on the bars for a sophisticated look.

Line

A line graph is similar to a bar graph, but instead of creating bars, a line is drawn from value to value. Line graphs are especially good at showing trends—your audience immediately grasps if

8

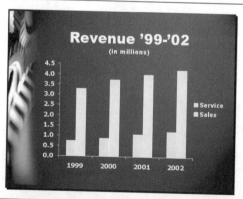

FIGURE 8-5   A simple column chart, the most common type of graph

the line is going up, down, or remaining flat. However, they are not as visually impressive as column or bar graphs.

You can add markers at each data point to make the actual values on the line graph stand out. The 3-D subtype creates ribbons instead of lines. Here you see a line graph using the same datasheet used for the bar and column graphs shown previously. For clarity, the lines have been formatted to make them thicker than the default line weight.

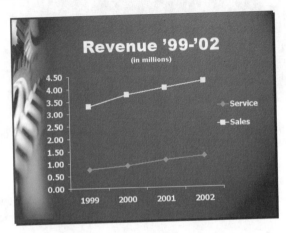

Pie

A pie chart shows which percentage each data value contributes to the whole pie. For this reason, pie charts are suitable for datasheets with only one row, that is, one data series. They are often used for breaking down revenues or expenses. Pie charts look great on slides, but keep the number of items to six or less, if possible. Here you see a datasheet and its corresponding pie chart.

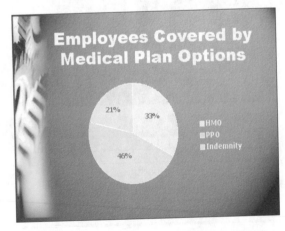

PowerPoint offers some great-looking 3-D pie charts. You can also create exploded pies (messy!) and pie charts that break down one of the chart's components into subcomponents.

Scatter

A scatter chart (also called an XY chart) is used when both the categories (columns) and the series (rows) are numbers, to draw conclusions about the relationships in the data. It is an effective way to present many data values at once. Here you see a datasheet showing average annual salaries based on age and years of college education completed.

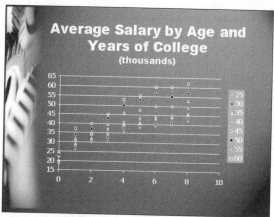

The scatter chart shows years of college education along the X axis and annual salary along the Y axis. Each marker type in the legend indicates a different age. You can clearly see how salary goes up with age and education, including a jump for those with four years of college. (This chart uses dummy data.)

Area

An area chart is plotted like a line chart, but the area under the lines is filled in. Because of the fill, an area chart shows up better on a slide. Another advantage of an area chart is that you can use one of the stacked subtypes, which show the relationship of the data series to their total. Here you see a 100 percent stacked area chart, which shows the trend in the percentage that each value contributes across the categories.

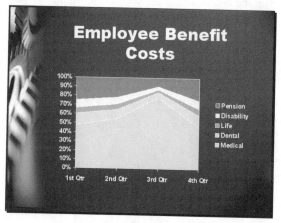

In this case, you clearly see how much each of the five employee benefits categories contributes to the total employee benefits cost over the four quarters of the year. Your audience would immediately understand that medical expenses are the largest part of the total cost, with pension expenses coming second.

Doughnut

A doughnut chart is like a pie chart, but you can use it for data with more than one series (row). You can also use the exploded doughnut option. Here you see an unexploded doughnut, showing medical plan choices made by employees in two offices.

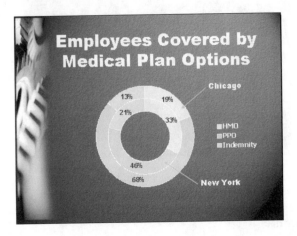

The point is to show the proportions between the choices, not the total numbers. Because the Chicago office has fewer employees than the New York office, a chart type emphasizing totals, such as a bar chart, would not make the point clearly.

Radar

A radar chart compares the values of several data series. Each category (column) has its own value axis radiating out from the center. Lines connect all the values in a series. A radar chart is usually used for scientific data and may be confusing for a presentation. Here you see a radar chart showing average annual temperature and rainfall for three U.S. cities.

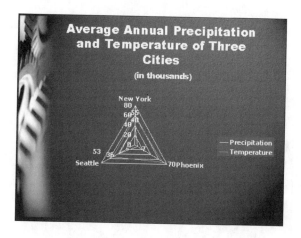

Surface

You can use a surface chart when you have two series (rows). The surface chart plots both series as it would with a line graph and connects lines to create a ribbonlike surface. The topology of the surface shows the combined value of both series. Here you see a surface chart showing quarterly sales of tapes and CDs. You can see that in the fourth quarter, the combined sales were the highest for the year.

8

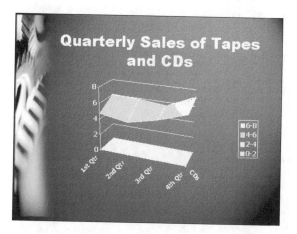

Bubble

A bubble chart lets you plot three series (rows) of data. The first row becomes the horizontal (X) axis, the second row becomes the vertical (Y) axis, and the third row is indicated by the size of the bubbles. In the next example, you see data for four U.S. cities—the X axis is precipitation, the Y axis is temperature, and the size of the bubbles indicates population (as of 1990) in thousands. In which city would you rather live? (Try to guess which city is which. The answer is at the end of the chapter.)

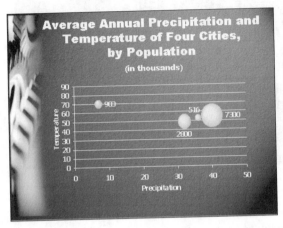

Stock

A stock chart is specifically designed to plot stock prices. The simplest version plots high, low, and closing prices, which must be located in rows in the datasheet in that order. The first row can be the names of stocks, sectors, dates, and so forth. Here you see a datasheet with dummy data for three sectors and the corresponding stock chart.

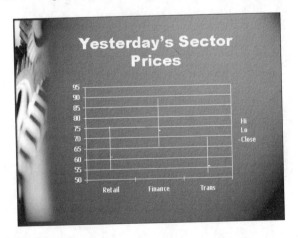

Cylinder, Cone, and Pyramid

These charts are just like bar or column charts, but PowerPoint uses cylinders, cones, or pyramids rather than bars to create the graph. These charts use 3-D effects that look good if the exact numbers are not important. In the next example, you see a cone chart displaying data about employee benefit costs. You get the main idea—medical/dental costs are the highest of the three costs listed and are most variable.

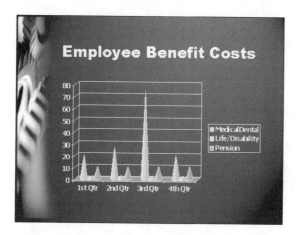

Format a Chart

Rarely is the default version of the chart acceptable for a slide. Sometimes the labels aren't readable. Perhaps the scale of the axes is not appropriate. The charts you have seen in this chapter were formatted after their initial creation. PowerPoint gives you a great deal of control over the format of a chart.

Charts have a number of elements that can be formatted individually. Not all charts have every element. For example, only 3-D charts have a floor. Other elements are optional, such as axis titles. The type of formatting available depends on the type of element. Obviously, you can change the font, font size, and font color only for elements that contain text. Table 8-1 describes the most often-used chart elements.

Element	Description
Category axis	Usually (but not always) the horizontal (X) axis
Value axis	Usually (but not always) the vertical (Y) axis
Series axis	A third axis (on some 3-D charts), labeled with the names of the data series being plotted
Chart title	A title for the chart
Axes titles, if any	Titles for the axes
Data labels, if any	Labels containing the actual values
Plot area	The area within the axes
Each series of data	Each row of data (there may be several) that is plotted on the graph
Chart area	The entire chart, including the plot area, the legend, and a chart title, if any
Corners	The corners of the floor and walls in 3-D charts
Floor	In a 3-D chart, the floor that creates the chart's depth
Walls	In a 3-D chart, the two walls that create two of the three dimensions

TABLE 8-1   Chart Elements

8

Element	Description
Legend	The labels that indicate the names of the series
Tick marks	Marks that divide the axes into regular units
Gridlines	Lines running perpendicular to the axes from the tick marks, which help the viewer visualize the values plotted on the graph

TABLE 8-1   Chart Elements *(continued)*

Figure 8-6 shows a 3-D chart and its elements.

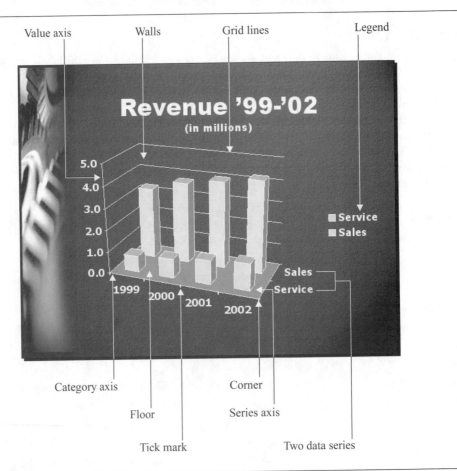

FIGURE 8-6   A chart is made up of many elements, each of which can be formatted individually.

Use the Chart Options Dialog Box

Perhaps the simplest way to change a chart's elements is to use the Chart Options dialog box, which gives you access to the entire chart and its many elements at once. To open this dialog box, shown in Figure 8-7, open a chart and choose Chart | Chart Options.

Each tab in this dialog box lets you format one of the features of the chart. As you make changes, the simplified image of the chart previews the effect of the change. The number of tabs depends on the type of chart you have. Here's how to use the tabs:

- **Titles**   Add an overall chart title or add titles to the series, category, and/or value axes.

- **Axes**   Check if you want each of the available axes. If you uncheck an axis, PowerPoint removes its labels, for example, the years on a category (X) axis.

- **Gridlines**   Check if you want major and minor gridlines for each axis. Major gridlines mark off larger intervals. Minor gridlines mark off smaller intervals between the major gridlines.

- **Legend**   Check if you want a legend and choose where you want it to be placed. (You can always drag it elsewhere.)

- **Data Labels**   Data labels usually show actual values. For example, you can place the actual number represented by a column at the top of the column. You can choose from several formats.

- **Data Table**   You can include with the chart a table of the data in your datasheet.

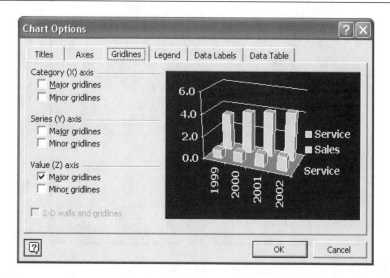

FIGURE 8-7   The Chart Options dialog box with the Gridlines tab on top

As a general guideline, include as few features as possible without sacrificing clarity. For example, titles, gridlines, and a data table often clutter up a chart without providing any additional necessary information. Save the fine details for a printed report.

Format Chart Elements

Once you have determined which features to include in your chart, you also want to individually format those features. Each element of a chart has its own customized Format dialog box that fine-tunes that element. To format an element, first make sure that the chart is open and active.

As you move the mouse cursor around a chart, ToolTips pop up telling you which object you are passing over. To get an idea of the available elements in your charts, click the Chart Objects drop-down list on the Standard toolbar when a chart is open. You can choose any element form this list to select it.

Double-click an element to open its Format dialog box. For example, if you double-click one of the axes, you see the Format Axis dialog box, shown in Figure 8-8. You can also right-click and choose Format Axis, or another appropriate element of the chart.

FIGURE 8-8   The Patterns tab of the Format Axis dialog box

All the Format dialog boxes have a Patterns tab that lets you change colors or change the line width or border style. Here are some of the other items you can format:

- **Axes**   You can format the scale of the axes on the Scale tab, setting the minimum and maximum numbers as well as the intervals for major and minor units. Use the Font tab for formatting the font of the axes labels. The Number tab lets you format exactly how numbers will appear. The Alignment tab aligns the text—great for fitting axis labels into tight spaces.

- **Data series**   The data series is the part of the chart that plots the values, such as the columns, bars, or lines. For certain charts, you can set which axis PowerPoint uses to plot the data series and format Y error bars, which indicate standard deviation or some other type of error value. You can format the data labels and set options for the spacing between the data series (for example, the columns). You will often want to change the color and width of bars or columns.

- **Chart area**   On the Font tab, you can format the font for text in the chart area, as well as background and foreground colors.

- **Legend**   You can format the patterns, font, and placement of the legend.

- **Gridlines**   You can format the patterns and the scale of the gridlines.

Figure 8-9 shows a chart before and after formatting. The following formatting was done:

- The titles and gridlines were removed to get a cleaner look.

- In the Format Data Series dialog box, the gap width was reduced on the Options tab, which has the effect of widening the columns.

- The legend was removed.

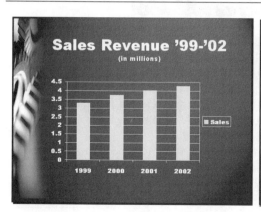 

FIGURE 8-9   Format your chart to make it simple and clear.

- A one-color gradient was added to the columns.
- The Shadow check box was checked on the Patterns tab of the Format Data Series dialog box to create a slight shadow effect on the columns.
- Data values were added.
- An AutoShape was added to emphasize important information and rotated slightly.

> **TIP** *If you still don't think your chart conveys the message adequately, feel free to add AutoShapes, arrows, or text boxes. You can also animate elements of a chart—see Chapter 9.*

On the other hand, sometimes you want to be dramatic. For example, PowerPoint's chart feature lets you fill columns or bars with a picture that can be either stretched to fill the column or bar or stacked as many times as necessary. Here you see an example of using a graphic of a book to indicate book sales.

To create a slide like this, first create a chart. Column and bar charts work best. Here a column chart was used. With the chart open, double-click one of the columns to open the Format Data Series dialog box. (If the Format Data Point dialog box opens instead, close the dialog box. This time, right-click one of the columns and choose Format Data Series. If you use the Format Data Point dialog box, your changes affect only the one column you selected.) On the Patterns tab, click Fill Effects, then the Picture tab. This procedure should be familiar from Chapter 6. Click Select Picture and choose a picture.

In the Format section of the Picture tab, shown in Figure 8-10, choose one of these options:

- **Stretch** Stretches the graphic to cover the entire column or bar
- **Stack** Tiles the column or bar with copies of the originally sized graphic
- **Stack and Scale To** Tiles the graphic but resizes it based on a scale

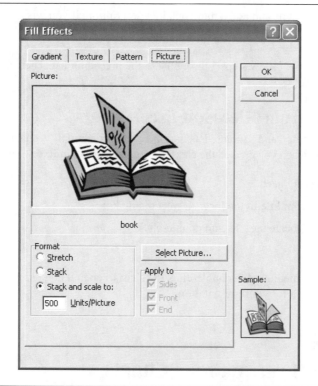

FIGURE 8-10   Use these options to format a graphic in a chart.

On the Options tab of the Format Data Series dialog box, reduce the gap width. This chart used a gap width of 20, which widens each column, making the graphic larger. In the Format Plot Area dialog box, the border was removed to make the chart as simple as possible. In the Category Axis dialog box, on the Alignment tab, the text was rotated to 45 degrees.

Save Chart Properties

You can save all your hard work formatting a chart if you think you might use the same formatting in the future. Follow these steps:

1. Open the chart.

2. Right-click the chart and choose Chart Type.

3. In the Chart Type dialog box, choose the Custom Types tab.

4. Choose User-Defined at the bottom of the dialog box.

5. Click Add.

6. Name the chart type and add a more detailed description, if you wish.

7. Click OK twice to return to your presentation.

To use this chart type, follow steps 1 through 4 in the preceding list. Then choose the chart type you created. Click OK.

Insert a Chart from Microsoft Excel

If you have already created and formatted a chart in Excel, for example, you can insert it onto a slide. This works best when you created the chart on a separate sheet in Excel. Follow these steps:

1. Choose Insert | Object.

2. Click Create from File in the Insert Object dialog box.

3. Click Browse, locate the file, and double-click it.

4. Click OK.

When you use this method, you double-click the chart to open it and use Excel's menus and toolbars to edit the graph for your presentation.

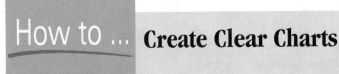

How to ...   **Create Clear Charts**

Charts are an essential component of many presentations. However, many charts are unclear and require extensive explanation before the audience can understand them.

A chart is created to make a point. Suppose you're creating a presentation about your company's financial results. You could put a summary of the company's balance sheet into the presentation. However, if what your audience really wants to see is the company's debt-to-equity ratio, which is buried somewhere in the balance sheet, a simple pie chart of the debt-to-equity ratio would be more effective.

Once you determine that the key point is to show the improvement in earnings per share, for example, you can create your chart, perhaps a column chart. But even a simple column chart should be designed to serve a purpose. Choose colors and fills so that the eye is drawn to improvement, rather than past losses. Decide if you want data values on the top of each column or values on the Y axis—but both are unnecessary and confusing. The border around the chart that PowerPoint creates by default is also unnecessary. Also, 3-D charts are notoriously hard to evaluate—it's difficult to see exactly where the top of the column is. If you wish, add an arrow to guide the attention to the latest earnings. If there is a recent improvement, add a text box or AutoShape and explain it in a few words. Shadows and shaded fills on the columns enhance visual appeal. Animation (discussed in Chapter 9) can be used to focus the attention of the audience on what the presenter is saying.

Here are some basic rules of thumb for charts:

- Guide the attention to your main point. Use an arrow, animation, or a contrasting color to guide the eye.

- Reduce the number of lines or bars. Try to use one data series (line or row of bars) per chart. If necessary, create two charts on separate slides to present all the data.

- Use an axis scale or data points, but not both.

- Remove details. Gridlines, footnotes, and other details detract from the message.

A well-designed chart needs very little explanation. The audience gets the idea quickly and can pay more attention to your analysis and follow-up discussion.

Present Data in a Table

Using a table is an easy way to present lots of text or to summarize complex information that you want your viewers to remember. Use a table to make your point quickly and succinctly when you are not trying to show relationships or trends, as shown here. Another good use of a table is to supplement a chart to show your audience the details. Show them the chart first so they get the main point, and then let them focus in on all the nitty-gritty.

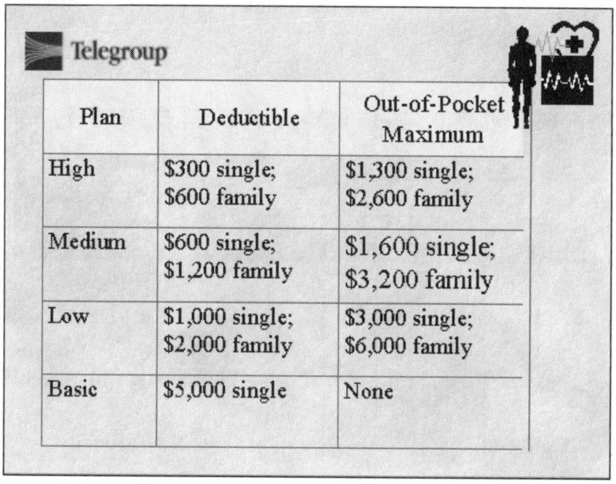

Telegroup		
Plan	Deductible	Out-of-Pocket Maximum
High	$300 single; $600 family	$1,300 single; $2,600 family
Medium	$600 single; $1,200 family	$1,600 single; $3,200 family
Low	$1,000 single; $2,000 family	$3,000 single; $6,000 family
Basic	$5,000 single	None

Create a Table

The simplest way to create a table is to create a new slide using one of the Content Layouts. Click the Insert Table icon and PowerPoint opens the Insert Table dialog box. Specify the number of columns and rows you want. When you click OK, PowerPoint creates the table on your slide.

You can create a table on a slide without a table placeholder by choosing Insert Table on the Standard toolbar. A grid appears. Drag down and to the right to fill in the number of columns and rows you want. You can always modify the table later.

You also use the Tables and Borders toolbar, shown in Figure 8-11, to create a more complex table, varying the size and shape of the columns and rows. Here's how to use the Tables and Borders toolbar to create a table on a slide:

1. Click Tables and Borders on the Standard toolbar. The cursor changes to a pencil. (If it doesn't, click Draw Table.)

2. Create the outer boundaries of the table by dragging from the top-left corner to the bottom-right corner. (Yes, you can do it from right to left if you want.)

3. Drag across to create rows. You can stop in the middle to create a partial row.

4. Drag vertically to create columns. Once you have created a row, you can similarly create a partial column.

5. To erase a line, click Eraser and drag across the line.

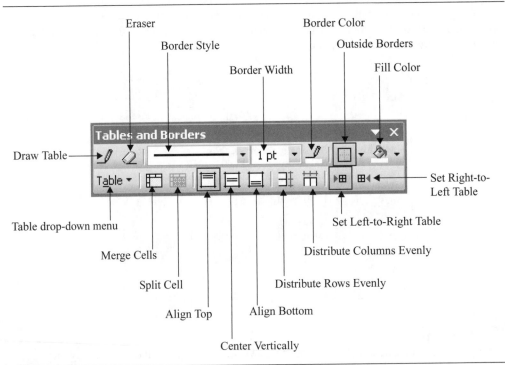

FIGURE 8-11 The Tables and Borders toolbar helps you format a table.

Here you see a table created using this method. This table would be difficult to create with the Insert Table button.

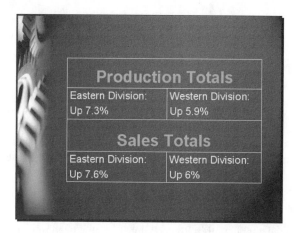

Once you have created a table, click in the first cell and start typing data. Press TAB to move from cell to cell. You can click in any cell to type in that cell. If you press TAB from the bottom-right cell, PowerPoint creates a new row so you can add more data.

If necessary, use the Tables and Borders toolbar to add, delete, split, or merge cells, rows, and/or columns. You can also use the Formatting toolbar to center text, make it bold, and so on.

Import a Table

As with charts, you don't have to reinvent the wheel. If you have already created the table in Word, Excel, or Access, for example, you can import it onto your slide. If you wish, you can start in PowerPoint, embed an object from one of those programs (or another program of your choice), and use the toolbars and menus of that program to create the table in PowerPoint. Remember these points when deciding which program to use:

- Word allows for more graphics formatting within its tables, including bulleted lists, numbering, and individual cell formatting.

- Use Excel when you want to include calculations, statistical analysis, or sorting and search features.

- If you need the power of a relational database, use Access.

Here's the procedure for importing a table:

1. Choose Insert | Object.

2. To create a new table, choose Create New and choose the type of object from the list.

3. To import an existing table, choose Create from File and type the filename or choose Browse to locate the file.

4. Click OK.

For more information about sharing information between PowerPoint and other applications, see Chapter 11.

To import a table that is part of an existing file, such as a Word document, open the file, select the table, and copy it to the clipboard. Display the slide where you want the table and paste it from the clipboard.

When you embed a table from another application into PowerPoint, you need to double-click it to open it. The other application's menus and toolbars appear so you can use them to edit the table.

Format a Table

Assuming you have created a table within PowerPoint, you now need to format it. The default table that PowerPoint creates, shown here, doesn't stand out at all!

Increase in Net Sales Over Previous Year	
2000	2001
8.9%	9.2%

One way to format a table is to use the Format Table dialog box, shown in Figure 8-12. With a table selected, choose Format | Table. On the Borders tab, you can change the style, color, and width of the borders. You can also use the diagram on the right to create and delete borders. The Fill tab lets you set the fill color. The Text Box tab is like the Text Box tab of the Format Text Box dialog box discussed in Chapter 3. Here you set the text alignment and internal margins.

On the other hand, you can also format a table using the Tables and Borders toolbar, which I recommend because it contains all the tools you need in one place.

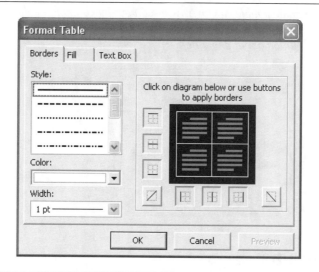

FIGURE 8-12   You can format a table in the Format Table dialog box.

The following are probably the minimum tasks you need to do to get a professional-looking table:

- Resize and place the table.

- Select the entire table and format the font, font size, and font color. Use the Formatting toolbar to center the text if you want. Use the Tables and Borders toolbar to center the text vertically, if desired.

- Change the borders: On the Tables and Borders toolbar, set the border style, width, and color. Then click the Pencil tool and redraw over the borders. You may want to make the outer borders thicker. If your table has a heading, it is common to place a heavier line under the first row or use a different fill for the first row. To delete borders, click the Border Style drop-down list and choose No Borders. You can also create individual borders using the drop-down arrow next to the Outside Border button, which opens to give you a choice of border arrangements.

- If you wish, use the Fill Color button to choose a fill. You can use any of the fill effects discussed in Chapter 6.

In the next illustration you see the simply formatted chart. The point is clear—we're going up, where do we go from here?

8

TIP *You cannot animate a table row-by-row or column-by-column. A solution is to create multiple tables next to each other and animate them as separate objects. See Chapter 9 for more information about animation.*

Increase in Net Sales Over Previous Year	
2000	2001
8.9%	9.2%

Dare we think 10%?

Work with Diagrams

PowerPoint 2003's diagrams offer a graphic way to display the relationships between elements of a process or organization. The diagram feature includes the following types of diagrams:

- **Organization chart**   Shows hierarchical relationships, often those of employees in an organization
- **Cycle diagram**   Shows a process that takes place in a continuous cycle
- **Radial diagram**   Shows the relationship between a core element and its surrounding elements
- **Pyramid diagram**   Shows relationships where each element is the foundation of the next
- **Venn diagram:**   Shows overlapping relationships
- **Target diagram:**   Shows steps toward a goal

TIP *PowerPoint's diagrams are not very flexible. Don't forget that you can create your own diagrams using AutoShapes, especially the flowchart and connector shapes.*

 To create a diagram, use one of the Content Layouts and click the Insert Diagram or Organization Chart icon, shown here. In the Diagram Gallery, shown in the following illustration, choose the type of diagram you want and click OK. To see a description of a diagram type, click its image.

 *To add a diagram to an existing slide, choose Insert Diagram or Organization Chart on the Drawing toolbar.*

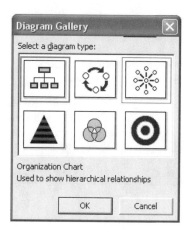

Here you see the result when you click the cycle diagram. Each diagram type similarly prompts you to enter text in the appropriate location. You can then edit the diagram to suit your needs. Organization charts are somewhat different from the other diagram types; I explain them separately in the following sections.

8

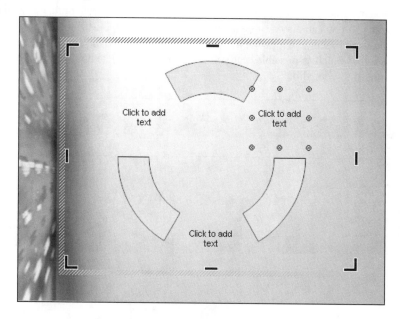

Format a Diagram

Once you insert a diagram, you often need to make changes. For example, you can change the number of elements. You also have several formatting options to change the look of the diagram. The best way to edit a diagram is to use the Diagram toolbar, shown in Figure 8-13.

Insert Shape—add
an element

Move Shape Forward—move
element to next position

Layout—expand
and scale diagram

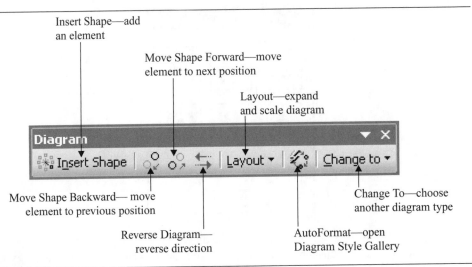

Move Shape Backward— move
element to previous position

Change To—choose
another diagram type

Reverse Diagram—
reverse direction

AutoFormat—open
Diagram Style Gallery

FIGURE 8-13 Use the Diagram toolbar to edit your diagrams.

When you select a diagram and choose AutoFormat from the Diagram toolbar, the Diagram Style Gallery opens so you can choose a style, as shown in Figure 8-14. Choose the styles and decide which you want based on the preview. You may want to match the style of other elements of your presentation as much as possible, but you do not have complete control over the style. Click Apply to return to your slide.

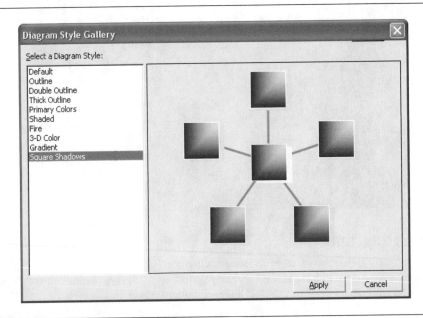

FIGURE 8-14 The Diagram Style Gallery

To delete an element from any type of diagram, click the element and press DEL. You can also select any text and change the font, size, and color. Here you see a formatted cycle diagram using the 3-D Color style.

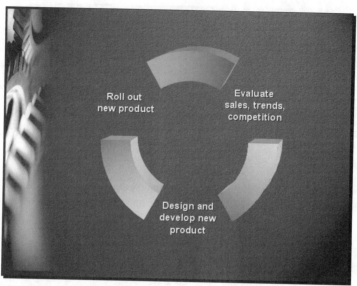

Format an Organization Chart

When you choose Organization Chart from the Diagram Gallery, as explained previously, you see the following chart on your slide.

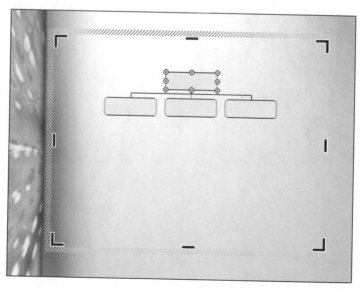

Use the Organization Chart toolbar, shown in Figure 8-15, to format your chart.

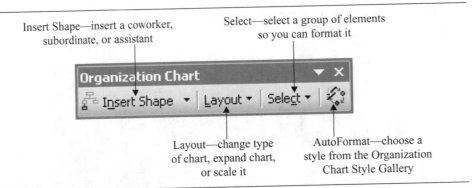

Insert Shape—insert a coworker, subordinate, or assistant

Select—select a group of elements so you can format it

Layout—change type of chart, expand chart, or scale it

AutoFormat—choose a style from the Organization Chart Style Gallery

FIGURE 8-15   The Organization Chart toolbar

To delete a box from the organization chart, click the box and press DEL. You can also select any text and change the font, size, and color. Here you see an organization chart using the Beveled Gradient style.

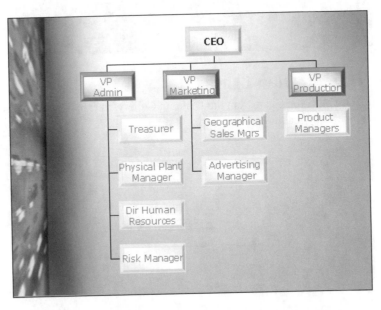

Summary

In this chapter, you learned how to present complex information clearly using graphs, tables, diagrams, and organization charts.

PowerPoint lets you create or insert a graph (or chart) to suit your presentation needs. To determine the type of chart, you need to understand the structure of your data and the specific qualities of the types of charts PowerPoint offers. Once you have chosen a chart type, you should format it for maximum simplicity and impact.

Tables add clarity to complex information, and PowerPoint lets you draw a simple or complex table to present information. You can also embed tables from other applications. Tables also need to be well formatted to deliver the message loud and clear.

Diagrams show relationships between elements. This new feature offers several types of diagrams. Organization charts show the structure of an organization. PowerPoint lets you insert and edit organization charts easily and quickly.

In the next chapter, you learn how to animate slides and create electronic transition effects between slides.

NOTE   *In the "Bubble" section, the cities shown in the chart are (from left to right) Phoenix, Chicago, Seattle, and New York.*

8

Chapter 9

Add Animation to a Presentation

How to...

- Animate text and objects
- Use animation schemes
- Create custom animation
- Edit animation
- Animate charts and diagrams
- Add animated GIF files
- Add Flash animation
- Add transitions from slide to slide

To add the finishing touches to a presentation, you can include two types of animation—within a slide and from slide to slide. Animation on a slide, often called *builds,* determines how and when objects on the slide appear. Animation from slide to slide, called *transitions,* specifies how a new slide appears after the previous slide disappears. PowerPoint 2003 includes powerful animation effects and features.

Create Professional Animation

To animate a presentation in a professional manner, it has to have a purpose beyond the Wow! effect. Animation can certainly enliven a presentation, but too much animation will distract your audience from your main message. All professional presenters make the same point about animation—pick one or two effects and stick to them. This principle applies to both animation on a slide and transitions between slides.

Animate Text and Objects

Animating objects has an additional purpose—to focus your audience's attention on what you're saying. To animate a slide, you need to know what you are going to say while that slide is displayed—and in what order. You then use that order to determine the order in which the objects appear on the slide. Object animation is sometimes called a *build* because the objects build up on the screen, one after another. You can control the following aspects of the animation:

- How the object appears.
- In what grouping the object appears. For example, text most often appears paragraph by paragraph but can appear by the word or even by the letter.
- Whether the animation occurs when you click the mouse or automatically after a preset number of seconds.

- Whether a sound plays during the animation.

- What happens, if anything, after the animation. For example, you can change the color of a previously displayed object when the next object appears or hide it completely.

Use Animation Schemes for Quick Results

For a quick solution, PowerPoint offers animation schemes—a complete group of settings that you can quickly assign to a slide or presentation. Animation schemes apply only to slide titles and text placeholders. To animate other objects, use custom animation, as explained in the next section.

NOTE *Several animation schemes also include slide transitions, which are discussed later in this chapter, in the "Transition from Slide to Slide" section.*

When you animate placeholder text, all the text in the placeholder is considered one object. However, it is automatically animated paragraph by paragraph—that is, bullet by bullet, which is usually what you want. To animate by word or even letter, use custom animation. You can add animation schemes either in Slide Sorter view or in Normal view.

The advantage to adding an animation scheme in Slide Sorter view is that you can easily select a group of slides at once and you see the results on all the slides after you choose the scheme. If you want to see the animation with the larger view of the slides, add it in Normal view. To add preset animation in either view, follow these steps:

1. Select the slide (or slides) for which you want animation.

2. Choose Design on the Slide Sorter or Formatting toolbar. The Slide Design task pane appears.

3. Choose Animation Schemes at the top of the task pane to display the animation schemes in the task pane, as shown in Figure 9-1.

4. Choose the animation scheme you want from the list in the task pane. You immediately see the results on the slides if AutoPreview is checked at the bottom of the task pane. If you don't like the results, click another animation scheme.

To see the animation again, click Play in the task pane. To see the animation full screen, click Slide Show.

To see the result of an animation effect, you have three options:

- As mentioned earlier, click Play in the Animation Schemes task pane.

 - In Slide Sorter view, click the Animation icon below the bottom-left corner of the slide, shown here.

- Switch to Slide Show view. Click the mouse to see each successive step of the animation.

9

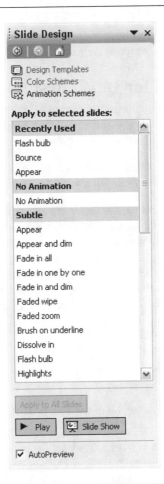

FIGURE 9-1 Use the Animation Schemes options of the Design task pane to create animation quickly.

Figure 9-2 shows the effect of the Appear animation scheme on a slide of bulleted text. Each bulleted item appears in order at the click of the mouse. At the end of the process, the entire slide's contents are visible.

Use Custom Animation for Maximum Control

For more control over animation, you need to create your own settings. It's not hard; once you've done it once or twice, you'll be able to get exactly the effects you want.

Don't forget that you can also animate objects such as AutoShapes and text boxes. Because these objects often serve to draw attention anyway, adding animation to them increases the effect. You can even animate WordArt text.

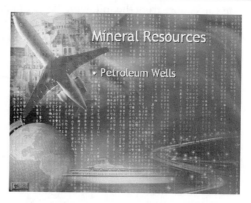
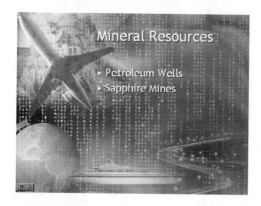
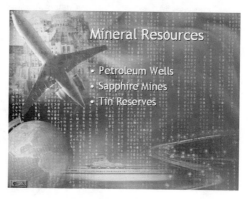

9

FIGURE 9-2   The Appear animation scheme is very simple. Each item appears, one after another, as you click your mouse. *Thanks to Geetesh Bajaj* (www.indezine.com) *for this presentation.*

To specify a custom animation, you must be in Normal or Slide view. Choose Slide Show | Custom Animation to open the Custom Animation task pane, shown in Figure 9-3.

Add Custom Animation

The first step to adding animation is to select an object on the active slide and click Add Effect in the Custom Animation task pane. You see the menu shown here, which provides you with four basic types of animation and then individual animation options.

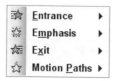

You can choose from the following types of animation:

- **Entrance**   Determines how the object appears on the slide
- **Emphasis**   Changes the object in some way to bring attention to it
- **Exit**   Determines how the object disappears from the slide
- **Motion Paths**   Moves the object along a preset or custom path

As you pass your cursor over any of the four types of animation, a submenu appears listing commonly used animation types. Each submenu also includes a More Effects (or More Motion Paths) item. Click this item to open a dialog box listing of all the animation effects available, as

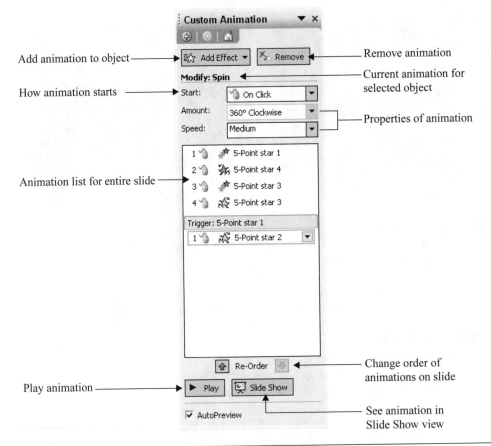

FIGURE 9-3   The Custom Animation task pane lets you create and manage animation.

shown in Figure 9-4. Each listing includes basic, subtle, moderate, and exciting effects. Scroll down to see them all. Overall, you have a huge number of effects to choose from.

You can add more than one animation to an object. For example, you can fade an object in (Entrance effect), change its color (Emphasis effect), or move it along a path (Motion Paths effect), and then let it fly off the slide (Exit effect). You can also create a custom motion path by choosing Motion Paths | Draw Custom Path and then choosing Line, Curve, Freeform, or Scribble.

TIP
When Preview Effect is checked in any of the More Effects dialog boxes, you can select any object, click any effect, and see the effect on your slide. Move the dialog box to the side of the slide to see the effect clearly. To learn about the effects, try them all!

Once you have chosen an animation effect, click OK. You now see the effect listed in the Custom Animation task pane. Your slide also displays numbered tags next to each animated object

9

FIGURE 9-4   The Add Entrance Effect dialog box lists all the Entrance effects. Similar dialog boxes list Emphasis, Exit, and Motion Paths effects.

to help you keep track of the order of animation, as shown here. These tags never show in Slide Show view and don't print. You see them only when the Custom Animation task pane is open.

When you click Play to view an animation, you see a timeline that shows the seconds passing throughout the animation. This timeline helps you gauge the total time that your animation takes.

Choosing an animation effect is not always enough. You can refine the animation effect in many ways. You can do the following:

- Specify when the effect starts.
- Set the speed of the effect.
- Add a dimming effect after the main animation effect.
- Specify other properties particular to an effect. For example, for the Spin effect, you can specify how many degrees the object spins.

Specify How Custom Animation Starts

Choose when an animation effect starts from the Start drop-down list in the Custom Animation task pane. (Refer back to Figure 9-3.) An animation effect can start in three ways. By default, animation starts only when you click the mouse. For example, if you animate bulleted text, you click the mouse to display each bullet of text. In this way, you control the timing of the animation.

To use the On Mouse Click setting or the Hide on Next Mouse Click setting on the Effects tab (discussed in the next section of this chapter), you must also have the On Mouse Click check box checked in the Slide Transition task pane. (It's checked by default.) If On Mouse Click is not checked, your mouse click will have no effect when you run the presentation. The Slide Transition task pane is covered later in this chapter, in the "Choose the Ideal Transition Style" section.

However, sometimes you want animation to start automatically, without requiring a mouse click.

- To start animation at the same time as the previous animation on the slide, choose With Previous from the Start drop-down list.

■ To start animation after the previous animation, choose After Previous. Then you need to specify how many seconds wait you want after the previous animation. You do this by setting the timing of the effect.

To set the timing of an effect, select the object whose timing you want to specify. You now see the effect also bordered in the animation listing in the Custom Animation task pane with a down arrow next to it. (Refer back to Figure 9-3.) Click the down arrow to display a menu, shown here.

Choose Timing to display the dialog box shown in Figure 9-5. The name of the dialog box varies according to the type of animation effect. Here you can set the following timing parameters:

■ **Start** You can change when the animation starts. You have the same three options described previously.

■ **Delay** Set the delay from the start. For example, if the start is set to After Previous and the delay is 2 seconds, then the animation automatically starts 2 seconds after the previous animation. (Adding a delay to the With Previous start setting has the same effect.) You can add a delay to the On Click start, in which case, the animation starts the specified number of seconds after you click the mouse.

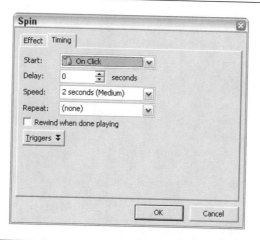

FIGURE 9-5 The Timing tab of the Spin dialog box lets you set the timing of the Spin animation effect. Similar dialog boxes let you set the timing of all the other animation effects.

- **Speed**   You can set the speed of the animation itself, from very slow to very fast.
- **Repeat**   You can specify the number of repetitions. You can also choose to repeat the animation until the next mouse click or until the next slide.

To return the object to its original condition or setting, check the Rewind When Done Playing check box.

You can create a *trigger,* which means that when you click another object (the trigger), the animation starts. For example, you could click a circle to turn a star purple, using the Change Fill Color emphasis effect. To create a trigger object, click Triggers on the Timing tab of the dialog box and choose Start Effect on Click Of. Then use the drop-down list to select one of the objects on your slide.

Click OK when you have finished setting the timing. A triggered animation displays the icon shown here.

Add a Sound, Dim Objects, and Set Text Options

To specify settings for an animation not related to timing, select the animated object and click its drop-down arrow in the Custom Animation task pane's listing. Choose Effect Options to open the Effect tab of the dialog box for the particular animation you have set, as shown in Figure 9-6.

The Settings section of the dialog box is available for only certain effects. As shown in Figure 9-6, the Spin animation effect offers you the opportunity to specify the amount of the spin and whether the spin is clockwise or counterclockwise. A number of animation effects let you create a smooth start and smooth end, by checking the appropriate check boxes in the dialog box. A smooth start slows the acceleration of the effect and a smooth end slows its deceleration. Check Auto-reverse to play the effect backward after it has finished, doubling the total time of the effect.

FIGURE 9-6   The Effect tab of the Spin dialog box lets you refine the Spin animation effect. Similar dialog boxes let you specify settings of all the other animation effects.

The Enhancements section of the dialog box for each effect lets you do the following:

■ Add sound

■ Dim the object after animation

■ Animate text all at once, by word, or by letter

Sound is especially useful for presentations that run automatically, without a presenter, such as presentations used at kiosks and trade shows. Chapter 10 explains how to add music, CD soundtracks, and narration to a presentation.

PowerPoint comes with a few sound effects, such as applause, a drum roll, or a cash register. These sounds tend to have a humorous effect, which is fine if that's what you want. For a presentation given by a real person, sound effects tend to distract from the presenter. They can also be annoying. The first and last slides are two places where sound can be useful. For example, you might want music to be playing as the audience trickles in before the presentation or as they leave after the last slide (if you won't be taking questions). A drum roll on the first slide can get your audience's attention in a humorous way—but leave it at that. PowerPoint can play any WAV sound file attached to a transition or animation effect.

TIP *Use the Windows Find feature (Start | Find | Files or Folders) to search for WAV files on your hard disk or network.*

9

To add a sound to an animation, use the Sound drop-down list on the Effect tab of the animation dialog box. (See Figure 9-6.) Choose Other Sound to search for sound files on your hard disk or network. When you have chosen a sound, click OK to close the animation dialog box.

Dimming text after animation is especially effective in focusing your audience's attention on the current point. You can dim to a lighter color, hide the object completely immediately after the animation (which doesn't leave it on the screen for very long), or hide it on the next mouse click. Just as your audience can wander ahead of you when all the text is visible at once, your audience may start thinking about the points you just finished if they are still clearly visible on the slide. While bulleted text is most often dimmed, you can also dim other objects on a slide, such as AutoShapes.

TIP *Dim to a softer, lighter color to emphasize your current point so that the previous items are still visible enough to discuss if someone in the audience asks a question about a previous point. Don't dim when your slide contains an entire process that your audience needs to see as a whole.*

To dim an object, click the After Animation drop-down list on the Effect tab and use the menu shown here. Choose a dimming color or one of the hide options—After Animation or On Next Mouse Click. Then click OK.

Figure 9-7 shows a slide that is animated with a dim to a lighter color. All the bulleted items are still visible, but the current item is much more obvious.

Finally, in the animation effect dialog box (see Figure 9-6), you can specify how text is animated. From the Animate Text drop-down list, choose to animate text all at once (the entire paragraph), by word, or by letter. If you choose to animate by word or letter, specify the speed by setting the delay between words or letters.

When you are animating text, the animation effect dialog box includes a Text Animation tab, shown in Figure 9-8.

Use the Group Text drop-down list to specify how text is grouped when animated. For example, you can animate text As One Object (the entire text placeholder), By 1st Level Paragraphs (the most common choice), By 2nd Level Paragraphs, and so on. In addition, you can use the following settings:

- **Automatically After *x* Seconds**   Set animation to occur automatically after the number of seconds you specify.

- **Animate Attached Shape**   Animate the shape with the text, if the text is in an AutoShape and you select the shape when specifying the animation.

- **In Reverse Order**   Animate the text from the bottom up.

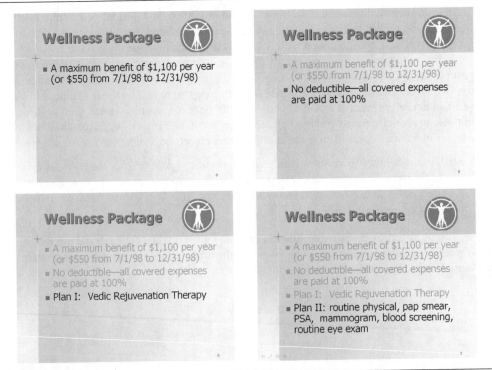

FIGURE 9-7   Dimming previously animated text helps to focus your audience's attention on the current point.

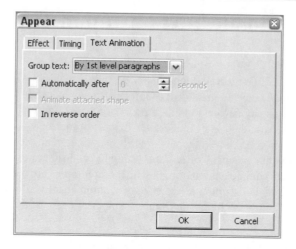

FIGURE 9-8   The Text Animation tab offers additional options for animating text.

9

When you're done with the settings, click OK to return to your slide.

Edit Animation

You may need to remove or change animation. When you are animating more than one object, you may also want to change the order of animation. You can perform any of the following tasks:

- **Remove animation**   Select the animated object and click Remove in the Custom Animation task pane.

- **Change animation effect**   Select the animation from the animation list in the Custom Animation task pane. (Do not select the object.) Click Change and choose a new animation.

- **Change animation timing or options**   Select the animation from the animation list in the Custom Animation task pane. From the drop-down list, choose Timing or Effect Options and make the desired changes in the dialog box. Click OK.

- **Change animation order**   Select the animation from the animation list. Click the up or down Re-Order arrow that is beneath the animation list.

- **Edit animation path**   If you draw a custom path, you can edit it. Select the animation from the animation list in the Custom Animation task pane. From the Path drop-down list, choose Edit Points. You see small squares along the path, which you can drag to a new location. Right click the path and choose Add Point to add a new point or choose Delete Point to delete a point.

Animation can be a major influence in a presentation that is not meant to tell a simple story but instead used to create a visual impression. For example, some presentations are used as an

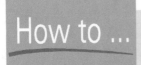 **Animate Text on Top of Text**

An interesting use of the Hide on Next Mouse Click feature, one of the After Animation options, is to enable you to cover a great deal of information on one slide. This technique lets you hide text and then display new text in the same location as the previous text, which is now invisible. You get to use the same "real estate" twice—or more.

Figure 9-9 shows a portion of a slide that uses this technique. The presenter wanted to discuss the products that his company offers, and wanted to add subtopics for each product. This slide includes some complex animation, in which major topics are animated on the presenter's mouse click and the subtopics are displayed automatically afterwards, and then hidden. See if you can follow the frames in Figure 9-9 to get a sense of the flow of the slide.

impetus for a subsequent workshop or brainstorming session. In these cases, you want to excite or inspire your audience, rather than systematically move from text item to item.

Figure 9-10 shows a presentation on one of Sharp Electronics' projectors. While it provides information, there is no bulleted text in the entire presentation. The word "introducing" flies in from top left, "a compact projector" flies in from top right, "with a" flies in from bottom left,

FIGURE 9-9   This slide uses the Hide on Next Mouse Click feature to display subtopics that could not otherwise fit on the slide.

FIGURE 9-10	Presentations can use animation to excite and inspire the audience. *Thanks to Gerry Ganguzza of Sharp Electronics Corporation*, http://www.sharp-usa.com, *for this presentation.*

and "high IQ" flies in from bottom right. The purpose of the presentation is to excite potential customers about a new product. In other words, this is advertising. Although you can't see the actual animation in the figure, you can get an idea of how the first slide presents the material. This presentation is meant to run automatically, with preset timing.

Animate Charts and Diagrams

You can animate a chart created within PowerPoint or with Microsoft Excel. As with other objects, animating a chart can help to focus your audience's attention on a specific portion of the chart. Because charts often represent growth over time, building the chart over several steps is appropriate. You can animate a chart in the following ways (refer to the chart that follows the list):

- ■ **All at Once**   The entire chart appears at once with the animation effect.
- ■ **By Series**   For a chart with more than one series (for example, your chart shows sales for both nuts and bolts), first one series appears, then the next, and so on, with the animation effect. All of the elements of the series (the breakdown by years) appear together as a group. Use this when you want to discuss each series separately.
- ■ **By Category**   Each category (for example, each year is a category) appears together. Use this option when you want to discuss the chart year by year.

- **By Element in Series**   This option breaks down the animation by each element in each series.
- **By Element in Category**   The elements of each category appear in order.

These options will not all be available if your chart doesn't contain all these features. For example, a simple pie chart will have only the All at Once and the By Category options.

If these options aren't enough for you and you must animate a chart in more detail, you can ungroup the chart. You can then animate each individual object as you wish. But beware, ungrouping a chart turns it into an Office drawing object, and it loses its connection with the underlying data. Also, any link to another file is severed. Another disadvantage is that you will probably end up with more objects than you want to deal with. But you *can* do it!

TIP   *If you want to ungroup a chart, first duplicate the slide and hide it. (See the "Create Slide Show Variations" section in Chapter 14 for instructions on hiding a slide.) An alternative is to duplicate the chart itself and drag the original off the slide area.*

To animate a chart, follow these steps:

1. Select the chart.
2. Open the Custom Animation task pane.
3. Click Add Effect and choose an animation effect. A typical choice would be Entrance | Wipe.
4. Choose the animation from the task pane's listing and choose Effect Options.
5. In the Direction section of the Effect tab, specify any settings. For example, you often want column charts to wipe from the bottom, so the column appears to grow up to its full height.
6. On the Chart Animation tab, choose an option from the Group Chart drop-down list. If you want each column to wipe up separately, try the By Element in Series option.

7. Uncheck Animate Grid and Legend if you don't want to animate these parts of the chart.

8. Click OK.

9. Click Slide Show in the Custom Animation task pane and check out the animation. Make any adjustments you think are necessary. For example, you may want to change the speed of the animation from the Speed drop-down list in the task pane.

You can animate other objects now. For example, in the chart shown in the previous illustration, after the columns appear with the Wipe Up effect, the arrow showing the percent increase wipes to the right. You can animate diagrams and organization charts like a chart. Instead of a Chart Animation tab in the dialog box (see step 6 in the previous procedure), there is a Diagram Animation tab.

NOTE   *When a composite object like a chart or diagram is animated, the listing in the Custom Animation task pane is sometimes collapsed. Click the double down arrow below the list to expand the list and see all its components.*

Add Animated GIF Files

Animated GIF files are graphics files that include animation. You see them often on web sites. You can easily download them from many web sites that offer free web graphics. Try a search in your favorite search engine for "free animated gif."

Among the more useful animated GIFs are animated bullets. However, be aware that, like sound, the effect will usually be humorous. If you want to use animated GIFs in a business presentation, keep it low key. You may be able to take an animated logo from your company's web site. Perhaps you could draw attention to one especially noteworthy or exciting item with an animated arrow. Too many animated GIFs make a presentation look like a cartoon.

You insert an animated GIF like any image. Follow these steps:

1. Display the slide to which you want to add the animated GIF.

2. To insert an animated GIF from a file, choose Insert | Picture | From File. Then navigate to the file, select it, and choose Insert.

3. To insert an animated GIF from the Clip Gallery, choose Insert | Picture | Clip Art or click Insert Clip Art on the Drawing toolbar. (For information on adding graphic files to the Clip Gallery, see Chapter 5.)

Animated GIFs move only in Slide Show view. In Normal or Slide Sorter view, they are frozen. You cannot edit an animated GIF image with the Picture toolbar in PowerPoint. To edit an animated GIF, you need an animated GIF editing program.

Add Flash Animation to a Slide

Macromedia Flash is an animation program that is usually used on web sites. Flash's capabilities are far beyond PowerPoint's. You can add Flash animation to any slide fairly easily to create any sophisticated effect you wish. If you wish to learn an advanced technique for creating animation, try this one out.

9

First, you need to create the Flash movie using Flash. The file you create has an .fla extension. However, you need to publish the movie, using the Publish command in Flash. The result is a movie file with an extension of .swf. You use the SWF file in PowerPoint. To view the results, you need the Flash Player. You probably already have it on your computer, but if not, it's a free download at www.macromedia.com/shockwave/download/index.cgi?P1_Prod_Version=ShockwaveFlash. Here are the steps:

1. Write down the location of the SWF file you want to use.

2. Choose View | Toolbars | Control Toolbox.

3. Click the Hammer button (More Controls).

4. Choose Shockwave Flash Object from the listing.

5. Drag a box across the screen to get the desired size and location. Don't cover the entire slide.

6. Right-click the box and choose Properties.

7. In the Properties window, click the top line, Custom. Then click the ellipsis at the right.

8. In the Property Pages dialog box, type the location of the SWF file that you wrote down earlier. Use the full path, for example, c:\animation\animlogo.swf.

9. Set the other parameters if you wish, for example, Quality: Best; Scale: Show All; Window: Window. Check Loop if you want the movie to continuously replay itself.

10. Click Embed Movie if you want to make sure the movie is always included with the PowerPoint presentation.

11. Click OK.

12. Close the Properties window using its close box.

13. Choose Slide Show view to see the movie. If your movie didn't appear on the slide in Normal view, it will appear when you return to Normal view after running the slide show.

You cannot create the Flash movie the full size of the slide because PowerPoint doesn't recognize mouse clicks on top of the Flash movie. So you need some blank space on the slide so you can click to the next slide. You can match the movie background to the background of your PowerPoint slide. Use a one-color background on your PowerPoint slide. In Flash, choose Modify | Movie (or Document, depending on the version of Flash) to change the background before publishing your movie and choose the same color as your PowerPoint slide.

If the Flash movie doesn't play, open the Properties window again and look at the Playing property. If it says False, click Playing, click the down arrow, and change the Playing property to True. Flash movies placed on the slide master will play continuously from slide to slide to create an animated background. (But that can get distracting.)

There is a bug that automatically changes the Playing property to False if the Flash movie is not set to loop. In this situation, the Flash movie simply does not play. Two solutions are helpful:

■ **Save the presentation as a PowerPoint show**   Reset the Playing property of the SWF file(s) to True: select the Shockwave Flash object, right-click it, and choose Properties. Click the Playing row, then click the down arrow and choose True. Then choose File |

Save As. From the Save as Type drop-down list, choose PowerPoint Show (*.pps). Keep the same filename and click Save. (A PowerPoint show automatically plays in Slide Show view when you open it.)

■ **Create Visual Basic for Applications (VBA) code to control the Playing property** On the Control Toolbox toolbar, click the View Code button or press ALT-F11. The Microsoft Visual Basic window opens. Choose Insert | Module. In the main window, enter the following code, where the number after ActivePresentation.Slides is the number of the slide containing the Flash movie. (The fourth and fifth lines are split here in the book, but you should type them on one line in the Visual Basic window.)

```
Sub OnSlideShowPageChange()
  Dim obj As ShockwaveFlash

  On Error Resume Next

  Set obj = ActivePresentation.Slides(2). _
    Shapes("ShockwaveFlash1").OLEFormat.Object
  obj.Playing = True
  obj.Rewind
  obj.Play

  Set obj = Nothing

End Sub
```

As you can see, the code simply sets the Playing property to True, rewinds the movie, and plays it. Even with this code, you may need to open the PowerPoint presentation from scratch for the Flash animation to play.

If you want more than one Flash movie in a presentation, you need to give additional movies unique shape names to replace ("ShockwaveFlash1") in the code. The second one could be "ShockwaveFlash2" for example. Then, in the Properties window, give the object the same name in the Name row (which is just under the Custom row).

NOTE *For more information see http://www.ellenfinkelstein.com/powerpoint_tip.html#flash, www.indezine.com/products/powerpoint/ppflash.html, and www.indezine.com/products/powerpoint/ppflash2.html.*

Transition from Slide to Slide

Another type of animation controls how each new slide appears. Because these effects control the transition from one slide to another, they are called *transitions*. While some of these effects have the same names as animations, they look quite different when applied to an entire slide.

Use Transitions Wisely

Transitions, like slide animation, need to be used with reserve. Many options are available, but that doesn't mean you should use them all in one presentation. One of the best solutions is to choose a simple transition and apply it to every slide in the presentation. If your presentation is divided into sections, you could use a second transition to introduce each new section.

Choose the Ideal Transition Style

The ideal transition style heightens your audience's attention without your audience noticing why. If the transition style is too active, your audience will get a headache looking at it. PowerPoint offers a transition style for every possible purpose.

You may want to set transitions in Slide Sorter view where you can get a sense of the flow of the entire presentation. PowerPoint places an Animation icon beneath each slide with a transition so you can easily see which slides have transitions and which don't. However, you can add transitions in Normal view.

When you add a transition to a slide, the transition determines how that slide appears after the previous slide is removed from view.

To add a transition, follow these steps:

1. Select the slide or slides to which you want to add a transition.

2. Choose Transition on the Slide Sorter toolbar to open the Slide Transition task pane, shown in Figure 9-11.

3. Choose a transition style from the list at the top of the task pane.

4. From the Speed drop-down list, choose Fast, Medium, or Slow.

5. From the Sound drop-down list, choose a sound if you wish. If you want the sound to be continuous, choose Loop Until Next Sound.

CAUTION   *Adding a sound to each slide transition can get very annoying. It can work for a self-playing presentation or else at the beginning or end of a presentation.*

6. In the Advance Slide section of the task pane, choose whether you want slides to advance on a mouse click, automatically after a specified number of seconds, or both. If you want to use automatic timing, it's a good idea to keep the On Mouse Click option checked as well.

CAUTION   *If On Mouse Click is not checked, your mouse will not work while you present! (You can still use the keyboard.) As a result, you should keep this box checked even if you also check the Automatically After check box.*

7. Click Apply to All Slides if you want to apply the transition to the entire presentation. Otherwise, the transition you chose (in step 3) is applied only to selected slides.

FIGURE 9-11   Use the Slide Transition task pane to create transitions from slide to slide.

TIP   *As you click a slide, the Slide Transition task pane highlights the slide's transition.*

You can view transitions in three ways:

 ■ In Slide Sorter view, click the Animation icon, shown here. (You see animation for the slide as well as the transition.)

Use Animations and Transitions Effectively

When presentation software programs introduced movement into their feature sets, it became the best of times and the worst of times. It's not enough to animate objects because you can; your audiences simply grow weary of the gratuitous use of any presentation element. The first time you animate some clip art, it gets a few oohs and aahs; the second and third time, some yawns. The flying objects appear to be nothing more than a multimedia shell game, causing audiences to wonder under which presentation component the real message resides.

That said, the proper use of movement can have a profoundly positive effect on how your audiences grasp, interpret, and retain your key messages. You can make a busy chart significantly easier to understand by introducing the content in animated stages. Mirroring how the presenter addresses the information (quarter by quarter or category by category) is essential in making the point.

Text-based information creates its own inherent challenges. When given a chance to read ahead, the audience is more likely to make quick judgments. By staging the bullets to enter on a mouse click, you get an opportunity to articulate the points before judgment is passed, providing the best chance of the audience staying with the flow of information.

The challenge in creating a quality presentation is to identify opportunities for making text-type information more graphical and introducing it in a way that best supports your needs. This could be processes, steps, chronologies, or other similar topics.

Transition effects fall into the same category. Presentation software provides many more options than will ever be appropriate. Look at transition effects as a tool for guiding the audience's eye or creating interest. For example, you could use a Wipe Up effect to guide the eye back to the top after each slide, or possibly a Wipe Left effect to reset the eye for more information. Pick a specific nondistracting transition and stick with it. Sort through the choices, eliminate those that fall into the cute category (audiences grow weary of "cute" very quickly), and throw in a change-up once in a while. Introducing a new topic in the presentation may be a time to box out a transition and then get back into your standard transition effect.

Let's face it: animations and transitions are just electronic effects. A wise presenter realizes that the stage lights don't make good presenters—compelling stories do.

Thanks to Jim Endicott, who is owner/manager of Distinction, a business communications company that provides creative and consulting support services. He assists business professionals in enhancing the content, tools, and techniques of effective presenting. Jim regularly writes articles for Presentations magazine. He can be reached at 503-554-1203 or jim.endicott@distinction-services.com.

■ Select a slide or slides and click Play in the Slide Transition task pane. You see both animation and transition effects.

■   In Slide Show view, view the presentation.

To remove a transition, select the slide or slides you want to work with and choose No Transition from the list in the Slide Transition task pane. To remove a sound, choose No Sound in the Sound drop-down list.

Summary

In this chapter, you learned how to animate text and objects on a slide, both to help focus your audience's attention on what you're saying and to add interest and excitement to a presentation. Animation options include building text and objects with various effects, dimming or hiding objects after animation, and adding WAV sound effects. PowerPoint 2002 has added many new animation effects. You can also add animated GIF files to a slide.

And you can add transitions from slide to slide for a professional effect. PowerPoint offers many transition effects to choose from. For both animation and transitions, the main principle is to keep it simple.

In the next chapter, I explain how to add more sophisticated sounds as well as music to your presentation. In addition, I cover using a CD soundtrack, video clips, and narration.

9

Chapter 10

Use Multimedia

How to…

- Add sounds and music
- Use media clips
- Play a CD soundtrack throughout a presentation
- Show movies with video clips
- Record narration

More and more, multimedia effects are showing up in PowerPoint. While PowerPoint does not yet offer the flexibility of creating a full-fledged video or movie, you can add some of the same features. You can add sounds, music, or CD soundtracks to your presentations. You can use short sounds with any presentation, but continuous music or soundtracks work best for unattended presentations, where the music doesn't compete with the presenter. For a self-running presentation, music can add a professional effect.

In addition, you can insert video clips onto a slide to be shown at any time during a presentation. They don't turn your presentation into a video but add the element of video where the static quality of a slide is not enough. These video clips are usually quite short—less than a minute—but they pack quite an impact.

For self-running presentations, you can record narration. Narration replaces what you would say if you were making the presentation and is appropriate whenever viewers will see a presentation on their own. As with music, the effect of the narration adds a professional quality to your presentation.

With Microsoft Producer, a free download from Microsoft, you can create multimedia creations that include presentations, still images, video, and audio. You can synchronize the audio with the images or presentation and play the resulting show in your browser or on the Internet.

Create a Mood with Sounds and Music

When you stand in front of an audience, you generally want the audience to pay attention to *you*. You talk, which is probably the best sound effect your presentation can have. But when you create a self-running presentation for a kiosk or the floor of a trade show, you often need to replace your words with some type of sound, music, or narration. Music, especially, creates a mood that can add a lot to the overall impression of your presentation. You've probably heard of research done by retailers showing that music played in stores increases sales. Music can have a powerful effect on your presentation because music has an emotional effect on people. Of course, you need to choose appropriate music for your message. In this section, I explain how to add sound and music to a presentation. In the "Record Narration" section later in this chapter, I explain how to add narration to a presentation. (Chapter 15 explains how to create a self-running presentation.)

Insert Sound or Music Files

In Chapter 9, I explained how to add WAV sound files to animation and transitions. For more options, you can insert a music or sound file into your presentation. You have more file type options when you use this method. Table 10-1 lists the most commonly used sound formats that you can insert into a presentation.

Filename Extension	Description
.aif, .aiff., .aifc	Audio Interchange File Format, developed by Apple, allowing for various sampling rates, sample size, and number of channels. An .aifc file is an AIFF, but compressed.
.mid, .midi, .rmi	Musical Instrument Digital Interface, primarily for musical instruments.
.mp3	Moving Picture Experts Group. Can achieve high rates of compression without a noticeable decrease in quality.
.wav	Windows WAVE format. Specifies an arbitrary sampling rate, number of channels, and sample size. It also specifies a number of application-specific blocks within the file. Has many different compression formats.
.wma, .wax, .asf	Windows Media Audio files provide quality comparable to .mp3 at nearly half the file size.

TABLE 10-1   Common Sound File Types

When you insert a sound file, PowerPoint places an icon on the slide. The music or sound can be set to play automatically or only when you click its icon. Here's how to insert music or sound on a slide:

1. Display the slide you want to add the sound or music to.

2. Choose Insert | Movies and Sounds.

3. On the submenu, choose either Sound from Clip Organizer or Sound from File.

   ■ If you choose Sound from Clip Organizer, you see the Insert Clip Art task pane. You can choose from a category or type in a keyword to locate a sound on your system or from the Office Online service. Drag the sound you want onto the slide.

   ■ If you choose Sound from File, locate the file, choose it, and click Insert.

    PowerPoint puts a sound icon, shown here, on the slide.

4. A dialog box opens asking if you want the sound to play automatically or when you click it. Choose the option you want. If you choose to play the sound when clicked, PowerPoint creates an animation setting for the icon. You can change it by choosing Slide Show | Action Settings and changing the setting in the drop-down list. You can also modify the timing by choosing Slide Show | Custom Animation, choosing the sound in the Custom Animation task pane, and choosing Timing from its drop-down list.

TIP *If the sound is played automatically, you don't need the Sound icon on the slide. Drag it off the slide so that it is invisible to your audience.*

See Chapter 5 for instruction on adding clips to the Clip Gallery. You add sounds in the same way. Most music files come in MIDI format. You can search for music or sounds in several places:

■ Search your hard disk and network for .mid files.

■ The Windows\Media folder has additional sounds and music that you can use.

10

- Don't forget to check the Office CD-ROM.
- You can find music and sounds from the Clip Art task pane by checking Sounds from the Selected Media File Types drop-down list.
- The new Office Online web site contains a large selection of sounds. From the Clip Art task pane, click Clip Art on Office Online. There you can search for sounds by keyword and download them.

Be especially careful when searching the Web for music—much of it is copyrighted.

 If you already have a Sound icon on a slide, PowerPoint usually places a new Sound icon on top of the previous one, making it hard to find. Just select it and drag it to a new location, and you immediately see that you have two Sound icons on the slide.

You can play the sound or music at any time by double-clicking the Sound icon. Here you see a slide with a Sound icon on it. You can insert two sounds that play at the same time on a slide.

Specify Play Settings

Once you have inserted a sound or music file, you can specify how it will play. These settings give you a great deal of control over the sound in your presentation. Here are your options:

- You can play the music or sound before or after other animation on the slide.
- You can choose whether to play the music or sound automatically or when you click the mouse button.
- You can continue the presentation while the sound or music is playing, or pause it.
- You can stop the sound or music after the current slide or after any number of slides that you specify. If you specify the last slide in the presentation, the sound or music plays to the end of the presentation.

■ You can choose to start the sound or music file from the beginning again when it reaches the end, called *looping*.

■ You can hide the Sound icon before and after it plays.

To set the options for playing sound or music, select the Sound icon. Then choose Slide Show | Custom Animation to open the Custom Animation task pane. Click the down arrow for the sound in the task pane listing and choose Effect Options to open the Play Sound dialog box, shown in Figure 10-1. On the Effect tab, you can decide where you want the sound to start (from the beginning or from where it left off the last time it was played) and if you want the sound to start after a delay. You can also specify when the sound will stop playing. Finally, you can set the volume and hide the Sound icon while it is not playing. Click OK when you're done.

Your decisions will depend on whether you are playing a short sound effect or a long piece of music. Is the sound or music appropriate for just this slide, or do you want to continue it throughout part or all of the presentation?

How do you find out how long the sound or music will last? One way is to right-click the Sound icon on the slide and choose Edit Sound Object to open the Sound Options dialog box, shown here. Notice that the playing time of the sound is displayed. You now have the information you need to decide if you want to repeat the sound or music over and over. For example, if you want the music to play throughout the entire presentation and the presentation will take longer

10

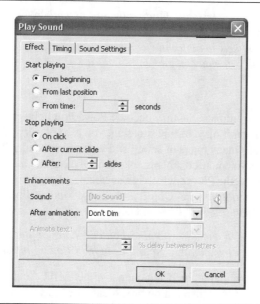

than the sound, you may want to loop it. (Don't forget to check out the result to see how it sounds.) Check the Loop Until Stopped check box and click OK.

Another way to check the timing of a sound is to display the timeline. Choose any sound from the Custom Animation task pane's listing and click its drop-down arrow. Choose Show Advanced Timeline. Then click Play at the bottom of the taskbar and watch the timeline pass by, showing seconds as the sound plays.

TIP *You can set a sound or music file to play when you simply pass the mouse cursor over the icon, without requiring a mouse click. Instead of using the Custom Animation task pane, choose Slide Show | Action Settings to open the Action Settings dialog box. (This dialog box is covered in detail in Chapter 11.) On the Mouse Over tab, check Object Action and choose Play. Instead of hiding the object while not playing it, you can format it with the same background color as your slide and hide most of it behind another object. Your audience is unlikely to notice the icon and if you set it to play on a mouse over, your audience will think you made magic!*

Use Media Clips

When you insert sound files onto a slide, they become PowerPoint objects. Sometimes you might have a file that PowerPoint can't play. In this situation, you can try using Media Player, a basic Windows program that plays many types of sound and video files. Media Player can play CD and videodisk music, and it offers you more control over playback of the sound file. Media Player shouldn't be confused with Windows Media Player, which is a separate and more complex program.

To insert a media clip, choose Insert | Object and choose Media Clip from the Insert Object dialog box. Leave Create New selected. Choose OK.

SHORTCUT *Use a slide layout with a media clip placeholder. Choose a file by double-clicking the placeholder. You can immediately go to files in the Clip Organizer using this method.*

Choose Insert Clip on the menu bar. Then choose either MIDI Sequencer (usually .mid files) or Sound (.wav files). In the Open dialog box, locate the file you want to insert and choose Open. PowerPoint reduces the size of the icon, and your screen now looks like Figure 10-2. (This figure shows the MIDI Sequencer icon. The Sound icon is different.) You can now try out the sound or music.

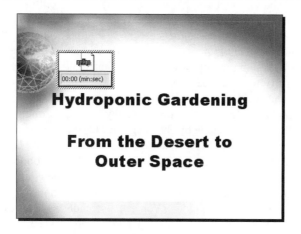

Hydroponic Gardening

From the Desert to Outer Space

![FIGURE 10-2]   You can insert media clip objects into your presentation.

Media Player works like a tape recorder. You can play, pause, stop, rewind, and fast forward. To play a portion of a multimedia file, called a *selection,* click at the starting point you want on the timeline and click Start Selection. Then click at the desired end of the selection and click End Selection. This edits out any portion of the file not within the selection.

The Media Clip window also tells you how long the clip is. Use this information to decide if you want to repeat the clip over and over. To set options for playing media clips, double-click the media clip object to open it and choose Edit | Options on the Media Clip menu to open the Options dialog box, shown here.

To automatically rewind the file, choose Auto Rewind. To automatically repeat the file (loop it), choose Auto Repeat. Click OK.

If you check Control Bar on Playback, Media Player displays a control bar with Play/Pause and Stop buttons while playing the sound or music. Leave this box unchecked to make the controls of the sound or music transparent to your audience.

Check Play in Client Document to play the file directly within PowerPoint without showing the Media Player controls. Playing the file within PowerPoint avoids showing your audience the source of the file and results in a smoother presentation.

You can also insert a media clip file into a document by copying it to the clipboard. You might want to do this when you have Media Player open to copy more than one file at once into a presentation. In Media Player, open the file by choosing File | Open, locating the file, and clicking Open. Set the options for playing the file as just described. Choose Edit | Copy Object. In your presentation, display the slide where you want the file and click Paste on the Standard toolbar.

Once you have closed Media Player, you can play the file by double-clicking its icon or frame. If you want to change some of the settings, right-click the icon and choose Media Clip Object | Open to open Media Clip as a separate window. You can also choose Media Clip Object | Edit to open Media Clip within PowerPoint. In that case, when you have finished specifying the settings you want, just click elsewhere in your slide to return to PowerPoint.

During a presentation, in Slide Show view, click the Media Clip icon to play the file. It changes color when you play it. If you choose Hide While Not Playing in the Play Sound dialog box (as explained in the "Specify Play Settings" section earlier in this chapter), and place the icon in a location whose color is similar to the media clip's color during playback, the icon will be barely visible. This type of technique hides the mechanics behind the playing of the media clip for a smoother-looking presentation.

> **TIP** *For a thorough discussion of PowerPoint and sound, go to http://www.indezine.com/ products/powerpoint/ppsound.html.*

Add a CD Soundtrack

As you may know, you can play an audio CD in your CD-ROM drive. Just put the CD in the drive, and it will start playing automatically. The controls available depend on which software you have installed on your computer.

You can insert a CD audio track on a slide. The sound that you'll get will be much superior to either WAV or MIDI files, for a more professional result. Like with other electronic files, be careful about copyright issues when using a CD audio track. Inserting a CD audio track is like inserting any sound. Follow these steps:

1. Display the slide on which you want to place the CD audio track.

2. Choose Insert | Movies and Sounds | Play CD Audio Track.

3. In the Insert CD Audio dialog box, shown here, set the options you want for playing the CD audio track.

4. You can choose to loop the CD until it is stopped. You can also specify the exact tracks with minutes and seconds that you want to play. You can generally find this information on the CD itself. Be sure to change the End Track setting. If you leave it at 1, PowerPoint stops and ends the play in the same place—that is, it doesn't play anything. To play the first track, start at track 1 and end at track 2.

5. PowerPoint asks if you want the CD to play automatically or when clicked when you display the slide. Choose the option you want.

PowerPoint places a CD icon on the slide. To listen to the CD audio track in Normal view, double-click the CD icon. Don't forget that you need to put the CD in your CD-ROM drive. If you are traveling, remember to take the CD with you!

You can change the play settings that you created:

■ To change the tracks you want to play or the looping setting, right-click the CD icon and choose Edit Sound Object.

■ To change when and how the music starts and stops, open the Custom Animation taskbar (Slide Show | Custom Animation) and click the sound object in the listing. Choose Effect Options. The Play Sound dialog box opens, shown in Figure 10-1.

Test your settings in Slide Show view to make sure you like the results.

NOTE *PowerPoint only remembers the track, not the actual CD. Therefore, if you set the options to play track 1, your presentation will play track 1 of whichever CD you place in your CD-ROM drive.*

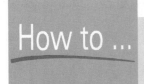 **Insert an AutoCAD Drawing into PowerPoint**

If you use technical drawings (CAD drawings), you can now put an AutoCAD drawing directly into PowerPoint. AutoCAD is the most widely used technical drawing (CAD) program in the world. Incredibly, with Autodesk Express Viewer (AEV), Autodesk's viewer (a free download from Autodesk at http://usa.autodesk.com/adsk/servlet/index?id=2787358& siteID=123112), you can zoom in and out and pan around the drawing to show the entire drawing in detail, all from within your PowerPoint presentation. First, you need to turn the AutoCAD drawing into DWF format using the PUBLISH command. These instructions were tested using AutoCAD 2004.

Here are the steps:

1. Create the DWF file.

2. In PowerPoint, choose a slide layout that gives you room for the DWF file.

3. Choose Insert | Object.

4. Click Create New and then choose Autodesk Express Viewer Control. Click OK. You see a box with handles on your slide.

5. If you want, resize or move the box. (If you deselect the box, it disappears. Click inside the box to select it again.)

6. Right-click the box and choose Autodesk Express Viewer Control Objects | Properties.

7. In the Autodesk Express Viewer Control Properties dialog box, on the SourcePath tab, type the path to the DWF file or click browse to browse to the file.

8. In your PowerPoint presentation, click the Slide Show View button to enter Slide Show view. You can now pan, zoom, and print from within your presentation.

This could make for a very nice presentation, zooming in and out to show the drawing. It's certainly more than you can do with a JPEG or any other static image format.

TIP   *For instructions on adding SVG (Scalable Vector Graphics) into PowerPoint, see http://www.indezine.com/products/powerpoint/ppsvg.html; for Macromedia Director, see http://www.indezine.com/products/powerpoint/ppdirector.html and http://www.indezine .com/products/powerpoint/ppdirector2.html; for QTVR/QuickTime, see http://www.indezine .com/products/powerpoint/ppqtvr.html.*

Show Movies with Video Clips

You can also play video clips in your presentations. Video clips are usually AVI or MPG (.mpeg, .mpe, or .mpg) files—electronic movies. They are usually videos of live scenes but can also be animated. Examples of videos you might use in a presentation are a short message from your CEO, a demonstration of a product, an example of how a product is produced, or a testimonial of a customer. Most videos should be custom-made to suit your needs. There are three ways to create a live video clip:

- ■ Internet video-camera kits let you record a video while sitting in front of your PC. They're intended mostly for sending videos of yourself while calling someone over the Internet. They include a small camera with a built-in microphone that you place on top of your monitor, facing you, and software to record the video into a digital file format. Prices range from under $100 to about $200.

- ■ You can use a video capture device that captures analog videos created with a video camera or camcorder and converts them into digital format. You need both an analog capture card (hardware that you insert in your computer) and software to transfer the video onto your hard disk. The software also compresses the video files, which is generally important because they quickly grow to an unmanageable size.

- ■ You can create a video with a digital camcorder, which is like a digital camera except that it creates videos instead of photographs. Canon, Sony, Hitachi, and Sharp, among others, make these camcorders, which are quite expensive. Even some digital cameras can record video clips. Just make sure you can end up with AVI, WMV, or MPG format. You still need an IEEE 1394 port in your computer, whether built-in or on an expansion card (hardware that you insert in your computer).

You may do none of the above and instead look for a professional service bureau that specializes in creating business or educational videos. To look on the Web, use a search engine to search for "digital video" and "service bureau." If you already have a video that you want to use, you can convert it yourself using one of the video capture devices or ask a service bureau to convert it for you. Be sure to explain that you want the video for insertion into a PowerPoint presentation.

Video capturing software transfers the video to your computer. Your video capture card may come with this software. Video editing software may include capturing features. You also use video editing software to edit the video, including trimming unnecessary frames or more elaborate effects. Finally, you export the files into a video format that PowerPoint can use, such as MPEG or AVI. Windows versions since Windows ME include the free Windows Movie Maker that can combine video and still images, add effects, and output a WMV video file.

Video clips are typically compressed because without compression, they are too large to store. There are many types of compression, called *codecs* (which stands for compression/decompression). The beauty of codecs is that they decompress your video on the fly and then display it. Once you have the video, you can add it to the Clip Gallery. See Chapter 5 for instructions.

To insert a video on a slide, follow these steps:

1. Display the slide.

2. Choose Insert | Movies and Sounds.

3. Choose Movie from Gallery if the video clip is in the Clip Gallery. Then locate the file you want, click it, and choose Insert Clip. Otherwise, choose Movie from File, locate the file, choose it, and click Open.

4. PowerPoint asks you if you want the movie to play automatically or when clicked. Choose the option you want.

You see the first frame of the video on your slide, as shown here. Once you have inserted the movie, you can watch it by double-clicking it.

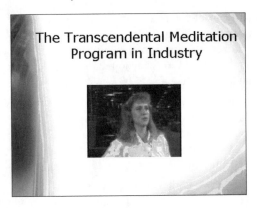

Thanks to Tom Carlisle of Maharishi Institute of Management for this animated video clip.

Note that if PowerPoint doesn't recognize the codec used by your video clip, you may still be able to insert it by choosing Insert | Object and choosing a different video player application. You can also use an AutoLayout that includes a video clip to insert a video.

A new feature of PowerPoint 2003 expands video to cover your entire slide. However, you generally lose resolution and the video can look grainy, unless your movie is already high resolution. To expand video to full screen and specify other play settings, right-click the movie and choose Edit Movie Object from the shortcut menu to open the Movie Options dialog box, shown here. You can

- Loop the movie to play it over and over
- Rewind the video, useful if you might play it more than once during a presentation
- Hide the movie when it is not playing
- Zoom the movie to full screen

Click OK when you are done.

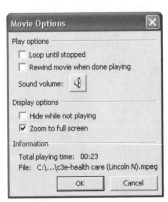

You can adjust the video clip for the resolution of your screen. This task is especially important if you are creating your presentation on a desktop with 1024×768 resolution but presenting it on a laptop with 800×600 resolution, for example. Follow these steps:

1. Select the video object.

2. Choose Format | Picture to open the Format Picture dialog box.

3. Choose the Size tab.

4. Check the Best Scale for Slide Show box. This box scales any picture to the best scale for your screen's resolution. Then choose the proper resolution from the resolution drop-down box.

5. Click OK.

Did you know?

Online Video Resources

When you start to use video, you'll need to collect resources for both hardware and software, especially if you want to create your own clips. Sources for video hardware include the following:

- **Pinnacle Systems**   http://www.pinnaclesys.com
- **Matrox Video Products Group**   http://www.matrox.com
- **Dazzle Multimedia**   http://www.dazzle.com/main.html

These are some of the video editing applications currently available:

- **Adobe Premiere**   www.adobe.com/products/premiere/main.html
- **Pinnacle Systems Studio**   http://www.pinnaclesys.com
- **Ulead Systems VideoStudio**   http://www.ulead.com/vs/runme.htm
- **Dazzle MovieStar**   http://www.dazzle.com/main.html

Other valuable resources include Cleaner 5, a highly regarded suite of tools for preparing video and audio files. It does an excellent job of compressing these files, works with most formats, and lets you convert a file from one format to another. It also provides tools for publishing your video or audio projects. For more information, go to http://www.discreet.com/products.

In addition, an excellent article on multimedia in PowerPoint is available at http://www.indezine.com/products/powerpoint/ppmultimedia.html.

10

Record Narration

For a presentation that will run unattended at a kiosk or trade show, you may want to add narration to replace what you would say if you were there. PowerPoint lets you record narration that plays when you run the presentation.

Narration can add a professional touch. The problem is that poor narration is usually worse than no narration. Unless you can sound like those announcers on the radio, you should seriously think about hiring a professional to record the narration for your presentation. Remember that an unattended presentation will play over and over again. Not only will a professional have a better-sounding voice, but he or she will likely have the use of a sound studio, professional recording equipment, and the best sound-editing software. You can contact a sound studio yourself to make the arrangements, although your narrator probably has good contacts.

If you are looking for a professional narrator, you can try doing a search on the Web—use the keywords "professional," "narrator," and "announcer." A number of individual narrators have their own web sites. You may also want to consider a professional scriptwriter. An experienced outsider can often more easily envision the point of view of your intended audience and avoid technical language that you use every day, but your audience may not understand.

You should ask for the recording in digital format, rather than on a cassette tape. (Otherwise, you need to digitize the tape yourself.) When you make arrangements for the narration, remember that you will eventually need a separate file for each slide. If necessary, you can divide the file yourself using sound-editing software, such as Creative WaveStudio that comes with some Sound Blaster sound cards. Most sound cards come with some sound-editing software.

While the exact steps depend on the software you are using, you can generally divide a file as follows:

1. Select part of the file and click Play. Do this, adjusting the amount you select, until you have the snippet you want.

2. Copy it to the clipboard.

3. Open a new file.

4. Paste the clipboard contents into the new file.

5. Save that file as slide 1, for example.

Once you have sound files for each file, you can attach them to the transition of each slide by choosing Slide Show | Slide Transition. On the Slide Transition taskbar, choose Other Sound at the bottom of the Sound drop-down list. In the Add Sound dialog box, locate and choose your sound file and click OK. PowerPoint plays the slide file.

If you do decide to record your own narration, here's the procedure:

1. Attach a microphone to the proper connector at the back of your computer, generally the Mic In or Line In connector of the sound card. You may have to check with your computer manufacturer.

TIP

A good-quality microphone will provide better results than the cheap one that probably came with your computer. You can also purchase a good preamplifier that picks up less outside sound. Plug the microphone into the preamplifier and plug the preamplifier into the Line In connector. Find a quiet place to record and get close to the microphone.

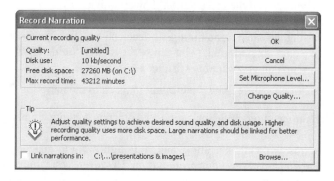

FIGURE 10-3   Start the narration process in the Record Narration dialog box.

2. Choose Slide Show | Record Narration to open the Record Narration dialog box, shown in Figure 10-3. This dialog box displays the amount of free disk space and the number of minutes you can record before using up that space.

3. Click Change Quality to open the Sound Selection dialog box, shown here.

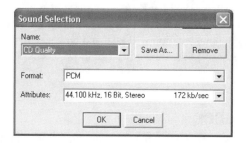

4. Choose a sound quality from the Attributes drop-down list. Then click OK. The higher the quality (CD quality is the best), the fewer minutes you can record. Sound files take up a great deal of space.

5. For the first time you record, choose Set Microphone Level and follow the directions to set the proper microphone level for recording. Click OK.

6. If you want to link narration as a separate file, check Link Narrations In and click Browse to choose the desired folder. If you use separate files, you have greater control, especially if you want to make changes in the file. Otherwise, narration is inserted on your slides as OLE (embedded) objects. Click OK.

7. PowerPoint puts you into Slide Show view automatically. Start narrating. Move through the slide show, narrating on each slide as desired. Note that other sounds do not play while you're recording. If you have other sounds in your presentation, run through the presentation afterward to make sure there are no conflicts.

10

8. When you reach the end of the presentation, PowerPoint asks you if you want to save the slide timings as well as the narration. If you save the timing, you can play the presentation automatically using the exact same timings for each slide. Click Yes to save the timings. Click No to save only the narration. (You can set or change timing later. Setting the timing for a presentation is covered in Chapter 14.)

9. Run the presentation in Slide Show view again to listen to the narration. It's a lot of fun!

In Chapter 14, I recommend recording narration as a practice technique when preparing for actual presentation.

It's easy to make a mistake while narrating, and you might want to make changes, just as you make changes to any other part of your presentation. However, you wouldn't want to have to record the entire narration over from the beginning. Because the narration for each slide is separate, you can edit existing narration. You display the first slide that you want to edit and use the regular narration procedure for the slides you want to edit. Then advance to the next slide and press ESC.

Let's say you want to redo the narration for slides 2 and 3. Display slide 2. Start narrating using the steps just previously listed. Narrate for slides 2 and 3. When you get to slide 4, press ESC.

You have the option to run the presentation without the narration if you want. For example, you might want to record narration only as a backup (when you go on vacation) for a presentation that you usually present yourself. You might also have a presentation that is sometimes run automatically and sometimes given by a presenter. Or you might record narration as a practice to see how long the presentation will take and how it will sound. To run the slide show without the narration, choose Slide Show | Set Up Show. Check Show Without Narration and click OK.

Use Microsoft Producer

Microsoft Producer 1.1 is a freely downloadable program that creates multimedia files. These files can include PowerPoint slides, still images, video, and sound. You can synchronize the sound with the slides, images, and sound. Producer can add video effects and transitions. When you are done, you can publish the production to an HTML file that you can view on a web site.

Start by downloading Microsoft Producer from Microsoft's web site. While the location was not final at the time of this writing, you should be able to download if from http://office.Microsoft.com/downloads. Choose PowerPoint as the product and look for Producer. Although the web page describes Producer as a PowerPoint add-in, it functions as a completely separate program. Follow the instructions to install the program.

Add Content to Producer

The first step is to add the content of the presentation, which includes PowerPoint slides, still images, video clips, and audio files, as shown in Figure 10-4. Before starting, you should know the location

Video   Slide

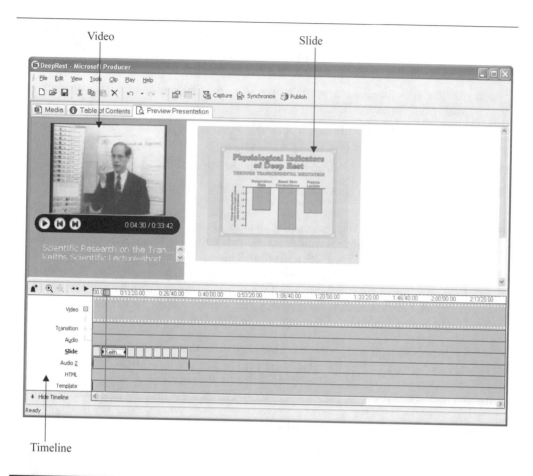

Timeline

FIGURE 10-4   This presentation contains a still image, video, the video's sound track, and music.

of the files you want to use. When you first open Producer, the Startup dialog box offers you a choice of using the New Presentation Wizard, starting a blank project, or opening an existing project.

If you use the wizard, follow the instructions for importing the elements of the presentation. To work on your own, choose to start a blank project. The first step is to add elements. Follow these steps:

1. Click the Media Tab.

2. To choose a template, click Presentation Templates from the Project Files list. Choose a template from the list that appears. A template is a configuration of video, audio, image, or slide files. If the template includes HTML, you can add an HTML file.

3. For each type of content that you want to add (video, audio, images, slides, HTML), do the following:

   ■ Choose the type from the Project Files list.

   ■ Double-click the icon that appears and choose the file you want from the Import File dialog box. Click Open.

   ■ When an icon for the file appears in Publisher, drag the icon to the appropriate track of the Timeline at the bottom of the screen.

4. To add a video effect, click Video Effects from the Project Files list.

5. To add a video transition between videos, click Video Transitions from the Project Files list.

6. If you have two or more images or slides on the Slide track of the Timeline, you can synchronize slides and images with audio and video. Choose Tools | Synchronize. In the Synchronize Slides dialog box, click Set Slide Timings. Then click the Play button to play the video and audio tracks. When you want the next slide to start, click Next Slide. Continue until you have synchronized all the slides and images with the audio and video tracks. Click Finish. You can also manually drag elements in the Timeline to change their start and ending times.

Use the Table of Contents tab to view the table of contents that will appear when you publish your presentation. Viewers can use the table of contents to navigate through the presentation. This tab also enables you to create an introduction page for the presentation.

After you have added and synchronized your elements, click the Preview Presentation tab to see the results. Click the Play button and watch your production! When you are satisfied, you are ready to publish your work to an HTML format. Follow these steps:

1. Choose File | Publish Presentation to open the Publish Wizard.

2. Choose the location for the presentation—your computer, a network location, or a web server. Click Next.

3. On the next screen, complete the specific location information, based on the choice you made in the previous screen of the wizard. Click Next.

4. On the next screen, name the file and how it should be saved. Click Next.

5. On the next screen, enter information about the presentation that is used for the introduction page. Click Next.

6. On the Playback Quality screen, choose a playback quality based on expected user Internet connection speed and/or screen resolution. If you choose more than one playback quality, Producer creates files suitable for all your choices.

7. Click Finish.

8. When the publishing process is complete, a window opens asking you if you want to view the published presentation. Click Yes to view it in your browser.

9. Click Close to close the Publish Wizard dialog box.

TIP *Take note of the address in the browser so you can easily find your presentation again later.*

Here you see the final presentation as displayed in a browser.

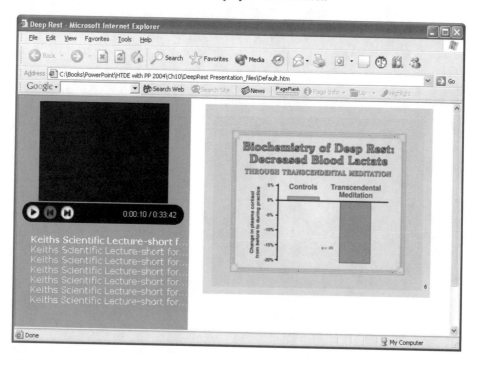

Summary

In this chapter, you learned how to add sounds, music, video, and narration to include multimedia effects in a presentation. You can use PowerPoint's sound effects, sounds or music from files, or sounds or music from the Clip Gallery. The most common type of sound and music files are WAV, MIDI, and MP3 files. You can insert on a slide a media clip object that the Media Player program can play. PowerPoint can play a CD soundtrack as well for a full-length, full-bodied sound.

You can show a small video clip on a slide. The video clip is attached to an individual slide and played when you display that slide. Video clips can add an extra dimension to a presentation, which is, in essence, mostly static.

10

You can record narration for all the slides in a presentation. Narration is usually used for self-running presentations. Your presentation will then play with that narration.

Microsoft Producer is a free program that enables you to combine slides, images, video, and sound into one synchronized presentation and then publish that presentation to an HTML file for display on the Web.

In the next chapter, I explain how to create hyperlinks, use action buttons to control your presentation, and move data in and out of PowerPoint.

Part III

Manage and Convey a Presentation

Chapter 11

Interact with Others

How to...

- Hyperlink to anywhere
- Create a web-style presentation
- Use action buttons to control your presentation
- Move data from application to application
- Collaborate with others
- Let others view your presentation without PowerPoint

These days, the whole world is interconnected. A presentation cannot stand isolated any longer. A question from the audience can create the need to access data from another presentation, another application (such as a spreadsheet), or from your company's web site. If you're making a presentation to a customer, your customer might express an interest in any number of other products you sell, and you need to be ready to provide pertinent information at a moment's notice. However, you don't want to create a huge presentation with all the possibilities and make your customer sit through everything. In this chapter, you learn how to use hyperlinks and action buttons to create the ultimately flexible presentation. You also learn how to manage data from other presentations and applications.

Add Flexibility with Hyperlinks

A *hyperlink* is a command to go to another location. That other location can be another slide in the same presentation, a slide in another presentation, a file in another application, or a location on a web site or intranet. You can even go to an e-mail address. You attach a hyperlink to an existing object—text, AutoShapes, a table, a chart, or a picture. In Slide Show view, click the hyperlink to go to the specified location. Hyperlinks are not active in Normal or Slide Sorter view.

When you attach a hyperlink to text, PowerPoint underlines the text and displays it in the accent and hyperlink color of the presentation's color scheme. When you click a text hyperlink, PowerPoint changes that text to the color designated in the color scheme for accents and followed hyperlinks. Be sure to check out how these two colors look in your presentation. They may lack the necessary contrast to show up clearly. Chapter 6 explains how to customize the colors in a color scheme.

Think of hyperlinks as a way of providing supporting information for a presentation. In the days of paper presentations, you carried along with you reams of additional data—perhaps sample swatches, price sheets, delivery schedules, and so on. Now you can include hyperlinks to the electronic versions (although nothing beats the feel of a real piece of carpet). Moreover, you can include hyperlinks to various pages on your web site to add a truly unlimited potential for information.

Create Hyperlinks

A common use for hyperlinks is to let you quickly jump around in a complex presentation. You may be able to anticipate that your audience will have additional questions on a topic when you're done. On the last slide, for example, you can provide hyperlinks back to each major section of the presentation. You can also create a custom presentation that lets you show some slides to one audience and other slides to another audience. Custom presentations are covered in Chapter 14.

Hyperlink to Another Slide in Your Presentation

To attach a hyperlink to an object that connects to a location in the current presentation, select the object to which you want to attach the hyperlink. You can choose any object or text on a slide. Then choose Insert | Hyperlink (or press CTRL-K) to open the Insert Hyperlink dialog box. In the Link To bar on the left of the dialog box, click Place in This Document to display the options shown in Figure 11-1. Choose the location you want to hyperlink to and click OK. To create a ScreenTip that appears when you place the cursor over the hyperlink object, click ScreenTip and type the text you want.

You should now switch to Slide Show view and test the hyperlink. If you selected text to create the hyperlink, make sure it is still readable in its new color, both before and after you click it, as mentioned earlier. If necessary, change the hyperlink and followed hyperlink colors in the color scheme, as explained in Chapter 6.

When you test the hyperlink, you will end up in the new location. You might wonder how you get back again. Usually you want to create a complementary hyperlink to bring you back to the original location.

There's an art to designing hyperlinks. You may want some hyperlinks to be obvious. You may wish others to be undetectable until you use them. (You may not want your potential client asking where each and every hyperlink goes to.) For example, you can place several obvious hyperlinks on a slide near the end of the presentation that simply says "Questions?" Here you pause and answer questions. You might have a series of text boxes, naming the topics you covered, hyperlinked back to those topics, as shown in Figure 11-2.

11

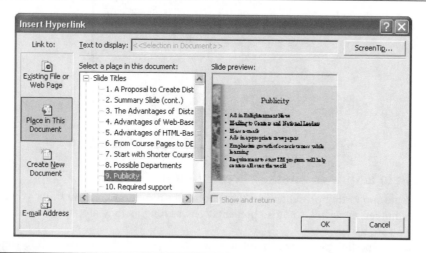

FIGURE 11-1   Use the Insert Hyperlink dialog box to create hyperlinks.

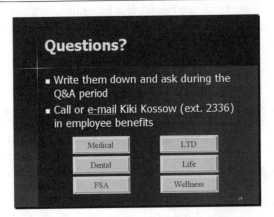

FIGURE 11-2   You can hyperlink to any slide in your presentation.

You should have hyperlinks on each of the slides to which you hyperlinked to bring you back to the Questions slide, but you wouldn't want them to be obvious because they might be distracting during the main portion of the presentation. You could therefore attach those hyperlinks to graphic objects on the slide. During the presentation, your audience would have no clue that the slides were hyperlinked until you used the hyperlinks during the question-and-answer period. In the slide shown next, the hyperlink is added to the graphic of the dentist.

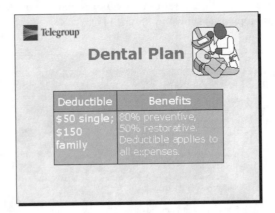

Hyperlink to a Slide in Another Presentation

You can create supporting presentations that contain information that you think you may need. You can then hyperlink to those presentations as long as they are available from the computer you are using.

To create a hyperlink to a slide in another presentation, select the text or object to which you want to attach the hyperlink. Choose Insert Hyperlink to open the Insert Hyperlink dialog box. In the Link To bar, choose Existing File or Web Page.

Choose the presentation you want to link to and click Bookmark. PowerPoint opens the Select Place in Document dialog box, shown here.

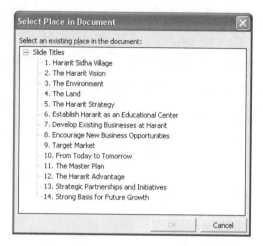

Choose the slide you want to hyperlink to and click OK. PowerPoint identifies the slides by their number and title. If your slides don't have titles, you'll need to know the slide number.

Switch to Slide Show view to test out the hyperlink. When you click the hyperlink, PowerPoint sends you to the specified slide in the other presentation. Press ESC to automatically return to your original point.

NOTE *When you hyperlink to another presentation, you can display as many slides in the presentation as you wish. Pressing ESC always brings you back to your original point in the first presentation.*

11

Hyperlink to Another File or a Web Page

You can hyperlink to any other file, even in another application. For example, you can hyperlink to a word processing document, a spreadsheet, or a CAD drawing that might contain additional details your audience may be interested in. You can also hyperlink to a web page, which is, after all, just another file.

Hyperlinking to another file or web page is similar to hyperlinking to another slide in a presentation. Follow these steps:

1. Select the object to which you want to attach the hyperlink.

2. Choose Insert | Hyperlink. (Refer to Figure 11-1 for the Insert Hyperlink dialog box.)

3. In the Link To bar, choose Existing File or Web Page.

4. Type the filename and path in the text box, choose it from the list, or click either the Browse for File or the Browse the Web button to browse to the file or web page. If you click Browse the Web, make sure you are already connected to the Internet. PowerPoint opens your browser. In your browser, locate the web page you want by typing the URL, using the Favorites/Bookmark feature, or using the list of recently visited web sites. Then switch back to PowerPoint by choosing your presentation's button on the Windows taskbar or by closing your browser. The URL is now displayed in the Address text box.

5. Click Bookmark to choose a named location in the file to which you are hyperlinking.

TIP   *The Bookmark feature does not always work. An effective workaround is to type the pound (#) character and the bookmark name after the address in the Insert Hyperlink dialog box. For example, if you have a bookmark in a Word document called "prices," link to the document and type **#prices** after the address. This technique also works for a named range in an Excel spreadsheet.*

6. Click ScreenTip to enter a label that will be displayed when you place the mouse cursor over the hyperlink. Without a ScreenTip, PowerPoint uses the path or URL of the file or web page.

7. Click OK when you're done.

As with all hyperlinks, you should go into Slide Show view and test the hyperlink. PowerPoint opens the file or opens your browser and links you to the URL. You can close your browser or the application to return to your presentation or use the Windows taskbar button.

Hyperlink to a New File

You can also use a hyperlink to open a new file. You might want to open a new file if your presentation is part of an in-house working session and you want to have a place to enter ideas as they come up. Here's how it works:

1. Select an object for the hyperlink.

2. Choose Insert Hyperlink.

3. In the Link To bar, choose Create New Document. In the Name of New Document text box, type the name of the file you want to create. You determine the type of document by the filename extension. For example, if you name the file **New Ideas.doc**, then you will create a Microsoft Word document. To change the location from the path listed, click Change. You can then find a new location and type a name for the file in a dialog box.

4. Choose when to edit the file. If you choose to edit the file now, PowerPoint opens the file. You can create a framework for inserting those new ideas, for example, such as headings of your major topics. Save the file and close it. When you show the presentation, your hyperlink will open the file again as you saved it. If you choose to edit the document later, PowerPoint will open it the first time you try out the hyperlink in Slide Show view—which should be before you actually give the final presentation.

TIP   *If you are opening a new PowerPoint presentation, choose to edit the slide now. If you try to edit it later in Slide Show view, PowerPoint creates a new presentation with no slides and immediately returns you to your original presentation.*

5. Click OK when you're done.

Once you create the new document, the hyperlink is connected to it. You can open the file any time you use the hyperlink. If you use the Windows taskbar to return to your presentation, be sure to choose the taskbar button that says PowerPoint Slide Show, not the button that says Microsoft PowerPoint, which returns you to Normal view or the view you last used.

Create an E-mail from a Slide

You have probably seen web sites that let you instantly e-mail the sponsoring company. You click an image on the web page, and your e-mail software opens with the correct e-mail address already

How to ...   Create a Web-Style Presentation

Most presentations are *linear* and give viewers no choice about what they see. When you deliver a presentation, you control what your audience sees. However, from experience viewing web sites, people are accustomed to choosing what they see from an array of hierarchically arranged information. You can create a presentation that functions like a web site. This style is ideal for presentations to small groups of clients—you can let them choose which information they want to see.

If you wish, start with a title page: in web jargon, this is called a *splash page*. Then create a home page with your logo, a brief explanation of what you are offering your audience, and a menu. Turn each menu item into a hyperlink to other slides.

To create the hierarchical structure, create a menu on each of the second-tier slides and link to yet more slides. These slides contain the information you want to present. Finally, create links on each of the slides to return to the tier above and to the home page, just like on a web site.

You can choose Slide Show | Action Buttons to insert premade web-style buttons on your slides, such as the house icon, to go to your home page.

When you give your presentation, present your home page and explain the information available using the menu. If your prospective clients indicate an interest, go that way. If not, you can use the links to direct the presentation yourself.

Why not just present your company's web site? There are many reasons:

- The web site probably doesn't contain all the specialized information you want to present and probably contains lots of information your audience doesn't need.

- Getting a fast, reliable Internet connection is tricky. You don't want prospects to have to wait for pages to download (or worse, not download at all).

- Web sites limit graphics and colors for downloading speed and consistency over various platforms and browsers. In PowerPoint, you can create the compelling look you want.

Hierarchical presentations take some getting used to for both the presenter and the audience, but you'll soon find that they offer incredible flexibility and power.

11

in the message window. You can do the same on a PowerPoint page. You can use this technique for self-running presentations when you want potential customers or other viewers to e-mail you with questions or for further information. Be sure to check that this system works properly. Obviously, you need an e-mail program and an active Internet connection. Once you get it working, this strategy is a great tool for creating an interactive presentation.

You can easily set up this kind of system over a company intranet. For example, you may have a networked computer set up with presentations on various topics for employees to view. Or you can place the presentations on an employees-only area of your company's web site or intranet. One could be a presentation on the new employee benefits plan—employees could e-mail their questions. Another presentation might present the employee suggestion program and ask employees to e-mail their suggestions. The possibilities are endless.

Here are the steps:

1. Select any object on a slide. Label it clearly—for example, "Click here to e-mail us your questions."

2. Choose Insert | Hyperlink.

3. In the Insert Hyperlink dialog box, choose E-mail Address from the Link To bar. In the E-mail Address text box, type the e-mail address you want the e-mail to go to.

4. In the Subject text box, type a subject. You can insert a general subject that will let you know which presentation the e-mail came from so that you can distinguish it from other e-mail you receive.

5. If you wish, choose ScreenTip and type a ScreenTip to appear when you place the mouse cursor over the hyperlink. Otherwise, PowerPoint uses the e-mail address and subject.

6. Click OK.

Look back to Figure 11-2 for an example of a slide with an e-mail link. Employees viewing the presentation on their own can click to e-mail the appropriate person in the Human Resources department.

Edit Hyperlinks

You sometimes need to edit a hyperlink. You can change any of the settings that you created in the Insert Hyperlink dialog box. To edit a hyperlink, right-click it and choose Edit Hyperlink. PowerPoint opens the Edit Hyperlink dialog box, which is the same as the Insert Hyperlink dialog box. Make any desired changes and click OK. To remove a hyperlink, right-click it and choose Remove Hyperlink.

You can play a sound or highlight a hyperlink to draw attention to its action. The next section explains how to attach actions to a hyperlink.

Use Action Buttons to Control Navigation

Action buttons are graphics on a slide that control actions you specify. You can use them to create hyperlinks, to play movies or sounds, or to open applications. Action buttons have the following advantages:

- They include familiar graphic symbols from web sites for going back, forward, to the first slide (home), and so on. Action buttons are therefore ideal for self-running presentations at a kiosk or on a web site because their controls are familiar to users.

- They often look more professional than graphics you would create yourself. When they are used during a presentation, they appear to be depressed, similar to buttons that have been clicked on web sites.

- You can play a sound while executing an action.

- You can use action buttons to run movies or play music.

- You can use action buttons to run macros or programs.

- You can choose whether clicking the button or passing the mouse cursor over it executes the action.

Navigate Within a Presentation

Action buttons don't need to be limited to self-running presentations. You can also use them for presentations that you deliver. The buttons are cute but professional looking. Whenever you want navigation in a presentation to be obvious, you can use an action button. Here's how to add an action button:

1. Display the slide where you want to place the action button.

2. Choose Slide Show | Action Buttons. On the submenu, shown here, choose one of the buttons. Each button has a ScreenTip so you can tell its intended purpose.

TIP   *You can also use the Draw toolbar and choose AutoShapes | Action Buttons. In either case, you can drag the palette of action buttons from the menu so that it stays open while you insert action buttons. (When you're done, you can just close the palette, which returns automatically to its original menu location.)*

3. To insert the button in the default size, click the slide. Otherwise, drag the shape to the desired size. You can adjust the size and shape later. You may want to change the color as well.

4. PowerPoint opens the Mouse Click tab of the Action Settings dialog box, shown in Figure 11-3, with a suggested hyperlink based on the action button you inserted. If necessary, click the Hyperlink To drop-down list and choose another option. Click OK.

5. When you use the Hyperlink To drop-down list, you can not only choose another slide option, but you also have all the options you would have if you attached a

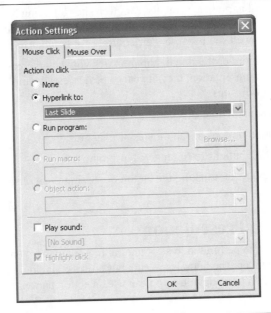

FIGURE 11-3   You can specify a hyperlink in the Action Settings dialog box.

hyperlink to an existing object, as described in the "Create Hyperlinks" section earlier in this chapter:

- **Slide**   Choose any slide in the presentation by its number and title.
- **URL**   Type a URL.
- **Other PowerPoint Presentation**   You can locate any other presentation and then choose any slide from that presentation.
- **Other File**   You can choose any file you have access to.

As with regular hyperlinks, you should always go to Slide Show view and test how the hyperlink works and how to get back to your presentation. Here you see a slide with a set of action buttons along the left side. It looks somewhat like a web page.

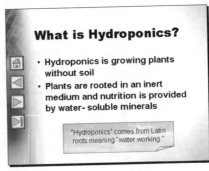

By default, the Action Settings dialog box opens with the Mouse Click tab on top. You activate the hyperlink you create by clicking it with the mouse. The Action Settings dialog box also has a Mouse Over tab, which is identical to the Mouse Click tab except that it creates actions that you activate by passing the mouse cursor over the action button.

Most of the time, you'll use the Mouse Click tab. You certainly don't want to accidentally move elsewhere in a presentation because you (or someone else if you have a self-running presentation) happen to move the mouse over the action button.

A good use for the Move Over tab might be to play a sound file that says, "We need your comment" or something similar.

At the same time that the action button executes a hyperlink, it can play a sound. While you can attach only one action to an object, playing a sound is an exception. To make an action button play a sound, check Play Sound on either the Mouse Click or the Mouse Over tab. Then choose a sound from the drop-down list. Choose Other Sound at the bottom of the list to locate any sound file on your system. A typical use for a sound would be to add a clicking sound to an action button to simulate the clicking of a button.

Use Action Settings

You can use the Action Settings dialog box for hyperlinks that you create with the Insert | Hyperlink command. Select the hyperlinked object and choose Slide Show | Action Settings. You can then add a sound, for example.

If the hyperlink is an object (that is, not text), you can highlight it when it is clicked or when the mouse cursor is passed over it. Check the Highlight Click checkbox in the Action Settings dialog box. This technique is a traditional way to emphasize a hyperlink. Here's how highlighting is generally used:

- If you choose to highlight the object when the mouse cursor is passed over it, the object blinks once in a contrasting color any time the mouse cursor passes over the object. The highlighting confirms to the user that this object is active and suggests that clicking it will perform some action.

- If you choose to highlight the object when it is clicked, the object blinks once when clicked and then immediately performs the action. This confirms to the user that the click "took," that is, was successful.

You can run a macro by clicking or passing the mouse cursor over an object. Using an object or an action button to run a macro lets you execute complex actions with a click of a button. To do this procedure, you first need to create the macro. For more about macros, see Chapter 12.

Here's how to use action settings to run a macro:

1. Select the text or object you want to use.

2. Choose Slide Show | Action Settings.

3. Choose Run Macro on either the Mouse Click or Mouse Over tab.

4. From the drop-down list, choose the macro you want to use.

   5. Play a sound if you wish.

   6. Click OK.

Test the macro in Slide Show view. Note that some macros do not work in Slide Show view. For example, macros that edit a slide will not work in Slide Show view because you cannot edit in that view.

You can also use action settings to run a program. This technique simply opens another application—you can't open a specific file. Follow these steps:

   1. Select an object.

   2. Choose Slide Show | Action Settings.

   3. Choose Run a Program.

   4. Click Browse.

   5. In the dialog box, choose the executable file (for example, winword.exe for Microsoft Word) in the Select a Program to Run dialog box.

   6. Click OK.

When you click the object in Slide Show view, PowerPoint opens the application. You can then use that application in any way you want. For example, you could record data in a spreadsheet file. Save the file and close the program to return to where you left off in your PowerPoint presentation.

Move Data

When you create a presentation, you often use data from other applications. You can copy data from other documents and paste it into PowerPoint, or you can drag-and-drop it. You can also import and export entire files. Another way to use data from other applications is to embed an object, such as a spreadsheet, into a presentation. Finally, you may want to investigate linking data from another document, so that it is always updated as the other document changes. Linking is especially valuable for price lists that change regularly.

Use the Clipboard and Drag-and-Drop

The Windows and Office clipboards let you copy data from place to place, whether within a presentation, from one presentation to another, or from one application to another. (See Chapter 3 for more about the Windows and Office clipboards.)

While I have already covered using the clipboard within PowerPoint, I have not talked much about using it to insert data from other applications. In order to decide how to best bring data into your presentation, you should understand how PowerPoint formats it.

When you paste data from another application via the clipboard, it becomes part of your presentation. PowerPoint creates PowerPoint objects. For example, if you paste data from an Excel spreadsheet, PowerPoint creates text boxes and groups them. You can ungroup them if you wish. You can then format them as you would any other text boxes. However, if you want to enlarge the text, a common requirement, you then lose all the nicely lined up rows and columns. For this reason, you'll get best results when importing only a small amount of data from a spreadsheet. When pasting in text from a word processing document, keep in mind that you can't fit very much text on a single slide. Remember that spreadsheet and word processing documents almost always contain text that is too small for a slide—you'll need to enlarge the text once you paste it into your presentation.

You'll have different considerations when pasting in graphics. You often can't determine the size the graphic will be until it's pasted into PowerPoint. Enlarging a small bitmap graphic may make it grainy. Sometimes there will be a background that you don't want. You may need to make the background transparent. An outside graphic-editing program may help you get the results you want. (See Chapter 5 for more details on editing graphics for PowerPoint.)

Drag-and-drop works just like the clipboard. You can select data, text, or a graphic from one application, drag it down to the Windows taskbar onto your presentation's taskbar button, and your presentation will open. Continue to drag the data onto the slide and release the mouse button.

You can drag-and-drop an entire file onto a PowerPoint slide from Windows Explorer. Locate the file in Windows Explorer and size the window so that you can see both your slide and the icon for the file. Then drag the file onto your slide. This technique works well for graphic files.

Import and Export Files

A different way of sharing information is to import and export files. For example, you might need to import a presentation created in another presentation program. You might also need to export a PowerPoint presentation into another format.

Import Files

You can create a PowerPoint presentation by simply opening a file from another application. This method doesn't provide satisfactory results in many cases, but occasionally, it will be just what you need to start you off on a presentation. For example, you can open a Microsoft Word document in PowerPoint, and PowerPoint converts it to a presentation. When looking for the Word document, don't forget to change the Files of Type drop-down list to All Files in the Open dialog box.

PowerPoint uses file converters to accomplish this conversion, and the converters are not all installed automatically. You may see a message offering to install the converter. Insert your Microsoft Office CD and click Yes. PowerPoint installs the converter and converts the file.

PowerPoint can also import presentations created in Harvard Graphics and Lotus Freelance. Usually PowerPoint can convert both the text and the graphics satisfactorily. If you have a presentation created in another program, you may have to convert the text and the graphics separately. You can probably save the presentation as a text (.txt) or Rich Text Format (.rtf) file. You can also use a graphics converter, but this converts an entire slide into a graphic file. You may not be able to edit or manipulate the slide in a meaningful way.

PowerPoint can open presentations saved as .wmf or .pct files. If the program can't save in those formats, try one of the other formats that PowerPoint can import.

PowerPoint can import the following graphic types without a filter:

■   Enhanced Metafile (.emf)

■   Graphics Interchange Format (.gif)

■   Joint Photographic Experts Group (.jpg)

- Portable Network Graphics (.png)
- Windows Bitmap (.bmp, .rle, .dib)
- Windows Metafile (.wmf)

PowerPoint can also open graphic files in the following formats, but these require a special graphics filter. These are generally not installed automatically. When you try to open them, PowerPoint usually displays a message offering to install the filter. If not, you can start Setup from the Office CD-ROM and install the filter yourself.

- Computer Graphics Metafile (.cgm)
- CorelDRAW (.cdr) — through version 6 only
- Encapsulated PostScript (.eps)
- FlashPix (.fpx)
- Hanako (.jsh, jah, and .jbh)
- Kodak Photo CD (.pcd)
- Macintosh PICT (.pct)
- PC Paintbrush (.pcx)
- Tagged Image File Format (.tif)
- WordPerfect Graphics (.wpg)

PowerPoint 2003 can import the following file types as charts. For more information on importing charts, see Chapter 8.

- Delimited text—text separated by tab characters, commas, or spaces (.txt, .csv)
- Lotus 1-2-3 (.wks, .wk1)
- Microsoft Excel worksheet or workbook (.xls)
- Microsoft Excel—versions 5.0 or earlier (.xlw, .xlc)

Export Files

PowerPoint can also export to different file types. Typically, PowerPoint is not as generous in export capabilities as it is in its importing capabilities. For example, it can't save a presentation as Harvard Graphics or Lotus Freelance presentations. However, you do have the following options when exporting to different file types:

- Web page (HTML)—for more information, see Chapter 12.
- Several older versions of PowerPoint so you can give your presentations to users who don't have the latest version. (Usually, you need to save in an older version only for someone using a version prior to PowerPoint 97.)
- Several graphic formats: GIF, JPEG, PNG, BMP, TIFF, TGA, and WMF. PowerPoint asks if you want to save the entire presentation or only the current slide. Whichever you choose, PowerPoint creates a graphic file from an entire slide. If you save the entire

presentation, PowerPoint automatically creates a subfolder with the same name as your presentation and places the graphic files in the subfolder.

- Rich Text Format (RTF). Saves only the text but preserves some of the text formatting.

These options are discussed in more detail in Chapter 1, Table 1-1.

Insert OLE Objects

When you insert an object into PowerPoint, you are embedding the object. The object, while part of your presentation, retains an "awareness" of its original application. When you double-click the object, the original application opens within PowerPoint and you use the menus and toolbars of that application to edit the object. To return to PowerPoint menus, click anywhere outside the object. Embed an object when you don't need to update the data from the original source document. There are three main ways of embedding an object:

- Choose Insert | Object. In the Insert Object dialog box, either choose Create New to create a new object and choose the type of object you want to create, or choose Create from File to embed an existing file and choose an existing file (using the Browse button). Click OK.

- Double-click a placeholder on a slide—chart, organization chart, media clip, or object.

- Go to the source document, select the data you want to embed, and copy it to the clipboard. Return to PowerPoint and choose Edit | Paste Special. In the Paste Special dialog box, choose Paste. In the As box, choose the type of object you want to create. Click OK. Use this method to create an object from part of a file.

Inserting objects has been discussed in several chapters in this book. For example, Chapter 8 discussed inserting organization chart and chart objects, and Chapter 10 covered inserting media clip objects.

Link Objects

If you need to update data from its original source, you should link an object. Linked data is not actually part of your presentation. Instead, PowerPoint stores the location of the data and only displays it. Linked objects can help reduce the size of a file, but the main reason to link is to keep your data current. Each time you open the presentation, PowerPoint reloads the file from the source, giving you the most current data. Also, if the source changes while the presentation is open, PowerPoint updates the data on the spot. There are two ways to insert a linked object:

- Choose Insert | Object. In the Insert Object dialog box, either choose Create New to create a new object and choose the type of object you want to create, or choose Create from File to embed an existing file and choose an existing file (using the Browse button). Check Link and click OK.

- Go to the source document, select the data you want to embed, and copy it to the clipboard. Return to PowerPoint and choose Edit | Paste Special. In the Paste Special dialog box, choose Paste Link. In the As box, choose the type of object you want to create. Click OK. Use this method to create an object from part of a file.

Links need to be well taken care of. Because PowerPoint stores the location of the source file, if that source file is moved, PowerPoint cannot maintain the link. If your slide doesn't properly display a linked object, or you get a message that PowerPoint cannot find the object, you have a broken link. Choose Edit | Links. Use the Links dialog box, shown in Figure 11-4, to reconnect the linked object. You can choose to update the link automatically or manually. If necessary, choose Change Source to reconnect a link to a file that you have moved. You can also break a link that you no longer require.

Manage Files

When you create presentations, you often collect numerous supporting files as well, especially graphic files. Managing your files is an important part of creating a presentation. Chapter 1 contains some tips for saving files so you can easily find them again. Here I discuss techniques for finding files.

Find Files

You can use the Open dialog box (choose File | Open) to search for files either on your hard disk or on a network. In the Open dialog box, choose Tools | Search to open the Search dialog box, shown in Figure 11-5. If you want to find only PowerPoint presentations, use the Results Should Be drop-down list to uncheck other types of files.

Once you have specified the criteria in the dialog box and clicked Search, wait for the results of the search. To open a presentation from the resulting list, double-click it. PowerPoint reopens the Open dialog box with the presentation listed in the File Name text box. Click Open to open the presentation.

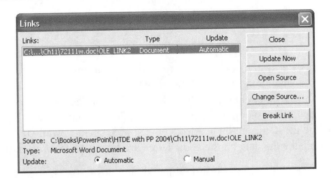

FIGURE 11-4   The Links dialog box

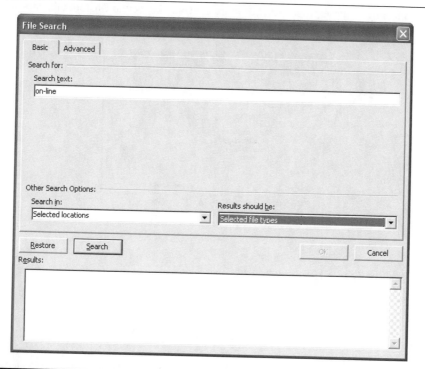

FIGURE 11-5   Find presentation in the Search dialog box.

Set File Properties

You can set properties for any Microsoft Office file to help you find the file again later, using the Find dialog box. You can open the Properties dialog box in three ways:

- From within the file, choose File | Properties.
- From another file, click Open on the Standard toolbar and navigate to the file. In the Open dialog box, choose Tools | Properties.
- Right-click on a file from Windows Explorer and choose Properties.

Most often, you use the Summary tab. Here you can add the properties listed, such as subject, manager, company, and category. You can also add keywords. You can then search for the presentation by any of these properties. For more control, choose the Custom tab, shown here with two custom properties added.

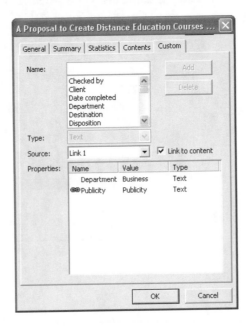

PowerPoint offers a long list of suggested properties, such as Checked By, Client, Department, Document Number, and Project. You can create your own properties as well. For example, you could use custom properties to assign project numbers.

An interesting feature of the Properties dialog box is the ability to link properties to text in your presentation. (Unfortunately, you cannot link properties to anything except text.) Once you create this link, you cannot only use the property to find the presentation, but you can quickly go to the linked text. Choose Edit | Go to Property. In the Properties dialog box, choose the property you want and click OK.

To add a custom property, choose File | Properties and click the Custom tab. If you want to link a property, select the desired text first. Then follow these steps:

1. In the Name text box, choose a property from the list or type in your own property name.

2. In the Type drop-down list, choose Text, Date, Number, or Yes or No.

3. In the Value text box, type the value for the property. For example, if your property is a project number, type the project number for the presentation. If you are linking to text, you can paste the text in here.

4. Click Add.

5. To link the property, check Link to Content. (This check box is available only if you previously selected some text in the presentation.)

6. Click OK.

Chapter 14 explains how to use Pack and Go to collect all the files you need when you go on the road with a presentation.

Using the Search and Properties features of PowerPoint will go a long way to helping you keep track of all your presentations.

Collaborate with Others

Whether you are creating a presentation for your company or for a client, you usually need to collaborate with others and share your ideas before the presentation is finalized. The old-fashioned way of collaborating involved printing out the presentation, mailing it to everyone, getting their feedback via return mail or phone, and making the necessary changes. Nowadays, you can collaborate online via a network or the Internet. These options make it easier to control the flow of comments. Collaborating online also allows you to keep up with the fast pace of today's electronically enabled businesses.

Many of the techniques described in this chapter require that you be connected to a network or an intranet. You probably need to work with your system administrator to put some of the techniques into place. However, some of the techniques are applicable to everyone, so browse through them and see what will work for you.

How you collaborate with others will depend largely on the systems you have where you work. In this section, I review some of the options you have to enable you to work with colleagues, managers, and clients on a presentation.

Share and Send a Presentation

Windows contains a built-in feature that lets you give others on a network access to files on your hard disk. It's called *file sharing,* and it creates a special shared folder. The steps vary widely depending on your version of Windows and the type of network you have. For instructions, ask your system administrator or check Help for your operating system.

You will often want to send a presentation via e-mail. You probably already have an e-mail system set up that you can use and you can simply attach a presentation file. You can also send a presentation via e-mail directly from within PowerPoint. This method also sends the presentation as an attachment.

To use this method, you need Microsoft Outlook or a MAPI-compliant e-mail program (MAPI is a common mail interface standard). This method also works with e-mail programs that are compliant with Lotus cc:Mail or VIM (another mail interface standard). If you have one of these, you have an e-mail button on the Standard toolbar.

To mail an entire presentation as an e-mail attachment, follow these steps:

1. Open the presentation and click E-mail (as Attachment) on the Standard toolbar.
2. PowerPoint opens a new message window. Complete the names in the To and Cc boxes.

3. If you wish, select the name of your presentation in the Subject box and type a new subject.

4. Click Send to send the e-mail.

Send a Presentation for Review

You can send a presentation to others for review. The recipients make changes and return the presentation to you. You then merge all the presentations, with the changes, into the original and view all the changes at once. You can accept or reject any changes to finalize the presentation.

Before sending a presentation for review, be sure to either embed linked files into the presentation (see the earlier section, "Insert OLE Objects") or know the location of linked files so that you can include them as attachments with your presentation. How you start the process depends on which e-mail program you use:

■ If you use Microsoft Outlook, choose File | Send To | Mail Recipient (for Review). A new e-mail opens. The presentation is already attached and the message says, "Please review the attached document." Complete the To and Cc boxes and click Send.

■ If you use another e-mail program or are not using e-mail to deliver the presentation, you first save the presentation in a special review format. Choose File | Save As and choose Presentation for Review (*.ppt) from the Save as Type drop-down list of the Save As dialog box. Then send the presentation as an attachment to the desired recipients. The review format saves the original copy of the presentation as well as changes made by reviewers so you can use the Compare and Merge Presentations command to create a final version of the presentation.

See the section "Compare and Merge a Presentation" later in this chapter for information about what to do when you receive reviewed presentations from others.

Fax a Presentation

A new feature for Office 2003 makes it easier to fax a presentation (and other Microsoft Office files) using an Internet-based fax service. You must have installed Outlook and Word on your computer to use this feature. Sent faxes are stored in Outlook like e-mails. Note that faxes are always in grayscale. Before sending a fax using this method, you need to sign up for an Internet-based fax service. To sign up, choose File | Send To | Recipient Using Internet Fax Service, as you would if you were sending an actual fax. Click OK at the message and follow the instructions on the Web site (www.venali.com) to sign up.

 The Web site, www.venali.com, offers a free 30-day trial. You must provide a credit card number and sign up for one of the monthly plans. If you don't cancel within 30 days, your credit card is charged according to the plan you chose.

To send a presentation by fax, follow these steps:

1. With the presentation open, choose File | Send To | Recipient Using Internet Fax Service. A new e-mail message opens in Outlook. Your presentation is already attached as a multi-page TIF file. (TIF is a bitmap image format. The new Microsoft Office Document Imaging program that comes with Microsoft Office supports viewing the multi-page TIF format. You can also use Irfan View (http://www.irfanview.com.) The message itself has a Preview button that you can click to preview the pages of the fax.

> **TIP** *You can right-click the attachment and choose Save As to save the multi-page TIF file. You can then e-mail it or use another method of delivery.*

2. In the To field, enter a name from your address book. You can click the To button and choose a name that has an associated fax number. At this time, you can create a new entry in your address book if necessary.

3. Complete the Subject field. You can also type a message, which becomes a cover sheet.

4. Click Send. The e-mail is sent and the fax service takes care of sending the fax for you.

> **TIP** *If you have fax software (many modems come with fax software), you may be able to use it to send a presentation by fax using your modem. Usually, you choose File | Print and choose your modem's print driver to open the software and send the fax.*

Let Non-PowerPoint Users View Your Presentation

You may need to send your presentation to someone who does not have PowerPoint. For you to be able to collaborate with clients, managers, or colleagues who do not have PowerPoint, they will need the PowerPoint Viewer, a free program for viewing PowerPoint presentations. You can send the viewer to them or direct them to where they can download it. A new viewer for PowerPoint 2003 is now available.

PowerPoint viewer is available from Microsoft's web site. A special update site—http://office .microsoft.com/downloads/—lists updates. Choose PowerPoint as the product and 2003 as the version. Find the listing for the PowerPoint viewer and click Download Now to download the viewer. Once installed, PowerPoint Viewer can be easily loaded and any PowerPoint presentation viewed. (Chapter 14 covers PowerPoint Viewer in more detail.)

Review a Presentation

What do you do with a presentation when it is routed to you? When you receive a presentation for review, double-click it to open it. (You may see a message asking if you want to open it or save it. You can choose to open it.) You can edit the presentation directly or just add comments.

Edit a Presentation Sent for Review

Make the changes you want and save the presentation. If you are sending the presentation via e-mail, reply back to the sender that you have reviewed the presentation and attach the presentation.

See the section "Compare and Merge a Presentation" later in this chapter for information about what to do when you receive reviewed presentations from others.

Add Comments to a Presentation

Instead of editing a presentation, you can add comments. Anyone can add comments to a presentation. Each comment contains the name of its author so you'll always know who made the comment. To insert a comment, choose Insert | Comment and type your comment.

When you insert a comment, PowerPoint automatically opens the Reviewing toolbar, shown here. The Reviewing toolbar lets you easily add comments, show/hide comments, delete comments, and move from comment to comment throughout a presentation.

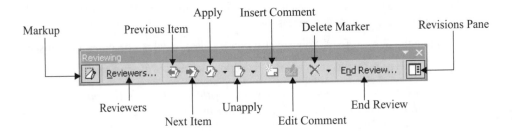

The Reviewing toolbar is most useful when you receive presentations back from review. After you have added comments, return the presentation back to the original sender, using the instructions explained in the earlier section "Edit a Presentation Sent for Review."

Compare and Merge a Presentation

When you receive reviewed presentations back, you need to combine them in a way that enables you to see the various changes that reviewers made and read any comments they have added. If the reviewed presentations were sent for review using Microsoft Outlook, you can double-click the attached reviewed presentation in the e-mail. When you see the message asking if you want to merge the changes, as shown in Figure 11-6, click Yes.

If you are using another e-mail program, open the presentation and click Yes when you see the message shown in Figure 11-6.

If you don't see the message, save the presentation to your hard drive, making sure not to overwrite the original presentation. Add a slight variation to the end of the presentation's name, such as "review1." PowerPoint usually recognizes similarly named presentations as variations of the same presentation.

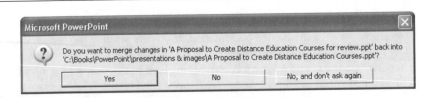

Use the Merge message to merge presentations.

You can now combine any reviewed presentations that you have saved with this presentation. Follow these steps:

1. Open the original presentation.

2. Choose Tools | Compare and Merge Presentations.

3. Choose the reviewed presentations.

4. Click Merge.

You now have a presentation that contains the information of both the original and the changes made by reviewers. Changes are shown by a marker on each slide, as shown in Figure 11-7. Click Revisions Pane on the Reviewing toolbar to display the task pane you see in this figure.

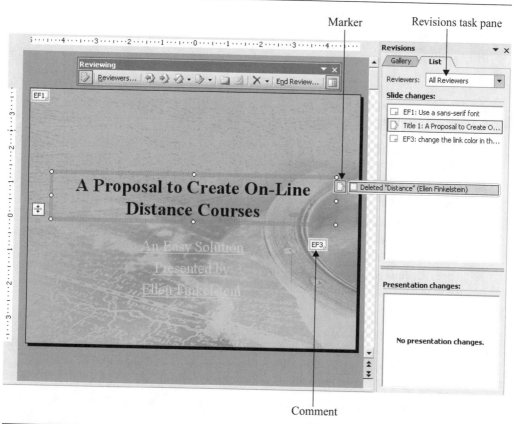

FIGURE 11-7   When you merge presentations, you can compare the original presentation with the reviewed one.

To see an itemized list of the changes on a slide, click either the marker or the listing of the changes in the Revisions Pane. You see an example here.

```
□ All changes to Text 2                        ▲
    □ Text ruler setting (Ellen Finkelstein)
    □ Inserted "Like all gardening,
      hydroponic" (Ellen Finkelstein)
    □ Deleted "Hydroponic" (Ellen Finkelstein)
    □ Text format: size (Ellen Finkelstein)
    □ Text format: size (Ellen Finkelstein)
    □ Text format: size (Ellen Finkelstein)
    □ Text format: size (Ellen Finkelstein)   ▼
```

You can then use the Reviewing toolbar to do the following:

■ Show comments (if they're hidden)

■ Move from comment to comment

■ Delete comments

■ Apply changes

■ Reject changes

Any changes that you don't apply are not incorporated into the original document. You have the flexibility to apply single changes or multiple changes at once:

■ **Apply an individual change**   Click a marker or a listing of a change on the List tab of the Revisions Pane. Select the check boxes of the changes you want to apply.

■ **Apply all the changes made to one slide**   On the Reviewing toolbar, click the down arrow to the right of the Apply button and choose Apply All Changes to the Current Slide.

■ **Apply all the changes made to the entire presentation**   On the Reviewing toolbar, click the down arrow to the right of the Apply button and choose Apply All Changes to the Presentation.

■ **Apply all changes made by a specific reviewer on one slide**   Click the Gallery tab of the Revisions Pane, choose a slide of the reviewer, and choose Apply All Changes by This Reviewer.

If a reviewer made changes to the slide master, display the slide master and then choose the changes you want to apply as described just previously for applying individual changes to a slide.

If you change your mind and want to unapply changes, you can do so. On the Reviewing toolbar, click the down-arrow to the right of the Unapply button and choose one of the options.

TIP   *You can show or hide comments and reviewers' changes. Choose Markup on the Reviewing toolbar.*

When you are completely finished updating your presentation, you can end the review process so the reviewed presentation is not available any more for comparison. Click End Review on the Reviewing toolbar. If you apply the reviewer changes that you want, delete all the markers, and save the presentation, PowerPoint automatically ends the review for you.

To delete markers, choose the down arrow to the right of the Delete Marker button on the Reviewing toolbar and choose Delete Marker or Delete All Markers on the Current Slide.

Collaborate Online

NetMeeting is a program for online meetings. While it is beyond the scope of this book to go into detail about how to use NetMeeting, you should know about its capabilities for collaboration. NetMeeting includes the following features:

- Audio capability so participants can talk to each other during the meeting
- Application sharing so participants can share access to the presentation
- Whiteboard that lets you paste data into the whiteboard and mark up the image for all to see
- Text chat where you can type comments that all can see and reply to
- File transfer so that participants can send presentations and other documents to each other

You can start NetMeeting from within PowerPoint by choosing Tools | Online Collaboration. Then choose either Meet Now or Schedule Meeting. To use the Meet Now option, all the participants need to have NetMeeting running and be on your network. When you choose Schedule Meeting, you use Microsoft Outlook to schedule the time of the meeting. Of course, you can also e-mail or phone people to set up the meeting. The first time you use NetMeeting, you need to complete the Microsoft NetMeeting dialog box where you fill out information that NetMeeting needs to connect everyone. You will probably need to contact your system administrator to complete the information.

Once you are ready to start the meeting, choose the Meet Now option to open the Place a Call dialog box, where you select people you want to invite. Then click Call. The people you invite receive a message inviting them to participate. When they accept, they are in on the meeting and can see the shared presentation on their screens. During the meeting, the host starts out with control over the presentation, although everyone sees it. When the collaboration feature is on, participants can take turns controlling the presentation, which means that they can edit it. Only one person can edit the presentation at a time. During an online meeting, you can send text messages to each other in the Chat window and work on the whiteboard, where you can type, draw, copy, and paste objects, and mark up text and graphics. The host of the meeting has controls for ending the meeting when everyone is done.

11

Create Discussions on a Presentation

Microsoft Office includes a discussions feature; however, it requires Microsoft Office Server Extensions, which can be set up only by your system administrator on a network. If you've ever participated in a newsgroup discussion, you are familiar with discussions.

Discussions let collaborators add comments to a presentation. Discussions are different from comments. They can be much longer, and they are *threaded,* which means that people can reply to the comments. Related comments and replies are kept together, so you can follow the thread of the discussion. If you have Office Server Extensions installed, you have a Discussions toolbar that facilitates sending and replying to messages in the discussion.

You can also use a browser to start a discussion about a presentation that you have posted on a web page. For more information about using discussions, speak to your system administrator.

Summary

In this chapter, you learned how to create hyperlinks to other slides, other presentations, other files, or the Web. You can even create a hyperlink that opens a new e-mail message. Action buttons provide a professional way to display hyperlinks as well as other actions, such as opening a program, playing a macro, or playing a sound.

Part of managing the relationship between your presentation and the rest of the world is knowing how to move data in and out of files. You can use the clipboard or drag-and-drop to paste in data. You can embed objects with or without a link to the source document.

Use the Search feature to find files. Set file properties using the Properties feature to help you find files more easily in the future.

Collaboration is often as simple as e-mailing a presentation to others. You can e-mail others a presentation for review. If you need to collaborate with someone who doesn't have PowerPoint, you can include PowerPoint Viewer along with the presentation. It can be downloaded free from Microsoft's web site. You can also fax a presentation.

You can add comments to a presentation. If you send you presentation to others, they can add comments to your presentation. When you get the presentation back, you can incorporate the suggestions in the comments. You can also merge a reviewed presentation that contains suggested changes and decide which changes you want to apply.

If you work on a network, you can use two other features: online meetings with NetMeeting, and discussions. Online meetings allow several people to view the PowerPoint presentation and communicate about it simultaneously. Discussions let you create newsgroup-type threaded discussions about a presentation. The next chapter covers the process of publishing a presentation on the Internet.

Chapter 12

Display a Presentation on the World Wide Web

How to…

- Create a presentation for a web site
- Publish a presentation on the Internet
- Save a presentation for a web page

PowerPoint 2003 makes creating web content easy. You can save a presentation in HTML format, the format used on the Web, and then open it in PowerPoint like any other presentation for further editing. Viewers can see your presentation on your web site, in some cases with all the animation and special effects intact. This chapter describes these features as well as some of their limitations.

Show Presentations on the Web

You can use PowerPoint to create web pages. In this situation, you are not creating a presentation at all; rather, you are using PowerPoint's ability to create fully graphic slides as a tool to design a web page. You must take into account the usual design features of a web site, such as a title, links to other pages, more (and smaller) text, and so on.

You can also add a presentation to an existing web site. In this case, you want your audience to be able to run the slide show while browsing the web site. You create a typical presentation, although you may add special design elements because it is shown on the web site.

Use PowerPoint to Create Web Pages

When you use PowerPoint to create a web page, you are using PowerPoint as your design tool. You then save the presentation in Hypertext Markup Language (HTML) format. *HTML* is a format that browsers can read.

Although designing web pages is beyond the scope of this book, here are a few simple guidelines:

- *Format the page's text and graphics appropriately.* Most web pages include graphics. However, too many large graphics make a web page slow to download. Text for a web site can be smaller than for an onscreen slide show.

- *Provide links on each page to go to other pages.* Figure 12-1 shows an example of a web page for a human resources department web site. Most pages should also have a link to your home (main) page. Create consistent navigational tools throughout the web site pages using action buttons or AutoShapes. Chapter 11 explains how to create hyperlinks in your presentation.

- *Keep the colors simple.* The rich, dark colors appropriate for an onscreen presentation are often overwhelming on a web site.

- *Include a way to contact the Webmaster and the organization that created the web site.* Add an e-mail link to the Webmaster on the first page. See the "Create an E-mail from a Slide" section in Chapter 11 for instructions on creating an e-mail link.

FIGURE 12-1   When you design a web site using PowerPoint, provide hyperlinks on each page to navigate to other pages.

■ *Before publishing your web pages, open them in your browser and check out all the links and graphics.* Once you send the web pages to your server or web site host, check them out again. Professional web designers also test web pages on both major browsers, earlier versions of browsers, various platforms (PC and Mac), and at varying screen resolutions.

You can include all the pages of the web site in one presentation using each slide in the presentation as a web page. You can also create a different presentation for each web page; you may end up with a large number of files, but each file is smaller and loads faster.

PowerPoint's AutoContent Wizard includes a presentation for a corporate web site. Choose File | New and choose From AutoContent Wizard in the New Presentation task pane. In the AutoContent Wizard, choose the Corporate topic, and then choose Group Home Page, which is designed to be an intranet home page for a workgroup or project.

NOTE   *Many programs are specifically designed for creating web pages, and they offer more features and control than PowerPoint. Microsoft FrontPage and Macromedia Dreamweaver are two examples.*

Before saving your presentation in HTML format, you can preview it as a web page. Choose File | Web Page Preview. PowerPoint opens your default web browser and displays the first slide in the presentation. Figure 12-2 shows a slide viewed in Internet Explorer. Using this preview, you can test all the links that don't require Internet access, such as links within the presentation.

Create a Viewer-Controlled Presentation

You can publish a presentation to a web site so that others can view the presentation. When you publish to the Web, the presentation appears in the browser with navigational tools so that users can view the presentation.

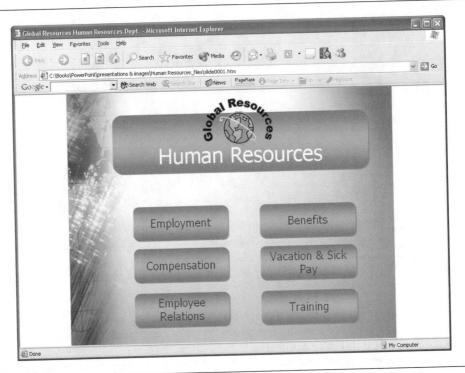

FIGURE 12-2 A slide previewed in Internet Explorer

Create a viewer-controlled presentation when you want to simply place your presentation on a web site and let viewers decide when they will view it. A presentation can be part of a larger web site. You may have seen web sites that included PowerPoint presentations.

When you publish the presentation to the Web, as explained in the next section, PowerPoint automatically creates the navigational tools your viewers need. (You can turn off the navigational tools, but you shouldn't do so for a presentation designed to be controlled by your viewers.)

Figure 12-3 shows the first slide of a presentation as it appears in a browser.

Remember that viewers may need instructions to get the most out of the presentation. The navigational controls at the bottom are not large, and some viewers may miss them. One solution is to include instructions for using the controls on the first slide.

If you include a video file, it may need to be double-clicked to run. Viewers will not know this, so you should include a text box with instructions to this effect.

You need to pay special attention when designing a presentation that is viewed on a web page. Here are some pointers:

- *Make sure that each slide has a meaningful slide title.* On a web site, these titles appear in a frame at the left side, listing each slide's title. Viewers can click any slide's title to go to that slide.

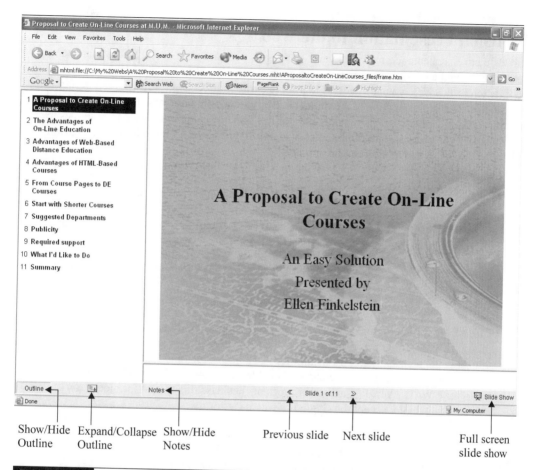

Show/Hide Outline   Expand/Collapse Outline   Show/Hide Notes   Previous slide   Next slide   Full screen slide show

FIGURE 12-3   A presentation on a web site contains navigational tools so your viewers can move from slide to slide and decide which slides they want to see.

- *Add alternative text for graphics.* Browsers use this text while pictures are loading because some people may use the Web with graphics turned off to speed load time. Alternative text offers impact even without the graphics. Search engines also use this text. To create alternative text, select the object in PowerPoint, right-click, and choose Format AutoShape (or Picture or Table). On the Web tab, type the text. (Text in a WordArt object is used by default for the alternative text.) Click OK.

- *Don't use builds or other animation that requires a mouse click.* Your viewers have no way of knowing about this animation. If you want to use animation, set automatic timing. (See Chapter 14 for details.) Even with automatic timing, animation (builds) may be confusing to viewers because they have no control over the timing. Dimming does not work well because viewers may not have finished reading a line of text before it dims.

Publish a Presentation to the Web

Once you have created and previewed your web pages, you save them in HTML format and save them to their final location on the Internet—a process called *publishing to the Web*. To save a presentation to the Web, you need access to a server, with a direct connection to the Internet. You can also save a presentation to an intranet server within your company. If you are saving to an intranet, your company's system administrator has the information you need to save files to the intranet. If you are saving to the Internet, you usually do so via an Internet service provider (ISP) who can give you the information you need.

When you save a presentation for viewing in a browser, PowerPoint offers two formats:

- Single File Web Page format (.mht or .mhtml) lets you save all the components of a web site into one file. (This format is also available for other Office applications.) Working with one file makes it easier to upload, send as an e-mail attachment, and store. This format is the default and works with Internet Explorer 4.0 or later.

NOTE *Some people have had problems using the MHT format when the presentation contains sound and video. You can convert an MHT file to an HTML file in Internet Explorer— choose File | Save As and choose one of the HTML options.*

- Web Page format (.htm or .html) creates many supporting files, including separate files for each slide, for graphic files, and for the navigational tools your viewers use to browse through the presentation. PowerPoint creates a new folder and places all the new files in that folder. One presentation creates a bewildering array of GIF and HTM files. You may also have WAV, AVI, JPG, and other types of files. Use this format for older browsers or servers that do not accept the single file web page format.

The procedure for publishing to the Web is the same whether you are using PowerPoint to create a web site or using the Web to present your slide show.

Before you publish to the Web, you need to consider which format you want to use. PowerPoint 2002 offers three options for converting a presentation to HTML format. Each format has its advantages and disadvantages:

- **Microsoft Internet Explorer 4.0 or Later (High Fidelity)** This option, which PowerPoint calls "high fidelity," retains almost all of the features of a presentation, including transitions, animations (builds), sounds, and video clips. Viewers can see your presentation in full-screen mode, which makes it look like a real presentation rather than just a presentation inside a browser. When you save a presentation in this format, you can open and edit it in PowerPoint like a regular presentation. The disadvantage is that many viewers use Netscape or earlier versions of Internet Explorer—they will probably get an error message or lose many of the features of your presentation. This option is ideal for intranets where you know that your viewers have Internet Explorer 4.0 or later.

- **Microsoft Internet Explorer 3.0, Netscape Navigator 3.0, or Later** This option loses many of your special effects. You still get a good basic presentation and more people can view it. You cannot open and edit this format in PowerPoint. Therefore, if you edit your presentation, you need to resave it using this HTML format. Use this format when you need to make your presentation available to a wide variety of people and don't need special effects—for example, when you are using PowerPoint to create a web site.

- **All Browsers Listed Above (Creates Larger Files)** This option creates a presentation with the capabilities of both of the previous options. Viewers with Internet Explorer 4.0 or later can see your special effects, and others get the basic version of your presentation. The disadvantage of this format is that it creates more and larger files.

Now you're ready to publish your presentation to the Web. Follow these steps:

1. Choose File | Save as Web Page. PowerPoint opens the Save As dialog box with special web publishing options, as shown in Figure 12-4.

2. In the File Name text box, type a name for the web page. By default, PowerPoint uses the name of the presentation.

3. In the Save As Type drop-down box, choose either Single File Web Page (the default) or Web Page.

4. In the Save In drop-down box at the top of the dialog box, choose a location for the web page. You should ask your Internet service provider or your company's network/web administrator for this location, as well as how supporting files (such as graphics) should be organized. If you usually save to a web site using an FTP program, you can save to your hard disk now and use the FTP program afterwards.

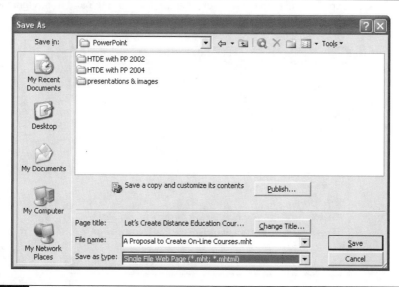

FIGURE 12-4 The Save As dialog box with special options for publishing a presentation to the Web

5. If you would like the web page title to be different from the filename, click Change Title. The web page title is the text that appears in the title bar of your web browser. (The page title also appears in the browser's history and favorites lists.) Make this title descriptive because many search engines use this title. In the Page Title box, type the new title and click OK.

6. Click Publish. PowerPoint opens the Publish as Web Page dialog box, shown in Figure 12-5. It has the following options:

■ In the Publish What? section, specify if you want to publish the entire presentation, certain slides, or a custom show (if available).

■ Uncheck Display Speaker Notes if you don't want your viewers to automatically see your notes. Leave this option checked if you are publishing the presentation for others to review or if you have used the Notes pane to provide additional information that you want your viewers to see.

If you include navigation controls (see the explanation of the General tab of the Web Options dialog box, next), viewers can choose to display notes. Therefore, you should not include Notes that you don't want viewers to see.

7. Click Web Options to open the Web Options dialog box, shown in Figure 12-6. Here's how to use the tabs on the Web Options dialog box:

■ **General tab** You can check Add Slide Navigation Controls (it's on by default) to include the Outline and Notes panes, as well as the navigational arrows at the bottom of the screen. (The Notes pane will not appear if you unchecked Display Speaker Notes, as explained in step 6.) Viewers can use the Outline pane to navigate around

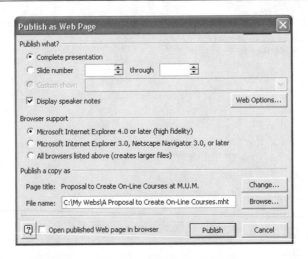

FIGURE 12-5 Use the Publish as Web Page dialog box to specify how you want to publish your presentation.

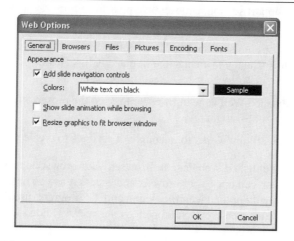

FIGURE 12-6   The Web Options dialog box lets you specify the details about your published presentation.

your presentation by clicking on any slide listed in the outline—just as you do in Normal view. PowerPoint gives you some color options in the Colors drop-down list. For example, you can use presentation colors, black on white, white on black, or your default browser colors. You can disable slide animation (builds). You can also disable the automatic resizing of graphics to fit the browser window.

■ **Files tab**   You can change the names and location of the files that PowerPoint creates. For example, you can disable the feature that puts in a separate folder all the files of a presentation published to the Web. You should disable this feature only if instructed by your Internet service provider or web administrator, because PowerPoint creates a large number of files for each presentation.

■ **Browsers tab**   You can make choices about the browsers that will be used to view the presentation and how graphic elements are handled.

■ **Pictures tab**   You can specify the screen resolution. If you are publishing to an intranet and know the screen resolution of your viewers' monitors, you should set it here. If you are publishing to the Web for anyone to view, you should try different resolutions and view them with different browsers to see the results. The default is 800×600, which works fine for the majority of web users.

■ **Encoding tab**   You can save your presentation in various languages and operating system formats. Use these options if text and symbols are not properly readable from your browser.

■ **Fonts tab**   Choose the default fonts you want to include with your presentation.

8. When you're done setting the web options, click OK to return to the Publish as Web Page dialog box.

12

9. In the Browser Support section, choose the type of web format you want to create. (See the descriptions of the different HTML formats earlier in this section.)

10. In the Publish a Copy As section, you have another opportunity to change the filename and text title. Click Change to change the title text. Click Browse to navigate to a new location.

11. Check Open Published Web Page in Browser to open the presentation in your browser immediately after publishing it.

12. Click Publish. PowerPoint works for a couple of seconds to create the new files.

If you checked Open Published Web Page in Browser, your browser opens and displays the presentation. Otherwise, you can open your browser and access it as you normally would access files on the Web. If you usually upload web files using an FTP program, use that program now to upload the presentation to the web site. Don't forget to re-create any folders that PowerPoint made in your presentation's folder structure.

Save a Presentation to an FTP Site

A File Transfer Protocol (FTP) site offers the capability of sending and receiving files. When you go to a web site and download a file, you are usually connected to an FTP site for the transfer. If your web server or Internet service provider offers access to an FTP site, you can save a presentation to it. Others can then download your presentation from that site.

To save to an FTP site, you need to add the site to PowerPoint's list of Internet sites. Follow these steps:

1. Click Open on the Standard toolbar.

2. In the Look In drop-down list, choose Add/Modify FTP Locations.

3. In the Name of FTP Site box, type the URL of the site.

4. If the site allows anonymous access, choose Anonymous. (No password is required.) Otherwise, choose User and type your name. Type your password if you are prompted for it.

5. Click Add, then click OK.

6. Click Cancel to close the Open dialog box.

You can now save presentations to the FTP site. Choose File | Save As. In the Save In drop-down list, choose FTP Locations. From the list of FTP sites, double-click the site you want, then double-click the folder within the site. In the File Name box, type the name of your presentation and click Save.

Test Your Web Site

Once you have published your web site, you should access it as your viewers would and test it out. Here are some things to test for:

- *Test any links that connect to sites outside your web site.* You may have forgotten to save supporting files to the Web, such as text files containing additional data.

- *Test any multimedia objects, such as sounds and video clips.* Are the means to open these objects clear to your viewer? If not, add instructions such as "Double-click to see the video."

- *Test any action buttons that you created.* These may have hyperlinks, may open programs, or may play a sound, for example.

- *If you added animated GIFs, make sure they work.*

If you can manage it, an extra precaution is to view your web site using both browsers (Microsoft Internet Explorer and Netscape Navigator), at varying screen resolutions, and with varying numbers of screen colors. These factors can affect how your web site appears.

NOTE *The Broadcast feature, which enables you to present a slide show in real-time over the Internet, has been removed from PowerPoint 2003. However, at the time of this writing, Microsoft was planning to offer it as a free add-in download, available after PowerPoint 2003 ships.*

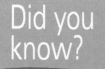

Broadcasting Your Presentation

12

When you publish a presentation to the Web, viewers see can the presentation whenever it's convenient for them. Another option is to present a slide show in real time over the Internet. PowerPoint calls this *broadcasting*. The broadcasting feature is available as a free download from Microsoft's web site. While the location is not final, I expect that you will be able to find it at http://office.microsoft.com/downloads. Choose PowerPoint as the product and look for the broadcasting feature. Follow the instructions to download and install it.

To broadcast a presentation, you invite your audience to view the presentation at a specific time, so they know when to go online. PowerPoint uses Advanced Streaming Format (ASF) technology to send the presentation to all your viewers at once. You need access to a server or other computer that can be accessed by everyone in your intended audience. The broadcast can be recorded and saved so that people who miss the meeting can view the presentation whenever they want.

Although broadcasting is an exciting concept, it has some limitations: Viewers must have Internet Explorer 5.01 or later, and if you want to broadcast to more than 10 locations at once, you need a Windows Media server available from Microsoft (or other third-party server). Broadcasting is most useful in an organization with an intranet, where you have access to a network administrator, have a means of contacting all the viewers, and know that all your viewers have Internet Explorer 5.01 or later.

Broadcasting involves the following steps:

1. Set up server options (you need to do this only once), including specifying the location of the broadcast.

2. Schedule the broadcast using Microsoft Outlook or your e-mail program.

3. Start the broadcast.

4. View the broadcast.

Broadcasting can be complicated to set up, but after you have worked out the details once, it is fairly easy to use and offers a new way to communicate to a group of people at one time.

Summary

In this chapter, you learned about creating a presentation for a web site. You can use PowerPoint to create a web site or you can place a presentation on a web site so that people can view it in a web browser. When you publish your presentation to the Web, PowerPoint creates the HTML and other files for you.

In the next chapter, you learn about customizing PowerPoint.

Chapter 13

Customize PowerPoint

How to...

■ Set PowerPoint's options to suit your needs

■ Customize menus

■ Customize toolbars

■ Use an add-in

■ Create and use a macro

■ Start programming PowerPoint

Most of the customization you do in PowerPoint is not visible in your final presentation; rather, it helps you work more quickly and easily. Customizing a menu or a toolbar makes it easy for you to find the features you use most. If you create a macro, you can automate some of your editing and turn a long task into a short one. But you can also create macros and Visual Basic for Applications (VBA) programs that change how your presentation appears or works—and the results are readily visible to your viewers.

Customization offers you great power to control PowerPoint. This chapter explains what you can accomplish without being a programmer and introduces you to the advanced capabilities of customization.

Customize PowerPoint's Options

One of the most basic ways to customize PowerPoint is to use the Options dialog box. (Choose Tools | Options.) Here, in one place, you can specify many of PowerPoint's features. Many people use PowerPoint for months, being frustrated with one feature or another, before discovering that they can change the way the feature works. The AutoCorrect dialog box also offers a number of helpful options for creating text.

Use the Options Dialog Box

The View tab of the Options dialog box, shown in Figure 13-1, enables you to customize many of the visible features of the PowerPoint screen while you work.

Most of the items are self-explanatory. Here are a few pointers. The first check box, Startup Task Pane, displays the Getting Started task pane when you open PowerPoint. You can choose whether you want the vertical ruler to appear when you display the horizontal ruler (using View | Rulers). The Windows in Taskbar check box lets you specify whether you want a separate button on the Windows taskbar for each open presentation.

The second section of the View tab applies only to Slide Show view. You can choose to display the shortcut menu when you right-click and display the shortcut menu button in the lower-left corner of the screen. You can also choose to end a slide show presentation with a black screen, so that you don't inadvertently show the audience the Normal view of PowerPoint at the end of a presentation. Finally, you can choose in which view PowerPoint opens. The default is the last view saved.

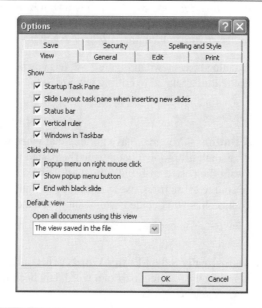

FIGURE 13-1   Use the View tab to specify how PowerPoint looks.

The General tab of the Options dialog box has the following options:

- **Provide Feedback with Sound to Screen Elements**   Available throughout Microsoft Office, this feature plays a sound when a message opens or at other specific events. You can change the sounds played for each event by going to Start | Control Panel and double-clicking Sounds.

- **Recently Used File List**   You can customize the number of recently used presentations listed at the bottom of the File menu and on the New Presentation task pane, from zero through nine.

- **Link Sounds with File Size Greater Than_KB**   You can determine at which point PowerPoint links sounds rather than embedding them, in order to avoid very large files. The default size is 100KB.

- **User Information**   You can customize your name and initials. User information is automatically placed in the Properties dialog box and used when you insert comments, for example.

- Click Web Options to specify default options for publishing a presentation to a web site. However, these settings are also available when you publish a web site and should be checked at that time. See Chapter 12 for more information.

- Click Service Options to specify settings regarding your connection with the Internet, Microsoft's web site, and Shared Workspace files.

A shared workspace is a location, hosted by a web server, where people can share files. Shared workspaces are based on a service offered by Microsoft called SharePoint Services. For more information, go to http://www.microsoft.com/sharepoint/ teamservices/.

The Edit tab of the Options dialog box, shown in Figure 13-2, lets you set some of PowerPoint's general editing features. (Some features related to editing text are in the AutoCorrect dialog box, discussed in the next section.)

Here is what each option does:

- **Show Paste Options Buttons**   You may have noticed that when you paste data from the clipboard, you see a small drop-down list next to the pasted material. This list lets you decide how you want the pasted material formatted. For example, if you are pasting text, you can keep the source formatting, use the design template formatting, or paste only plain text. This option lets you decide if you want to see these buttons.

- **Use Smart Cut and Paste**   You can add or delete spaces before and after pasted text, as appropriate.

- **When Selecting, Automatically Select Entire Word**   This option is one that drives some people nuts when they try to select part of a word. Uncheck this check box to give yourself more control over selecting text.

SHORTCUT   *Double-click any word to select it.*

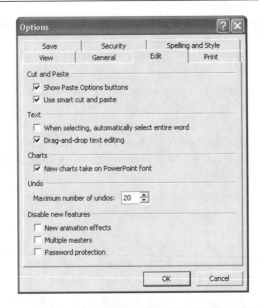

FIGURE 13-2   The Edit tab of the Options dialog box

- **Drag-and-Drop Text Editing**   If this check box is checked (and it is checked by default), when you pause the mouse cursor over selected text, you see an arrow. Then you can click and drag the text to move it. To copy it, press CTRL as you drag. Uncheck this box if you want dragging to extend the selection instead.

- **New Charts Take On PowerPoint Font**   This option sets fonts in inserted charts to Arial, 18 pt, or the current default that you can set in the Fonts dialog box. (Choose Format | Fonts.) If you clear this check box, the charts retain their original fonts.

- **Maximum Number of Undos**   This option sets how many actions PowerPoint remembers so that you can undo them. A larger number takes up more memory.

- **Disable New Features**   In this section of the Edit tab, you can disable the new animation effects, multiple masters, and password protection to maintain compatibility with previous versions of PowerPoint. These features were added in PowerPoint 2002.

The Print tab of the Options dialog box lets you turn background printing on and off. Background printing makes it easier to do something else while you are printing. You can also print TrueType fonts as graphics (to make sure they will display as they look on all computers), print inserted objects at your printer's resolution, and preset print settings that you would normally set in the Print dialog box.

The Save tab of the Options dialog box, shown in Figure 13-3, provides options for where and how you save presentations.

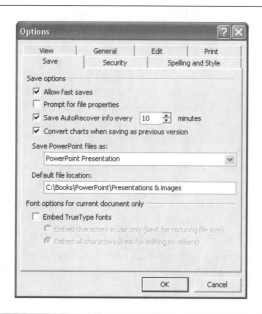

13

FIGURE 13-3   The Save tab of the Options dialog box

Here are the options for this tab:

- **Allow Fast Saves**   You can check this option to speed up saves, but at the cost of file size. You can then uncheck this option on your last save before closing the presentation to reduce file size.

CAUTION   *The Allow Fast Saves option can sometimes cause data file corruption. If you are having problems with corrupt files, try unchecking this option.*

- **Prompt for File Properties**   Use this feature in an environment where everyone is supposed to create file properties for document management purposes.
- **Save AutoRecover Info Every *x* Minutes**   By default, PowerPoint saves recovery information every 10 minutes. If your electrical supply is often cut off or you want to avoid doing even 10 minutes of work again, lower this number.
- **Convert Charts When Saving as Previous Version**   You can convert charts when you save to an earlier version of PowerPoint so that the charts will display properly.
- **Save PowerPoint Files As**   You can specify the version of PowerPoint you save to.

CAUTION   *If you save to the hybrid PowerPoint 97-2003 and 95 formats, file size increases. If you save to an earlier version of PowerPoint, such as PowerPoint 95, you lose any features introduced in later versions.*

- **Default File Location**   You can specify the default location where PowerPoint saves files.
- **Embed True Type Fonts**   Embeds fonts so that people on other computers can see the original fonts, even if the fonts are not installed. Otherwise, PowerPoint substitutes similar installed fonts. The setting applies only to the current presentation.

On the Security tab, you can set a password for opening and editing a presentation. If you have a digital signature service, you can apply a digital signature to a presentation. You can also remove personal information from a PowerPoint presentation, such as the name of reviewers. Finally, you can adjust the security for macros, to help avoid getting viruses. A number of viruses come as macros in Microsoft Office applications. You have the following security options:

- **High**   Disables all macros except those that you have specified are from trusted sources. This is the default setting.
- **Medium**   Notifies you if macros exist when you open a presentation. You can then choose whether you want to enable or disable them. You should enable macros only if you expect them. Of course, if you disable macros, they don't function.
- **Low**   Enables all macros. Use this option only if you are confident about your virus-scanning software or are sure all your presentations are free from viruses.

CAUTION   *If you add a password, people using PowerPoint 97 or 2000 will not be able to open or edit your presentation, even if you give them the password. You can save the presentation in an earlier version format, but then you cannot add a password.*

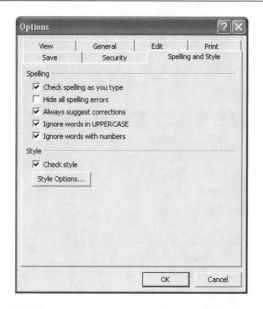

FIGURE 13-4 You can set spelling and style options for PowerPoint on the Spelling and Style tab.

On the Spelling and Style tab, shown in Figure 13-4, you set options for checking spelling and style. These options are self-explanatory.

Click Style Options to open the Style Options dialog box, shown here with the Case and End Punctuation tab on top. (These options are explained further in Chapter 2.)

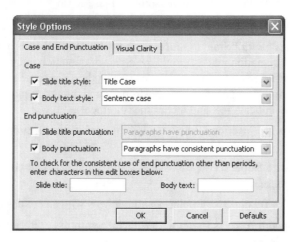

Use this dialog box to specify the case (capitalization) and ending punctuation for slide text.

13

Click the Visual Clarity tab, shown here, to set rules for the number and size of fonts as well as the amount of text on a slide. The purpose of these rules is to ensure that you don't have too many fonts, use text that is too small to read easily, or put too much text on a slide. Click OK when you are done. PowerPoint checks the slide using all the style rules and displays a lightbulb if your text deviates from the rules, as long as you display the Office Assistant (Help | Show the Office Assistant).

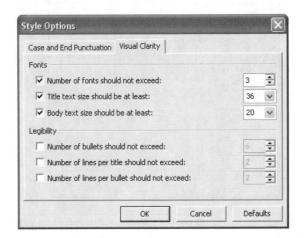

Use the AutoCorrect Dialog Box

The AutoCorrect dialog box contains settings relating to automatic adjustments to text. Choose Tools | AutoCorrect Options. The AutoCorrect and Smart Tags tabs are covered in Chapter 3.

The AutoFormat As You Type tab specifies how PowerPoint automatically changes certain types of text as you type it. You may have found some of these settings to be annoying—here's where you can turn them off. The options are the following:

- **"Straight Quotes" with "Smart Quotes"** Automatically changes a double quotation mark to a curved quotation mark. If you type a pair of quotation marks (around a word or phrase), the quotation marks automatically face each other. The same goes for apostrophes. Uncheck this option if you need to use apostrophes and quotation marks as primes and double primes (to indicate feet and inches measurement).

- **Fractions (1/2) with Fraction Character** Replaces a typed fraction with a built fraction ($\frac{1}{2}$).

- **Ordinals (1st) with Superscript** Replaces ordinal numbers that you type with their superscript versions (1st).

- **Hyphens (--) with Dash (—)** Replaces two hyphens with an em dash.

- **Smiley Faces :-) and Arrows (==>) with Special Symbols** Creates smiley faces (☺) and arrow symbols (➔).

■ **Internet and Network Paths with Hyperlinks**   Creates a hyperlink when you type an Internet URL or network path.

■ **Automatic Bulleted and Numbered Lists**   Starts a bulleted list when you type an asterisk (*) or dash and then a space or tab. When you type a number, a period, and then a space or tab, starts a numbered list.

■ **AutoFit Title Text to Placeholder**   Automatically changes the size of slide titles to fit the text placeholder. If you type more text than can fit in the placeholder, PowerPoint makes the text smaller. If you then delete some text, PowerPoint enlarges the text again. Uncheck this option if you want all your text to be the same size and prefer instead to move some text to another slide or shorten your text.

■ **AutoFit Body Text to Placeholder**   Automatically changes the size of body text to fit the text placeholder.

If you like this feature but want to turn it off sometimes, you can. When you want to turn off the text resizing, click the AutoFit Options button, shown here, and choose Stop Fitting Text to This Placeholder or one of the other options.

■ **Automatic Layout for Inserted Objects**   Adjusts the slide AutoLayout to accommodate inserted objects such as pictures. For example, if you are using an AutoLayout that includes only bulleted text and you add a picture, the AutoLayout changes to include bulleted text plus a picture placeholder. You can undo the change by using the options of the Automatic Layout Options button.

When you have finished setting the features in the AutoCorrect dialog box, click OK.

Configure Voice Recognition

Using the voice recognition feature, you can dictate text or commands instead of using the keyboard and mouse, although you will still use the keyboard and mouse sometimes. To set up voice recognition, choose Tools | Speech. If you don't see this menu item, you need to install it. (Choose Start | Settings | Control Panel, and double-click Add/Remove Programs. Choose Microsoft Office 2003 and follow the instructions for adding features to your original installation.)

The first time you use this feature, you are prompted to test your microphone. (A good-quality microphone helps.) Then a wizard brings you through the process of training Office to recognize your voice—you read some text about voice recognition for a few minutes. The entire process takes 15 minutes or less and as a bonus, explains the concepts behind voice recognition as you go. Once you have completed this training, you can use voice recognition in all Microsoft Office applications.

Once you have set up voice recognition, turn it on by choosing Tools | Speech again. This item is a toggle to turn the feature on and off. You'll see a check mark next to the Speech menu item when it is on. When voice recognition is on, the Language bar is displayed, as shown here.

Click Dictation on the Language bar to dictate text. Click Voice Command to use the feature to execute menu and toolbar items, as well as to navigate dialog boxes. For example, in Voice Command mode, say "New Slide" to insert a new slide. Dictating in PowerPoint requires some getting used to, because you constantly move from one text placeholder to another and from one bulleted item to another. By combining dictation with the use of the mouse and keyboard, you can easily dictate an entire presentation.

Customize Menus

You can create new menus or add menu commands to toolbars. These commands can be macros that you have created or existing PowerPoint commands. You can also customize shortcut menus. Customize your menus to put commands where you can access them quickly.

Some toolbars have menus. The best example is the Drawing toolbar, which has Draw and AutoShapes menus. I discuss these toolbar menus in the "Modify Existing Menus" section, later in this chapter.

You can choose if you want to display only the most often-used menu items or always display the full menus. Right-click any toolbar and choose Customize. Click the Options tab of the Customize dialog box. Check Always Show Full Menus if you want to display the full menus. Uncheck this check box to display only often-used menu items. This setting applies to all Office applications.

Create Your Own Menus

You can add a new menu on the menu bar and populate it with any menu commands, including custom commands. You can even hide a built-in menu, although it remains available so that you can add it back again. You can also change a menu's name and add your own dividing lines on the menu bar.

You can add commands to a menu or delete commands that you never use. PowerPoint has a long list of appropriate commands that do not normally appear on even the expanded menus but might be just what you need.

The advantage of adding a menu (over a toolbar) is that the menu is always displayed and doesn't take up space on your screen. Here's how:

1. Choose Tools | Customize.

2. Click the Commands tab, shown in Figure 13-5.

3. In the Categories list, scroll down and choose New Menu from the list of menus.

4. In the Commands window, select the New Menu item that appears there.

5. Drag this item to the menu bar. As you drag on the menu bar, PowerPoint places a vertical I-beam cursor to show you where the new menu item will appear.

FIGURE 13-5   Use the Commands tab of the Customize dialog box to create new menus and add commands to existing menus.

6.   With the Customize dialog box still open, right-click the new menu, which is now called New Menu, to display the shortcut menu shown here.

7.   In the Name text box, rename the menu. A menu name should be only one word and should not be too long.

Modify Existing Menus

If you wish, you can change the name of one of the existing menus on the menu bar.

 *Be especially careful about renaming menus if you share your computer with others. They may be quite mystified!*

Open the Customize dialog box and click the Commands tab. Right-click the menu that you wish to change. Change the menu's name in the Name text box and click Close in the dialog box. Opening the Customize dialog box may seem strange because you don't actually use it; however, having this dialog box open activates all the menu and toolbar customization features.

You can also delete a menu. Again, I urge caution. Anyone else using your computer may have a difficult time indeed! In general, you should delete only custom menus that you have added. However, a new word of caution: when you delete a custom menu, it's really gone! To delete a custom menu, open the Customize dialog box and drag the menu anywhere off the menu.

 *To remove a menu, menu item, or toolbar button without opening the Customize dialog box, press* ALT *and drag the item off the menu or toolbar.*

Now that you have created a new menu, you need to add commands to it. You could move your most often-used commands to one menu for convenience. A common use for a new menu is for macros that you have created. Here you see a menu with two commands on it that format AutoShapes with a gradient using a company's special colors. You can select any AutoShape and format it exactly like you have specified in the macro by choosing one of the two items on this menu. Macros are covered later in this chapter in the section "Work with Macros."

You can also add commands to existing menus. PowerPoint offers a long list of available commands that don't normally appear on the menus. For example, you can add often-used AutoShapes to a menu. You can also add custom commands that you or someone else wrote using Visual Basic for Applications (VBA) or another programming language. To add a menu item to a menu, follow these steps:

1. Choose Tools | Customize.
2. Click the Commands tab.
3. In the Categories box, choose a category. To add a macro, choose Macros.
4. Drag the command or macro you want from the Commands box to the menu you want to add it to. The menu opens. Drag to the desired location on the menu. PowerPoint places a horizontal I-beam cursor to show you where the menu item will appear.
5. Release the mouse.
6. Click Close in the Customize dialog box.

Deleting a menu item is easier than adding one. As usual, you need to open the Customize dialog box. Choose the menu with the menu item you want to delete. It opens up. Drag the menu item anywhere off the menu and release the mouse button. Voilà—it's gone!

Oddly enough, you can place a menu on a toolbar. As I mentioned earlier, the Drawing toolbar contains menus. You can customize these menus in the same way that you customize menus on the menu bar. Here you see the same menu shown earlier but placed on the Drawing toolbar. If you usually keep the Drawing toolbar open, you might want to place a menu there that contains commands that relate to drawing.

Work with Shortcut Menus

A shortcut menu is the menu that appears when you right-click somewhere in PowerPoint. You can't add or delete a shortcut menu, but you can remove and add menu items to it. Many of these menus display both text and icons; you can customize how these menu items are displayed. You can rename a menu item on a shortcut menu just like you can for regular menus.

Before customizing a shortcut menu, try to figure out where you right-click on the screen, and in which view, when you display that menu. For example, here you see the menu that appears when you right-click the background of a slide in Normal or Slide view.

Let's say you often wish you could get to the slide master from this shortcut menu. Perhaps you sometimes open the menu to format the background of a slide and then realize that you should change the slide master instead of the individual slide. So you want to add the Slide Master menu item (on the View menu) to the shortcut menu. Here's how:

1. Choose Tools | Customize.

2. Click the Toolbars tab of the Customize dialog box.

13

3. In the Toolbars list, check the Shortcut Menus check box. PowerPoint displays the Shortcut Menus toolbar with four items on it, as shown here. All the shortcut menus can be accessed from this toolbar.

4. Find the shortcut menu you want to change. You may have to search around a bit. For example, you can find the shortcut menu that appears when you right-click the background of a slide by choosing Draw | Slide Background from the Shortcut Menus toolbar. PowerPoint displays the shortcut menu.

5. To add a menu item, click the Commands tab of the Customize dialog box.

6. Choose a category from the Categories list. For example, to add an item to go to the slide master, choose View because you get to the Slide Master menu item from the View menu.

7. Find the command in the Commands list and drag it to the desired location on the shortcut menu. In our example, you would choose Slide Master.

8. Click Close in the Customize dialog box.

Here you see the new shortcut menu with its new item.

To delete a menu item, follow steps 1 through 4 above. Then drag the item you want to delete off the shortcut menu. Click Close when you have finished using the Customize dialog box.

A useful menu to customize is the Slide Show shortcut menu that appears when you right-click during a slide show. In the following example, First Slide and Last Slide commands (from the View category) have been added to the viewing options. In addition to individual commands, you can add VBA macros to help you navigate during a slide show.

A shortcut menu can contain both text and icons. PowerPoint enables you to customize whether you see text, icons, or both. Having both available means you can put a command on either a menu or a toolbar (or both) for maximum flexibility.

To control the appearance of a menu, open the Customize dialog box. Click the menu to open it. For a shortcut menu, choose Shortcut Menus from the Toolbars list on the Toolbars tab, and navigate to the shortcut menu until PowerPoint displays it. Right-click the menu item you want to change. PowerPoint displays the menu shown here.

13

Most of the items pertain to button images, which I discuss in the next section on customizing toolbars. However, you have four options that are appropriate for menus:

- **Default Style** Displays the button image and the text if the command is in a menu, but displays only the image if you move the command to a toolbar
- **Text Only (Always)** Displays just the text
- **Text Only (In Menus)** Displays just the text in a menu but the button image if the command is on a toolbar
- **Image and Text** Displays both the button image and the text, whether on a menu or on a toolbar

You cannot display only an image on a menu. Some commands do not have images associated with them.

Customize Toolbars

Toolbars are customizable in much the same way that menus are. You can add or delete items from a toolbar. You can create a new toolbar and add existing or custom commands to it. Chapter 1 explains how to add or remove buttons from the standard choices of buttons as well as how to display and hide toolbars.

In addition, you can customize those little button images to your heart's content. If you create a new command, you can use any graphic image for the button, or you can edit an existing button image.

Manage Toolbars

Some simple display tactics can help keep your screen useful, yet uncluttered. For example, when you first install PowerPoint, both the Standard and the Formatting toolbars may be on the same row, freeing up a row of screen real estate. The result is that a number of buttons are not displayed. This arrangement may work for you. On the other hand, you may find it annoying to have to click the arrow at the end of the toolbars to find the missing buttons. You can move the toolbars so they are in two rows, but you can also change this setting in a dialog box. Choose Tools | Customize and click the Options tab. Then check the Show Standard and Formatting Toolbars on Two Rows check box.

You move a toolbar by dragging its *move handle*—a dotted bar at its left or top edge. If the toolbar is floating, it has a title bar that you can use to move it. When you drag a toolbar to the edge of the application window, PowerPoint docks it so that it cannot cover up any of your work.

You can resize and reshape a floating toolbar. Move the cursor over any edge until it changes to a double-headed arrow, and then drag the edge either inward or outward. For example, you can change a long, skinny toolbar into a compact box shape.

Of course, you can display any of PowerPoint's toolbars (including custom toolbars you create or install through a commercial add-in) by right-clicking any toolbar and choosing it from the list of toolbars.

A great trick is to detach a submenu from a toolbar to create a floating palette. For example, if you want to work with fill colors on several objects, you might find it annoying to constantly have to open up the Fill Color submenu on the Drawing toolbar. If you could turn it into a floating toolbar, it would stay open on your screen, and you could access the buttons immediately. It's easy. Choose the submenu so it opens. PowerPoint displays the submenu with a small move bar at the top. Then drag the move bar to anywhere on your screen, as shown here.

NOTE   *Another menu that is useful as a toolbar is the Align or Distribute submenu from the Draw menu of the Draw toolbar.*

To remove the floating palette, click its Close button. The submenu remains available from its original toolbar.

Add and Remove Toolbar Buttons

Adding and removing a toolbar button is similar to adding and removing a menu item. It's easy to add an existing button, but you can also create your own.

Remove Buttons from a Toolbar

If you never use a toolbar button, you can hide it. The button is still available if it is a built-in button—that is, if it came with PowerPoint. First, display the toolbar. Then display the Add or Remove Buttons menu in one of two ways:

- If the toolbar is docked, click the Toolbar Options down arrow at the right edge of the toolbar, then choose Add or Remove Buttons.

- If the toolbar is floating, click the down arrow at the upper-right corner of the toolbar's title bar and choose Add or Remove Buttons.

PowerPoint displays the list of buttons. Uncheck any button or buttons that you want to hide from the toolbar.

Add Buttons to a Toolbar

You can add a toolbar button to a toolbar, either from another toolbar or from PowerPoint's long list of toolbar buttons. You can also create a custom button for a custom command and add it to a toolbar.

13

To add a button from another toolbar, display both toolbars and open the Customize dialog box (Tools | Customize). If necessary, move the dialog box out of the way. To move the button (remove it from one toolbar and add it to another), drag the button from one toolbar to the desired location on the other toolbar. To copy the button, press CTRL while you drag.

You can add a toolbar button to a menu, too. Just drag the button to the menu, wait until the menu opens, and continue to drag to the desired position on the menu. PowerPoint automatically adds the appropriate text to the button image.

The opposite also holds—you can drag a menu item to a toolbar. You can even put one of the built-in menus (File, Edit, View, and so on) on a toolbar. Here's how:

1. Display the toolbar.

2. Choose Tools | Customize.

3. Click the Commands tab.

4. From the Categories box, choose Built-in Menus. You see a list of the built-in menus in the Commands box.

5. Drag the menu that you want to the toolbar.

Most often, you simply want to add a menu item or two to a toolbar. To add a button from PowerPoint's list of commands, follow these steps:

1. Display the toolbar you want to customize.

2. Choose Tools | Customize.

3. Click the Commands tab.

4. Choose a category from the Categories box.

5. In the Commands box, find the command you want and drag it to the toolbar.

It's worth the time to look through the available commands. You may find some useful ones!

Create a New Toolbar

Adding and removing buttons on existing toolbars may not be enough for you. You may want to create your own toolbar from scratch. You can place existing buttons together there, for convenience, or you can add custom buttons containing custom macros. Follow these steps to create the toolbar.

1. Choose Tools | Customize.

2. Click the Toolbars tab, shown in Figure 13-6.

3. Click New.

4. In the New Toolbar dialog box, type a name for the toolbar and click OK. It can have spaces, but try to keep the name fairly short and meaningful. PowerPoint creates a tiny toolbar, all ready for some buttons.

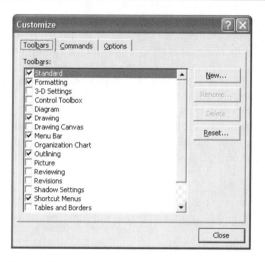

FIGURE 13-6 Use the Toolbars tab of the Customize dialog box to create a new toolbar.

The procedure for adding buttons of existing commands to a custom toolbar is the same as described previously for adding buttons to existing toolbars—open the Customize dialog box and drag commands to the toolbar.

If you have created a macro, as discussed in the "Work with Macros" section later in this chapter, you can add it to a custom toolbar. With the Customize dialog box open, choose the Commands tab. From the Categories list, choose Macros. Then drag the macro you want from the Commands list to the toolbar. PowerPoint creates a toolbar button from the name of the macro.

13

Customizing the Way Toolbars and Menus Work

The Options tab of the Customize dialog box lets you customize several features of toolbars and menus. You can enable or disable the display of only often-used menu items and toolbar buttons. You can also specify that you want the Standard and Formatting toolbars on two separate rows, so that all of the buttons are always available. Check Large Icons if you have a very high screen resolution and the toolbar buttons are too small to see clearly. This feature is also useful for people with visual impairments. By default, font names in the Formatting toolbar's Font drop-down list are displayed in their font. If you find that this feature slows the display of fonts, you can disable it on the Options tab. You can turn on and off the display of ScreenTips (labels that appear when you hover the cursor over a toolbar button). If you like to use keyboard shortcuts but often forget them, check Show Shortcut Keys in ScreenTips.

TIP

One use for a custom toolbar is to hold custom buttons and menus that you don't want to display. If you remove a custom button or menu, it's gone forever. Instead, you can create a new toolbar and move custom buttons or menus to the holding toolbar. Then hide the toolbar. The toolbar stores them for you in case you ever need them again.

To help organize toolbars into sections, you can create separator bars. Look at the Standard or Formatting toolbars in PowerPoint and you see several separator bars. To add a separator bar, with the Customize dialog box open, right-click a button and choose Begin a Group. You now have a new separator bar to the left of the button. You can remove a separator bar by simply dragging a button to the right of the bar closer to the button to its left.

You can also turn PowerPoint into a browser by attaching hyperlinks to toolbar buttons. Follow these steps:

1. Open the Customize dialog box and drag any button on a toolbar.

2. Right-click the button and choose Assign Hyperlink | Open.

3. In the Assign Hyperlink: Open dialog box, specify a hyperlink. The hyperlink replaces the original button's command.

4. Click OK. If you want, change the button's image as described in the next section.

Create Toolbar Buttons

Once you start creating your own custom toolbars and custom commands (like with macros), you need to create your own buttons. Here's your chance to get artistic! You can even change existing built-in button icons to suit your whims.

Choose from PowerPoint's List of Buttons

You can avoid the artistic route by using one of PowerPoint's buttons, but they aren't suitable in most circumstances. Here's how:

1. Display the toolbar containing the button you want to change.

2. Choose Tools | Customize to open the Customize dialog box.

3. Right-click the toolbar button you want to change.

4. Choose Change Button Image from the shortcut menu.

5. Choose one of the button images from the submenu. PowerPoint uses that image for the toolbar button.

From the same shortcut menu, you can choose to display the button image only, the text only, or both the text and the image.

Edit an Existing Image or Create an Image from Scratch

You may want to slightly change a button image or use an existing image as the basis for a new one. It's easier to edit an existing image than to create one from scratch. To edit an image, with the Customize dialog box open, right-click the image on the toolbar to open the shortcut menu. Choose Edit Button Image to open the Button Editor, shown in Figure 13-7. Note that you cannot edit a button that displays a list or a submenu.

Use the Move arrows to move the entire images in any direction. To erase, click the Erase box and then click in the picture image where you want to erase.

To create a new button image from scratch, click Clear in the Button Editor, click a color, and then start clicking those little boxes. You can drag across boxes to create a line.

Use a Graphic Image

You can find an image you like and use it for your button. For example, many web sites offer free graphic images that you can legally download and use. You can also use an image that you create in a graphic program. For best results, use an image that is 16 × 16 pixels, the size that PowerPoint normally uses. Larger images are scaled down and may become unclear or distorted.

The first step is to copy the graphic to the clipboard. If you have downloaded an image, you need to insert it into any program—PowerPoint is fine. Then select it and choose Copy on the Standard toolbar. If you have created the graphic in a program, you can select it and copy it to the clipboard directly from that program.

Display the toolbar and open the Customize dialog box. Right-click the toolbar button and choose Paste Button Image. PowerPoint replaces the current image with the image on the clipboard.

Don't forget that you can use button images for menus and shortcut menus as well. As explained earlier, you can customize whether the menu shows just text or text along with an image. For toolbar buttons, you can show just the image or text and the image.

13

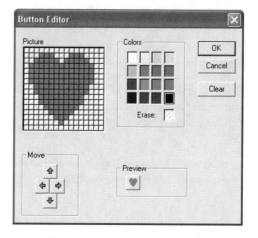

FIGURE 13-7   Use the Button Editor to edit button images, pixel by pixel.

Using Add-Ins

Add-ins are programs (written by a programmer) that add a feature to PowerPoint. You install an add-in and then load it into PowerPoint. PowerPoint add-ins are files with the filename extension .ppa.

Microsoft's web site has several add-ins that you can download and try out. Go to http://office.microsoft.com/downloads/ and choose PowerPoint as the product. Among the available PowerPoint downloads are the add-ins. If the add-in is compressed, you need to decompress it. Microsoft provides self-extracting .exe files. Double-click the file to install the add-in. Follow the simple instructions to complete installation. The installation program tells you where it is installing the add-in. Write down this location because you may need it later. To load the add-in, follow these steps:

1. Choose Tools | Add-ins.

2. Click Add New.

3. In the Add New PowerPoint Add-In dialog box, locate the add-in. Here's when you need to remember where you installed it. Choose it and click OK.

4. If you see a message that says the Add-In contains macros, choose Enable Macros if you want the add-in to work.

5. Click Close in the Add-Ins dialog box.

Of course, how you use an add-in depends on the add-in. Most add-ins come with a text file or some other method to provide you with instructions. (You may see instructions at the web site that you can print.)

You can also unload an add-in when you are finished using it. Choose Tools | Add-Ins and select the add-in. Click Unload.

If you have some VBA code, you can save it as an add-in. Type the code in the Visual Basic Editor (discussed later in this chapter in the section "Program with VBA"). You can use any presentation to do this. Close the Visual Basic Editor and then choose File | Save As from PowerPoint's File menu. In the Save as Type drop-down list, choose PowerPoint Add-In (*.ppa). Type a name in the File Name text box and click Save.

CAUTION   *When you save your presentation as an add-in, do not delete the original presentation (.ppt) file. You'll need the .ppt file if you ever need to edit your add-in.*

Work with Macros

A *macro* is a series of PowerPoint commands that you save. You can then run the macro and execute all the commands in the macro. A macro can save you hours of time doing repetitive tasks. All macros are written (or recorded) in Visual Basic for Applications (VBA).

There are two ways to create a macro. If you can execute the commands for the macro in PowerPoint to get the result you want, you can record the macro. For example, let's say you need to format fills in a certain way. You find yourself going through the same formatting steps over and over. Instead, you can select an object, start recording, and go through the same steps. When you stop recording, you have a macro. From now on, you can select any object, run the macro, and let it do the work for you.

Other macros cannot be recorded. If you want a procedure to be executed under only certain conditions, you need to write the macro using VBA. Macros used in Slide Show view also need to be written, because Slide Show view doesn't have menus and toolbars to let you run through the macro's commands. In these cases, you need to learn how to program in VBA—or find someone who knows how.

In this section, I explain how to record and run macros. I also provide an introduction to writing VBA macros with the assumption that you are not a programmer. If you are, the "Program with VBA" section will provide you with an introduction to the programming tools available in PowerPoint 2003.

Record a Macro

If you want to record a macro, it often pays to practice the macro steps first. If the macro is long, you might even want to write down the steps you need to take. Otherwise, if you make a mistake, you may need to record the macro again. It's a little like rehearsing a presentation!

When you know what you need to do, set up the initial conditions first. For example, if you want to write a macro to format the fill of objects, you need to select an object first. It doesn't make any difference which object you select. If the macro will be run in Slide Sorter view, go into Slide Sorter view. Macros may not work if you try to run them in a different circumstance than the one you recorded them in.

The macro recorder is a wonderful tool, almost magical, but it cannot track where you move or click your mouse on the part of the screen that contains your presentation. Therefore, if you try to select an object while recording a macro, the results will not be what you expect. Sometimes this requires learning new ways of doing familiar tasks. However, you can record using the mouse to click a toolbar button or choose a menu item.

To record a macro, follow these steps:

1. Choose Tools | Macro | Record New Macro. PowerPoint opens the Record Macro dialog box, shown here.

2. In the Macro Name text box, type a name for the macro. Macro names may not have spaces, and the first character must be a letter. You can use an underscore. Examples of macro names are FormatFill and Format_Fill.

3. If you want, add a description of the macro in the Description box. You can describe exactly what the macro does.

4. Click OK. PowerPoint places the Stop Recording button, shown here, on your screen, both to remind you that you are recording and so that you can stop recording when you're done.

5. Execute each command that you want to record. If you make a little mistake, you can correct it. For example, if you choose the wrong color, you can go back and choose the correct color. PowerPoint records both the mistake and your correction, but the end result is OK, although the macro might take a couple of milliseconds longer to run.

6. When you are done, click the Stop Recording button.

If you make a big mistake while recording, stop recording and start over. Use the same macro name. PowerPoint asks if you want to replace the existing macro. Choose Yes and continue the process. You may also be able to edit the macro text directly, as explained later in this chapter in the section "Manage Macros."

Use a Macro

Once you have recorded a macro, you should test it. If necessary, re-create the situation you want to start with first. Then follow these steps:

1. Choose Tools | Macro | Macros. PowerPoint opens the Macro dialog box, shown in Figure 13-8.

FIGURE 13-8   Choose your macro from the Macro dialog box.

2. Choose the macro from the list.

3. Click Run.

If the macro does not work properly, try recording it again. If you get an error message, it may be because the environment has changed, as mentioned earlier. If the Run option is not enabled when you try to run your macro, unsigned macros may be disabled. PowerPoint 2003 defaults to a high level of security, where only signed macros from trusted sources are permitted to run. This setting can prevent your computer from being infected by viruses, but it prevents you from running your own macros unless you sign and trust them first. To run your own macros without signing and trusting them, choose Tools | Macro | Security and set the security level to Medium. When PowerPoint is closed and started again, you will be prompted that macros are in the presentation and asked whether to enable macros or not. If you choose to enable macros, you will be able to run your macros.

For quick access to a macro, you may want to place it on a toolbar button or menu. You can also attach it to an object. In Slide Show view, the only way to run a macro is to attach it to an object. Placing a macro on a toolbar button is discussed earlier in this chapter, in the "Create a New Toolbar" section. Use the same procedure for both menus and toolbars. For details on attaching a macro to an object, see the section "Use Action Settings" in Chapter 11.

 **Sign and Trust Your Macros**

You should never set your security level to Low, but you can have the virus protection that high security provides while still being able to run your own macros. To run your own macros while using high security, you must sign and trust them. Just follow these steps:

1. Create a code-signing certificate using the Selfcert.exe utility that comes with Office 2003. To create a certificate, run Selfcert.exe, which by default is located in the C:\Program Files\Microsoft Office\Office 11 folder. (You may need to install this feature first.) Enter your name in the Create Digital Certificate dialog box and click OK to create your new digital code-signing certificate.

2. Open the Visual Basic Editor by choosing Tools | Macro | Visual Basic Editor (or press ALT-F11).

3. Choose Tools | Digital Signature to open the Digital Signature dialog box.

4. Click Choose to see a list of all digital certificates registered on your computer and select the certificate you just created. Click OK twice to close the Digital Signature dialog box.

13

5. Close the Visual Basic Editor and exit PowerPoint.

6. When you open the PowerPoint presentation that is signed with your certificate again, the Security Warning dialog box will list your new signing certificate as unauthenticated. Check the check box to always trust macros from this source and click the Enable Macros button.

7. Choose Tools | Macro | Security to open the Security dialog box, and click the Trusted Publishers tab. Click OK. Your certificate is now listed as trusted. If you now choose to set the security level back to High, you will still be able to run your macros when you open the presentation again. You won't see the Security Warning dialog box when PowerPoint starts, but you will have the protection that high security provides.

Thanks to Ken Slovak for this information. Ken (http://www.slovaktech.com) *is an Outlook MVP (Most Valuable Professional).*

Manage Macros

The more you understand about how VBA code works, the more easily you can manage your macros. Sometimes it's easier to go into the code and edit it than to rerecord a macro. In addition, looking at VBA code created by recording a macro is a great way to learn about VBA.

Edit Macros

To edit a macro and view the code, choose Tools | Macro | Macros, choose the macro you want to edit, and click Edit. Figure 13-9 shows a macro. You are now in the Visual Basic Editor, where you can write your own code.

The Editor window contains a *code module,* which stores VBA code. You can have several code modules in a *project,* which contains all the pieces necessary for a VBA program.

Here's how this simple macro works:

- The first line starts the macro. A VBA macro always opens with the word *Sub.* (It stands for subroutine.) The name of the macro follows. The line always ends with a set of parentheses, in this case, empty.

- The next three lines start with an apostrophe. The apostrophe tells VBA that what follows is a comment, not code. You can, and should, place comments in your code to explain what the code is doing. When you record a macro, PowerPoint automatically places a comment containing the date and your name.

- The next line starts a With block of code. Because a shape was selected, the code states that the next few lines apply to the ShapeRange (one or more shapes) that is selected in the active window.

- The next four lines specify the gradient, set the fill to be visible, specify the two colors, and create the two-color gradient and its variant (represented by the number 3 in this case).

- Now the code ends the With code block.

- The last line ends the subroutine, with the expression *End Sub.*

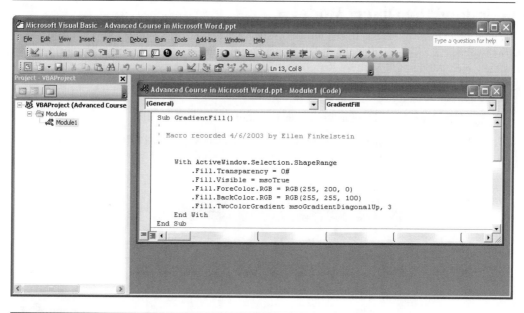

FIGURE 13-9   The Visual Basic Editor

You can see that you could easily fix the colors if you knew their red-green-blue numbers. You could also change the variant—most gradients offer variants from one through four.

If you edit a macro, click Save on the Visual Basic Editor toolbar to save your changes. To close the Visual Basic Editor, click its Close button.

Copy Macros

You can create a duplicate of a macro by copying and pasting. You can then edit the new macro to create a different macro, instead of creating it from scratch. To create a duplicate, open the Visual Basic Editor to display the macro. Select all the text and copy it to the clipboard. Then choose Insert | Module to create a new code module window. Paste the macro into the new window and edit it. You can also paste the text at the bottom of the same window to create a new macro.

You can use the Project Explorer (the top left window of the Visual Basic Editor in Figure 13-9) to copy a macro module to another presentation. Open both presentations. If necessary, click the plus (+) sign next to the presentation to display its modules. Then drag a module from one presentation to the other, all within the Project Explorer. If the Project Explorer isn't visible, you can open it by choosing View | Project Explorer.

Program with VBA

Learning how to program in VBA is quite a large undertaking. Here I explain some basic information to get you started. The chapter concludes with some examples that you can use in your own PowerPoint presentations.

13

Understand the Object Model

VBA uses a hierarchy of objects to enable you to specify an object. Each object also has its own hierarchy. In this way, you can distinguish text in a text placeholder from shapes or pictures. To view the Object Model, follow these steps:

1. Choose Tools | Macros | Visual Basic Editor.

2. Click the Help button on the Visual Basic Editor Standard toolbar.

3. In the Search box, type PowerPoint Object Model. Chose the PowerPoint Object Model item to open the Object Model schematic shown in Figure 13-10.

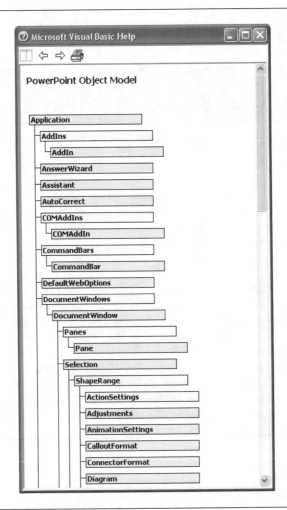

FIGURE 13-10   The PowerPoint Object Model

The top of the hierarchy is always the application—in this case, PowerPoint. You can click on any object listed here to get further help on that object.

Another way to follow the line of a hierarchy is to use the Object Browser, shown in Figure 13-11. To open the Object Browser, follow these steps:

1. Click the Object Browser button on the toolbar, shown here, or press F2 to open the Object Browser.

2. From the Object Browser's Project/Library drop-down list, choose PowerPoint.

3. Select any PowerPoint object and click the Help button inside the Object Browser window.

For example, if you want to find out about the ActiveWindow object used in the macro explained earlier, you can type **ActiveWindow** in the Search Text box (just under the Project/Library drop-down list) and press ENTER. The results are displayed in the Search Results window. (If you get more than one result, click the item you want.) Click Help to get information on that term.

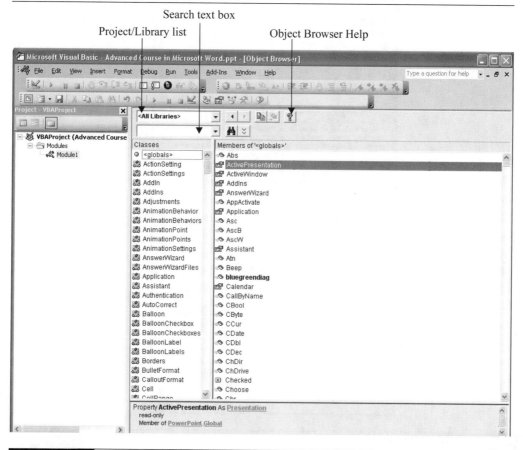

FIGURE 13-11 The Object Browser helps you find out about objects.

13

Use Methods and Properties

It's not enough to specify objects—you need to do something with them. In VBA, objects have methods and properties. A *method* is an action that you perform on an object or an action that an object can perform itself. A *property* is an attribute of an object, such as the fill color of an object or the font of text. After looking up any object (type it in the Search Text window and click Help), you can find its methods and properties. You usually also get some examples of code using that object. In Figure 13-12, you see the Help page for ShapeRange.

When you choose an object on the left side of the Object Browser, the right side shows its sub-objects, methods, and properties. When you click ShapeRange on the left and then Fill on

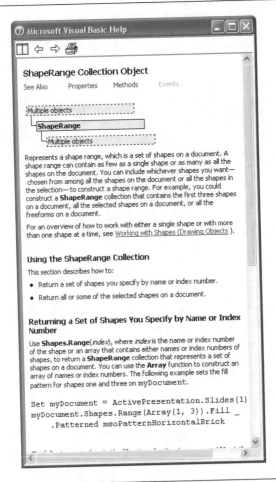

FIGURE 13-12   The ShapeRange Help page

the right, you can click Help in the Object Browser window to view Help for the Fill Property used in the example shown in Figure 13-9.

All VBA code uses this structure of the object hierarchy and accomplishes tasks by means of methods and properties. You can also use built-in functions, such as If and For Each or For...Next.

You can create dialog boxes that appear when you run a macro. This topic is more involved, but to start, choose Insert | UserForm from the Visual Basic for Applications menu. A *UserForm* is the raw material for a dialog box. The toolbox appears, letting you draw in the dialog box typical controls such as buttons and text boxes. You can double-click any control to write code that specifies how the control functions. To create a form that viewers can use in Slide Show view, choose View | Toolbars from the PowerPoint menu and choose Control Toolbox. You can choose a control and drag it on a slide.

Use VBA in Your Presentations

Programming in PowerPoint with VBA first appeared in PowerPoint 97. However, in many ways, programming PowerPoint has proved a challenge for both PowerPoint experts and VBA programmers. While programming Excel or Word is fairly straightforward, writing VBA for PowerPoint programming requires not only programming knowledge, but also an understanding of the graphical nature of PowerPoint. But every day, PowerPoint programmers learn new strategies for using VBA in PowerPoint.

This section discusses three real-world examples of what VBA can accomplish in PowerPoint. You'll find sample VBA code at the end of the chapter for two of these examples. You can use VBA to accomplish three types of processes in PowerPoint:

- Speed up routine production tasks that would otherwise be time-consuming or prone to error.
- Automate the integration of tasks in other Office (or VBA-aware) programs when the task is better done in another program.
- Add interactive capability to PowerPoint to gather data from a person viewing a slide show.

Accelerate Routine Production Tasks

Many routine production tasks take a lot of time or are just not straightforward in PowerPoint. For example, presentation designers often need to keep track of the filename and where that presentation is located during and after the production process. Users have often asked for a way to include the path and filename of a presentation on draft printouts.

You could type the filename and the path into the footer, but that information is not updated if you change the filename or the location of the presentation. A simple VBA routine can help you accomplish this goal quickly and dynamically. The first code example at the end of this chapter is a simple macro that toggles between showing and not showing a complete path and filename in the footer. You can use this VBA macro to print presentations for draft purposes (with path and filename). You can then turn it off for either the real presentation or real printouts. Click to turn the footer on or off.

Similarly, you can improve other time-consuming, repetitive, or error-prone tasks with a VBA tool created and customized for your own specific needs.

13

Automate the Integration of Tasks in Other Programs

While PowerPoint is a good presentation tool, it does not have many of the advanced features of Microsoft Excel. For example, you cannot indicate the minimum or maximum values on a series of charts or automatically recalculate scaling as your data changes.

You can use VBA to automate the deletion of the old chart and the copying and pasting of the new charts back into PowerPoint. In some cases, you could legitimately perform this task without VBA and use linking. But if you need to add charts or change the scaling, you might be best off automating the task and controlling Excel from PowerPoint.

Add Interactive Data-Gathering Capability to a Presentation

Suppose you are at a trade show and have set up a presentation to show in kiosk mode. You want to make it easy for someone to give you information or request to be added to your mailing list. Create the entry form on a PowerPoint slide and export the information from that slide into an Excel workbook. This simple application both controls Excel from within PowerPoint and uses PowerPoint as a way to capture and store information. The user never sees Excel. PowerPoint opens Excel in the background, captures the data supplied by the viewer, and tells Excel to place those values into an Excel worksheet. PowerPoint then tells Excel to save that file and wait for the next viewer's input. See the second code example at the end of this chapter.

Thanks to Brian Reilly, owner of Reillyand, Inc., a consulting firm that specializes in automating MS Office applications, for the information in this section "Use VBA in Your Presentations" and for the original creation of the VBA code at the end of this chapter. Brian is a Microsoft MVP and frequent contributor to the Microsoft PowerPoint newsgroup. He can be reached at 212-683-5969 or brian@reillyand.com.

You can find more VBA resources on Steve Rindsberg's web site, http://www.rdpslides.com. Steve is another Microsoft PowerPoint MVP and coauthors a variety of PowerPoint production toolbar utilities with Brian.

Code Example 1: Place a Path and Filename in a Footer

The following VBA code shows the code for the application described in the "Accelerate Routine Production Tasks" section of this chapter.

This example creates a one-button menu that is placed just after the Help menu. When you click it, PowerPoint displays the presentation's path and filename as a footnote in the slide master. Click it again, and the footnote disappears.

VBA code that is meant to run while not in Slide Show view cannot be run by assigning a macro to an object. That means you have two choices:

- Choose Tools | Macro | Macros and choose the macro to run.
- Assign the macro to a custom toolbar button.

The code that follows creates the menu when you run the Create_Menu macro. To remove the menu, run the Remove_Menu macro. You can type this code in the Visual Basic Editor of any new or existing presentation. You can also download the Join Our Mailing List.ppt by going to http://www.osborne.com and clicking the "free code" link. This presentation contains the VBA code for both this example and the example that follows.

```
Option Explicit

Sub Create_Menu()
'Purpose:Creates a custom menu
'Created: Brian Reilly 12-26-2001
'Modified: Ken Slovak 01-16-2002
    Dim cmPres As CommandBar
    Dim cbctrMnu As CommandBarControl

    With Application.CommandBars(1).Controls
        Set cmPres = Application.CommandBars(1)
        'Make sure the previous instance of this menu
        'is not still around
        'On Error Resume Next continues even with an error
        'if this menu is not found
        On Error Resume Next
        cmPres.Controls("Reillyand, Inc.").Delete
        'Next line resets error trapping to be back on.
        On Error GoTo 0

        Set cbctrMnu = cmPres.FindControl(, , "Reillyand, Inc.")
        If Not cbctrMnu Is Nothing Then
            Exit Sub
        End If

        With .Add(Type:=msoControlPopup, before:=.Count + 1)
            .Caption = "Reillyand, Inc."
            .TooltipText = _
              "Contains the Reillyand, Inc. Custom Menu items"

            'Add the first menu item to attach an OnAction to
            With .Controls
                With .Add(msoControlButton)
                    .DescriptionText = "Toggle Path"
                    .Caption = "Toggle Path"
                    .OnAction = "Toggle_Path"
                    .Style = msoButtonIcon
                    .FaceId = 29
                End With
            End With

            'You can add additional items to the menu.

            'To add additional items, uncomment the following code and
```

13

```
'change the control captions to the button names you want
' and the OnAction property to the macros you want to run
'when the buttons are pressed.

'With .Controls
'     With .Add(msoControlButton)
'         .Caption = "Import New Month"
'         .FaceId = 1096
'         .OnAction = "Macro_1"
'     End With

'     With .Add(msoControlButton)
'         .Caption = "Create Report"
'         .FaceId = 956
'         .OnAction = "Macro_2"
'     End With

    'End With
  End With
End With

'Now release the objects we created to release the memory they use
Set cmPres = Nothing
Set cbctrMnu = Nothing
End Sub

'Add the code to be called from the menu button
Sub Toggle_Path()
    'This will only put the path on the slide master and
    'not on the title master
    'You would have to put it specifically on the title
    'master if you wanted it there.
    Dim strfullname As String

    strfullname = ActivePresentation.FullName
    'will carry 'the value for the .sourcefullname

    ''''''This checks to see if the footer is on or off
    'and switches off or on''''''''''''

    'Note: this only looks at the slide master
    'and not the title master
    With ActivePresentation.SlideMaster.HeadersFooters
```

```
        If .Footer.Visible = False Then
            With .Footer
                .Visible = msoTrue
            End With
        Else
            With .Footer
                .Text = strfullname
                .Visible = msoFalse
            End With
        End If
    End With
End Sub


Sub Remove_Menu()
    Dim cmPres As CommandBar

    With Application.CommandBars(1).Controls
        Set cmPres = Application.CommandBars(1)
        On Error Resume Next
        cmPres.Controls("Reillyand, Inc.").Delete
    End With

    'Now release the object we created to release the memory it uses
    Set cmPres = Nothing
End Sub
```

One very good way to create a menu or a toolbar, especially if you are going to have many special production tools, is to create an add-in with a custom toolbar or menu and assign each macro to a button on that toolbar or menu.

The preceding code could reside in that add-in and automatically build the menu every time PowerPoint is started. Instructions for saving VBA code as an add-in are in the "Using Add-Ins" section earlier in this chapter. To automatically create the menu when the add-in starts, the Auto_Open sub would call the Create_Menu macro. To automatically remove the menu when the add-in shuts down, the Auto_Close sub would call the Remove_Menu macro:

```
Sub Auto_Open()
    'In PPT Auto_Open only runs automatically if in an add-in
    Create_Menu
End Sub

Sub Auto_Close()
    'In PPT Auto_Close only runs automatically if in an add-in
    Remove_Menu
End Sub
```

13

Code Example 2: Collect Data from a Slide Show

Here is the VBA code for the application described in the "Add Interactive Data-Gathering Capability to a Presentation" section, earlier in this chapter.

This code example gets the values of the text boxes and a combo box on a PowerPoint page, and then it places those values into a workbook in Excel—completely in the background. The user never sees Excel open because it is invisible. The Excel file is saved, and Excel is closed. If you listen to your hard disk, you may hear the activity, but you won't see it on the screen.

To use this code, you need two files: Join Our Mailing List.ppt and Submit to Mailing List.xls. You can download these files from the Osborne web site by going to http://www.osborne.com and clicking the "free code" link. The presentation already contains the necessary VBA code for both this example and the previous one. Place both files in the same folder. Open the presentation and switch to Slide Show view. Click in the text boxes and type the requested information. Click the Submit for Mailing List button. You can try typing in several names and addresses. Then open the Excel worksheet, and voilà!—you see the data on the spreadsheet. Figure 13-13 shows both the presentation and the Excel worksheet.

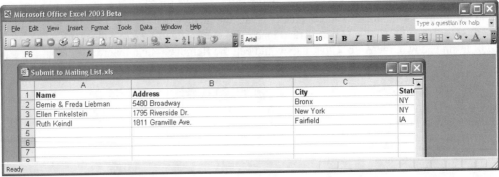

a

b

FIGURE 13-13   (a) A slide containing a form for collecting names and addresses and (b) the resulting Excel worksheet that collects the information

```
Option Explicit

Private Sub btnSubmit_Click()
    Dim oAppXL As Object        'Declare the Excel application object
    Dim strName As String       'Holds the Name text string
    Dim strAddress As String    'Holds the Address text String
    Dim strCity As String       'Holds City
    Dim strState As String      'Holds State
    Dim strZip As String        'Holds ZIP code
    Dim strPath As String        'Lets the database location be in same
                                 'location as presentation
                                 'no matter what drive you are on
'First check if all the required fields are completed
    If tbName.Text = "" Or tbAddress.Text = "" Or tbCity.Text = "" _
        Or cboState.Text = "" Or tbZip.Text = "" Then
          MsgBox "A necessary field is empty. Please check your " _
          & "entries and submit again.", vbExclamation

        Exit Sub
    Else
        'Will use the current path of this presentation to look
        'for the Excel file in the same folder.
        strPath = ActivePresentation.Path
        Set oAppXL = CreateObject("Excel.application")
        With oAppXL
            'Each Excel command is preceded with an extra "."
            'compared to normal code in Excel
            'since PPT is actually telling Excel
            'to run the code in Excel.
            .workbooks.Open FileName:=strPath & "\" & _
              "Submit to Mailing List.xls"
            'We don't want to see Excel and it doesn't have
            "to be visible to run
            .Visible = False

            'Now run Excel and place the values
            'This next line refers to the first open cell in
            'column A that is blank
            'It will accept up to 65536 entries and if this
            'were a really intelligent application
            'it would check for the .row <> 65536 and
            'create a new sheet to add more names.
            If .Sheets("Database").Range("A65536"). _
```

```
                    End(xlup).Offset(1, 0).Value = "" Then
                        With .Sheets("Database").Range("A65536"). _
                            End(xlup).Offset(1, 0)
                            'Now get the values from the text boxes and
                            'combo box in PowerPoint
                            strName = tbName.Text
                            strAddress = tbAddress.Text
                            strCity = tbCity.Text
                            strState = cboState.Text
                            strZip = tbZip
                            'Add the values from the PPT page
                            .Value = strName
                            .Offset(0, 1).Value = strAddress
                            .Offset(0, 2).Value = strCity
                            .Offset(0, 3).Value = strState
                            .Offset(0, 4).Value = strZip
                        End With
                    End If
                End With
            End If
            'Turn off warnings in Excel since the file is
            'overwriting an existing file
            oAppXL.Application.DisplayAlerts = False
            'Wouldn't need to close or quit if the upfront code
            'handled that differently but it still
            'all happens quickly, so it might be a good idea anyway.
            'Close and save the file, the (True) tells Excel to save it.
            oAppXL.activeworkbook.Close (True)
            oAppXL.Application.Quit
            'Clear the memory used by Excel
            Set oAppXL = Nothing
            'Now clear the existing values and be ready for a new entry.
            tbName.Text = ""
            tbAddress.Text = ""
            tbCity.Text = ""
            cboState.Text = ""
            tbZip.Text = ""
End Sub
```

As you can see, VBA is an extremely powerful tool for customizing PowerPoint.

Thanks to Brian Reilly, a PowerPoint MVP (reilly_and_associates@compuserve.com), *and Ken Slovak, an Outlook MVP (Most Valuable Professional), for helping with the VBA programming in this chapter.*

Summary

In this chapter, you saw how to customize menus and toolbars. You can change the way menus and toolbars look and function. More importantly, you can add your own menus, menu items, toolbars, and toolbar buttons. This chapter also explained how to use add-ins. The second part of the chapter explained how to record and use a macro, and then introduced you to programming in Visual Basic for Applications (VBA).

In the next chapter, you prepare to deliver your presentation.

13

Chapter 14

Prepare to Deliver Your Presentation

How to...

- Decide on the best slide format
- Choose the right equipment
- Create a timed presentation
- Set slide show parameters
- Rehearse, rehearse, rehearse
- Create slide show variations
- Use the road warrior's tools

You have completed your presentation. Now is not the time to run out and deliver it. Now is the time to prepare. You need to decide on some of the mechanical aspects of your presentation, such as which type of slide format and projector you will use. Will you manually forward each slide or let PowerPoint do it for you? Then it's time to rehearse until you are thoroughly familiar with your presentation. You may want to create custom shows so that you can vary your presentation based on your audience's reactions. Finally, if you will be traveling, you need to collect in one place all the files you need for your presentation.

Decide on the Best Slide Format

Your first decision is how you will present your slide show. Your decision should be based on the equipment you have available, what type of impression you want to give, and the venue of the presentation.

Print Handouts

If you want or need a low-tech method, you can print handouts from your presentation and give them to your audience. You don't need any equipment (or even any electricity). You should consider this method if you will present outdoors or in a country where you can't count on electricity. However, in all other situations, your audience probably expects you to take advantage of the electricity!

Of course, handouts are a great aid to your audience members, helping them remember what you said after they have gone home. In most cases, use handouts as an addition to your presentation. Research shows that handouts increase the effectiveness of a presentation in a sales situation. In Chapter 15, I explain more about printing handouts and using them during your presentation.

Use 35mm Slides

You can send your presentation to a slide bureau to have 35mm slides made and show the slides from a slide projector. Using 35mm slides has two advantages:

- They generally provide the clearest, sharpest picture, with very bright colors.
- A 35mm slide projector is inexpensive and easy to use.

If you have only a 35mm slide projector available, you may want to go this route. Of course, remember that 35mm slides are static; you lose all your animation and transitions. You also lose any video, sounds, or music.

To create 35mm slides, choose File | Page Setup before starting the presentation to open the Page Setup dialog box, shown in Figure 14-1. In the Slides Sized For drop-down list, choose 35mm Slides. PowerPoint sizes your slides appropriately for 35mm slides.

Once you have completed your presentation, you send it to a service bureau that makes the actual slides. Look in the Yellow Pages for "Photographic Color Prints and Transparencies" or "Slides and Filmstrips." Otherwise, search for "35mm slides" using any Internet search engine. Don't hesitate to ask your colleagues for referrals. You should check the following:

- Do they use Macs or PCs, and does their platform match yours?

- Can you send them your PowerPoint 2003 presentation as is, or do you have to convert it? If you have to convert it to a previous version, you will lose new features.

- Can you e-mail them your presentation?

- How quickly will they send your 35mm slides back to you? (Expect to pay more for rush service.)

New technology now enables you to make your slides in-house using a 35mm slide scanner. Some of these scanners sell for less than $1,000 and do an excellent job of making slides. If you make 35mm slides often, you can save a great deal of money this way.

Use Overhead Transparencies

You can make overhead transparencies from your slide show and project them with an overhead projector. Overhead projectors are much less expensive than LCD or DLP projectors. (Projector terms are explained in Table 14-1.) You are more likely to find an overhead projector in an educational setting. Overhead projectors usually need dimmed lights to work well, especially in larger groups.

Overheads are easy to create. Many printers can print directly onto a special transparency acetate that stops the ink from creating puddles. If you do not have this special transparency acetate, you can also print onto paper and use a photocopier to copy onto acetate. Of course, you would

14

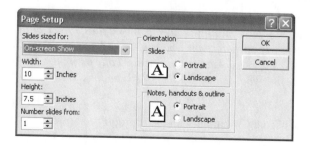

FIGURE 14-1   Use the Page Setup dialog box to set the size of your slides.

ideally use a color printer or copier to make the transparencies. Service bureaus can also create transparencies for you.

Generally, overhead backgrounds should be light. You can even create overheads with no background at all. Remember, all the color on the slide needs to be printed onto the acetate. To create a quick, inexpensive color background, you can buy colored acetate that acts like the background.

To create overheads, before starting your presentation, choose File | Page Setup. In the Slides Sized For drop-down list, choose Overhead. While 35mm slides and onscreen presentations almost always use a landscape orientation, overhead transparencies often use a portrait orientation. In the Page Setup dialog box, choose the orientation you want. PowerPoint then sizes your slides appropriately for overhead transparencies.

Overheads are a great backup for an onscreen presentation; you can use them if your projector or computer dies. Of course, like with 35mm slides, you lose any animation, video, or sound when you print to overheads.

Present Directly from a Computer

Nowadays, most presenters show presentations directly from a computer using an LCD or DLP projector. The general term is a *data projector* because it transmits data from your computer onto a screen. You could possibly use an LCD panel over an overhead projector, but LCD panels are rarely used any more—they are not bright enough for most situations.

For very small groups (1–5 people), you can present directly from a laptop with no projector. If you use a large monitor, you can show a presentation to a group of 15 or so. You could do a new employee orientation like this. You can also buy very large display systems, such as 80-inch televisions and plasma screens, that will present to larger groups—but they are quite expensive. For most groups, you need a projector and a screen. For more information on choosing a projector, see the section, "Choose the Best Equipment."

Run a Presentation on an Autorun CD

One way to deliver a presentation, especially one that is meant to be self-run, is on a CD. You can copy a presentation onto a CD along with an *autorun* file that automatically starts the presentation when a viewer inserts the CD into a CD-ROM drive. You also include the PowerPoint viewer on the CD in case the viewer doesn't have PowerPoint.

NOTE   *The Package for CD feature is new for PowerPoint 2003. This feature enables you to include one or more presentations, plus any linked files, on a CD-ROM. You can include the PowerPoint viewer so that people who don't have PowerPoint can view the presentation. You can also have the presentations run automatically from the CD. As an alternative, you can copy all the files you need to a folder. Package for CD replaces the earlier Pack and Go feature.*

To create a CD, you need a CD burner with the appropriate software and a blank CD. Follow these steps:

1. Choose File | Package for CD. The Package for CD dialog box, shown here, opens.

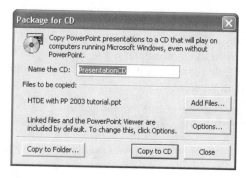

2. Type a name for the CD in the Name the CD text box.

3. The dialog box lists the active presentation. To add other presentations or other files, click Add Files, choose the files, and click Add. Any linked files and the PowerPoint viewer are included by default. (See Chapter 15 for more information about the PowerPoint viewer.) If you add files, you can change their play order by selecting a file and clicking the Up and Down arrows.

4. To specify whether to include the PowerPoint viewer, linked files, and embedded TrueType fonts, choose Options to open the Options dialog box, shown here. Choose which types of files you want. To choose how your presentations play (automatically or not), choose one of the options from the Select How Presentations Will Play in the Viewer drop-down list. You can also password protect presentations. When you are done, click OK.

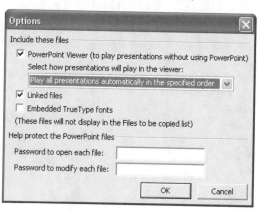

14

NOTE *To make sure that you always have the latest version of the PowerPoint viewer, go to http://office.microsoft.com/downloads. Choose PowerPoint as the product and check only the Converters and Viewers checkbox. Click Update List. Find the PowerPoint viewer and follow the instructions to download and install it.*

5. If you want to copy the files to a folder (instead of to a CD), click Copy to Folder. In the Copy to Folder dialog box, choose a location and name the new folder. (If you are using an operating system earlier than Windows XP, you cannot copy to a CD-ROM; you need to use this feature and then use your CD burning software to copy the files to a CD-ROM.)

6. If you want to copy the files to a CD, insert a blank CD-ROM (CD-R or CD-RW) in your CD-ROM drive. (If you use a CD-RW that contains files, PowerPoint overwrites them.) Click Copy to CD. PowerPoint immediately copies the files to the CD and creates the autorun.inf file that causes the presentation to run automatically when the CD is inserted in a CD-ROM drive.

7. When the files are copied, you see a message asking if you want to copy the files to another CD. Click Yes to repeat the process or No to finish.

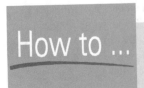

A common problem occurs when movies and sounds don't play once the presentation is on a CD. Make sure you place on your hard disk all of the movies and sounds in the same folder as your presentation before inserting them into the saved presentation.

8. If you created an autorun CD, eject and reinsert the CD, and your PowerPoint presentation should start! (If you have disabled the CD autorun feature in Windows, you need to start the CD manually.)

How to ... Reuse a Presentation in Another Format

Most presentations contain content that you can reuse, either in new presentations or as e-mail or in other software formats. Chapter 10 covered the Microsoft Producer add-in for PowerPoint. Chapter 12 explained how to export a presentation to HTML to display it on a web site or intranet. For more options, try PPT2HTML, developed by Steve Rindsberg (www.rdpslides.com/pptools, $49). You'll have more control over how your presentation appears in various browsers.

Several programs convert PowerPoint presentations into Macromedia Flash SWF format. Flash is a program for creating web-based animation. These programs are server-based or desktop-based. Three desktop-based options are PowerCONVERTER (www.presentationpro.com), iCreate (www.wanadu.com), and Macromedia Breeze (previously Presedia, www.macromedia.com/products/breeze).

Impatica for PowerPoint (www.impatica.com) converts PowerPoint files into Java presentations with faithful rendition of most transitions, animation, sound, and narration. Viewers may need to download Sun Microsystem's Java Virtual Machine to view the presentation (http://java.sun.comgetjava/download.html).

Another possibility is to capture a presentation as it runs in a movie format. TechSmith's Camtasia Studio (www.camtasia.com) and Hyperionics Technologies HyperCam (www.hyperionics.com/hc) can accomplish this task so that you can play a presentation as RealMedia or Windows Media content. You can also convert these presentations to video CDs or DVDs for display on a television screen.

If you have Adobe Acrobat, you can convert your PowerPoint presentation. Acrobat puts a PDF icon within your PowerPoint application window to quickly convert the presentation to a PDF. While PDF is generally a static format, the newest version, 5.0, does the best job of including hyperlinks and some slide transitions. For a more faithful translation, try Prep4PDF (www.rdpslides.com/pptools) from RnR, which works with Adobe Acrobat.

Perhaps you *really* present on the run and would like to have your presentation on your handheld PC or PDA. Dataviz's Documents To Go (www.datavizonline.com/palm_powerpoint .htm) has a Slideshow To Go component, which you can use to edit and rehearse your presentation at the last minute. Other options on the PocketPC 2002 platform are CNetX's Pocket Slideshow (www.cnetx.com/slideshow) and Conduits Technologies' Pocket Slides (www.conduits.com/products/slides). To actually deliver your slideshow from your Palm, PocketPC, or Sony Clie, try Margi's Presenter-To-Go (www.margi.com) for the hardware you need.

Thanks to Geetesh Bajaj, PowerPoint MVP and the technical editor of this book, for this information.

Choose the Best Equipment

LCD and DLP projectors are quite complex. To buy one, look under "Projection Apparatus" in the Yellow Pages. Projectors are rarely sold in computer stores, but that is changing as prices come down. Before you buy a projector, you need to understand the terminology involved, as explained in Table 14-1.

Term	Definition
LCD projector	LCD stands for *liquid crystal display*. An LCD projector electronically takes the data from your presentation and displays it on a screen.
DLP projector	DLP stands for *Digital Light Processing*. Developed by Texas Instruments, a DLP projector uses a technology involving over a million micromirrors, each attached to a micromotor. The motors move the mirrors to help focus the image. DLP projectors generally produce a brighter, smoother image and are especially valued for video and photographs, where accurate color fidelity is most important.
LCD panel	An LCD panel fits on top of an overhead projector. The overhead projector provides the light, optics, and focus, and the LCD panel reads the data from your computer. LCD panels are less expensive than projectors.
Projector	A projector includes a light source and lens, and the ability to read data from your computer. Most include speakers.
Overhead projector	Overheads are mostly used for transparencies, with no computer involved. You can combine an LCD panel with an overhead projector to project a PowerPoint presentation.

TABLE 14-1   Projector Terminology

14

Term	Definition
Passive LCD	Passive LCD is the oldest technology for projectors. It is lower in cost, but the color contrast is unsuitable for video clips.
Active LCD	This is the current technology for LCD projectors, providing higher color contrast. Suitable for video.
Resolution	This is the number of horizontal × vertical pixels displayable on a screen. There are three major types: SVGA (800 × 600), XGA (1024 × 768), and SXGA (1280 × 1024).
Lumens	This is a measure of the brightness of light.

TABLE 14-1   Projector Terminology *(continued)*

Using a projector is generally simple: you connect its cable to the external display port of a laptop or computer and plug it into an outlet. A projector will come with a manual that you can read when you need to adjust color, focus, etc. You may need to read your computer's documentation for details on displaying the picture both through the projector and on the computer's monitor at the same time. If your presentation includes sound, you need to connect speakers to the projector, which you do with the included cables. Most projectors come with a remote controller so that you can move around the room as you control the presentation.

Projectors have a *native* resolution, a resolution that is built into the projector. If your computer screen uses the same resolution, no adjustments are necessary. Many projectors automatically adjust for differences in resolution.

When buying a projector, which is an expensive piece of equipment, it pays to do some homework before and during the process. Consider these points:

- *How much can you afford?* Prices have come down recently, but you'll still find that the newest lightweight ultraportables cost a little more. Of course, you'll have to pay a higher price for more performance, features, or brightness. You can often find refurbished rental-return units and closeout models at a significant discount, some with respectable warranties.

- *How will you use the projector?* If you expect to carry it around every day, the weight of the projector is a very important issue. But if you're not going to lug it around very often, the weight isn't as crucial. A sturdier, heavier projector with more features will work perfectly well—and you can get it for the same price or less. You'd be surprised how many features you can get by adding a few more pounds.

- *Where will you put the projector and what size screen you will you use?* These questions are important because there is no universal standard for projector placement and image size. Some projectors are designed to be used close to the screen, and others come with a wide-ranging zoom lens so that you have the option of being either close to the screen or farther away. You also need to consider *keystoning,* the image distortion caused by projecting at an angle that the projector wasn't designed for—you see an image that is wider on the top than on the bottom. Most projectors offer "keystone correction."

■ *How bright should the projector be?* Of course you want to have the brightest image possible. However, there's a catch—the size of the image a projector is displaying greatly affects your perception of its brightness. A 600-lumen projector looks great on a 60-inch screen (measured diagonally), but the same projector looks quite dim when you need to fill a 120-inch screen, because it has four times the area. You may find hundreds of lumens of difference between the claims of the manufacturer for the model line and the actual brightness of individual projectors in that model line. Look for a reputable, trustworthy salesperson who is honest with you about these discrepancies.

■ *How long will the lamp last and how much does it cost?* Generally, the lamp is your projector's light source—and burns out just like any lightbulb. Replacement bulbs can be expensive and are a hidden cost of owning a projector. Find out how often you'll need to replace it and consider that answer in your buying decision. You may find that buying a more expensive projector with a longer lamp life is less expensive in the long run than buying a cheaper projector that burns bulbs faster. Ask three questions: How many hours of use can you expect to get from the lamp? How bright will the projector be after the lamp has been run for several hundred hours (it often dims dramatically)? And how bright will it be near the end of its life? Don't forget to ask about the lamp's rated power in watts. Let's say you're trying to decide between two projectors with similar lumens of brightness, but one uses a 500-watt lamp to produce its light and the other uses only a 100-watt lamp. In that case, you should choose the 100-watt lamp projector—it will stay bright longer, produce less heat, require a less noisy cooling fan, use less energy, and last longer because it is inherently more efficient.

■ *What is the projector's resolution?* A projector's resolution is a key factor in a projector's price. As described in Table 14-1, there are three options: SVGA (800 × 600), XGA (1024 × 768), and SXGA (1280 × 1024 or higher). Before you start shopping, know which resolution you need. You probably don't need the highest resolution if you're going to use your projector just for simple, bulleted-text PowerPoint slides. SVGA may be fine. On the other hand, you'll need the highest resolution possible—SXGA or better—if you will be presenting a circuit design you created on a workstation. Find out from your salesperson the projector's native resolution. Most new projectors can shrink or expand a computer's image to fill the fixed matrix of pixels of the projector. With most images, when this resizing is accomplished skillfully, you will have a hard time discerning the projector's exact native resolution. But if you try to project a detailed CAD drawing on that same SVGA projector in full SXGA resolution, some of the lines will be missing and other lines will be blurry. These resizing problems will not occur if you project the same image with a projector that has a native SXGA resolution.

■ *What are the lens specifications?* Besides knowing whether you need a motorized zoom lens (only a few projectors are zoomless these days), what else is there to know? Besides the *zoom range* (the amount of change you can get in image size), look for a lens with all-glass elements. To save weight, many projector lenses are made of plastic or of a plastic composite, but the onscreen image from a good glass lens cannot be beaten; it will be sharp and in focus, even in the corners. If you are buying a projector for a conference room, an optional projection lens is important to consider. To allow projectors much greater flexibility to "throw" images farther and wider, many manufacturers are starting

14

to offer a range of lens options. If the projector's manufacturer doesn't provide them, a third-party lens company such as Buhl Optical probably does.

- ■ *What contrast and color saturation do you need?* Most projectors have more than enough contrast for the majority of situations. Contrast shouldn't be much of an issue unless you're very picky about video quality, which looks better with lower black levels. For today's projectors, a three-panel LCD projector or a three-chip DLP projector provides the best color saturation, compared to a one-panel LCD or one-chip DLP projector. CRT projectors deliver a level of color saturation somewhere between the three-panel and one-panel projectors. The big light-valve projectors are close behind the LCD and DLP units but show more color variation across their images. Check color intensity under various lighting conditions to get an idea of the projector's performance in the real world.

- ■ *What is the projector's weight and what are its other features?* To start with, find out how many inputs, outputs, and onboard speakers the projector has. Other capabilities, such as a motorized zoom, focus, and lens shift, should be added to the list. Additional features are related to ease of use: easily operated elevator feet, handles that are comfortable and sturdy, easy-to-use onscreen menus, and a lightweight carrying case for portables and ultraportables. If weight is important, you need to consider the total carrying weight of the unit, case, and accessories. When you add in all the required cables and accessories, you'd be surprised how much different projectors' carrying weights are equalized. Besides the weight of the carrying case, the signal cables and remote-control unit usually add about two pounds to a projector's overall heft.

- ■ *What should you expect from the warranty and service?* Let's say you're out in the field and the projector suddenly quits on you. What now? Now your warranty kicks in—and you'd better make sure you have one. The good news is that, because the overall quality of projectors is now so good, many manufacturers are competing to offer the best warranty and service options. Some manufacturers now even offer free overnight replacement of a dead unit, no questions asked. If you're a road warrior, that's the kind of service you need. Otherwise, warranties of one, two, or three years are the rule. Still, you should read the fine print carefully, because there is a wide range of service plans to choose from, depending on the manufacturer and dealer. In particular, check out how long the lamp is covered under the warranty; it may be for only a few months. As always, get everything in writing, and keep a file with your warranty and other projector-related materials in it. When you need to use that warranty, you'll know where it is.

The best way to learn about a projector is to see it perform. So ask for a demo—or better yet, a number of demos. To judge a full range of image-quality parameters, bring a disk of professional test patterns and images, such as Sonera Technologies' DisplayMate (http://www.displaymate.com). If you don't have a professional test pattern available, just use a disk of your favorite images and see what that new projector can do. A great way to decide between two competing models is to ask your salesperson to arrange a "shootout," so you can view both projectors with the same image at the same time. Practically every projector looks good by itself; but make a direct comparison, and all its warts appear.

Thanks to William Bohannon, chief scientist at Manx Research (760-735-9678), for the material on evaluating a projector.

Time Your Presentation

When giving a presentation, you can manually control the timing of each slide by clicking the mouse, or you can set timing and let PowerPoint forward each slide for you. Usually, timed slides are used when your presentation will run unattended at a conference or kiosk. However, if you are presenting, you can always pause a presentation that has timed slides to maintain full control. Timing was more important before the days of ubiquitous remote controllers. In that case, automatic timing freed the presenter from being tied to the computer. Nowadays, with a remote mouse, you can control the computer and still walk around the room without restriction.

Timing slides can be used as a technique for rehearsal. When you rehearse timings, PowerPoint lets you know the length of the entire presentation, which is extremely useful information. You also learn how long you are spending on each slide. From this data, you might decide to divide a slide into two, to break up the message into smaller bites. On the other hand, you might realize that two slides should be combined.

Set the Timing

There are two ways to set timing for a presentation. When you use the first method, you run through your presentation as a rehearsal and time the slides based on your rehearsal. In the second method, you directly assign a number of seconds to each slide. If your presentation is designed to run unattended, you can still use the rehearsal method to get an idea of how many seconds to assign to each slide. Then you can assign timings directly.

Rehearse Timings

Before rehearsing timings, especially if you will be presenting your slide show, gather together any notes you might need so that you are ready to present. You are about to rehearse your entire presentation for the first time! Follow these steps:

1. Open your presentation and make sure that the first slide is displayed.

2. Choose Slide Show | Rehearse Timings. If you are in Slide Sorter view, choose Rehearse Timings from the Slide Sorter toolbar. PowerPoint switches you to Slide Show view and opens the Rehearsal toolbar, shown here.

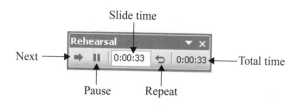

3. Start talking! Present your slide show like you plan to when you are actually presenting.

4. When you are finished with the first slide, click Next on the Rehearsal toolbar (or just click as usual).

5. Continue until you have finished the last slide, clicking Next after each slide.

6. After the last slide, PowerPoint displays the time of the entire presentation and asks if you want to record the timing and use it when you view the slide show, as shown here. If you do, click Yes. PowerPoint switches you to your previous view and ends the rehearsal.

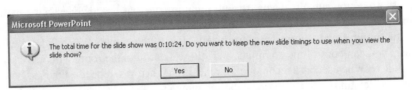

While timing a presentation, you have two other options on the Rehearsal toolbar. To pause the timing process, click Pause. Click Pause again to continue timing the slide. If you make a mistake and want to start a slide over, click Repeat.

After you have recorded the timings, you can see the time beneath each slide in Slide Show view, as shown here.

Assign Timing to Slides

You can directly assign timing to slides without going through the rehearsal process just described. You can also rehearse the presentation and then use the timings you obtain as a guideline for assigning your own timings. To assign timing to the slides in your presentation, follow these steps:

1. Switch to Slide Sorter view.

2. Select the first slide. If you want other slides to have the same timing, select them as well.

3. Choose Slide Transition from the Slide Sorter toolbar (or choose Slide Show | Slide Transition). PowerPoint opens the Slide Transition task pane, shown in Figure 14-2.

4. In the Advance Slide section of the task pane, check Automatically After. Then use the text box or the arrows to set the number of seconds you want the slide(s) displayed. The timing is applied to the active slide.

5. To apply the slide timing to all the slides in the presentation, click Apply to All Slides.

Continue to set timing for other slides if necessary, using the same procedure.

FIGURE 14-2   Use the Slide Transition task pane to manually set slide timings.

Use Timing When You Present

To automatically advance slides with the timing you set, you should make sure that the slide show is set up to use the timings. Here's how:

1. Choose Slide Show | Set Up Show.

2. In the Advance Slides section of the Set Up Show dialog box, click Using Timings, If Present, as shown in Figure 14-3.

3. Click OK.

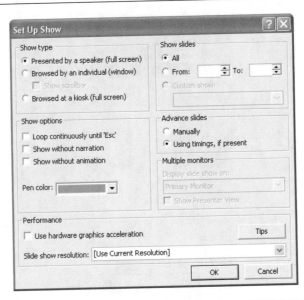

FIGURE 14-3   Use the Set Up Show dialog box to specify how your presentation runs.

Now, when you run your presentation in Slide Show view, PowerPoint uses your timings. You can go back and choose Manually in the same section of the dialog box if you decide not to use the timings you have set.

Set Slide Show Parameters

Before running a slide show, you can set a number of parameters that determine how your presentation runs. These settings give you last-minute control over your presentation. To set these parameters, choose Slide Show | Set Up Show to open the Set Up Show dialog box, shown in Figure 14-3.

The Show Type section of the dialog box determines the type of show you want to present. By default, your presentation is shown full screen. However, if the presentation will be browsed by an individual at a kiosk or computer station, you can choose Browsed by an Individual (Window) to have the presentation run in a window and include a scrollbar that people can use to run through the presentation at their own pace or Browsed at a kiosk (full screen) if your presentation will use automatic timings.

> **NOTE**   *If you chose the kiosk option, mouse clicks do not work. If you want to allow viewers control over the presentation, you must either include a scrollbar or add hyperlinks or action buttons that move the presentation to the next slide.*

For self-running presentations at trade shows and conferences, choose Loop Continuously Until 'Esc'. As soon as the presentation ends, PowerPoint starts the presentation from the beginning again.

If you chose Browse at a Kiosk (Full Screen), the presentation is automatically looped.

Choose Show Without Narration if you have recorded narration but don't want to use it. This is a great option for presentations that are sometimes run without a presenter and sometimes with one. You can also record narration for practice purposes and then check this box when you are ready to give the presentation.

Choose Show Without Animation to show the presentation at the end of any animation on each slide. Use this option when you want to allow individuals to browse the presentation themselves. Because they are not familiar with the animation, they could find it confusing to have to click several times before going to the next slide.

In the Show Slides section, you can choose to display all the slides or only a group of slides. Specify which slides you want to display. If you have created a custom show (covered in the "Create a Custom Show" section later in this chapter), you can choose it here.

You can use multiple monitors to display a presentation. In the Multiple Monitors section, choose which monitor displays the slide show. The other monitor can display the next slide or speaker's notes for your own private viewing during the slide show. This feature is available only if you have multiple monitors.

In the Performance section of the dialog box, you can choose to use the capabilities of graphics acceleration if your video card offers this feature. You can also choose the resolution of the slide show.

Click OK when you are done.

Prepare Your Notes

It's now time to think about what you will say when you stand up in front of your audience. If you haven't already done so, before going any further, research your audience. How much do they know about the topic? What do they want to get from your presentation? Even if the slides are the same, your explanation of the slides will change for varying audiences. Always get as much information about your audience as you can.

NOTE
The best time to research your audience is before you start writing your presentation, so you can design the content around your audience's needs and level of knowledge.

14

As a last resort, if you can't get any information in advance, you may be able to ask questions of your audience just before you start presenting. You may need to make some quick changes to your planned talk based on the answers you receive.

If you will work from notes, print them out and use them when you rehearse. If you didn't create notes as you worked, now is the time to go back and add presentation notes for each slide. To print notes from the Notes pane in your presentation, choose File | Print to open the Print dialog box. From the Print What drop-down list, choose Notes Pages and click OK.

Practice in front of a live person. Others can pick up potential problems more easily than you can. A useful technique is to leave out your overview and summary slides and see what the person remembers as your main points. Ask your test audience what was interesting, appealing, or confusing.

Before you actually deliver your presentation, prepare a backup plan. Every presenter has experienced or heard stories about equipment catastrophes. Practicing with your equipment not only benefits you, but it tests your equipment. Then think what you would do if your computer

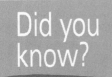

The Three Stages of Rehearsing

Before you present, you need to rehearse your presentation until you are thoroughly familiar with it. You should know your presentation so well that you almost have it memorized, but not well enough that you can repeat it by rote.

Practice delivering your presentation in three stages. The first stage is to talk through the presentation in front of your computer. You can look directly at your slides, which is OK for a first run. Repeat this step a couple of times. Next, attach your mike to your computer and use PowerPoint's narration feature to record what you have practiced saying, going through the entire presentation. (See Chapter 10 for details.) Now, sit back and run through the presentation again, just listening to the presentation. How was the tone? Did you speak too fast or slow? Were you clear? You are sure to find room for improvement. Make adjustments and go through the cycle of practicing, recording, and listening until you are happy with the results.

The second stage is to run through the presentation using the equipment (laptop, projector, and so on) you will use when you actually deliver the slide show. New elements at this stage are becoming comfortable with the equipment, talking without looking directly at the slides for more than a second, and standing up, even walking around a bit, while you talk. You should practice your opening remarks, when you will turn the lights up and down (if at all), how you will start and end the presentation (for example, opening and closing remarks; ending with a final slide or black screen), answering questions, and so on. A great idea is to rehearse in front of a real person to get feedback. If you can videotape yourself, do so. Just like narration lets you listen to how you sound, video lets you see how you look as you present.

The final stage is to run through your presentation in the actual physical environment you plan to use, if possible. (If you are presenting in-house, you can combine stages two and three.) If you will use a projector and screen, set them up and use them. Where will you stand? Check out the view from the last seat. Can you read the smallest text? Learn everything you can about the room—where the lights and thermostat are, where to get more chairs, where the outlets are, and so on.

Once you have completed these steps, you will be well rehearsed and ready for anything! The confidence you have gained from being prepared will shine through.

died, your projector conked out, or your remote controller stopped working. Practice your backup plan, too. Here are some musts:

- Always have printed handouts or overhead transparencies for the worst-case scenario—no electricity, a dead computer, and so on.
- Make sure you have a regular mouse if your remote controller doesn't work or gets lost.
- Always carry at least one spare bulb for your projector.
- If you are traveling, call ahead to see which equipment is available locally.

Create Slide Show Variations

Sometimes you want to vary a presentation. If you present a slide show more than once for different audiences, you can hide a slide in your presentation that isn't suitable for a specific situation. You must hide the slide in advance, so you need to think ahead.

To hide a slide, select the slide you want to hide and choose Slide Show | Hide Slide. In Slide Sorter view, select the slide and click the Hide Slide button, shown here.

Create a Custom Show

You can create a presentation that includes slides for more than one situation. You can then specify which slides you will use for one situation and which ones you will use for another. These variations are called *custom shows*. Let's say you are giving a presentation on a new employee benefit package but the packages vary slightly for two different groups of employees. You can create slides appropriate for each group and include them all in the presentation. Then you create custom shows that present only the slides you need.

Often, you start with a set of slides that are common to both groups. When the presentation must diverge, you jump to the custom show.

Another use for a custom show is to allow for more than one possible response from your audience. You could include some slides with more details if you find out at the last minute that your audience is more sophisticated than you expected.

To create a custom show, you must first create all the possible slides you will need. The variations should be together in a group so you can jump around as little as possible.

Choose Slide Show | Custom Shows and then click New in the Custom Shows dialog box to open the Define Custom Show dialog box, shown in Figure 14-4. In the Slide Show Name text box, name the custom show.

Select the slides for the custom show from the Slides in Presentation list and click Add to move them to the Slides in Custom Show list. To select a contiguous group of slides, click the first slide in the group, press SHIFT, and click the last group. To select a noncontiguous group

14

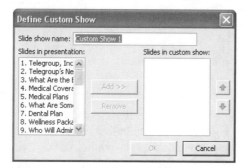

FIGURE 14-4   In the Define Custom Show dialog box, specify which slides go in the custom show.

of slides, press CTRL, and then select each additional slide. Click OK to create the custom show. PowerPoint now displays the Custom Shows dialog box with your new custom show listed. To preview the custom show, select it from the list and click Show.

Edit a Custom Show

To modify a custom show, choose Slide Show | Custom Shows and select the show you want to edit. Click Edit. PowerPoint opens the same Define Custom Show dialog box you used to create the custom show originally. Use the same tools to add or remove slides or to move them around in the custom show.

To delete a custom show entirely, choose Slide Show | Custom Shows and select the show you want to delete. Click Remove. Note that the slides are not deleted from the presentation.

Use a Custom Show

To set up your presentation so that PowerPoint displays only the slides in the custom show, choose Slide Show | Set Up Show. In the Set Up Show dialog box, choose Custom Show in the Show Slides section. This option is available only if the presentation includes a custom show. Then click OK. Now, when you start your presentation in Slide Show view, only the slides in the custom show are displayed. To display all the slides of the presentation again, open the Set Up Show dialog box again and choose All in the Show Slides section.

In most cases, you want to display slides not in the custom show with the option of using the custom show slides when you choose to. Using a custom show is like hyperlinking. There are three ways to jump to a custom show during a presentation:

- Select an object on the slide where you want to create the option to jump to the custom show. (The object can be a text placeholder.) Choose Slide Show | Action Settings. On either tab, choose Hyperlink To. From the drop-down list, choose Custom Show. PowerPoint opens the Link To Custom Show dialog box, shown here.

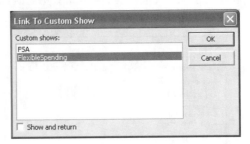

Now choose the custom show you want. If you want to return to the same slide after displaying the custom show slides, click Show and Return. (Otherwise, PowerPoint displays the custom show and ends the presentation.) Click OK.

- Select an object on the slide where you want to create the option to jump to the custom show. Choose Insert | Hyperlink. Click Place in This Document. Under Custom Shows, choose the custom show you want. If you want to return to the same slide after displaying the custom show slides, click Show and Return. Click OK.

■ During a presentation, right-click, choose Go | Custom Show, and choose the custom show you want. When you use this method, you can't return to the current slide.

You can create several custom shows if you wish, but be careful not to make your navigation possibilities too complex. It's easy to get confused during your presentation!

To print a custom show, follow these steps:

1. Choose File | Print.

2. In the Print Range section of the Print dialog box, choose your custom show from the Custom Show drop-down list.

3. Click OK.

Summary

In this chapter, you reviewed all the necessary steps involved in preparing for a presentation. You need to decide which medium you will use: handouts, 35mm slides, overhead transparencies, or onscreen projection. You can copy all of your files to a CD-ROM, either to transport them or to create a presentation that runs automatically from a CD. The chapter covered information about choosing and using a projector.

You can rehearse timing for your presentation or directly assign timing. You can choose whether to use your timing when you actually present.

Before you start to rehearse, you should prepare notes that you will use. Then rehearse, rehearse, rehearse!

To create variations on your presentation, you can hide slides or create a custom show. If you create a custom show, you can choose when delivering your slide show whether or not to use the custom show.

The next chapter covers the process of delivering a slide show.

14

Chapter 15

Present Your Slide Show

How to...

■ Print and use handouts

■ Send your presentation to Microsoft Word

■ Use the PowerPoint viewer

■ Learn professional presentation skills

■ Control your slide show

■ Let your slide show run itself

The time is at hand! You have completed your presentation, practiced and timed it, and now you're finally ready to present it to an audience. You need to decide if you want to print handouts. You may want to work on your presenting skills. Think about what will happen during the presentation—how will you control your presentation? Will you want to mark up slides to emphasize certain points? This chapter discusses these issues and more.

Print and Use Handouts

Of course, handouts are a great memory aid for your audience members, helping them remember what you said after they have gone home. In most cases, use handouts as an addition to your presentation, not as a substitute.

If you are going to make your presentation using only printed handouts, you don't need any equipment except a printer, which you almost certainly already have. You should invest in a color printer if you don't already have one. It's a shame to create color slides in PowerPoint and then print them in black and white.

Even if you want to give handouts to your audience only as take-home material, make them look as professional as possible. Your handouts will be sitting on their desks long after your voice has faded. Don't forget to package the handouts. Provide a pocket or binder folder at the very least. Make sure to include your business card or contact information.

PowerPoint lets you print your presentation to use as handouts. When you print handouts for your audience, you are simply giving them a copy of your presentation, minus the animation and transition effects. You may also want to print handouts simply to show your colleagues and supervisors. To format your handouts, use the handout master. Don't forget that you can add a logo or other graphics to the handout master. (See Chapter 7 for an explanation of the handout master.)

Once you have formatted your handouts, click the Close button on the Master toolbar. You are now ready to print. Follow these steps:

1. If you wish to change the orientation of the page for printing, choose File | Page Setup. Under Notes, Handouts & Outline, choose Landscape or Portrait. Click OK.

2. Choose File | Print to open the Print dialog box.

Did you know?

View Your Presentation in Grayscale

If you need to print in black and white, you can view your presentation in grayscale to see how it will look. To do so, choose View | Grayscale. Unfortunately, if you use the common technique of using a template that includes a bitmap image or if you insert a bitmap image using Format | Background, your background does not appear, making it hard to judge the final look of your presentation. On the other hand, if you use a template that does not include any bitmap images or if you open the Slide Master, use Insert | Picture, and then choose Draw | Order | Send to Back from the Draw toolbar, you do see your background.

3. In the Print What drop-down list, choose Handouts.

4. If you created a handout master, PowerPoint sets the Slides per Page drop-down list accordingly, but if you change your mind, you can change the setting here. You can print up to nine slides per page.

5. If you choose four or more slides per page, choose Horizontal or Vertical to specify the order in which PowerPoint places the slides on the page. The Print dialog box provides a diagram to show you the results of your choice, as shown in Figure 15-1.

6. If you don't have a color printer, choose Grayscale to optimize the look of your color slides for your printer.

7. If you wish, uncheck Frame Slides to remove the border around the slides. (The dialog box diagram does not display the result of this choice.)

8. Click Preview to see what the handouts will look like.

9. Click OK.

TIP   *You can also make the presentation or handouts available to people for download from a web site. Also, many people create handouts using the Adobe Acrobat Reader PDF format. For more information on handouts, including information on using the PDF format, go to http://www.indezine.com/products/powerpoint/pphandout.html.*

15

Send the Presentation to Microsoft Word

You may feel that printing handouts does not provide you with enough options. Perhaps you want to provide more information than you can fit using the handout master. For example, you may want to add supporting documentation or include references to the sources of your material. Perhaps you want your audience to take home only the text outline. For whatever reason, you should consider sending the presentation to Microsoft Word. In Word, you can make changes,

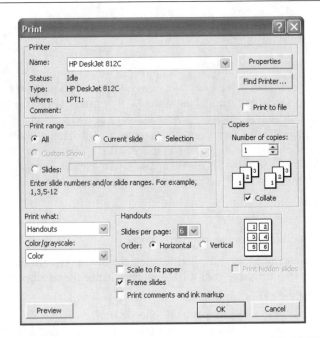

FIGURE 15-1   Use the Print dialog box to print handouts.

additions, or deletions. You can also format the text differently. PowerPoint offers a number of options for sending your presentation to Word. Here's how:

1. Choose File | Send To | Microsoft Word. PowerPoint opens the Send to Microsoft Word dialog box, shown in Figure 15-2.

2. Choose one of the options. The options that include notes with the slides print the contents of your Notes pane. Most of your notes may be for your eyes only. However, remember that you can change the contents of these notes once you have sent them to Word. For example, you could replace your notes with supporting information you would like your audience to take home.

3. At the bottom of the dialog box, choose either Paste or Paste Link. If you paste link the slides, the Word document is updated whenever you make changes in your presentation and then open the Word document. If you are sending your presentation to Word to print handouts for a one-time presentation, you don't need to link the slides.

4. Click OK.

Microsoft Word opens with your presentation in the format you specified. It's a good idea to save the document before making further changes.

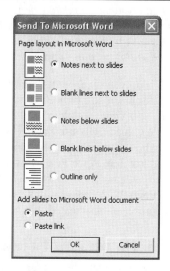

FIGURE 15-2   You can set options when you send a presentation to Microsoft Word.

Once you have created your file in Word, you can use Word's more advanced features to edit the text as you wish. Here are some ideas for additions to your handouts:

■ Thank your audience for attending.

■ Tell your audience how they can contact you if they have any questions or want further information.

■ Offer access information for web sites and other resources where audience members can obtain further information.

■ Add supporting data such as a price list, delivery schedule, your resume, your company's history and accomplishments, and so on.

■ Offer your audience a means of providing feedback on your presentation.

Use PowerPoint Viewer

PowerPoint Viewer is a program that can run a slide show on a computer that doesn't have PowerPoint. PowerPoint Viewer is an essential part of the road warrior's equipment. While you are on the road, your computer's hard disk may crash. If you have your presentation and PowerPoint Viewer on a removable storage medium (such as a Zip drive), you can still show your presentation on any available computer. In another scenario, your client might have told you in advance that there is no time for a presentation or you may not be planning to show a slide show at all. However, if you have Viewer and a presentation with you, you can still show your presentation if the opportunity arises.

15

PowerPoint 2003 comes with a brand new updated viewer, the first in a while. In PowerPoint 2002, the viewer could not display some of the newer features. You can now create presentations and be assured that all your animations and other effects will be displayed in PowerPoint Viewer.

The main PowerPoint Viewer file is pptview.exe, but it requires several other files as well. You should have it in your Program Files\Microsoft Office\Office11\Office11 folder, but your location may be different. If you can't find Viewer on your hard disk, you can download the file from http://office.microsoft.com/downloads. Choose PowerPoint as the product and check only the Converters and Viewers checkbox. Click Update List. Find the PowerPoint viewer and follow the instructions to download and install it. PowerPoint Viewer is free and can be distributed with no license required. For example, you can send it to a client along with a presentation. With Viewer, you can view not only PowerPoint 2003 presentations, but also PowerPoint 95 through 2002 presentations. It also works with presentations created on a Macintosh (but viewed on a PC).

Present a Slide Show with PowerPoint Viewer

The easiest way to use PowerPoint Viewer is to use the Package for CD feature, as explained in Chapter 14, saving either to a folder or a CD. If you don't choose the CD and automatic start options, you need to start PowerPoint Viewer. To start PowerPoint Viewer, locate pptview.exe in the folder or on the CD and double-click the file to start Viewer, shown in Figure 15-3. Choose the presentation you want to play and click Open. If you choose the automatic start options, PowerPoint creates a play.bat file, which you can double-click to start viewing the presentations. This play.bat file is useful when you save to a folder or if the auto-run feature for CD-ROMs is disabled.

As of this writing, PowerPoint Viewer does not support multiple monitors, VBA (programming), ActiveX (certain objects from other applications), pen annotation, or navigation to a custom show.

When you use the Package for CD feature and choose more than one presentation to include, viewers do not automatically see all the presentations if they start PowerPoint Viewer by double-clicking pptview.exe. Instead, they see the dialog box shown in Figure 15-3, where they can choose which presentation they want to view. This might occur if viewers have disabled the Autorun feature in Windows or use Windows Explorer to browse the CD-ROM.

If you think you may show your presentation using PowerPoint Viewer, practice presenting using the program. Make sure you can easily open Viewer—you don't want to have to fuss to find it in front of your audience. Check that the closing of your slide show is smooth and professional so that your audience doesn't see the mechanics behind the magic.

If you want to play more than one presentation at a time automatically, use the Package to CD feature. PowerPoint Viewer no longer plays playlists, which were previously used to play multiple presentations.

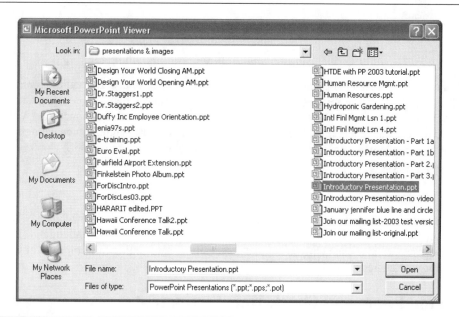

FIGURE 15-3   PowerPoint Viewer

Learn Professional Presentation Skills

Most of the skills required for an effective presentation apply whether you use PowerPoint, paper handouts, or no visual aids at all. These skills are based on the relationship you create with your audience. A successful presentation includes the following characteristics:

- The audience has a need—for information, for a product, for training, and so on.
- Your presentation meets the audience's need.
- The audience understands and appreciates how your presentation meets its need.

As you can see, to create an effective presentation, you need to know what your audience needs. You also need to meet that need in a way that your audience can understand and appreciate.

Sometimes, you are the one who determines your audience's needs. If you are a sales manager presenting your company's latest products to your sales representatives, you have decided that your audience needs to know your company's latest products. All you need to do is present in a way that your sales representatives can understand and appreciate. The information you present in a clear manner provides the understanding. The excitement you generate helps your audience appreciate your message.

In many instances, however, you need to do some research to determine your audience's needs and level of understanding. If you are speaking to a large group, you should try to find out from

15

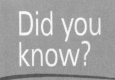

Arrive Early

Professional speakers generally plan to arrive about two hours early to check out the room and their equipment, make any necessary adjustments, and do a dry run of their presentation. If you find that the room doesn't have enough chairs, how long will it take to get them? Will you have to help carry them in and set them up yourself? If so, will that leave you enough time to check out your equipment? (This is the stuff that nightmares are born of.) Don't be afraid to ask others for help setting up.

the group's organizers something about the audience members. How much do they already know about the topic? What is their level of education and expertise? Why are they attending? The answers to these questions can help you avoid a presentation that is either too simplistic or too advanced for your audience, or one that misses the mark entirely.

Set Up the Room and Check Your Equipment

One of the best ways to prepare for a presentation is to get a good night's sleep the night before. Feeling fresh and rested makes you feel and appear brighter, happier, and more enthusiastic.

If you're nervous, settle down just before your presentation. If you know how to meditate, do so. If not, sit quietly for a few minutes with your eyes closed. Get up slowly and then start moving about and making preparations to gear up for the presentation.

Sometimes, you have no control over a room. If you are presenting in a potential client's office, you are probably not at liberty to move the furniture. When you are presenting in a larger group situation, such as in a classroom, convention center, or auditorium, you may have more leeway.

Here are some ideas for checking out a room:

- *Do you feel too hot or too cold?* Find the thermostat or the windows. Cooler is better than hotter.

- *Does the air smell stuffy?* Open the windows. Leave the doors open until your presentation starts.

- *Do you have enough chairs?* Are they comfortable? If necessary, get more chairs or move existing chairs farther apart. Hopefully, you won't have to replace all of the chairs, but an uncomfortable audience has a hard time appreciating anything.

- *Can people get to the chairs?* Perhaps the rows are too close together. A center aisle can help if the rows are too long. Depending on the number of people attending, you may want to set up the chairs all facing front or in a U shape. A U shape is more conducive to interaction, especially among the participants.

- *Does everyone have an unobstructed view of your screen?* If the room has columns, move the chairs that are behind them.

- *Will latecomers have to pass between you and your audience?* Perhaps you can create an aisle going toward the back of the room.

- *If you will use a microphone, is it working?* How do you turn it on and off? Can you remove it from the podium or its stand if you want to walk around? Try it out before the audience arrives to make sure it doesn't squeal. If you have a pin-on mike, make sure you can put it on and take it off easily.

- *Where are the lights?* If you need to turn down the lights to start your slide show, can you do so without walking to the back of the room or asking an audience member to do it for you? (A well-designed presentation room should have light controls at the podium, but you might not be in a well-designed presentation room.)

- *Where are the electrical outlets?* Are there enough of them? Do you need extension cords? If you have to run extension cords across the room, it is a good idea to tape them down with duct tape.

- *Where are the restrooms?* You should know the answer in case anyone asks.

Once you have checked out the room, set up your equipment. Set up your slide show as you want it to appear when your audience walks in. If you want to speak a while before turning on the slide show, open the presentation and simply turn off the projector or toggle off its image. Then you can start your slide show with one simple motion.

Now, with the slide show displayed, make sure the slide looks straight and centered on the screen. Decide where you will stand and where you will walk.

Finally, run through your presentation. Practice going back one slide and using your hyperlinks and action buttons. If you are using equipment provided by the facility, find out where the spare bulbs and batteries are kept, who can replace them, and how you can contact that person at a moment's notice.

When you are done, you can heave a sigh of relief. While the unexpected can always happen, at least you did everything you could to ensure a problem-free presentation.

Speak in Front of a Group

15

Many people are afraid of speaking in front of a group. While being 150 percent prepared helps, the truth is that once you strike up a relationship with your audience, much of your fear will dissipate. An actor cannot create a relationship with his or her audience in advance because the requirement of acting is to stay in character, but you have a lot more control over the situation when you present. Here are some tips:

- *Chat with audience members as they come into the room.* Smile and introduce yourself. If they traveled, ask them how their trip was. Say anything to start up a brief conversation. You may even be able to use this opportunity to find out more about your audience.

- *Start your presentation with some humor, a quotation, or a personal experience.* This personal touch creates a pleasant relationship between you and your audience immediately (unless your jokes aren't funny or are in bad taste).

- *Dress conservatively.* You can never go wrong and you'll feel more comfortable.

- *Don't hide behind a podium or your computer.* Face your audience. If you are going to turn down the lights, start talking before you do so to let the audience see your face and get to know you.

- *Look at one or two individuals in more detail.* Pick a person to talk to, then another, and so on, so that you can focus on something. You will also get some feedback during your presentation—such as someone sleeping! You should be able to give your presentation with only occasional glances at your slides or notes.

- *Don't mumble.* Express your enthusiasm for your topic. It's infectious.

Remember, your audience members are just people, like you. They probably empathize with you. They want you to succeed because they want to learn something. So they're with you, not against you. Just start!

Cope with Disasters

Sometimes a disaster occurs. Your computer crashes or the projector dies. You leave your projector on the plane. You rip your sleeve. Well, anything *can* happen.

For technological mishaps, always come with an alternative—overhead transparencies if you will have an overhead projector available, or simple paper handouts. Bring a change of clothes. Make sure you have a comb with you and any other personal articles that you might need. A bottle of room-temperature water is useful in case your throat needs clearing or you start to cough.

Oh, and always use the bathroom before you start your presentation.

The Internet offers a number of useful web sites for presenters. These sites offer tips and advice for everything from organizing your presentation text to standing up in front of an audience. The following are some Internet resources for presenters:

- ***Presentations* magazine**   Offers lots of resources, including articles from past issues. From the home page, click Delivery for a list of articles on delivering presentations. http://www.presentations.com

- **Presenters Online**   Offers loads of articles and tips for presenters. http://www .presentersonline.com

- **3M Meeting Network**   Includes articles and advice on delivering presentations. Although run by 3M, there's lots of general information here. http://www.3m.com/ meetingnetwork/presentations/index.html

- **Wilder Presentations**   Includes lots of visual examples and tips for your presentations. You can sign up for a monthly newsletter that includes ideas and tips for designers and presenters. http://www.wilderpresentations.com

- ■ **SpeakerNet News**   Contains lots of helpful information for those who stand up in front of audiences. A weekly e-mail newsletter for professional speakers. http://www.speakernetnews.com

- ■ **InfoComm News and Information Network**   Includes articles on presenting and other presentation-related topics (some of mine), equipment advice and sales, and more. http://www.infocommnews.net

- ■ **PowerPointers**   Includes articles on the various aspects of presenting and using PowerPoint. http://www.powerpointers.com

- ■ **PresentersUniversity**   Includes loads of articles on every aspect of presenting. An excellent site. http://www.presentersuniversity.com/index.cfm

- ■ **Indezine**   Articles about PowerPoint and presenting. A very wide-ranging site. http://www.indezine.com

Be Prepared When Using Computer Projection

Projectors paired with laptop computers have undeniably changed the way presentations are delivered. They encourage the use of color, photography, animation, and even three-dimensional effects. The portable and ultra portable models have led on-the-go presenters to take along their own equipment for assurance that proper equipment will be available and for ease of familiarity no matter what far-flung outpost they are visiting.

If you've recently adopted such technology, you're likely to read at least part of the user's manual to learn how to configure and adjust the system. Once you've mastered the physical connections and the software, remember to go these extra 10 steps to make presenting with computer projection smooth and comfortable for both you and your viewing audience.

1. *Check colors for accuracy.* Colors vary among the desktop on which you design the presentation, the laptop screen, and the projection screen. If an exact color is important (for example, in a company logo), test and adjust the color in its final projection form ahead of time.

2. *Keep the colors and special effects simple.* Use no more than six colors on each side. Use slide transitions and builds to entertain without detracting from your message.

3. *Test your slides for size and readability.* Stand 6 feet away from your computer monitor. If you can read the monitor, your audience will likely be able to read the screen.

4. *Turn off all screen savers.* Remember to disable the screen savers on your computer—any that are part of the computer software, plus the one that comes with the laptop. You would be embarrassed if you were talking about important points on the screen only to realize that your audience is staring at flying toasters. It would be even worse should your energy-saver kick in and shut down the whole presentation.

5. *Learn how to use the toggle switch.* Find the switch that shows the image on both the computer and projection screens. Often the toggle is a function key; it controls whether your laptop, your projector, or both are on (showing an image). You want both to be on so you can look at the laptop while the audience watches the same image behind you on the screen.

15

6. *Arrive early and test everything.* Reread this line—again!

7. *Stand on the left as the audience sees you.* Because in English we read from left to right, if you stand to the audience members' left, they can look at you, follow your gestures to the screen—read left to right—and return their eyes to you. If you present in Hebrew or Arabic, reverse the approach.

8. *You are the show.* Too many people hide in the dark behind the laptop. You should stand away from the computer and in the light. Use a remote mouse so you can walk away from the computer. Arrange the lighting in the room so you are in the light while the screen is dark. You might even need to unscrew some of the lightbulbs.

9. *Motion attracts people's eyes.* Gesture to the screen when you want audience members to look there. Use moving text to grab their attention. Stand still when you want them to focus on the screen. Then move when you want to capture their attention again.

10. *Murphy's law applies to technology.* Any little thing might go wrong, so be ready to give your presentation without the hardware. If your presentation absolutely must be given by computer projection, have a backup system. Be prepared with backup files, a power source for the laptop and projector, and batteries for your remote mouse.

Thanks to George Torok, host of the weekly radio show, Business in Motion *for this information on working with computer projectors. He specializes in helping sales and marketing people present themselves effectively. He can be reached at* http://www.torok.com.

Control Your Presentation

As mentioned earlier, you should display the first slide on the screen in Slide Show view before your audience arrives. You can turn off the projector or the switch that projects to the screen before you start, if you wish. If you cannot set up in advance, like when you present in someone else's office, you can open the presentation and switch to Slide Show view before turning the monitor around for others to see. The general guideline is to create a clean start.

Once you start, simply click the remote mouse to move from slide to slide.

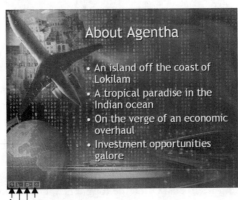

Back | | Next
Annotation menu Navigation menu

For more controls, you use the Slide Show View menu. As you move the mouse around, the menu bar, shown in the illustration on the previous page, appears at the lower-left corner of the screen. The menu bar contains four buttons:

■ **Back**   Goes to the previous slide or animation step on a slide.

■ **Annotation menu**   Contains options for annotating your slides. You can also access these options by right-clicking and choosing Pointer Options. See the next section "Mark Slides as You Present."

■ **Navigation menu**   Contains options for navigating throughout your presentation. You can also access these options by right-clicking to display the shortcut menu.

■ **Next**   Goes to the next slide or animation step on a slide.

Right-click anywhere on the screen to open the Slide Show shortcut menu shown here. (See the "Work with Shortcut Menus" section in Chapter 13 for information on how to customize this menu to add additional items.)

You should be very familiar with this menu so that you can quickly navigate anywhere in your slide show. Here are some of your options on this menu:

■ **Next**   Moves you to the next slide or the next animation step.

■ **Previous**   Moves you to the previous slide or the previous animation step, if any.

■ **Go to Slide**   Opens a submenu that lists all the slides in your presentation.

■ **Custom Show**   Lists custom shows. (See Chapter 14 for details on creating a custom show.)

■ **Screen**   Provides options that control how your screen looks and functions:

■ **Black Screen**   Displays a black screen. If you don't want to leave the last slide on the screen at the end of your slide show, a black screen is an alternative to returning to the PowerPoint screen. Returning to your application looks unprofessional because your audience sees the nuts and bolts behind the presentation.

■ **White screen**   Displays a white screen.

■ **Speaker Notes** Enables you to add notes during the presentation. In the Speaker Notes dialog box, shown next, click Close when you are done, and these notes are saved with the presentation. These notes subsequently appear in the Notes pane in Normal view. You can use this feature to save action steps during a meeting in place of the Meeting Minder, a feature that has been eliminated in PowerPoint 2003.

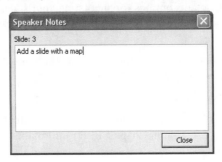

■ **Switch Programs** Displays the Windows task bar (usually at the bottom of your screen) and the Microsoft Office Shortcut bar (if you have it open) so you can switch to a different program while still in Slide Show view.

■ **Pointer Options** Offers options for the cursor arrow and for annotating slides. See Figure 15-4 in the next section.

  ■ **Arrow** Changes the cursor from a pen back to the default arrow.

  ■ **Ballpoint Pen** Changes the cursor to one of the three annotation modes. The ballpoint pen draws the thinnest line.

  ■ **Felt Tip Pen** Changes the cursor to one of the three annotation modes. The ballpoint pen draws a mid-weight line.

  ■ **Highlighter** Changes the cursor to one of the three annotation modes. The ballpoint pen draws a wide translucent line that looks like a highlighter.

  ■ **Ink Color** Opens a color palette where you can choose the color for one of the annotation modes.

  ■ **Eraser** Changes the cursor to an eraser. Drag the eraser over any annotation to erase it.

  ■ **Erase All Ink on Slide** Erases all annotation on the slide.

  ■ **Arrow Options** Sets the way that the arrow functions. Automatic displays the arrow but hides it if you don't move the mouse for 3 seconds. Moving the mouse re-displays the arrow. Visible displays the arrow all the time. Hidden hides the mouse all the time.

NOTE *Hiding the arrow removes any distraction for your audience. All they see is your slide show. To use the Slide Show shortcut menu with the pointer hidden, you need to right-click. (The cursor reappears on the menu so you can choose menu items.)*

- **Help**   Provides help, which hopefully, you won't need during a slide show. After all, you are supposed to come across as knowledgeable about PowerPoint. However, this option can be a lifesaver if your remote mouse dies. PowerPoint displays a list of keyboard shortcuts (see Table 15-1) that you can use to navigate through your presentation. Click OK to close the Help screen.

- **Pause**   Pauses a slide show that is running automatically using slide timings. (See the "Time Your Presentation" section in Chapter 14.)

- **End Show**   Immediately ends the show. You can also press ESC.

Table 15-1 lists the many keyboard shortcuts that you can use if your mouse fails or if you like to use the keyboard.

Shortcut	Result
N, ENTER, PAGE DOWN, right arrow, down arrow, or SPACEBAR	Advance to the next slide or perform the next animation build.
P, PAGE UP, left arrow, up arrow, or BACKSPACE	Return to the previous slide or perform the previous animation build.
Any slide number-ENTER	Go to that slide number.
B or .	Display a black screen or return to the slide show from a black screen.
W or ,	Display a white screen or return to the slide show from a white screen.
S or +	Pause or restart an automatic slide show.
ESC, CTRL-BREAK, or -	End a slide show.
E	Erase existing annotations.
H	Go to the next hidden slide.
T	Set new timings (use while rehearsing).
O	Use original timings (use while rehearsing).
Both mouse buttons for two seconds	Return to the first slide.
CTRL-P	Redisplay hidden pointer; change the pointer to a pen.
CTRL-A	Redisplay hidden pointer; change the pointer to an arrow.
CTRL-H	Hide the pointer and menu icon immediately.
CTRL-U	Hide the pointer and menu icon in 15 seconds (or less).
SHIFT-F10 (or right-click)	Display the shortcut menu.
TAB	Go to the first or next hyperlink on a slide.
SHIFT-TAB	Go to the last or previous hyperlink on a slide.
ENTER while a hyperlink is selected	Perform the mouse click action of the hyperlink.
SHIFT-ENTER while a hyperlink is selected	Perform the mouse over action of the hyperlink.

TABLE 15-1   Keyboard Shortcuts to Use When Delivering Your Presentation

15

Mark Slides as You Present

As a presenter, you have several techniques for focusing the audience on a specific item. The simplest is to use words, for example, "Look at the sales in the Northeast Division for last year." However, can you be sure that everyone in your audience has found the correct bar in your chart?

Many presenters use a pointer—either the old-fashioned wooden kind or an up-to-date laser one. A laser pointer is a necessity, of course, if you can't reach the screen.

PowerPoint offers the ability to annotate a slide directly. For example, you can circle a word or draw an arrow to that bar on your chart. The advantage of using annotation is that the audience can't miss it. The results are striking and immediate. The disadvantage is that annotation sometimes looks messy; with a mouse, you don't have much control over your circles and arrows. Figure 15-4 shows an example of the three annotation modes.

NOTE   *PowerPoint 2003 adds new annotation modes (pen widths) and new colors.*

To annotate a slide, you need to change the pointer from its default arrow to a pen. If you are close enough to the keyboard, press CTRL-P because it is less distracting to your audience. Otherwise, right-click to open the Slide Show menu, choose Pointer Options, and then choose one of the options. The cursor now looks like a pen. To draw, move the cursor to where you want to start and hold down the mouse button as you move the mouse. Release the mouse button to stop drawing.

You can't leave the mouse cursor as a pen if you want to use the mouse to navigate through your slide show. If you try to click the mouse button, you just keep getting little dots on your screen! To change the cursor back to an arrow, choose Pointer Options | Arrow or CTRL-A. If you want to keep the pen and can use the keyboard, you can use N, ENTER, PAGE DOWN, or one of the other keyboard shortcuts to navigate through your slide show.

FIGURE 15-4   It's hard to keep the lines straight, but annotation can draw your audience's attention to a point on your slide.

As mentioned earlier, you can hide the mouse cursor, whether it is an arrow or a pen. From the Slide Show menu, choose Pointer Options | Arrow Options | Hidden.

Use the Slide Show menu to control the annotation color. The default color may not contrast clearly against your slide. Choose Pointer Options | Pen Color. Choose Pointer Options | Pen Color | Automatic to return to the default pen color.

When you leave Slide Show view, you see a message asking if you want to keep your annotations. Click Yes to turn them into PowerPoint drawing objects that you can edit and save in your presentation. This feature is new for PowerPoint 2003.

You can also preset the pen color before starting your slide show. Choose Slide Show | Set Up Show. From the Pen Color drop-down list, choose the color you want to use. Choose More Colors to open the Colors dialog box for a wider range of color choices. Click OK.

Use Hyperlinks and Action Buttons

If you have created hyperlinks and action buttons to help you navigate through a presentation, now is the time to use them. While most hyperlinks and action buttons work with a mouse click, some may be set to work when you pass the mouse cursor over them. Watch out that you don't end up somewhere else by mistake!

You also need to be careful that you don't get lost! It can be embarrassing if you go from slide to slide and forget how to return.

What you need is a compass. As discussed in Chapter 11, each hyperlink and action button should provide a return trip mechanism, but you need to make sure you know what it is, because not all hyperlinks and action buttons are obvious. In addition, you can forget that an object on your screen is a hyperlink or action button, especially if you have camouflaged it.

Create a list of hyperlinks to help you out or include the information in your speaker notes. List the location of the hyperlink or action button, what it looks like (if necessary), where it goes to, and how to get back. If you have action buttons that use a mouse over effect, be sure to note it. Make sure to take the list with you when you present, but just as important, become very familiar with the list so that you don't need to refer to it except in a rare lapse of memory. The more complex your slide show, the more you need to know its myriad paths.

Summary

In this chapter, you saw how to create and use handouts for maximum effect with your presentation. This chapter also explained how to present a slide show using PowerPoint Viewer. A good part of this chapter covered the basics of professional presentation skills—you can use these skills whether or not you are showing a PowerPoint presentation.

Once you start presenting, PowerPoint offers a number of controls that let you navigate wherever your presentation might lead—even if off the beaten, linear track. You can also use any hyperlinks or action buttons that you have created.

You now have the knowledge you need to create and give professional presentations. I wish you all success. Enjoy!

Index

INTERNATIONAL CONTACT INFORMATION

AUSTRALIA
McGraw-Hill Book Company
Australia Pty. Ltd.
TEL +61-2-9900-1800
FAX +61-2-9878-8881
http://www.mcgraw-hill.com.au
books-it_sydney@mcgraw-hill.com

CANADA
McGraw-Hill Ryerson Ltd.
TEL +905-430-5000
FAX +905-430-5020
http://www.mcgraw-hill.ca

GREECE, MIDDLE EAST, & AFRICA
(Excluding South Africa)
McGraw-Hill Hellas
TEL +30-210-6560-990
TEL +30-210-6560-993
TEL +30-210-6560-994
FAX +30-210-6545-525

MEXICO (Also serving Latin America)
McGraw-Hill Interamericana Editores
S.A. de C.V.
TEL +525-1500-5108
FAX +525-117-1589
http://www.mcgraw-hill.com.mx
carlos_ruiz@mcgraw-hill.com

SINGAPORE (Serving Asia)
McGraw-Hill Book Company
TEL +65-6863-1580
FAX +65-6862-3354
http://www.mcgraw-hill.com.sg
mghasia@mcgraw-hill.com

SOUTH AFRICA
McGraw-Hill South Africa
TEL +27-11-622-7512
FAX +27-11-622-9045
robyn_swanepoel@mcgraw-hill.com

SPAIN
McGraw-Hill/
Interamericana de España, S.A.U.
TEL +34-91-180-3000
FAX +34-91-372-8513
http://www.mcgraw-hill.es
professional@mcgraw-hill.es

UNITED KINGDOM, NORTHERN,
EASTERN, & CENTRAL EUROPE
McGraw-Hill Education Europe
TEL +44-1-628-502500
FAX +44-1-628-770224
http://www.mcgraw-hill.co.uk
emea_queries@mcgraw-hill.com

ALL OTHER INQUIRIES Contact:
McGraw-Hill/Osborne
TEL +1-510-420-7700
FAX +1-510-420-7703
http://www.osborne.com
omg_international@mcgraw-hill.com

Know How

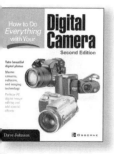

How to Do Everything with Your Digital Camera
Second Edition
ISBN: 0-07-222555-6

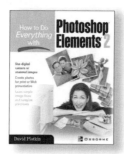

How to Do Everything with Photoshop Elements 2
ISBN: 0-07-222638-2

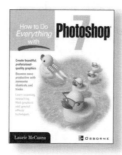

How to Do Everything with Photoshop 7
ISBN: 0-07-219554-1

How to Do Everything with Your Sony CLIÉ
ISBN: 0-07-222659-5

How to Do Everything with Macromedia Contribute
0-07-222892-X

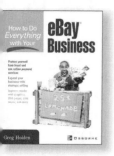

How to Do Everything with Your eBay Business
0-07-222948-9

How to Do Everything with Your Tablet PC
ISBN: 0-07-222771-0

How to Do Everything with Your iPod
ISBN: 0-07-222700-1

How to Do Everything with Your iMac,
Third Edition
ISBN: 0-07-213172-1

How to Do Everything with Your iPAQ Pocket PC
Second Edition
ISBN: 0-07-222950-0

Mc

Sound Off!

Visit us at **www.osborne.com/bookregistration** and let us know what you thought of this book. While you're online you'll have the opportunity to register for newsletters and special offers from McGraw-Hill/Osborne.

We want to hear from you!

Sneak Peek

Visit us today at **www.betabooks.com** and see what's coming from McGraw-Hill/Osborne tomorrow!

Based on the successful software paradigm, Bet@Books™ allows computing professionals to view partial and sometimes complete text versions of selected titles online. Bet@Books™ viewing is free, invites comments and feedback, and allows you to "test drive" books in progress on the subjects that interest you the most.

Mc